D1195669

Leading the Parade

Conversations with America's Most Influential Lesbians and Gay Men

Paul D. Cain

The Scarecrow Press, Inc.
Lanham, Maryland, and London
2002

SCARECROW PRESS, INC.

Published in the United States of America
by Scarecrow Press, Inc.
4720 Boston Way, Lanham, Maryland 20706
www.scarecrowpress.com

4 Pleydell Gardens, Folkestone
Kent CT20 2DN, England

British Library Cataloguing-in-Publication Information Available

Library of Congress Cataloging-in-Publication Data

Cain, Paul D., 1961–
Leading the parade : conversations with America's most influential lesbians and gay men / Paul D. Cain.
p. cm.
Includes bibliographical references (p.) and index.
ISBN 0-8108-4139-8 (cloth : alk. paper)
1. Lesbians—United States—Interviews. 2. Gays—United States—Interviews.
I. Title.
HQ75.6.U5 C345 2002
305.9'0664'0973—dc21 2001054167

The paper used in this publication meets the minimum requirements of American National Standard for Information Sciences—Permanence of Paper for Printed Library Materials, ANSI/NISO Z39.48-1992. Manufactured in the United States of America.

Veronica Guerin and *Cassie Bernall,*
Two women who counted the cost—yet told the truth

CONTENTS

PART III: The Written Word

PART IV: Political Creatures

PART V: Creating a New World

FOREWORD

The best writers, in my opinion, are those who've embarked on a spirited quest. They are seekers eager to explore the varied sides of those ideas and individuals about whom they write, relying not on hearsay, but on personal contact.

Paul D. Cain is such a writer. Without first bothering to obtain a pricey author's contract for *Leading the Parade*, he set out alone on his quest, traversing the nation, spending his personal savings to visit the far-flung movers and shakers of America's lesbian and gay civil rights movement. Into each of his interchanges with these pioneers, activists, and artists, he brought with him a considerable knowledge he'd gained from voluminous reading.

More important, Cain took care to avoid imposing his own ideology as he wrote. Able to describe each of his colorful interviewees without being judgmental, he presents many strong and startling personalities within their own conceptual contexts. Upon meeting him, I found myself speaking uninhibitedly, knowing intuitively that he would honorably utilize whatever it was I might say.

As he talked at length with me about other pioneers, it quickly became clear that they were not just subject-matter fodder, but that in many cases they'd become his mentors, friends, and confidantes. *Leading the Parade* wouldn't simply be quoting these women and men, but would artfully reflect, through Cain's breadth of knowledge about them, that individualistic magic only gadflies, reformers, heretics, radicals, and revolutionaries can emit.

In fact, as the author appreciates, these leaders of the parade have, during a remarkably short time frame, conceived and effected much-needed social changes of a magnitude wholly unimaginable only a few decades ago. The reach of these changes, worrisome now to the movement's losing foes, has extended into the councils of the world's governments, into the planet's highest courts, into every major religious institution, into schools and colleges, and into films, books, and the news media where gay and lesbian issues have become daily fare.

What could have impelled those who'd instigated such a revolution? Paul Cain wanted to know. What had made them flout the great taboo, bravely climbing over seemingly impregnable barricades, demanding uncompromising equality for same-sex love and affection?

In previous centuries those who'd dared to make same-sex love had been tied to stakes, their bodies torturously consumed in flames, wooden sticks called "faggots" being lit beneath their feet. Others were hunted down like escaped convicts. During the past century many who'd openly celebrated the love that once had dared not speak its name had, like Oscar Wilde, suffered imprisonment. As late as the '60s, city and state government crusades in Idaho and Florida exposed same-sex lovers to public ostracism and job loss. Fifteen years ago, in 1986, a gang of five on the U.S. Supreme Court ruled that police in Georgia were within their rights to invade a private bedroom and arrest two men making love.

Who, in this present day, can imagine the courage, the devotion to principle, the intellectual and moral grandeur it once required to be an openly homosexual advocate for change? It has been my privilege to live and learn in the presence of such pioneering men and women, among the noblest sons and daughters of our nation. They had become, I realized, genuine saviors, running to the rescue of the downtrodden, building escape hatches for the persecuted, destroying cruel superstitions, and creating institutions to release ordinary citizens from the brutal prisons of ignorance.

Leading the Parade is not only an inspiring foray into the lives of these amazing revolutionaries, but also, through their own words conveyed with passion and clarity, a means to preserve their memories for future generations.

Jack Nichols, writer

PREFACE

I have always been a voracious reader, ever since my mother taught me to read. (She used to regale me with stories about my reading to total strangers from the time I was three years old.) Many special books along the way assisted me in my journey to accept myself as a gay man. As I began to accept my sexuality, I found myself especially interested in lesbian/gay history, and more specifically, the people who created and influenced it.

After seven and one-half years of serving the Phoenix lesbian/gay community, I found myself "burned out" on direct activism, and I wanted to find a way to serve the community I love while developing talents that lay dormant within me.

I realized that as a result of two factors—age and AIDS—we would forever lose the stories of many pioneers and others who influenced the movement if someone didn't document their oral histories, and some we did lose. And without so much as a single contact, I believed I could do it.

Lesbians and gay men from my generation who have little, if any, knowledge of contemporary American gay and lesbian history frustrate me. (In 1989, Phoenix's slogan for gay pride was "Stonewall Remembered." I cannot begin to tell you how many people, openly gay for many years, asked, "What's that mean?") Unlike most cultural minorities, lesbians and gay men seldom receive affirmation of their minority status (or any sense of community history) from their families of origin as they mature, and in my experience, many gay men and lesbians are intellectually lazy about seeking that information (or they fail to believe such a lack of knowledge has any impact upon their lives). Additionally, I feel far too few gay and lesbian people really understand what has come before them, assume the progress we have achieved happened spontaneously, and believe that further changes aren't occurring quickly enough to suit them, despite their unwillingness to participate in making them reality.

Given all of this, I decided to compile a comprehensive (but by no means all-inclusive) book of biographic profiles presenting the lives of lesbians and gay men[1] who I believed influenced (or were perceived to have influenced) "the gay movement" in the United States between 1945 and 1995. I specifically chose U.S. history because I knew it well enough to make some intelligent choices, and the time period to celebrate fifty years of activism in this country. I did some initial research by copying pertinent sections from the gay- and lesbian-themed books I already owned, and from almost ten years of *Advocate* magazines, a national gay publication I had collected since 1984. Then I began contacting total strangers, asking them to permit me to interview them.

That part of the job proved both the most difficult and the most personally rewarding. I conducted forty-three interviews with men and women (thirty-nine of which are included herein) who have possessed and displayed incredible courage, enviable skills, and unwavering tenacity. While they may have little else in common, all have demonstrated the ability to risk, whether reputation, family, church, or society. As a result of this book, I traveled to sections of the United States I might never have chanced to see (having never before traveled in the United States east of Arizona), and made many incredible friends along the way. Sharing a meal with Holly Near, Rita Mae Brown, Jim Kepner, Frank Kameny, or Del Martin and Phyllis Lyon, was a little slice of heaven for me.

I have tried my very best to treat fairly everyone included herein. I compiled and read books, magazine articles, and newspapers, and/or viewed movies and videos by and about them all. Despite my best efforts, I'm sure some mischaracterizations and errors have crept into these pages. Let me know if you see any, and I'll correct them in the next printing. Sometimes the records are unclear, or contain conflicting information. I tried to verify any disputed fact with multiple sources, but that's not always possible; for many, this is the first time anyone has profiled their lives in this manner, and unambiguous information is either sketchy or absent. Also, any names that appear in boldface in a chapter's text belong to individuals who have their own profile included in this book.

Although many of mine are included, I have not compiled a list of my personal heroes, nor is this list designed to recognize the most accomplished gay people during this time period. While I attempted to cast a wide net to showcase the diversity of important contributors to the movement, some folks had already died; some eluded my attempts; some simply refused; and some initially welcomed me, only to change their minds toward the end of the process. To a certain degree, this book celebrates visibility and willingness to openly identify as lesbian or gay when it required (as it often still requires) daring and risk, as well as personal sacrifice. Most of the individuals I selected achieved noteworthiness as a result of many years of hard work. In some cases, I recognized a couple as one entity, either because their work was often done as one entity, or to recognize their contribution as a couple instead of as two individuals.

If you believe I have failed to emphasize folks currently active in the movement, you're correct. One of my criteria for selection and placement is that it was much harder to espouse or promote gay activism or visibility in the '50s than in the '70s, and more so in the '70s than in the '90s. By now, a self-acknowledged "role model" or pioneer has emerged in nearly every American endeavor, short of the presidency. And how things have changed since I began this journey! Melissa Etheridge was just beginning her ascent to cultural icon, Ellen DeGeneres was still in the closet—and Matthew Shepard was still alive. But their time in the limelight came post-1995, which is why they and some other prominent lesbian/gay folks are not profiled here.

I accept the criticism that my selections are colored by my experiences as a forty-year-old, West Coast-born, gay white Christian male. However, I have worked conscientiously to include experiences and influences different from my own while maintaining the integrity of this book as an accurate historical representation. I accept the criticism that this book is not "politically correct." However, my life is more "PC" than my book and, in my experience, *life* often does not conform to politically correct standards. I hope to write other books with frameworks that permit me to cast a broader net, but this is the book I was compelled to write at this time.

Nevertheless, I am extremely proud of this book, and the efforts that have gone into it. I hope it will help you to see those who have come before us as a community; the struggles, the successes, the failures, the personal victories. I also hope this awareness spurs you on to risk, and to dare to accomplish, great things in your life.

I know few fields that need more workers than the lesbian/gay/bi/trans community. Perhaps this book will inspire you to grab a scythe to cut down the weeds of sexism, racism, patriarchy, and apathy in your community, and help those of us whose hands have driven the plow for years to rest a moment and savor our accomplishments. If it accomplishes nothing else, then writing this book will have been worthwhile.

Last, dear reader, I want to know what you think. In my view, this book remains a work in progress regarding this era of American lesbian/gay history, which I hope to revisit (and revise) five or ten years from now. What did you like? What didn't you like? Whom should I have included? Whom should I have omitted? Please write and tell me; I really want to know your opinions.

Enjoy!

Note

1. One may technically define some of those profiled as "bisexuals," but they did not shy away from identifying with (and usually as a member of) the lesbian/gay movement.

ACKNOWLEDGMENTS

Thanks, first of all, to the men and women I interviewed during 1994 and 1995. Your willingness to share your stories and your insight gave me a crucial and often overlooked element in our history. Personally, I consider many of you new and dear friends.

Thanks to everyone who hosted me along the way: Steve Palmer; Jon Ewaniuk; Morris Kight; Bret, Laura, and Mary Jacobowitz; Barbara Grier and Donna J. McBride; Dick Schwartz; Jack Nichols; Bill Byrd; Allan Spear and Jun Tsuji.

Thanks to all my readers, who read draft chapters and gave me critical (and valuable) feedback: Sheryl Schwartzenhauer; Jody Ohradza; Mark Elliott; Donna Foy and Haris Blackwood; David Horowitz; Trey Hunt; Bret Jacobowitz; and Jeff Ofstedahl.

Thanks to Robrt L. Pela for his advice and support at several crucial junctures during this process.

Thanks to my research assistant and general "go-fer," Jon K. Thompson, for tracking down materials, transcribing interviews, and taking care of the cats during out-of-town trips.

Thanks to all the people who believed in me and this project in its earliest stages, especially Dennis Fleurant, Dixie Guss, Thom Holly, Ellen Edwards, and Meg Mac Mullen.

Cover art © 1994 by Ron Anderegg. All photographs courtesy of Robert Giard except Jack Nichols, courtesy of Jack Nichols, Robin Tyler, courtesy of Rex Wockner, and Barbara Gittings and Kay Tobin Lahusen, courtesy of B. Proud. All illustrations courtesy of Don Bachardy. Illustration of Frank Kameny courtesy of Don Bachardy and the Division of Rare and Manuscript Collections, Cornell University Library.

Thanks to Pat Allen at IGLA for his gracious assistance; to Karen Applegate for lending me women's music I needed to hear but couldn't find; to Roger Rea for inviting me to meet Harry Hay; to Greg Jackson for lending me a book I otherwise couldn't find; to Markita Martinez, librarian *extraordinaire*; to the staff of Obelisk bookstore in Phoenix (and numerous other bookstore clerks and librarians around the country); and to the folks who run Movies on Central, where I obtained rental copies of several videos I couldn't afford to buy.

Thanks to Rev. Brad Wishon for providing the inspiration for this book's title.

Finally, thanks to my husband, Kurt L. Jacobowitz-Cain. Through all the highs and lows of this project (driving the length of Florida and back in a four-day weekend; driving from D.C. to New York City until 2 A.M.; buying and wearing the "Help! I'm living with an unpublished writer" button; waiting for me to finish another interview, scheduling computer time, knowing where and how to find information on the Internet), you have stood by me. I am both lucky and blessed to have had you as my partner for twelve years, and I believe the best is yet to come.

ABBREVIATIONS AND ACRONYMS

AB-1	Assembly Bill 1 (California)
ACLU	American Civil Liberties Union
ACT-UP	AIDS Coalition to Unleash Power
AIDS	Acquired Immune Deficiency Syndrome
ANGLE	Access Network for Gay & Lesbian Equality
APA	American Psychiatric Association
ARC	AIDS-Related Complex
AREA	American Run for the End of AIDS
BACABI	Bay Area Committee against the Briggs Initiative
CBC	Club Bath Chain/Club Body Centers
CFS	Chronic Fatigue Syndrome
CLAGS	Center for Lesbian and Gay Studies
CORE	Congress of Racial Equality
c-r	Consciousness-Raising
DOB	Daughters of Bilitis
EAGLES	Emphasizing Adolescent Gay and Lesbian Education Services
ECHO	East Coast Homophile Organizations
ERCHO	Eastern Regional Conference of Homophile Organizations
FTA	Free the Army
GAA	Gay Activists Alliance
GAU	Gay Academic Union
GCN	*Gay Community News*
GLAAD	Gay and Lesbian Alliance against Defamation
GLAD	Gay and Lesbian Advocates and Defenders
GLBT	Gay/Lesbian/Bisexual/Transgender
GLF	Gay Liberation Front

GRNL	Gay Rights National Lobby
GWMs	Gay White Males
HIC	Homosexual Information Center
HIV	Human Immunodeficiency Virus
HRC	Human Rights Campaign
HRCF	Human Rights Campaign Fund
IASHS	Institute for Advanced Study of Human Sexuality
IGLA	International Gay & Lesbian Archives
IWY	International Women's Year
KS	Kaposi's Sarcoma
LCE	League for Civil Education
LFL	Lesbian Feminist Liberation
LHA	Lesbian Herstory Archives
LLC	Lesbian Liberation Committee
MCC	Metropolitan Community Church
MECLA	Municipal Elections Committee of Los Angeles
MMOW	Millennium March on Washington
MOW	March on Washington
MSNY	Mattachine Society, New York
MSSF	Mattachine Society, San Francisco
MSW	Mattachine Society, Washington, D.C.
NAACP	National Association for the Advancement of Colored People
NACHO	North American Conference of Homophile Organizations
NCOD	National Coming Out Day
NGLTF	National Gay and Lesbian Task Force
NGRA	National Gay Rights Advocates
NGTF	National Gay Task Force
NOW	National Organization for Women
P-FLAG	Parents, Families, and Friends of Lesbians and Gays
SIR	Society for Individual Rights
SPREE	Society of Pat Rocco Enlightened Enthusiasts
TVC	Traditional Values Coalition
UFMCC	Universal Fellowship of Metropolitan Community Churches
USC	University of Southern California
USO	United Service Organizations

PART I

STARTING FROM SCRATCH

1

DORR LEGG

ONE . . . does not claim that homosexuals are better or worse than anyone else, that they are special in any but one sense. And in that one sense ONE claims positively that homosexuals do not have the civil rights assured all other citizens. ONE is devoted to correcting this.

ONE . . . means to stimulate thought, criticism, research, literary and artistic production in an effort to bring the public to understand deviants and deviants to understand themselves as the two sides are brought together as one.

—*ONE Magazine*, 1950s

In the American gay movement, organizations have come and gone with alarming frequency. If one defines influence by longevity and continuity, no organization had greater influence than ONE, Inc., founded in 1952 and presided over by the iron will of perhaps the most doctrinaire martinet (self-described in 1975 as "one of the few radical homophile Republicans in existence") under whom the movement ever chafed. While Harry Hay and others founded Mattachine and **Del Martin** and **Phyllis Lyon** played instrumental roles in the inception of the Daughters of Bilitis (DOB), of these three homophile organizations begun in the '50s no activist became so closely identified for so long as did Dorr Legg and ONE, Inc. As executive director from ONE's inception, Legg personified its very spirit. Fortunately, I interviewed Legg in

March 1994: He died less than six months later, just shy of his ninetieth birthday.

"Dorr Legg"[1] appears to have been born William Lambert in the summer of 1904, and grew up in the Ann Arbor, Michigan, area. **Jim Kepner**, in his July 1995 newsletter, mentioned that Legg "was orphaned at [an] early age and adopted by close relatives," and that he hailed "from a Christian Science background," the sum total of Dorr's early personal history I could unearth. In a 1976 interview with Brad Mulroy, Dorr acknowledged coming out in Florida at nineteen after having sex with a man. As Kepner also explained to me, "Dorr said that when he came out, he began to think that every other homosexual was just looking for a trick, or Prince Charming. And he was looking for a community!"

In college Dorr displayed ingenuity by simultaneously studying a pair of nonrelated fields, telling me, "I was enrolled in two professional degrees at the same time at one university. And they didn't have computers to call it up. So I got a masters, a bachelor of music in piano, and a masters in design and urban planning." Legg graduated in 1928, and he used his urban planning degree to earn a living for most of the next thirty years, relocating to New York, Florida, and Oregon before settling in greater Los Angeles in the late '40s. Over the course of his lifetime, Legg entered several relationships with non-Caucasian men,[2] which resulted not only in his experiencing racial prejudice firsthand (as he told **John D'Emilio** in *Sexual Politics, Sexual Communities*, an interracial pair of men "would be stopped on the streets. . . . The police simply assumed criminal purposes"), but led him to participate in one of the most fascinating gay social experiments before or since.

Knights of the Clock, founded by African-American Merton Bird, reportedly incorporated in California in 1950 (although the group may have met the previous year). According to *Homosexuals Today—1956*, it aimed "to promote fellowship and understanding between homosexuals themselves, specifically between other races and the Negro, as well as to offer its members aid in securing employment, and suitable housing. Special attention was given to the housing problems of interracial couples of which there were several in the group." The Knights also provided a unique service in that "parents, brothers, sisters, and other relatives of homosexuals were generally present at the meetings, and a number of these held office." Legg told Dean Gengle in a 1976 *Advocate* article that the Knights

> were interracial, intergenerational, and included both homosexual and non-homosexual people. . . . They'd hold dances and holiday parties and whatnot. But they did have a service aspect, too. . . . The Knights were an important part of that early Los Angeles history in the homo-

phile movement. Mattachine, ONE, Inc., and a lot of other things can trace their origins to the Knights.

The audacious and comprehensive organization lasted until 1953; before then Legg, its president for a time, became involved in other fledgling gay groups in southern California.

Dorr attended his first Mattachine meeting in 1951, and he first led a cell group in 1952. On October 15, 1952, during a Mattachine discussion group meeting, that evening's group leader suggested that the assemblage create a monthly magazine to provide a forum through which they could more widely disseminate information about homosexuality. While the host thought better of the idea the next day, and quickly resigned, his chance remark spurred several in attendance to create such a magazine. Selecting the publication's name stymied the group, until one of the magazine's founders, African-American Bailey Whitaker (pseudonymously identified as "Guy Rousseau"), discovered a quotation from Thomas Carlyle: "A mystic bond of brotherhood makes all men one." Their dilemma solved, they entitled the new magazine *ONE*, and the state of California chartered ONE, Inc., on May 27, 1953.

The first issue of *ONE* came off the presses in January 1953. At the beginning, Legg served as its nonpaid business manager; when he later became executive director, he deferred his salary until the debt reached six figures. The little magazine grew slowly until a legal hurdle provided one of the most important legal decisions in early movement history.

As Dorr recounted the story to me, the Postmaster of Los Angeles "seized the October '54 issue of *ONE Magazine* and declared it obscene and unmailable. And it took four years for us to fight that verdict." Despite losing at every step along the way,[3] on January 13, 1958, the U.S. Supreme Court reversed the Ninth Circuit's decision in *ONE v. Olesen* without allowing either side to argue its case. Dorr continued, "We took on the whole federal government for a period of four [years]—and they spent big money, with top lawyers brought from Washington, to squash us. And they didn't! We won. Which was unheard of."

In the August 1958 issue of *ONE*, Legg (under the pen name "Hollister Barnes") submitted an essay, "I Am Glad I Am Homosexual," discussing the revolutionary idea that there was nothing inherently shameful about acknowledging one's homosexuality. It concluded:

> Do these concepts seem shocking, or startling? If so, the reader should prepare himself to continue being shocked, for ideas such as these are present today in the minds of many homosexuals. They will be expressing them more and more vigorously as time goes on. Their

> day is on the march. They are actively, resiliently proud of their homosexuality, glad for it. Society is going to have to accustom itself to many new pressures, new demands from the homosexual. A large and vigorous group of citizens, millions of them, are refusing to put up any longer with outworn shibboleths, contumely and social degradation.
>
> Like the rest of my brothers and sisters I am glad to be a homosexual, proud of it. Let no one think we don't mean business, or intend to enforce our rights.

Asked by *GAY* newspaper's Thane Hampten in a 1971 article what reaction his essay prompted, Dorr exclaimed, "Oh, my! You have no idea. Most of the reaction was *very* much against it. Many, many people cancelled their subscriptions. I was severely criticized. Believe it or not, it hasn't stopped yet."

Through the '50s and into the early '60s, *ONE* remained a major player on the homophile scene. As reported in the summer 1964 *Mattachine Review*:

> One magazine has appeared since January 1953 and today can lay claim to being the largest in circulation and the slickest as well. Its fiction has been called everything from a disgrace to perfect, its poetry and art have at times been daring and far out, but it has nevertheless maintained a lively pace editorially and drawn an equally lively response from its readers.

However, in *Unspeakable*, Jim Kepner took *ONE* to task, criticizing that "Dorr had no interest in editorial quality. It would have been fine with him simply to reprint the phone book." Surprisingly, Legg agreed with that assessment, telling Rodger Streitmatter, "Jim's right. The *ONE* I edited was of despicably poor quality. I was building the finest library and educational institution for homophile studies the world would ever know. I had no interest in the publication."

Despite philosophical differences and occasional squabbles, in John D'Emilio's *Sexual Politics, Sexual Communities* Dorr also explained ONE's relationship with DOB and Mattachine during this period: "We had to stand shoulder to shoulder because the movement was so small, and we knew we had to protect each other." D'Emilio remembered Legg from their encounters in the mid-'70s as "very opinionated. Very convinced that no one had ever done anything more significant than he had. . . . But, on the other hand, he was very cooperative." Phyllis Lyon lightly described Legg as "an old mule," and **Randy Wicker** recalled, "Dorr was dreadful." Harry Hay once acknowledged, "I could never look at Dorr without thinking of the carved wooden handle of my grandmother's umbrella." Yet in *A Few Doors West of Hope*, ONE vice chairman Tony Reyes described Dorr as "a witty speaker. Everyone loved to hear his lectures." Kepner wrote a balanced appraisal in his July 1995 newsletter:

> I found Bill knowledgeable about history, art, science and sociology, perceptive if too quick and inflexible in judging people, politically extremely conservative, but a charming conversationalist until we began to deal together with corporate business. He was devious and dictatorial in corporate affairs, and with visitors could be either engaging or coldly hostile—for reasons I could rarely fathom.

ONE always emphasized education regarding homosexuality, although ONE, Inc., also encompassed publication, research, and social science divisions. ONE began its periodic Midwinter Institutes in 1955 (continuing through 1980), and began several short-lived chapters, most notably in Chicago and Detroit. From 1964 to 1981 ONE also successfully promoted overseas tours through ONE Institute Overseas, visiting several European, Asian, and South American countries. It also owned the world's largest collection of gay materials in the Blanche Baker Memorial Library, about which principals contested one of the nastiest internal bitch fights in movement history.

In *The Trouble with Harry Hay*, Stuart Timmons elucidated the underlying reasons behind "The Heist":

> In [Don] Slater's words, 'Here it was, 1964. We'd been going along since '52 and ONE was still talking about what it had done back then. But we as editors of the magazine were looking ahead. We had to. New organizations were forming out there. But when we brought up new issues, Bill Lambert [aka Dorr Legg] would not deem them appropriate.'

As Kepner put it, "[Slater said] 'ONE is in the same position it was when we started it twelve years ago. And the world is moving, the world is changing! We're still coming up with the same stuff, and it's out of date!' Well, I thought that was awfully surprising, coming from Don, who hardly notices change in the world." ONE's Board of Directors split ideologically, half favoring Legg's slow but steady approach, while the other half favored Slater's desire to take chances in order to facilitate organizational growth and health. After legal consultation, and given the board's division, Slater utilized a legal measure known as "self-help"; in the course of a weekend he and his sympathizers relocated the contents of ONE's Los Angeles offices. Confronting a stunned Legg later that day, Slater allegedly countered, "I'm willing to forget what you tried to do to me. Restore the legally elected Board, and agree to resume ONE's activities on the old footing. We'll meet with my attorney tomorrow morning to sign the papers. And I'll bring back everything I took." Legg's reply? "Never." Hansen continues the narrative: "[S]ix manic months later, when the dust had settled, Bandito Don still had control of everything he'd trucked out to Cahuenga Pass that night, and [Legg] had managed to salvage only the right to exclusive use of the name ONE."

Harry Hay referred to the Heist as "a matter of two dinosaurs spitting at each other and not realizing that dinosaurs had become obsolete." Jim Kepner explained, "I can agree with his provocation, but not with what he did." When I visited with Dorr in March 1994, I asked him about The Heist. Legg told me, "We don't talk about it much. Because we don't see any point in doing it. It's a matter that's been legally settled, and the records are clear. I don't know how clear Don is himself, to this day, out of it."

After Stonewall, the gay movement changed radically. Dorr and ONE, however, did not. (Although he sagely told Mulroy in 1976, "I hate this 1969ing everything as if there weren't twenty years before a hell of a lot of hard work by hundreds and hundreds of dedicated people who put their lives and their jobs and everything else on the line.") As a result, ONE lost its position on the cutting edge of the movement, choosing to continue its focus on education instead of turning to arguably more pressing tasks. As Legg explained to Mulroy,

> Pragmatically speaking, no one in the world can take on all issues. . . . That is one thing that I feel has led to the longevity of ONE. We have refused to take our eye off the ball. We don't go into politics, we don't go into religion, we don't do any of these things that many of the groups are doing. Not that they don't have merit, it's just that you're losing track of what you set out to do.

Legg's and ONE's focus became both a strength and a weakness: While one cannot easily disregard nearly a half-century's work, as movement tactics evolved, Dorr's stubbornness in many ways rendered ONE irrelevant. Even **Hal Call**, who told me two months before Dorr's death that Legg was "a marvelous, marvelous man," admitted, "I understand the people that had ideas and want to do some things around ONE, they get shot down by Dorr. He just won't give up control of anything down there."

Despite the inception of the ONE Institute Graduate School of Homophile Studies in 1981, a wonderful thirtieth anniversary celebration in 1982, ONE's move from its long-time Venice Boulevard home to the grounds of Arlington Hall in Los Angeles on June 1, 1983, and the continuation of its Sunday afternoon monthly lecture series, ONE sadly became a shell of its former militant activist self. **Barbara Gittings** accurately assessed that Legg's

> outreach hasn't been commensurate with his beliefs that information and education are the key. I understand an argument can be made for that, but then what you have to do is go out and do something to reach the people that need it. If you simply sit back in a library and wait for the world to come to you, you're not gonna reach very many people.

Frank Kameny, more bluntly, told me, "If they were to suddenly vanish from the scene now, or any time in the last decade or decade and a half, there wouldn't be so much as a ripple."

After Legg's death from natural causes on July 26-27, 1994 (leaving his lover of thirty-two years, Johnny Nojima), ONE's primary legacy became its library. Before the year ended, ONE's library and the International Gay & Lesbian Archives's (IGLA) collection merged, and both moved from their respective facilities to USC. And in the summer 1998 *ONE/IGLA Bulletin*, Ernie Potvin reported that following Don Slater's death, the Homosexual Information Center library merged with the ONE/IGLA materials at USC. Tragically, it took the deaths of all three library principals (IGLA's Jim Kepner, HIC's Don Slater, and Legg) within three and one-half years of one another to reunite materials separated for over three decades.

Even when Dorr and ONE lost their effectiveness to create change, Legg remained aware of changes in the movement. "From the very start, almost, we spoke of the four horsemen of the apocalypse, the enemy. Which were the legal, the church, the social, and the scientific. And we didn't know which was the most vicious." Which did the movement most effectively change? "Possibly religion. Because things have happened in religion that I never expected I would ever see. . . . I just couldn't believe they would be able to adapt." Perhaps the churches adapted better than Dorr himself.

Notes

1. In *A Few Doors West of Hope*, Joseph Hansen wrote that over the many years of *ONE*'s publication, "Bill Lambert came up with a dozen, maybe a score [of pseudonyms] for himself . . . . In the end, Lambert would try to disappear completely behind his bizarre favorite, W. Dorr Legg."

2. Hansen uncharitably described Legg's "survival tactic [of] living off . . . a succession of hardworking black men."

3. "In 1955, the U.S. District Court in Southern California decided that the magazine was non-mailable since the 'stories are obviously calculated to

stimulate the lust of the homosexual reader.' The decision was appealed to the Ninth Federal District Court of Appeals, where in November 1956 [sic—February 27, 1957] the original decision was sustained." *Homosexuality: A History*, Vern L. Bullough.

2

LISA BEN

I have never considered *Vice Versa* as a "courageous venture" . . . I can not feel, however, that the time and effort I devote to *Vice Versa* is in vain because I believe that there is a definite need for such a magazine among the gay folk. *Vice Versa* was long a fond dream of mine ere it came into reality in June, 1947. It is my personal contribution to others of my ilk, meant to provide an outlet for the creative self-expression so often, of necessity, pent up within us.

—Lisa Ben, last comments of the final *Vice Versa*, February 1948

More than half a century ago, one of the less heralded young women influential to the gay and lesbian movement first set pen to paper (or fingers to manual typewriter) to compose, edit, publish, and distribute nine issues of a newsletter, *Vice Versa.* In deference to her work, at a January 1972 ONE banquet, **Dorr Legg** introduced her as "the father of the gay movement." While she told me, "I don't remember that! Or if he did say it, I didn't hear it. I think I would have thrown my guitar at him!," the young woman, who adopted the pseudonym "Lisa Ben" (an anagram of "Lesbian"), almost single-handedly assembled a charming magazine targeting the lesbian community. It was my great pleasure to speak with her at a suburban Los Angeles school (where she feeds the animals on weekends) during the spring of 1995.

Lisa Ben[1] was born in San Francisco, California, on November 7, 1921, and at age three moved with her parents to a thirty-three-acre fruit ranch in Los Altos, California. There she lived for the next eighteen years, enduring a rather stifling childhood. She "grew up with lots of animals. Not very many friends, but lots of animals." An only child, she suffered at the hands of her mother, and from the more benign neglect of her father: "If I spoke back to my mother, she'd slap me across the face so hard! My dad never raised a hand to me, but he could make me feel about two inches high with his putdowns." Describing her mother, Lisa said, "She was nice in many, many ways—she sewed my little clothes, and she was a wonderful mother in many ways, but there were other ways she wasn't." She also told Zsa Zsa Gershick in 1998's *Gay Old Girls*, "I was very passive. As long as I was passive and didn't make waves, I got along fine with [my parents]," but also added, "they discouraged me in every possible way from being creative." Lisa also admitted to me that her father was an alcoholic, although she didn't realize it until many years later.

Quite early in her life, she discovered her attraction to women: "I know I loved my mother's dear housewife friend. She had four children herself, and she was always so nice to me. I was about five or six at the time, and I always used to call her Mary My Angel. . . . I loved her because she was nice to me, because she loved children—that kind of thing." At fourteen, Lisa developed her first serious crush, on a female classmate: "Helen was the one that introduced me to hugging and kissing."

Despite her desire to leave her parents' home, Lisa never intended to become a "career girl." Instead, she told me, "I had always supposed I would be playing in a symphony orchestra. . . . I worked very hard at that violin." Instead, after two years at Mills College, her parents cavalierly forced her to attend business college because "they wanted to keep me at home and rent me out as an office girl, and then take a third of my salary in gratitude." When she balked at that arrangement, her parents banished her:

> I remember my father saying, "I think you'll find that it's more expensive to live away from home—you should stay here." And I thought, "That's why they're doing this—they're going to expect me to come back, and say, 'please take me back,' or, 'Daddy, can I borrow some money,' or something." Well, I never borrowed a cent from the day they put me out to Palo Alto. I nearly starved to death, but I didn't borrow from them—I didn't ask them for *anything*.

At one point, Lisa's weight dropped below one hundred pounds:

> My mother knew what time I would be off work, walking to the room where I lived, and sometimes would just show up in her car. She

> would ask, "Hello, little girl. Would you like a ride home?" Exhausted and having had no dinner (there were no fast food or Chinese takeout places in those days), I would scurry into her car, to be driven to the room where I was staying. She would ask, "Have you had dinner yet? Aren't you *hungry*? Wouldn't you like to take Mother out to dinner?" And I said no, and I expected a slap across the face when I said that, but she didn't say anything. But what cruel things to say! Sometimes if I saw her car before she saw me, I would hide behind a tree.

She moved first to Palo Alto in northern California for two and one-half years, then departed for Los Angeles to get farther away from her parents' clutches.

> My father said, "Oh, you're making a big mistake." And I thought, well, maybe I am, but I've gotta get out of this situation. I think I was making about $31 a week up there for an eight-hour day and half-days Saturday. So I came down here and I lived in rented rooms for a while, and then I bought my own little house finally. I realized if I didn't buy a house, I'd still be working at my age, you know.

She remains in that little house in the San Fernando Valley to this day, surrounded by eleven loving cats, and a sweetly protective gay male neighbor.

Once Lisa arrived in Los Angeles in 1945, away from her parents' disapproval, she blossomed. She discovered a science fiction readers' club, where she met others like herself interested in horror and fantasy stories, including **Jim Kepner**. (However, despite published reports that she achieved a minor name for herself as a science fiction writer, she told me, "I definitely was not a minor star of science fiction. Debunk it, because I wasn't.") Then, quite by accident, she met a group of girls who lived in her apartment complex whose sexual orientation matched hers, and they introduced her to women's softball and the Los Angeles gay clubs open to women, including the If Club. Finally, the young woman who had earlier believed herself "a misfit all the way around" found a welcoming home in the arms of L.A.'s lesbian community. As she exclaimed in the movie *Before Stonewall*, "They took me to their collective bosoms—and boy, was that fun!"

In the '40s, books and movies generally portrayed lesbians and gays as "damaged goods." Asked by Gershick how she perceived her feelings at that time in light of such attitudes, Lisa replied,

> the only thing I thought was, *Maybe we never grew past the teenager stage*. Perhaps we were—what's the word I want?—not retarded in our emotional growth but along in there. . . . I was young then and

> got around a lot, and why should I be unhappy about [my sexual orientation]? You know, it brought me nothing but fun and games and laughter . . . . I wasn't going to change because some book said I was a certain way. What do they know? They aren't me. So I was never particularly militant about it; I was just sort of self-accepting.

Young Lisa soon took a secretarial job at RKO Studios; despite her dislike of office work,[2] she loved her private office:

> In that time, I was still impressed by seeing movie stars in person, you know. And I saw Robert Mitchum, and Cary Grant, and some of the girls—Jane Greer and Gloria Graham. And I got a big kick out of that for a while. And then it began to pall on me. . . . But for a while, it was fun.

Her boss didn't produce a full day's work for her every day, but he wanted her to look busy: no reading or knitting at her desk. How could a creative girl like herself occupy her time?

To attract attention to herself within her circle of friends and acquaintances, in 1947 she decided to create her own little magazine. Lisa told Eric Marcus in *Making History* that *Vice Versa*

> was just sort of a gesture of love—of women loving women, and the whole idea of it. It was an enthusiasm that boiled over into these printed pages, and I wanted to give them to as many people as possible. It was a way of dividing myself into little bits and pieces and saying, "Here you are, take me! I love you all!"

The magazine's distribution swelled each month through word of mouth. In *Happy Endings* she recalled, "When I turned out my first copy, I probably knew about four people. And the next month, they introduced me to some more, and I knew ten people. And so on and so on and so on. So it grew. And eventually it grew to more girls than I had copies!"

While not originally intending to publish *Vice Versa* monthly, she never missed a month from June 1947 through February 1948. She distributed it for free, telling Gershick, "I never charged for it because it was a labor of my heart, and I felt that it would be almost like being a prostitute to charge." She kindly lent me a copy of the whole series; while naturally dated, it still reads very well, and predated all the major gay news magazines of her generation (DOB's *The Ladder*, *Mattachine Review*, and *ONE Magazine*) by at least five years. In the pre-Xerox era, Lisa told me she could create only twelve copies of each issue (with five carbons per original, typed twice). Given her distribution restrictions, she asked recipients to pass each *Vice Versa* around to friends and others sympathetic to its contents. In *Unspeakable*, Rodger Streitmatter editorialized, "*Vice Versa* looked more like a term paper than a newspaper, and it made no pretense of attempting to answer who? what? when? or where? regarding the news of the day. Yet it set the agenda that has dominated lesbian and gay journalism for fifty years."

For a magazine produced in the '40s, *Vice Versa* surprisingly bore no hint of apology. Its issues included book, movie, and theater reviews, poetry, letters to the editor, original fiction, and commentaries on the state of things gay. An excerpt from the last issue, dated February 1948, demonstrates Lisa's theoretical soundness in countering the widespread "sickness" theories about homosexuality prevalent at the time:

> I believe that the current influx of psychiatric literature is largely responsible for a great many of us attempting to analyze ourselves and why we are as we are. Such inward "psychological" reflection, while enabling us to understand ourselves better, also too often offers a convenient crutch with which to support a lot of half-baked theories. Frequently we would rather lean on the crutch than stand on our own two feet and face reality.

In a 1976 interview with Brad Mulroy, Dorr Legg gave credit where credit was due:

> Now Lisa Ben is *it* as far as the continuous movement is concerned. . . . I marvel at how this one young girl conceived of a publication which for many years was the prototype for what we all did: book reviews, editorials, articles, short stories, poetry, and theatre reviews. Lisa Ben had them all. 1947-48 she did that. So that is the apostolic succession.

Contrary to reports that she stopped publishing *Vice Versa* because the work load became too heavy, Lisa told me that when Howard Hughes bought RKO in 1948, the studio terminated her employment (as it did many others). She followed with a series of "horrible" office jobs, including at Universal Studios, but "had to quit [producing the magazine] because there was no opportunity to type privately or anything. So that's why *Vice Versa* bit the dust." Streitmatter also reported Lisa's remarks: "I was getting a little social life, too—becoming a sly little minx. I was discovering what the lesbian lifestyle was all about, and I wanted to live it rather than write about it."

After the magazine folded, Lisa continued her involvement in the lesbian/gay community in Los Angeles as an active member of the

Daughters of Bilitis and through her interactions with several gay male friends:

> An awful lot of fellas knew me socially because in those days, if they had an annual dinner at Christmas time or something, they always had to show up with a girlfriend. And of course, my phone was really busy: "Can you be my girlfriend at our office dinner?" And I'd say, "Oh, of course!" And I'd love to go to those banquets, and they'd show up with little me, and all their office people would show up with their wives and their girlfriends and look just marvelous, and then afterwards they would take me home and then they'd go down to these gay spots for boys, and I didn't care. It was wonderful. And of course, I loved all the boys. They always treated me like a lady, and none of them were raunchy or rude. And I know one time somebody interviewing me said, "Well, didn't you want to be separate from the gay boys?" And I said, "No, not at all!" I said, "I thought of them as my brothers."

In part, she received those invitations because no one would mistake her for a butch. Femmes in the lesbian community reaped certain benefits and encountered certain problems, as Lisa recounted to me:

> It's natural for me to be a girly girl, and I love it, and I'll never change! . . . I can remember dancing at a gay spot one time with a real handsome, tall butch, and she looked down at me, and said, "Are you here just to see how the other half lives?" And of course, here I was in my little dress with my jewelry and little high heels and everything, and I looked at her and I said, "No!" I said, "Why, I'm just as gay as you are. It's just that I don't like to wear men's clothing." And she kind of looked embarrassed, you know. But I've never felt the urge to dress other than I do.

Lisa also sang for a short time with the Sweet Adelines (women's barbershop quartets). By the end of the '40s and into the '50s and '60s, she wrote new, gay words to popular songs, and sang them in gay clubs. Lines such as "I'm gonna sit right down and write my butch a letter / And ask her won't she please turn femme," and "The girl that I marry will probably be / As butch as a hunk of machinery!" are only two examples of her repartee. As she stated in *Happy Endings*,

> I was absolutely appalled at the gay male entertainers who would, on stage, make derogatory remarks and dirty jokes about themselves to entertain the non-gay people who came there to be entertained and "see how the queers lived." No wonder society had such a bad opinion of us. So, I started writing parodies which would be *gay*, but not dirty or demeaning to us. I sang a few of them at one gay bar where

> we would all gather for afternoon dancing, before the nighttime non-gay crowd came in. I did not care to share my songs with a non-gay audience. I wrote strictly for *us*. This is my interpretation of separatism.

While in DOB, Lisa cut a 45 rpm record containing two songs, "Frankie and Johnny," and "Cruising Down the Boulevard," on the short-lived DOB recording label in 1960. She also performed her parodies for various lesbian and gay gatherings for several years, but age has taken its toll on her singing voice, and she can no longer vocalize as she would like.

Curiously, she didn't adopt her moniker "Lisa Ben" until the '60s. She wrote an article for *The Ladder*, and signed it "Ima Spinster." The powers-that-were disliked that pseudonym, and asked her to submit her article under another name. "Now, if that had happened today, I'd say, 'Take it or leave it—I want to use that name. If you don't like it, I'll take my stuff back.' But in those days, as I say, I still was kind of passive about things like that. So I used the name Lisa Ben."[3]

Does she think it easier or harder to be gay now than when she first came out? She referred me to another of her poems, "Nostalgia," in which she wrote, "Back then, there was subterfuge . . . harassment . . . raids. Now, there's wide-open closets, the drug scene—and AIDS!"

While she never developed a long-term relationship with another woman, she explained to Gershick that she feels quite comfortable about her life: "I have a pretty good life the way things are. I'm not bored. I don't feel frustrated or left out of things. I can be into things just as much as I want to, and I don't want to. I like it here. . . . I don't want anybody around me twenty-four hours a day. I *love* my friends, but I want them to go home at night, you know? [Laughs]"

After I finished interviewing her, we went to dinner near her home, and I took her to visit A Different Light bookstore in West Hollywood, a place she had long wanted to visit. Her presence startled several patrons—not because they recognized her (I doubt any did), but because they didn't expect to see a septuagenarian who looked like my grandmother browsing the shelves of alternative literature! It was also my distinct pleasure to speak with her briefly at Jim Kepner's memorial tribute in May 1998, where she clearly sparkled amid the assembled activists and others interested in contemporary gay American history. We have maintained a warm (if irregular) correspondence since our interview, and I will keep the memories close to my heart of an exuberant yet reserved woman who left her indelible mark on our community.

Notes

1. While other works have published her name, she asked me not to reveal it, and I have chosen to honor her request. As she told me, "It's not that I'm ashamed, or anything. But I like my privacy."

2. She also shared with Gershick, "I worked thirty-nine years at the very thing I hated, but I was a darn good secretary. . . . I feel sorry for those people who retire and feel lost. I love being at home, reading, playing with my cats, talking to friends. . . . If I could have retired a day sooner, I would have."

3. However, Lisa allegedly told Gershick that her pen-name resulted from a request to sing one song for a gay album produced by Capitol Records, where she dared not use her given name.

3

JIM KEPNER

There was a fairly common idea, down to some fairly fine details, on how to do [gay community organizing in the early '50s] in the presence of fear, in the presence of real danger, and in the presence of the general feeling that it's impossible. Now, I tried for ten years; Harry [Hay] had tried for twenty; and Dorr [Legg] tried for however many he will tell you, I don't know. . . . When I came out, as soon as I finished the wrestling holds—and I hadn't expected that! The movies I had seen didn't show people in bed together, when they fell in love. At best, they went off onto a hillside arm-in-arm and watched the aurora borealis. [Laughs] Something much more spiritually exciting. Even though I was an atheist at that time. But as soon as we finished the wrestling holds—"When do we organize?" This seemed a natural thing for me. But it did not seem natural for most gays.

—Jim Kepner, 1994

My first step outside my own efforts on the road toward writing this book was a November 1993 letter I sent to Jim Kepner. I had met him at Long Beach Pride in May 1991, and greatly enjoyed speaking with him there. When I wrote him, I knew no other potential interviewee, and knew Kepner only tangentially. Nor did I know how I might contact others I wished to interview. Had Jim turned down or ignored my request, I likely never would have written this book. But Jim welcomed me to visit him in Los Angeles, becoming my first interviewee of over two score during 1994 and 1995. Kepner's handy database also provided me with addresses for about twenty potential interviewees, and I began the project in earnest. I remain eternally grateful for his kindness, and for his invaluable help in making my book a reality. Not only that, he poured out his life's story during five hours on a long Saturday night at his West Hollywood apartment in January 1994.

James Lynn Kepner, Jr. couldn't tell me his birth date. Unlike some others, he was neither coy nor evasive: As he later wrote, it was on September 19, 1923, at the age of approximately seven months, that

> I was found under an oleander bush in Galveston, Texas, a happy, gurgling infant who, as the local press said, enjoyed the familiarities of the officers who took me to the station, then to the hospital, where I was a celebrity for three days before being adopted by idealistic parents whose marriage soon declined to drinking, battering, infidelity and frequent unemployment.

Jim did not discover until he was nineteen that Mary Christine Peterson and James Lynn Kepner, Sr. had adopted him as an infant. Like many children of alcoholics, he assumed significant family responsibilities, helping care for his (also adopted) sister Ella Nora, several years his junior.

Jim recognized his attraction to men before he turned four, although at the time he couldn't identify his feelings as sexual. Religion also played a significant role in Jim's childhood; a Presbyterian, he desired to serve as a Congolese missionary until his teens, when he perceived conflicts among the Bible, history, and science, which caused him to embrace atheism. While some sources reported that Kepner graduated magna cum laude from Ball High School in Galveston, Texas, in 1940, many of his movement peers believed Jim dropped out of high school.

Shortly after his parents divorced in 1942, Jim moved with his sister and father from Galveston to San Francisco. There he eventually discovered the City's gay bar scene (after the draft board rejected him because of his admitted homosexuality). He also happily shed his virginity. As he recollected plurally in *Pursuit & Symposium*'s first issue,

> He kissed us then, wetter than we ever imagined a kiss would be, and longer, first inserting his tongue, then drawing ours deeply into his mouth, till we were desperate for breath. His fingers gently explored, and his other hand, warm, soft, moist, found our hand and guided it south. We'd never felt one, besides our own, before, and this was more impressive than our own. . . . Our lesson lasted past midday, with an adjournment for afternoon breakfast. He was tireless, versa-

> tile, astonishingly flexible. We were silly about it all, sentimental and unbelievably clumsy—we haven't changed too much in those particulars. We were decidedly incompetent in some matters, but all of it was excitingly romantic, the fulfilment [sic] of undared dreams, though some of it also was shocking or painful. To put it in the most banal way, and we were then oozing banalities, we enjoyed every minute.

Around that time Jim also began collecting books and materials about the nascent gay community, which eventually grew into the International Gay & Lesbian Archives.

Not only did Kepner discover the beginnings of a community in 1943, he suddenly found himself secretary of a gay organization before he was permitted even to join it! As Jim told Eric Marcus in *Making History*, Wally Jordan, Kepner's Wisconsin pen pal,

> asked if I had ever heard of the Sons of Hamidy. After another two or three letters, he described this as a secret national homosexual rights organization started in the 1880s that fell apart due to bitch fights, which is naturally what gay groups do. He said it was reorganized in 1934 and again fell apart during bitch fights and was now being reorganized with some senators and generals in leading roles. Through three or four letters I asked, "How do I join?" And he kept being vague. . . . I began receiving visits and letters from some of my pen pal's other correspondents and learned that I was national secretary of the Sons of Hamidy! Well, that was a jolt because, poor little me, I was a nobody. With all of these senators and generals, what the hell was I doing as national secretary?[1]

By the '90s, Kepner revealed that "[y]ears later, Wally admitted Hamidy was just a dream, no strategies, no big shots—just a hunger for justice."

Surprisingly, Jim recalled that even in the early '40s twenty to thirty gay bars thrived in San Francisco, even if most were short-lived. During Stonewall 25 in 1994, Kepner told **Randy Wicker**,

> You'd enjoy yourself at a bar for a few weeks, and then the next night you'd go there, and there's a guard at the door—"We don't want your kind here." So there was always some enterprising queen who would go dancing down the street. Look in every bar. Wave at the bartender. And if he didn't get thrown out, that was a gay bar within a half-hour.

Kepner never fully adjusted to gay life during that time, chafing at external pressure "to be either queen or trade. I didn't fit either role."

In 1943 Jim moved to greater Los Angeles, where for a time he retreated from exploring gay life into his beloved science fiction, editing a magazine (*Towards Tomorrow*), dabbling in socialism, and promoting civil rights for African-Americans. He moved to New York for a few years, where he became a Communist Party member and *Daily Worker* columnist until his homosexuality resulted in his expulsion. After managing a bookstore in San Francisco, Jim returned to southern California in the early '50s. There Kepner eventually participated in the burgeoning Mattachine Foundation in December 1952, and he volunteered with ONE, Inc. for several years beginning in 1953. Shortly before this time, Jim attempted to organize gays and lesbians to begin either a magazine or some other enterprise, but homophobia and the beginnings of McCarthyism conspired to thwart his ambitions. Despite Harry Hay's contentions to the contrary, Kepner perceived even the early Mattachine participants as "very conformist," and Mattachine's insistence on secrecy frustrated him. When Mattachine's founders resigned at its May 1953 convention after rumors spread that they were Communists, the organization grew even more timid.

As a result, Jim gradually shifted his focus to ONE. He wrote articles for *ONE Magazine* beginning in April 1954 (often under pseudonyms such as Dal McIntyre, Lyn Pedersen, and Frank Golovitz) and a regular column, "Tangents," which covered news items of interest to gays and lesbians. In 1956 Jim also cofounded ONE's gay studies program, developing such now-established community theories as reclamation of gay and lesbian history, respect for diversity, and institution building. Kepner also edited the *ONE Institute Quarterly of Homophile Studies* from 1958-60, and Volume II of *An Annotated Bibliography of Homosexuality* in the mid-'70s.

He and ONE stalwart **Dorr Legg** had a serious falling out in 1960; as Legg explained to me, "Jim has had his books in and out of ONE's library for years. . . . And then he would, every time there was some kind of a disagreement, he would jerk 'em out and go home, and then finally, I think he just felt that he could never be comfortable until he formed something of his own." But Kepner countered in July 1995 in his personal newsletter (*Song & Dance*) that Legg's withholding an IRS letter from him regarding ONE's nontax-exempt status (in light of Jim's deduction for books donated to ONE and his personal liability as corporate president) caused the rift: "Dorr said I was immature enough to take the letter seriously. Damn right I took it seriously!" Kepner dissociated himself from both the magazine and the organization, becoming a taxi driver and Los Angeles City College student in the early '60s, and chairman of a short-lived Los Angeles Mattachine in 1963, but he returned in 1972 to become president of the board of ONE, Inc.

In the summer of 1963, Jim and Harry Hay began and ended an ill-fated relationship. At that time each found himself on the outs with the various gay groups in Los Angeles; as Jim said, "I couldn't become a Daughter of Bilitis." Regarding Harry, Jim told me, "I'm super-awed by him, and always have been. I love him, and I was almost inclined to say I can't stand him. . . . I think he does not let himself realize how domineering he is." Hay, in contrast, praised Kepner in the summer 1998 *ONE/IGLA Bulletin*: "Jim was a provocative thinker who got me to re-examine a lot of my own thinking. . . . We developed a brotherhood that was as sacred as anything I've ever known. Jim had great vision and dreams, and I loved him for it."

Jim kept his hand in journalism through the '70s, writing for *The Advocate* (even when, before Dick Michaels purchased it, it served merely as an L.A. community organization's newsletter). Kepner also created his own magazine, *Pursuit & Symposium*, in the mid-'60s. After "the Heist" and the split at ONE (see Dorr Legg), coupled with *Mattachine Review*'s decline, Jim told me, "I figured there was an open field. I hadn't really noticed *Drummer*." He also hadn't counted on a significant price increase from the days of editing *ONE Magazine*; instead of $500 per issue, suddenly Kepner found "it cost $2,000 for six thousand copies of the first issue." He attempted to negotiate a loan on his house to pay the additional unanticipated costs. Initially the bank approved the loan, but then reversed itself (after Jim spent the unreceived proceeds on various incidentals needed to produce a high-quality magazine). By the time Kepner resolved the bank issue, "all of a sudden the loan company owned my house for just enough to pay for the printing of one issue." Only two issues appeared: March-April 1966 and June 1967. In effect, *Pursuit & Symposium* was stillborn. Despite the difficulties and frustrations, almost thirty years later Jim smiled and spoke of the experience fondly: "It was fun! It was really fun."

From the '50s through the '70s, Kepner constantly provided useful service to the expanding gay movement. In addition to his journalistic forays, Kepner codirected the Southern California Council on Religion and the Homophile in 1966, and cofounded several other southern California groups, including SPREE (the Society of Pat Rocco Enlightened Enthusiasts), Christopher Street West, and the Gay & Lesbian Community Services Center (now known simply as The Center). Jim also taught initial courses at the ONE Institute in 1956 and its first extension classes (in San Francisco) in 1957, and he led four gay studies classes at UCLA beginning in 1974. Of the latter, he remarked he received "no credit, no pay. [Laughs] I didn't even get free parking. But they were fun."

Around this time **Dick Leitsch** interacted with Kepner. Leitsch's impressions? Jim "was this old queen who always wanted to hang out with the youngest people, and be right on the cutting edge, the newest, the most radical things!" While Kepner valiantly attempted to weather the movement's shift from homophile identification to gay liberation, he admitted to me, "I think Dorr [Legg] would count it a discredit for me, that I have tended to change largely with the times." Jim also acknowledged in his final *Song & Dance*,

> I'm not the only Gay activist who once held a lead position, and now finds himself often way behind, trying to figure out where the movement went, and why. . . . I've done a better job of riding with the changes than most old activists—but I get winded easily now, and have a harder time keeping up with the jackrabbits as they rush uphill.

In the '40s, years before Harry Hay conceptualized Mattachine, Kepner began collecting miscellaneous gay ephemera. By 1972, Kepner opened his home to display his collection, and in 1975 he named it the Western Gay Archives. By 1979, the collection moved to Hollywood's Hudson Street; renamed the National Gay Archives, **Frank Kameny** and **Barbara Gittings**, among others, lent their names and their time to the project. In 1981, Kepner explained to Charles Faber in an *Advocate* article,

> The chief purpose of the Archives is to serve the needs of self-definition—finding out who we are. . . . We want the resources of the Archives to be an active and creating agency in the community, to be the flowering of that understanding of ourselves. We see the Archives as a catalyst in the community, not just a pile of old papers and books that gather dust.

According to Legg, Kepner discussed merging the Archives with ONE's materials in the mid-'80s, "but Jim set up such an utterly impractical set of regulations for such a thing. Such as that we would have to be open until 2:00 in the morning on weekends, and all this sort of thing. I mean, he really believed this! Because there would be people getting out of the bars who might like to come." Assuming the statement's veracity, and despite its virtual impossibility, it sounds entirely in character for the optimistic Kepner, who eagerly desired to make his materials accessible to everyone. By 1986 the collection was renamed the International Gay & Lesbian Archives, and in 1988 IGLA moved from Hollywood to West Hollywood (on Robertson Boulevard). In 1995 the Archives formally merged with the ONE Institute of Homophile Studies' collection, now housed at the University of Southern

California. Jim also relocated to USC, where he could attend to his precious collection, over which he served for many years as curator, and where he was last listed as "Research Historian." At the end of 2000, Billy Glover of the Homosexual Information Center announced that all three collections had merged "under the general new name of One Institute and Archives" at 909 West Adams in Los Angeles, only a few blocks from USC's main campus.

While Jim's health had been generally good, doctors diagnosed him with colon cancer in 1983, for which he underwent a colostomy. He told a SPREE crowd after his surgery that "'while I no longer had an asshole, I could still be one.' Some listeners applauded, some were shocked. I'd decided not to be closeted about it."

Kepner never really sought the limelight, and in many ways this self-effacing man remained humble to a fault. Of the senior movement-based men I met, he possessed the least ego; I spoke with Kepner more easily than with the others, with whom I often felt as if I was polkaing with porcupines. Even in his last *Song & Dance*, dated August 1997, Jim spoke of his ideological flexibility: In contrast to his movement peers, Kepner acknowledged, "I am not omniscient. I may strongly defend whatever I believe at the moment, but I always recall the evolution of my views from some that I now reject, and if I live long enough, I'll rethink or drop some ideas I now hold firmly."

Most of his movement peers respected and admired him and his work. As I traveled the country, **Jack Nichols** described Jim as "just an all-around good person"; **Barbara Grier** remembered him as "always diffident, and charming, and easy to work with"; **Hal Call** remarked, "Jim's a good man. I've always liked Jim"; **Mark Thompson**, who wrote a glowing preface to Kepner's only publisher-printed work, *Rough News—Daring Views*, declared, "I think so highly of Jim, and his work. . . . Certainly, in my book, Jim Kepner is sort of deserving of gay sainthood if anybody is." Randy Wicker was most effusive: "Jim Kepner is one of the most fantastic and impressive human beings I've ever known. . . . What's so impressive with Jim Kepner was, he was so warm and knowledgeable."

Kepner and I interacted occasionally after our interview, including at Stonewall 25 in New York in 1994 and through cordial correspondence. Providence allowed me one final conversation with Jim about a month before he died. In his last *Song & Dance*, Kepner noted that he hoped to do some traveling to promote his upcoming publication, *Rough News—Daring Views*. Accordingly, I called and invited him to stay with me in Phoenix if his plans led him toward the desert Southwest. Despite his frustration that his publisher had not yet released the book, he hoped to visit to promote book sales, and he sounded in very good spirits. Sadly, fate squelched our plans—on November 15, 1997, Jim Kepner died following emergency surgery for a perforated intestine.

I consider myself privileged to have attended Jim's memorial service in Beverly Hills on May 22, 1998, where Jim's friends and fellow pioneers gathered to praise his tireless efforts to shape the movement. Barbara Gittings eulogized, "Jim was a sweet, low-key person who kept on plugging at his dream, never abandoning it, always tending it. The notion of burnout wasn't even in his cosmos. And even when his health faltered, Jim didn't. He put his time and his energy and what little money he had into creating a better life for us." From another generation, **Urvashi Vaid** described Kepner's legacy as "aware, helpful, thoughtful, humble, considerate, and above all, deeply intelligent. And quite radical, to the core." Co-emcee **Robin Tyler** read a letter from **Troy Perry**, unable to attend at the last minute, which proclaimed, "We can all be thankful that Jim was determined to preserve our history, and for that we should be eternally grateful. . . . [H]is work will continue to be a blessing to generations of gay men and lesbians in the centuries to come." **Malcolm Boyd** remembered Jim's joy in his avocation: "He loved his [Archives] work. A single reference of a page in a book, or a press clipping, had immediate salvation for him. It made him smile, laugh, feel good about himself, and our lesbian and gay stories provided his energy and pride." **Lisa Ben**, Hal Call, Harry Hay, Frank Kameny, **Kay Tobin Lahusen**, **Phyllis Lyon**, **Del Martin**, Jack Nichols, **José Sarria**, and Mark Thompson, among many others, attended to pay their respects to Kepner's memory and community service, perhaps the most illustrious assemblage ever of gay movement leaders.

Jim was that rarest of jewels, the worker bee concerned less with his own status than with the good of the movement, willing to serve in any capacity to make things happen. Not a born leader, Kepner was a born follower; in 1993, he obliquely acknowledged the same, writing, "I get frustrated with Boards of Directors, in time serving on scores of boards, and often end up at odds with groups I helped start. I'm never sure how much that's my fault. Even with the Archives, I often feel trapped in a bad marriage." But "loyal follower" is often a more difficult role than "fearless leader," and Jim probably followed better and more dutifully than any other man in the gay movement.

Harry Hay biographer Stuart Timmons said eloquently of Kepner, "He is our Claudius. He has seen everything, at least in the West, and jotted all of it down. His legacy is crucial: Extroverts fade, scriveners endure." For more than half a century since his first timid searches to find his community, Jim Kepner endured—and endeared himself to those whose lives his efforts improved.

Note

1. Curiously, the Sons of Hamidy received a nearly two-page spread in *Homosexuals Today—1956*. This article explained the Sons of Hamidy's "'apocalyptic program of retribution against a hostile society.' Political aims were foremost, centering on civil rights for homosexuals and the punishment of all who opposed or persecuted them. . . . Large membership was desired in order to acquire political power. The next step projected was 'to take over' government offices and other positions of authority. There is no evidence that these somewhat fascistic goals had any political or ideological bias other than that of justice for homosexuals. . . . At the peak of its activity there were said to be thousands of members. Meetings, probably social in character, were held by chapters in Philadelphia, Asheville, Chicago, Milwaukee and other Wisconsin cities, Los Angeles, and in various places in Arizona. By 1943, and after hints of financial irregularities, the men of note and wealth deserted."

4

HAL CALL

> **I would like to be remembered as one of the P.R. people who helped spread the word in the early days about the plight of the homosexual, and endeavored to ease the problems of the homosexual in our midst, and bring him an opportunity to come to grips and live with himself, understand himself better. And also, I would like to think that I contributed some to the erotica scene, with kind of a glorification of the male member. [Laughs]**
>
> —Hal Call, 1994

San Francisco has long enjoyed its reputation as the world's "gay Mecca." As a result, many people assume it always has been so. "The love that dared not speak its name" may have been practiced in San Francisco, but it was really no gayer than any other large U.S. city until the '40s and '50s. As the primary U.S. military port on the Pacific during World War II, servicepeople came to San Francisco from all over the country. A combination of San Francisco's allure and the service's "blue discharges" for homosexuality swelled the ranks of gay men and lesbians in the City. Within a few years, gay visibility increased, and the City's lesbian/gay community began to develop political clout. Arguably, the seminal figure of San Francisco's gay movement was Hal Call, a strong-willed, controversial, conservative/radical transplant who permanently impacted the U.S. gay movement during the '50s. I met with Hal at his place of business, San Francisco's Circle J Cinema, in May 1994. It was the most unusual setting among my interviews; while

Call proudly displayed the original Mattachine banner on the wall of his office, ten video screens simultaneously displayed hard-core male erotica. (It took all my concentration to focus on Hal!)

Although Hal limited his movement activity after the '60s, recollections by his contemporaries reflect Call's controversial role during the homophile era. Those who worked with him or knew him during his heyday shared vivid memories with me. **Jim Kepner** felt that Hal's sexual attitudes reflected his poor self-image; **José Sarria** inferred that Hal ill-concealed ulterior motives in helping young, wayward gay men; **Randy Wicker** described Hal as "tacky," "sleazy," and "a crook"; **Jack Nichols** recalled Hal's bickering with him and Richard Inman over use of the "Mattachine" name in Florida in the mid-'60s. On the other hand, Nichols encountered Call face-to-face in the '80s and found him "very pleasant and very personable;" **Frank Kameny** remained on friendly terms with Hal; **Dick Leitsch** "liked Hal immeasurably, and thought he was one of the few people who had his feet on the ground about the movement. [He was] the only one that had any sense of proportion [about sex];" **Harry Britt** described Hal as "a remarkable human being;" and **Troy Perry** described someone "so articulate." What kind of polarizing figure managed to generate such strong and conflicting emotions?

Harold L. Call was born in north-central Missouri in September 1917, the eldest of three sons. While Hal "never was taught anything about sexuality at all from Mother and Dad," he discovered his sexual attraction to males during the onset of puberty. The U.S. Army inducted Call in 1941; he served in the Pacific theater, and he rose to the rank of captain. One of the most traumatic days of Call's life occurred on the island of Saipan in August 1944, when the enemy attacked his battalion; while approximately forty men lost their lives, Call luckily "got through it unscathed," and earned a Purple Heart. After completing his stint in the service in 1946, Call obtained his journalism degree from the University of Missouri in 1947, and he worked in the advertising department of the *Kansas City Star*, which eventually transferred him to Chicago.

In August 1952, police arrested Hal, along with three other men, on morals charges. After paying $800 to dismiss his case, Call promptly left Chicago for San Francisco. As Eric Marcus recorded in *Making History*, Hal said,

> I decided after my arrest that instead of going where the job took me, I was going to go where I wanted and find my own career. So my lover and I drove from Chicago to San Francisco with all of our possessions in the autumn of 1952, and I've been here since. Now, we didn't choose San Francisco because it was some kind of gay

> mecca. Back then, it wasn't. But from when I first saw San Francisco during World War II, I thought it was the best place to live in North America because of its beauty and location.

Call's decision to heed Horace Greeley's famous advice ("Go West, young man") proved fateful for the homophile movement.

While the original Mattachine Foundation originated in Los Angeles in November 1950, and briefly blossomed in the East Bay city of Berkeley through the efforts of one Gerry Brissette in early 1953, the concept had not yet taken root in San Francisco. After connecting with Brissette, Call attended a Mattachine discussion group in Berkeley, and quickly became active in developing a Mattachine branch in the City. Amazingly, by Mattachine's April and May 1953 conventions, he and three other Mattachine newcomers (David "Nellie" Finn, Marilyn "Boopsie" Rieger, and Kenneth Burns) transformed the secretive Mattachine Foundation into the more open, democratic Mattachine Society.

At the May convention, as rumors of communism among Mattachine's leaders swept through the assemblage, Burns, Rieger, Finn, and Call, among others, pressed Mattachine to end its secrecy and create a statement renouncing communism among its members. Ironically, while that faction's motions failed, Mattachine's founders (several of whom had communist ties) knew the time had come for them to step down and turn the organization over to the new vanguard. In *The Trouble with Harry Hay*, Timmons quoted Mattachine co-founder Chuck Rowland as saying, "When we announced that we were resigning, a lot of people yelled, 'Oh, no, no.' But the Hal Call faction was delighted."

When the original founders left Mattachine, they took with it much of its activist spirit, and for a time the organization's membership declined precipitously. In Call's defense, anti-communist witch hunts reached fever pitch during the early '50s, and many Mattachine members besides Call feared the compounded repercussions that could ensue if either potential members or the larger society that Mattachine hoped to influence should discover the communist sympathies of Mattachine's founders. In Rodger Streitmatter's *Unspeakable*, Hal explained that before Mattachine "went public, we had to make sure we didn't have persons in our midst who were communists and would disgrace us all. The Reds had to go." Hal also told me that

> Harry Hay and Chuck Rowland and those boys in the Fifth Order of the secret Mattachine Society, they had the idea for the society, but they had not the slightest grasp of public relations, or how to promote something, or how to sell an idea! It was their idea, and I'm the one that developed the sales of it. . . . They had no concept of what to do to expand it, and to protect the security of those who came to it, and

> at the same time, connect with people in the major society, in the professions, in law, the judges, the courts, in law enforcement, in the academic world, and in the world of writing and literature and research, behavioral sciences, and so on. We had to work with people in all those. And as I have been quoted, sort of derisively at times, I've said, "We have to ride on their shirt-tails." Well, God damn it, we did! . . . We had to get the recognition from established elements in the total society that we were human beings, different mainly only in our choice of a sex object. And there was nothing that anybody else had to fear.

In addition, significant philosophical differences developed between the original founders and Call's faction:

> Harry Hay and his friends, they wanted Mattachine and its people, gay people, to be another subgroup in society. We didn't feel that way. We wanted to blend into total society, and be assimilated, and accepted by all. . . . We treated our technique mainly as an educational project, and our concept was to eliminate the prejudice and ignorance about homosexuality so that the homosexual in our midst could be assimilated in total society, as a responsible person, simply different in the choice of sex object. That was about the only difference he or she really put forth. And that otherwise, the problems of the homosexual in society, when that was achieved, when that status of acceptance and understanding was achieved, the "problem" of the homosexual would fade away, and there wouldn't be any, and Mattachine could disband!

Yet in *Rough News—Daring Views*, Jim Kepner countered that the "second Mattachine" leaders (including Call)

> took a conformist, assimilationist approach to our issues. They hoped to persuade influential hetero friends that homosexuals were all respectable citizens in two-button roll suits, and that the few embarrassing queens, dikes [*sic*], and hustlers would disappear once legal persecution ended. They sought researchers to find out what had gone wrong with us.

The debate regarding gay assimilation has scarcely changed since the movement's virtual inception.

Once Call and like-minded members wrested control of Mattachine from its founders, what did they do with it? Call described the futility of the task to Marcus:

> We were doing a $300,000-a-year—in 1950s dollars—public relations job on $12,000 a year income with three or four people doing the work. And what we needed to do was a $3 million-a-year PR job.

> We were overwhelmed by what we needed to do. So we had to pick out what we could do with the resources that were available.

Perhaps Call's greatest contributions to the movement involved his efforts as publications director/editor (and occasional pseudonymous writer) for *Mattachine Review*, begun in January 1955 and continuing through 1967. Along with ONE, Inc.'s newsletter, begun in 1953, and followed by the Daughters of Bilitis's newsletter, *The Ladder*, begun in 1956, *Mattachine Review* informed its subscribers of pertinent news affecting gay men and lesbians. In the summer of 1954, Call and others, including longtime business partner Don Lucas, created Pan-Graphic Press,[1] which printed *Mattachine Review*. Why Pan-Graphic Press? "We wanted a printing press that was not subject to the whim of the newest wave of voting members of the Mattachine Society."

Call also assisted gay men who risked arrest solely for frequenting a gay bar. Hal recounted to Eric Marcus that "[t]he cops knew there was a Mattachine Society, a group of queers that was daring to stand up and work on behalf of other queers whom the police were busting." Mattachine also sponsored national conventions, bringing like-minded people together to discuss problems and seek solutions. In 1957, *Mattachine Review* reported its actions to date in education, research, public relations, and social services. Call also participated in a New York City television program, "Showcase," on March 10, 1958, and in a radio discussion of homosexuals and their relation to society that November. During this era, local Mattachine chapters engaged in peer counseling and referred members and others to sympathetic professionals.

Combined with DOB's inception in 1955, Mattachine's presence in San Francisco resulted in the City's reputation as the capital of gay and lesbian America. As other organizations emerged and flourished, power struggles ensued. When the Mattachine Society of New York's membership began to surpass San Francisco Mattachine's, Hal exerted his influence to convince a majority of Mattachine's national board of directors to revoke all area chapter charters on March 12, 1961, leaving each chapter to fend for itself and develop a direction unique to its environs. The results, however, proved disastrous: the Boston and Chicago chapters dissolved; the Denver chapter transformed into "The Neighbors" before fading from the scene; the Los Angeles chapter became the Homophile Assistance League of Southern California; the Philadelphia chapter reorganized as the Janus Society; and the Mattachine Society of New York stubbornly retained its name and vision. As Hal interpreted the revocation, "some of the leading New Yorkers wanted to take over Mattachine and carry it back to New York City. . . . New York City can never be the branch office of anything! It's either head office or nothing. Well, by God, they didn't accomplish it. I didn't let 'em."

Since Hal permitted no challenges to his leadership of Mattachine, new groups, such as Guy Strait's League for Civil Education and the Society for Individual Rights (SIR), surfaced in San Francisco in the early '60s. These entities effectively limited Call's influence in matters affecting the nascent gay community.[2] Despite this, Call denied opposing SIR:

> Some of its organizational meetings were held in my flat, up on Pine Street. So I'm not anti-SIR. . . . We always cooperated with SIR. There was not any heavy antagonism between SIR and Mattachine. Mattachine had sort of done its thing. And our group of leaders were sort of diminishing in our influence and activity, while theirs was growing and expanding.

From 1964 to 1966, Hal produced a new publication, *Town Talk*, which featured ads for bars and erotica among its articles, which were more sexualized than those found in *Mattachine Review*.

Having fought the battle for gay visibility and respectability for a decade and a half, Call switched his focus to sexual liberation. Hal took credit for a 1967 federal court victory that "opened the door for the male nude to go through the United States mails." Around this time, Hal opened the Adonis Bookstore, and later he directed what remained of the Mattachine Society into Cinemattachine. The latter eventually became the Circle J Cinema, an adult male theater currently operating at 369 Ellis Street. Chuck Rowland referred to this period in *Making History* as the time when "this rotten son of a bitch turned our sacred Mattachine into a cock suck-off club. It made me sick to my stomach when I first heard about that. And he simply used the Mattachine all these years as a device for supporting himself."

Call's unwavering positive stance on private/public male sexuality may have contributed to the negation of his prior accomplishments among his contemporaries. Hal's twofold reasoning for providing men's private sex clubs (with guidelines developed in concert with the San Francisco Police Department, the district attorney's office, and the mayor's office)? They reduced the risk of gay men encountering public arrest by providing a private, safe place to express one's sexuality with others, and "they were good for mental health." In CBS's 1967 documentary *The Homosexuals*, Call spoke on behalf of San Francisco Mattachine, stating that "the laws which forbid certain types of private, consenting sexual behavior among adults need to be changed. So that what adults do willingly in private is their own affair." Call also took great pride in providing the first live gay male stage performances in the mid-'70s. As Hal told me, "I'm a sexualist. I've always said, 'We're fighting for sexual freedom. Let's have some.'"

In contrast to the precarious state of many gay pioneers' finances, the Circle J's financial success provided Call a very comfortable income, and he supported many organizations serving the gay community. Following Call's $50,000 donation to ONE, Inc., in 1994, **Dorr Legg** effusively praised Hal's generosity. Call, who continued to serve on ONE, Inc.'s board of directors until its merger with the International Gay & Lesbian Archives in 1995, spoke very modestly about his contribution: "I felt it was time to put my money where my mouth was." Call also contributed generously to local AIDS organizations from Circle J's profits, telling me in 1995: "In the last decade, I've contributed fifteen or twenty thousand dollars to AIDS organizations and enterprises, project groups in this city, including the hospice and the feeding project, and the AIDS Foundation and the like." And by 1998, Hal contributed another $50,000 to ONE/IGLA to endow the Hal Call/Mattachine Scholarship Fund, which ONE's Dr. Walter Williams proclaimed "has already helped several graduate students write their dissertations, found ways to reduce homophobia, and has brought many scholars [to Los Angeles] from throughout the world." Those actions changed Randy Wicker's perception of Call, as he noted in an e-mail to Jack Nichols: "I was obviously wrong to believe that he was just an 'exploiter' and 'pornographer' in the movement. The fact that he made such significant contributions to keep a cash-strapped institution viable redeems him in my eyes. . . . I regret having been so critical."

Hal also enjoyed travel; by the end of 1993, he achieved his goal of traveling to every continent in the world (he also visited every U.S. state capital). The vigorous Call enjoyed excellent health into his eighties, but he died of congestive heart failure on December 18, 2000. Despite Call's intelligence, he did not espouse today's "politically correct" positions; Hal remained unenlightened regarding racial issues, and many women endured his chauvinistic attitudes.[3]

In *Out of the Closets*, referring to Call and Dorr Legg, author Laud Humphreys wrote, "although both men may be described as 'articulate and outgoing,' neither is particularly 'charismatic' in the sense of being capable or desirous of stirring a crowd to action. They inspired confidence, chiefly due to their willingness to devote themselves to the movement on a full-time basis. . . . These men did not *found* a movement, they were *found by* it." While not completely untrue, I feel such assertions shortchange both men. In large part, Call powered the second wave of activism following the initial work of Mattachine's founders, and he laid the groundwork for what followed his efforts. Today's movement leaders owe a debt of gratitude to this pioneer, whose peers often overlooked his accomplishments in light of his unconventional character.

Notes

1. Pan-Graphic Press existed through 2000; Hal described it as "the oldest gay business established for gay service in San Francisco."

2. Through the '90s, the Mattachine Society of San Francisco remained an active entity. As Call described it, "I don't know whether it's really, absolutely, technically alive in the state of California, but we still operate as the Mattachine Society, Inc. It's a corporate entity that does service, particularly things like these interviews, which are important for the early history of the gay movement." MSSF holds an annual meeting "to officially try to say that Mattachine is still alive." At least as of 1995, Hal served as executive director, and Don Lucas remained a member.

3. **Del Martin** shared with me that Call "was always so opinionated. And bossy." Little wonder Martin felt that way, since Hal dared print in the November 1959 *Mattachine Review*, "The Daughters of Bilitis are sort of a woman's auxiliary to Mattachine."

5

JOSÉ SARRIA

People say that I have been ahead of the times. They listened to me and I believed that I had a direct line to the truth. My getting up and doing what I did will hopefully give younger people an incentive to say what's on their minds. They don't ever have to keep their mouths shut.

—José Sarria, *Advocate* interview with **Mark Thompson**, April 3, 1980

Unless you have studied gay history, you probably have never heard of José Sarria. However, Sarria earned his prominent place in gay/lesbian history for several reasons: As an entertainer who performed in women's clothing at the bohemian Black Cat bar in the '50s and '60s, San Francisco's burgeoning gay/lesbian community drew strength from his symbolic performances; in 1961, he ran for public office, the first openly gay person to do so in the United States; and he created the Imperial Court system, which has provided funds for a multitude of charities since its 1965 inception.

José Julio Sarria (aka Marquesa Josefina de Sarria, The Bay Street Songbird, The Male Anna Russell, Empress I de San Francisco Empress of the United States, Protectoress of Columbia, First Protectorate of Mexico, Dowager of the West, Madame of Salina's Parlour, etc.) was born at San Francisco's St. Francis Hospital,[1] the son of Colombian Maria Dolores Maldonado and Nicaraguan (of Spanish descent) Julio Sarria, maitre d' at the Palace Hotel. Discussing his mother, Sarria told Michael Gorman, "My mother paid her whole life for my birth.

She could have married some very big millionaires here in San Francisco, but she never married . . . for fear that they would mistreat me because of my illegitimacy. . . . She paid a bigger price than I ever did." José saw his father only once, just before he returned to Nicaragua. José began cross-dressing very early in his aunts' and cousins' clothing, and he had his own "drag closet" by age four. Otherwise, José's early life seems somewhat unremarkable, although he self-identified as gay by fourth grade, and he explained to Gorman, "I've never really lived a double life. It's not that I tell everybody, but people know; you're not fooling anybody." As a child, he had no intention to make his mark in life as an entertainer. He performed well academically, and served as a student body officer in both his junior and senior years.

Shortly after graduating from high school, Sarria joined the U.S. Army in 1942, and he eventually served in Europe. While the armed forces needed every able-bodied person willing to serve during World War II, José had difficulty persuading any branch to take him. Sarria's barrier was not his sexual orientation, but his size; at that time, he stood just under five feet tall and weighed less than one hundred pounds. After attending college for a year in Biarritz, France, Sarria enrolled at San Jose State University, studying French, German, and history, but he did not obtain a college degree. During that time, José easily found men willing to have sex, whether in San Francisco, San Jose, or even on campus, if he acted discreetly. (But that didn't mean San Francisco had a gay community per se before World War II. In *The Other Side of Silence*, José explained, "There may have been a 'sub-culture' of some kind . . . but there was not what I would call a gay society. I know. I looked!") After college, José worked as the first male waiter at the San Francisco airport and he also taught part-time when he met the love of his life.

The Black Cat, located at 710 Montgomery Street in San Francisco, developed a reputation as a bohemian bar for "free" people (including, but not limited to, gay men and lesbians). Upon meeting Black Cat bartender and waiter Jimmy Moore there, José bet his sister Teresa $10 that he could get Jimmy to his dinner table in Redwood City before Teresa could get Jimmy to her dinner table in Hillsborough. As so often happened, a determined José proved successful. Sarria also began working at the Black Cat as a waiter, and José and Jimmy lived together for nine years in a loving but turbulent relationship until Jimmy committed suicide resulting from his drinking problems. Early in José and Jimmy's relationship, police arrested Sarria in a public restroom at the St. Francis Hotel on a trumped-up morals charge. As a registered sex offender, José lost his teaching job. Needing another source of income to supplement his waiter's earnings, Sarria sang at several Bay Area nightclubs before he began performing at the Black Cat.

On nights when Moore drank too much, José worked Jimmy's shift. One Saturday night in 1958, the Black Cat's piano player performed excerpts from *Carmen*. Sarria spontaneously performed an abbreviated (and gay-themed) version of the opera for delighted patrons. José so impressed Black Cat owner Sol Stoumen that he asked José to perform similar operettas at the bar on Sunday afternoons. As a result, Sarria earned one of his many nicknames, "The Nightingale of Montgomery Street." Sarria continued those performances until the bar closed in the early morning hours of October 31, 1963.[2] While José wore women's costumes during his performances, he adamantly refused the appellation "drag queen": "When I put a dress on, it's because you paid me. I did not put on a dress because I needed sexual gratification. Or I was going to try to fool you. I put on a dress because it added to the show that I did. It helped you fantasize what you were seeing."

José also involved himself in San Francisco gay politics. Disdaining Mattachine's efforts (telling Gorman, "the Mattachine Society is catering to the lawyers and the doctors and the Indian chiefs, and not to the peasants. They are the ones who are getting arrested. They are the ones who don't know the law. They are the ones who don't have the money to buy their way out"), José joined Guy Strait and others in forming the League for Civil Education in 1960. He explained to Gorman, "Everyone thought that Guy Strait was the one who organized it. I let them think that, but I was the one that organized it, who was responsible for it." A few years later, LCE split into two entities: *Cruise News and World Report*, a gay community publication, and the Society for Individual Rights, a gay group that emphasized education and service.

Prior to the Black Cat's closing, José ran for a seat on San Francisco's Board of Supervisors in 1961. Sarria never anticipated victory: "Had I won, I think I would have died." He intended his candidacy to show San Francisco's elected officials that a significant gay vote existed, and he wanted to encourage gay men and lesbians not to accept second-class citizenship in San Francisco.[3] After declaring his candidacy, José struggled to obtain enough signatures to place his name on the ballot. (Sarria told me, "I needed $25 and thirty-five signatures. The $25 was easy. But I couldn't get the signatures. Many told me they were behind me, but that they just could not sign. Nobody wanted to endorse a known homosexual, and I ran an open campaign." He elaborated to Gorman, "How I finally got the people to sign was that I picked people out that were closet queens who had a little dirt on them. I told them, 'You sign the papers or I'll expose you.'") José also struggled during the campaign to find a sufficiently respectable male wardrobe;

he explained in a May 23, 1985, *San Francisco Sentinel* interview with Tom Murray,

> Because I worked full-time at the Cat, I dressed as a character. My wardrobe would be considered common today, but in 1961 it appeared outrageous. I did not own a complete man's outfit. My rommate [*sic*] solved the problem: he loaned me a shirt, tie and coat so a [campaign] picture could be taken from the waist up; no one would suspect that I wore boxer shorts below.

Ironically, Sarria actually might have won one of the five available supervisorial seats had twenty-four San Franciscans not declared their candidacies within twelve hours of the filing deadline; José believes City officials, fearing a Sarria victory, encouraged these eleventh-hour candidates to run. On November 7, 1961, receiving more than 5,600 votes, Sarria finished ninth in the thirty-three-person field, the most crowded ballot in San Francisco electoral history.

When the Black Cat closed, Sarria found himself without a setting to display his talents; with the LCE/SIR split, he also discovered a diffusion of his community's energy. As José admitted to Mark Thompson in 1980, "I lost the election, my mother died, the Cat closed. What else could happen to a person? Not even the doctor bill made me get out of bed." But he persevered, and he introduced an audacious idea that proved enormously successful.

To unite the community, José created for himself a character, Empress José I, the widow of self-proclaimed Emperor Joshua Abraham Norton, an eccentric legend of late nineteenth-century San Francisco history.[4] Sarria crowned himself empress in 1964 and devised the Imperial Court system, made up at that time of members from several of San Francisco's community organizations, including DOB, SIR, the Tavern Guild, and Mattachine.[5] While the straight community supported José's efforts, many in the gay community balked. José had to modify his initial plans, agreeing neither to wear a dress (he wore a cape and crown instead) nor to receive any personal financial assistance. During his reign,[6] he raised funds for many charitable works, supporting both gay and nongay organizations. Empress José may fairly be described as a benevolent dictator in his dealings with his Imperial Court: "I'd propose what I was going to do. And it usually ended up that I'd need seed money. And so, then, I would give [the Court] two minutes to decide whether to give me the money. 'Cause if they didn't give it to me, I'd get it anyway." The concept worked too well for José to let it lapse after his first year of service; he expanded the charitable program, and in so doing he created an institution. In a February 1996 *Frontiers* article on the Imperial Court system, Sarria explained that the concept spread to other cities, beginning in Vancouver, British Columbia, Canada, and led to more than eighty courts worldwide, including courts in Mexico and New Zealand.[7] Of the court system, Sarria said, "I never expected this to go beyond San Francisco. I never imagined the enduring interest and enthusiasm. People have grown up within the court system."

Not unlike Miss America contestants today, each empress chooses a primary platform of charities for which she provides financial assistance; after José's reign, subsequent empresses' efforts supported such diverse projects as funding a lesbian/gay community center, obtaining guide dogs for the blind, providing psychological counseling and youth services, and assisting several feeding projects. Empress XIV Nicole Ramirez-Murray described the court's function: "One can compare the gay court system to the Shriners, Elks, or any such similar service organization." Equally important, José saw little benefit in hiding the court's good works under a bushel: "I always preached that when you do something, I want you to be handing that check, I want the cameras to roll! I want it in the paper! I said, we must blow our own horn. You have to let the world know that it was *you* who did it!" The Imperial Court concept spread quickly along the West Coast, and later reached the Rocky Mountain states, the South, and the Midwest.

Those segments of the community concerned with "appropriate" gay image and appearance have often looked askance at the drag community. However, José defends its place in gay society: "In the beginning it was very rough, because you had the older, uptight queens, that thought that drag was simply terrible, and they weren't gonna put up with it. However, they very rarely realized that it was the drags that were gonna make the money that paid for them!" Even if initially viewed as a necessary evil, the Imperial Court's financial support of the larger community's service projects helped gradually shift the emphasis toward "necessary," and away from "evil."

In addition to his busy Imperial Court schedule, and despite the vicissitudes of aging (telling the audience at **Jim Kepner**'s May 1998 memorial, "I've been very ill, but I've managed to come out of it. They almost had me buried. . . . But I'm not ready to go, because there are a few people I want to bury first"), José remained active through the end of the '90s. He attended New York's Stonewall 25 in 1994 (which led to a brief cameo appearance in *To Wong Foo, Thanks for Everything, Julie Newmar*); traveled to Berlin, Germany, in 1997 to celebrate the one hundredth anniversary of Magnus Hirschfeld's founding of the Scientific Humanitarian Committee (the first recorded gay organization); and received an invitation to serve as Grand Marshal for Minneapolis's gay pride celebration in the summer of 1999.

Since Black Cat days, José has consistently preached, "United we stand; divided, they catch us one by one." Why does José think our community has resisted uniting?

> We cannot put our differences to one side, and yet we'd better. . . . It's all because they all want to be the big cheese. Well, you can't all be the big cheese! . . . I fight very hard. I'm a very determined person. You've got to get up very early in the morning to outwit me, but I will win. I will win. And when I die, then you can do what you damn well please. But until then, this is the way you're going to play the game.

To today's gay/lesbian activists, weaned on demonstrations and confrontations, Sarria's legacy may seem somewhat assimilationist. However, people often fail to comprehend how much American attitudes regarding homosexuality have changed since the '50s. San Francisco's **Hal Call** told me that "José is very much a well-respected crusading gay man here. And long has been." Mark Thompson described Sarria as "simply a man who serves both his community and his city with an unwavering commitment to honesty and uplift, couched always with style, charm, and above all else, humor." Activist George Mendenhall often saw Sarria perform at the Black Cat, and he described José's impact on him in the 1978 book *Word Is Out*:

> I didn't really relate to [men wearing women's clothes], but José could get away with it because we knew there was more to José than that—that the real José was not just making camp; he wasn't just silly. José was being silly with a purpose, and the purpose was to make us aware that we were worthy people and that society was wrong.

In the 1977 documentary of the same name, Mendenhall added,

> At the end of every concert, [José] would have everybody in the room stand, and we would put our arms around each other and we would sing [tears up], "God Save Us Nelly Queens." I get very emotional about this, and it sounds very silly, but if you lived at that time and you were aware of the oppression coming down from the police department and from society, and there was nowhere to turn—to be able to put your arms around other gay men, and to be able to stand up and say "God Save Us Nelly Queens"—We were really not saying, "God Save Us Nelly Queens." We were saying, "We have our rights too."

A 1978 booklet describing the history of the Black Cat noted,

> José is probably the most publicized gay personality in the state. People who have known him or know of him are either very loyal and supportive or very negative. For the loyalists, nothing more need be said. For the negativists, let this be said, José was not afraid to stand up and be counted, criticized, and castigated in a time when mose [*sic*] homosexuals could not or would not be visual or vocal. Through his efforts, and a handful of other gay and straight friends, the acceptance of homosexuality as a positive life style, among the citizens of the bay area and in part throughout the world, has been made a reality.

As a community, we continue to fight for our rights. But it took the actions and the determination of people like José Julio Sarria to help insecure lesbians and gays both to believe in their intrinsic worth and to refuse to accept the stigma of homosexual inferiority.

Notes

1. In Michael R. Gorman's 1998 Lambda Literary Award-winning book, *The Empress Is a Man*, José revealed, "My birth certificate was not issued until 1932, because of my illegitimacy. . . . When the birth certificate was issued, my mother put the dates on it that she wanted. I think I was born in 1922 because I can remember people speaking of President Harding being alive after I was born, and he died in office in 1923. . . . On paper, my birthday is December 12, 1923."

2. Gorman reports that "[t]he Cat limped along into the new year serving food and nonalcoholic drinks, but it finally had to close at the end of February 1964."

3. **Del Martin**, however, recalled that whether José was "out" at that time is open to debate and interpretation: "He was out to people at the Black Cat. But not out to anybody else. . . . He billed himself as an entertainer. And he didn't say anything about being gay. . . . If you're running for office, city-wide, you know, they're not gonna know you're gay unless you say so!" Yet Martin acknowledged that the Black Cat served as his campaign headquarters, indicating that those "in the know" could put two and two together to deduce Sarria's sexual orientation.

4. Norton was born around 1819, and he died January 8, 1880. Sarria continues to mark the occasion of Norton's passing every year at Norton's gravesite, located at Woodland Cemetery in the southern San Francisco suburb of Colma ("I go out and dust off his grave once a year and let him know that his widow has not forgotten him.") The Imperial Court purchased the plot next to Norton's for Sarria's final resting place.

5. However, in *Making History*, Eric Marcus stated, "The court system got its start in 1959 when bars in Portland, Oregon, elected the city's most popular drag queen 'Empress.'" Sarria explained to me that Portland gays devised an early takeoff on the Rose Queen Parade, but that he established Portland's Imperial Court in 1970.

6. While titles are bestowed in perpetuity, Sarria agreed to serve for only one year before permitting others to become empress.

7. In contrast, a 1999 article in San Francisco's gay pride magazine countered that "[t]he Imperial Court system has spread to over sixty-five cities throughout the United States, Mexico, Canada, and the United Kingdom."

6

DEL MARTIN/ PHYLLIS LYON

I like a challenge. Phyllis and I both like the challenge, and we both keep saying, as things develop, you know, it was a process of evolution. And we just went along with changes. And we've grown with the movement, too. And our philosophy is one that, you do whatever you can, where you are. . . . We had to build self-esteem, 'cause if we were illegal, immoral, and sick—I mean, that was heavy-duty. So what we needed to do was develop self-esteem, and self-acceptance being the real key. And then, once you have accepted yourself, then you can start coping in a hostile society.

—Del Martin, 1995

We figured, eventually, there would no longer be laws against us. That we would be, you know, accepted. And things would be OK. We didn't expect it to happen in our lifetime.

—Phyllis Lyon, 1995

Among the eight women who met on September 21, 1955, to form the Daughters of Bilitis, the nation's first social club for lesbians, sat a shy young couple. While they did not conceive DOB, when asked to participate they jumped at the idea; they knew relatively few other lesbians, and the bar scene was not conducive to establishing friendships for them. From such humble beginnings Del Martin and Phyllis Lyon influenced the homophile movement for over a decade as DOB's driving force before they transferred their considerable energies and efforts from coalition with gay men to coalition with straight women. While they maintain they simply found themselves in the right place at the right time, in reality they carved a place for lesbians in the chauvinistic milieu of the American homophile movement. DOB became the vehicle that provided lesbian legitimacy and empowered lesbian leaders from **Barbara Gittings** to **Barbara Grier** to **Rita Mae Brown**.

Del Martin was born Dorothy Erma Corn on May 5, 1921, in San Francisco. Del recognized early her difference from other girls, telling me, "Girls always played house, and I always played the male role. I think that what I observed was that men got their way. They ran things. And I was having trouble identifying with the feminine role. . . . I recognized sexism at a very early age. And that's why I had so much difficulty identifying as a woman." As she matured it became no easier, telling **Kay Tobin** in *The Gay Crusaders*, "I usually went on double dates and was much more interested in the other girl than my own date. It was a feeling I was aware of. I knew I wasn't reacting as others did, but I thought I was the only one to feel this way and I kept it to myself. I had no name for it or any idea of what to do with it." Martin graduated from high school at age sixteen before spending a couple of years as a journalism major, first at U.C. Berkeley, then at San Francisco State College (later SFSU). But Del could not overcome society's pressure for women to marry men; knowing no other options, in December 1940 she married James Martin and bore a daughter, Kendra, two years later. (Martin never completed her college education, much to her chagrin.) The marriage did not endure; the catalyst for its termination came when Del "met a woman who attracted me. And I knew for sure that was the direction I was going in." When they divorced, Del obtained custody of Kendra; when James remarried soon thereafter, Del relinquished Kendra to the couple and moved to Seattle, Washington, in 1949. While working for a construction trade journal there as its daily editor, Del met the love of her life.

In contrast to Martin, Phyllis Lyon, born November 10, 1924, in Tulsa, Oklahoma, avoided the considerable angst of dealing with her lesbian identity; as she told me, "I didn't find out I was a lesbian until I met Del. Or, no, until we got together, really, if you think about it. So I didn't have a lifetime to worry about it." Lyon and her family (like Del, Phyllis's only sibling was a sister six years her junior) migrated to California, and Phyllis graduated from U.C. Berkeley in 1946 with the wartime class of 1947. (Later, Lyon earned a doctor of education degree in human sexuality from the Institute for Advanced Study of Human Sexuality [IASHS], an independent graduate school she co-founded.) Again like Del, Phyllis chose journalism, but this Nellie Bly found most of the newspaper jobs open to women too tame for her tastes: "All they had, it seemed like, was the society page jobs. And I wasn't interested in that stuff." Since she had to work, she applied to the *Chico* [California] *Enterprise*; the editors offered Phyllis a job as a general reporter, a position she eagerly accepted. Toward the late '40s, Lyon also moved to Seattle, where she and Martin met on the job. At this time, Lyon had no clue as to her sexuality, telling Tobin, "Heterosexuality was fine, kind of fun, and I went along with these things because it never occurred to me there was any option. If you were a woman, you had to have a man! There was no other way." At one point, she was engaged to marry a man, but no marriage came to pass. Instead, she remarked to Maureen Odonne in an October 1977 *Advocate* article, "When I met Del, I was still dating men . . . married men. Women had always seemed like much more fun to be with, but it never occurred to me there was more I could have with them than friendships." Soon she not only discovered another way, she found it suited her quite well.

Del and Phyl worked together in Seattle for three years; there they became good friends, but not lovers. In *The Girls Next Door*, Lyon recalled first meeting Martin: "The day Del arrived, she was wearing her little suit and carrying a briefcase. I'd never seen a woman with a briefcase! I was overwhelmed." Not until Phyllis decided to relocate to San Francisco did Del muster up the courage to approach her "straight friend," with whom she had fallen in love. Happily, Phyllis agreed to give the relationship a try, and they moved in together in San Francisco on February 14, 1953.

While Del had participated in one previous relationship with a woman, neither knew much about their new journey, and few roadmaps existed. As **John D'Emilio** wrote in *Sexual Politics, Sexual Communities*, "for a short while [Lyon and Martin] adopted the butch-femme roles that were 'the only models we knew. . . . We played the roles in public, and then we went home and fought about them.'" Phyllis humorously recounted those days in Paris Poirier's *Last Call at Maud's*:

> When we started living together [butch-femme] really didn't work out. I mean, if you figured that the butch was supposed to be the, quote-unquote, masculine person, then she should be doing a lot of the, quote-unquote, masculine things, like driving the car, mowing the lawn, whatever. Which she didn't do any of. And I did all of. Right? So it seemed like I could have been butch, too.[1]

Further complicating matters, Phyllis still occasionally dated a man, and Kendra returned home to spend some time with her mother. Phyllis recalled with me that first year: She and Del "were either fighting or loving, one or the other. [Laughs] I finally determined that we were going to stay together for at least a year, if it killed us." They also suffered from isolation—until a gay male couple in their neighborhood befriended them, they socialized with no other same-sex couples. Not only that, while each told her sister, who proved supportive, neither ever told her parents about her lesbianism: "We decided, rightly or wrongly, that it would be easier for us to cope with their not knowing than it would be for them to cope with knowing." Having initially moved into an apartment on Castro Street, then a quiet Irish neighborhood, they moved into their home in the San Francisco hills in 1955 (which they dubbed "Habromania Haven"), where they still lived forty years later when I interviewed them there. Later that year, however, they received a phone call that forever changed their lives.

While often reported otherwise, Del and Phyllis did not conceive DOB (although they were among its founders). According to their award-winning 1972 book, *Lesbian/Woman*, a Filipina "envisioned a club for lesbians here in the States that would give them an opportunity to meet and socialize outside of the gay bars." Not only could the group provide Del and Phyl the opportunity to meet other lesbians, Lyon told D'Emilio "what we were looking for was a *safe* place, where we could meet other women and dance . . . an alternative to the gay bar scene." The group took its name from "Songs of Bilitis," an 1894 love poem written by Pierre Louys. (Scholars believed Bilitis a contemporary of Sappho on the Greek isle of Lesbos.) The name also provided the group an appellation similar to other women's organizations, such as the Daughters of the American Revolution or Daughters of the Golden West, although Bilitis's daughters served a distinctly different function. While no one anticipated the small lesbian social club would ever transmute into anything else, years later, Barbara Gittings explained to me, "I still think [DOB] was a poor choice of names. Unpronounceable. Meaningless to anybody who wasn't already on the 'ins.' And meaningless even to people who might be looking for something. It just, to me, didn't have any of the elements, even for those closeted days, that you should have."

The new group held its first open meeting on October 19, 1955; when three newcomers arrived, Phyl and Del became DOB's spokeswomen by default (the other six founders disappeared into the kitchen to make coffee). The women began holding three monthly meetings: a business meeting, a social, and a discussion session, which they called a "Gab 'n Java." As with Del and Phyllis's relationship, DOB's first year was rocky, as its founders debated the group's mission. Those who wanted to focus on socialization left to form two new clubs,[2] and DOB developed into a lesbian support group, with political overtones. Over a decade and a half later, Martin and Lyon "realized that the DOB split was among worker/middle class lines. The blue-collar workers who left DOB wanted a supersecret, exclusively lesbian social club. The white-collar workers, however, had broadened their vision of the scope of the organization." At DOB's founding, neither Del nor Phyllis had heard of Mattachine or ONE, Inc., but, by the end of 1956, DOB became one of the "Big Three" in the forefront of the homophile movement until Stonewall.[3]

Its position developed mostly due to Lyon and Martin's tireless efforts; as they recounted, "so desperate were we for members in the early days of DOB that we coddled, nursed, and practically hand-fed every woman who expressed the least interest." But a year later, DOB remained on life support; its membership had increased to just fifteen (and only one of its founders besides Phyllis and Del remained). In a fevered push to increase membership, the women not only began to hold "public" discussion meetings in San Francisco[4] but also decided to publish a newsletter, which they sent to every lesbian or sympathetic woman they collectively knew (as well as psychologists, attorneys, and other local professionals). DOB birthed *The Ladder* in October 1956, and the bold gamble paid off. One year later, DOB boasted forty-five members, and *The Ladder* counted four hundred subscribers. In the October 1958 *Ladder*, the San Francisco chapter praised both women for their work:

> It has been the striving, the courage, and the determination of [Martin and Lyon] who formed the glue (composed of tears, sweat, pride, prayer and stick-to-it-ism) that has held this embryo together through the tough (and sometimes disappointing) early years. . . . The countless hours and enormous energy of Del and Phyl have always been unselfishly and graciously given.

During its sixteen years of publication, *The Ladder*'s jumble of homophile news, poetry, fiction, history, biography, and personal narratives—as well as its sheer existence—positively impacted the lives of thousands of lesbians who discovered options other than lesbian bars and virtual isolation. Surely there were many like **Robin Tyler**, who recalled: "Reading one little article in '59 by Del Martin and Phyllis Lyon . . . got to me and changed my life, from being a [potentially] suicidal kid in Canada, to being out of the closet immediately, never knowing what it was like to be in the closet." *Lesbian/Woman* described *The Ladder*'s special impact on an isolated or small-town lesbian: "For her a magazine is the only real contact she has with 'her people': those who understand, who share her problems, who hold out hope for her dreams." In volume 1, number 1 of *The Ladder*, DOB spelled out its purpose:

> 1. Education of the variant, with particular emphasis on the psychological and sociological aspects, to enable her to understand herself and make her adjustment to society in all its social, civic and economic implications by establishing and maintaining a library of both fiction and non-fiction on the sex deviant theme; by sponsoring public discussions on pertinent subjects to be conducted by leading members of the legal, psychiatric, religious and other professions; by advocating a mode of behaviour and dress acceptable to society.
>
> 2. Education of the public through acceptance first of the individual, leading to an eventual breakdown of erroneous conceptions, taboos and prejudices; through public discussion meetings; through dissemination of educational literature on the homosexual theme.
>
> 3. Participation in research projects by duly authorized and responsible psychology, sociology and other such experts directed towards further knowledge of the homosecual [*sic*].
>
> 4. Investigation of the penal code as it pertains to the homosexual, proposal of changes to provide an equitable handling of cases involving this minority group, and promotion of these changes through due process of law in the state legislatures.

As Martin and Lyon wrote in 1978's *Our Right to Love*, "To today's more militant and secure lesbians it must seem like a complete sellout. But, for the most part, lesbians of the fifties were not secure in either fact or self-image." Phyllis edited *The Ladder* from its inception until 1960; Del followed through 1963.

During the pre-Stonewall era, DOB's members participated in myriad research projects, held their own biennial conventions (beginning in May 1960), and developed chapters around the country beginning in 1958 (most notably in New York City, as well as Los Angeles and Chicago). DOB also worked to improve the individual lesbian's lot in life as well as to educate society into eradicating its prejudices toward lesbians. Despite DOB's impressive achievements, other male-dominated homophile organizations often treated DOB as the ladies' auxiliary of the homophile movement. Martin felt compelled to address the issue as early as 1959, at Mattachine's Denver convention:

> At every one of these conventions I attend, year after year, I find I must defend the Daughters of Bilitis as a separate and distinct

> women's organization. . . . [I]t would appear to me that quite obviously neither [Mattachine nor ONE, Inc.] has recognized the fact that Lesbians are *women* and that this twentieth century is the era of emancipation of woman. Lesbians are not satisfied to be auxiliary members or second class homosexuals. . . . One of Mattachine's aims is that of sexual equality. May I suggest that you start with the Lesbian? This would certainly be a "new frontier in acceptance of the homophile."

Such tensions ebbed and flowed as a not-so-leitmotif for the next decade. Placed in proper historical context, however, these battles were probably inevitable: The homophile vanguard consisted of gay men, in large part no more sympathetic to protofeminism than their straight counterparts.

Additionally, DOB struggled internally in its attempt to provide all things for all lesbians. As Martin told Tobin for *The Gay Crusaders*, DOB's

> problem throughout its history has been that it was until recently the only lesbian organization in the country and had to serve the needs of all varieties of lesbians. So we had very scared lesbians who just wanted to meet others and then we had some people who wanted to get politically involved. And we had the intellectual and the non-intellectual woman. DOB was always being pulled in different directions. We tried to get across the idea that everybody could be involved and do her own thing.

There were other style differences as well. Barbara Grier told me,

> Del Martin and Phyllis Lyon were absolute *rulers*! I mean, to the point of where everything in DOB was run by them. It was run, like, by an army! I mean, they were the commanders. Everyone *obeyed* them. And if you didn't, you were dead meat. I mean, in simple, uncomplicated terms. . . . And people *worshiped* them. That's really true. I mean, everyone—including me—*everyone* worshiped them. If Del had ordered the lesbians under her command, in effect, to march into the ocean one by one, they'd've gone.[5]

Despite Grier's midwestern locale during most of *The Ladder*'s run, this may be her interpretation of East Coast vs. West Coast methodological differences. As Martin described to me, "What we found is that New Yorkers are 'by-the-rules' freaks. And they wanted rules and regulations." Phyllis spoke of their receiving letters from Barbara Gittings, operating from Philadelphia, in the early days: "'Can we do this? Can we do that? Can't we do this? Why can't we do that?' Point, point, point." In 1964's *The Lesbian in America*, Donald Webster Cory summed up DOB's influence on lesbians: "Whatever DOB's failings and shortcomings—and they have been numerous—its very existence is an expression of the belief by some women that to be lesbian is not a disgrace. It would be difficult to exaggerate the importance of such a fact."

In addition to law and psychiatric reform, DOB also strove to change organized religion's antihomosexual attitudes. After years of attempting to establish a meaningful dialogue with the clergy, in 1964 Del and Phyllis found an ally in Rev. Ted McIlvenna, then a Methodist youth minister. As a result, fifteen Protestant ministers held an historic meeting with fifteen homophiles (including Phyllis and Del) from May 30 to June 2, 1964, at the White Memorial Retreat Center in Mill Valley, California. (Lyon and Martin fought vehemently with McIlvenna to ensure that five DOB women would participate.) Martin later wrote that the retreat "opened unexpected avenues of communications and an expression of continued cooperation between the two groups." As a result, retreat participants formed the Council on Religion and the Homosexual ("CRH"). To raise funds for the group, seven San Francisco homophile groups planned a masquerade ball for January 1, 1965, at San Francisco's California Hall. None anticipated the impact such an ostensibly peaceable gathering later created.

In an attempt to inform police about the event beforehand, several CRH ministers met with San Francisco police for two "strained" sessions. On the night of the event, in a naked display of intimidation, police arranged for "a line-up of police cars, one paddy wagon, plainclothes and uniformed officers, and police photographers [to greet] over six hundred patrons of this supposedly gala event."[6] Police also harassed many attending the ball, including the ministers and their wives, and arrested six attendees: two for disorderly conduct, and four (including two heterosexuals) for obstructing police officers who repeatedly demanded to see the group's permit and inspect the hall to ensure it complied with city fire regulations. (Phyllis and Del only barely escaped arrest when Nancy May relieved them of their ticket-taking duties.) Gays and lesbians were familiar with the police's Gestapo-like tactics, but not so the ministers, who had never witnessed such treatment first-hand. At the trial the following month, the court dropped the obstruction charges on a technicality. However, as Del recounted in *Last Call at Maud's*, the day after the event "seven very angry ministers held a press conference, and really made a scene about how the police treated us." As a result, the ball and its aftermath received international publicity. Del told San Francisco's *Bay Area Reporter* a quarter-century later that "we consider that ball to be our Stonewall." Phyllis and Del's efforts to facilitate communication created a new comprehension from the societal branch (religion) many felt might never alter its antigay stance; this success in turn encouraged influential persons in other disciplines to rethink their positions on homosexuality.

As the '60s progressed, and the second-class treatment of lesbians in the homophile movement ceased to abate, the women's movement continued to influence Martin and Lyon. By 1967, Martin began to explore in print the possibility of DOB's building bridges to NOW, and of renouncing its unwavering allegiance to the gay (men's) movement. Del wrote in the June 1967 *Ladder*,

> There are many other phases of the American Sexual Revolution to which Lesbians may address themselves than to get bogged down in the defense of promiscuity among male homosexuals and of public sexual activity in "tea rooms." There are many other organizations with which the Daughters of Bilitis may align themselves in the good fight for civil rights. The Lesbian, after all, is first of all a *woman*—an individual who must earn her own livelihood, who must provide her own household. She is much more concerned with problems of inequality in job and educational opportunities than in the problems of male hustlers and prostitutes.

Despite internal debate within DOB over such a stance, by the end of 1968 Martin and Lyon shifted their emphasis and energy from DOB to the women's movement.[7] Their action foreshadowed the lesbian separatist movement of the '70s. As they also noted in *Lesbian/Woman*, "We felt that the Daughters needed to stand unsupported by its two 'mammas.' If it couldn't, then maybe it hadn't been such a hot idea after all."

At DOB's sixth national convention, held in July 1970 in New York City, members voted to abolish its bylaws, officers, and formal structure, leaving only a loose federation. Earlier that year, Barbara Grier and Rita Laporte "stole" *The Ladder* from the organization. This one-two punch left little reason for the chapters to remain as the post-Stonewall era proceeded. Of the few remaining chapters at that juncture, only Boston's DOB survived (and continues at this writing).

Also in 1970, Martin bade farewell to the male homophile community in a scathing essay, "If That's All There Is—" Despite the essay's militancy, even a conservative like **Randy Wicker** (*The Ladder*'s first back page "cover boy") praised it, telling me, "I understand where it was coming from, and I really respected her for writing it, and I liked it. 'Cause I thought some of the points she made were very good." When I asked Del if she felt the failure of gay men to understand lesbian issues had been resolved in the ensuing twenty-five years, she responded, "The old guard never got it. . . . But it's certainly not resolved, any more than it's resolved in the larger society. . . . They started adding 'lesbian' to gay in 1980. It took us that long to be mentioned." Lyon explained her position on lesbian separatism at the Minnesota Conference on Gay Rights in May 1974:

> The men say, "Why don't the women work with us? We tried." And it's true that a lot of men are trying to deal with their sexism. But at one gay conference recently, for example, the men panicked at the last minute when they realized they didn't have any women involved, and they called me long-distance to invite me to fly in and speak. . . . Working with the women's movement means going to the women at the beginning, when we're organizing or planning. Women don't want to be nags or shrews, but we're tired of playing the traditional role of being subservient to men.

In the meantime, Phyllis cofounded the National Sex Forum in 1968 and IASHS in 1976. She became a leader in the national sex education movement from 1965 to 1987. Additionally, she played an instrumental role in pioneering the use of explicit sexual films as educational tools and the development of Sexual Attitude Restructuring programs (with McIlvenna and Laird Sutton). Through the '70s, Martin became increasingly active in NOW, becoming the first open lesbian elected to the national NOW Board of Directors in 1973, and cofounding Golden Gate NOW in January 1974. The NOW work culminated in the IWY Conference victory in 1977 (see **Jean O'Leary**).

Fortunately, in Lyon and Martin's case the saying "a prophet is without honor in her own country" proved untrue. Using their Democratic Party connections,[8] both received political appointments from San Francisco mayor George Moscone in 1976: Phyllis to the Human Rights Commission (where she served until 1987), and Del to the Commission on the Status of Women (serving until 1979). Also in 1976, Del released *Battered Wives*, noted by author Susan Brownmiller as "[t]he first American book on domestic violence."[9]

In 1978 the couple celebrated their twenty-fifth anniversary, but not before the occasion became a political hot potato. San Francisco supervisor Carol Ruth Silver asked the board to honor both women for their years of civic service, as well as to mark their anniversary. Even given the time and location, the supervisors debated heatedly before passing the motion 8-2. And in 1980, a San Francisco medical clinic created to serve the lesbian community honored both women by taking the name Lyon-Martin Women's Health Services. However, by 1999, an *Echo Magazine* article reported that "the clinic is $140,000 in debt, disorganized and on the brink of extinction." Aware that today only about one in three of Lyon-Martin's clients is a lesbian, Phyllis exclaimed that Lyon-Martin should concentrate its services "on lesbians, dammit. That's where it started, but somewhere it lost that focus."

Have these two dynamos retired from community service? Hardly. In the '90s, both advocated for rights of lesbian and gay senior citizens, and they participated in several gatherings of Old Lesbians Organizing for Change as well as the 1995 White House Conference on Aging (where they shepherded passage of a nondiscrimination resolution including "sexual orientation" discrimination among its protections, and they tried unsuccessfully to add a resolution specifically targeting gay rights issues). Did they ever suspect society would change so much in their lifetime on lesbian/gay issues? "No way!" Martin replied. After being named among *Curve*'s Top 15 Most Influential Lesbians in July 1998, they wrote in a September letter to the editor, "Keep up the good work—and we'll keep on trying to be helpful to Lesbians."

In four decades of work on behalf of lesbians and gays, no women (and no couple of either gender) exerted more influence on movement leaders following in their footsteps than these two. In a July 1998 *Curve* sidebar, Roberta Achtenberg declared of Lyon and Martin, "They're influential because everyday for forty years they've stood up for this community. . . . [T]hey've never hesitated to confront bigotry head on and without regard to personal consequence." Five years earlier, in an *Advocate* interview, Achtenberg gushed, "I'm very, very fortunate to have come up in the San Francisco community, where Phyllis and Del are such a loving, nurturing presence for young women and men." (Indeed, **Cleve Jones** mentioned them among the people who most influenced his life.) Of Del and Phyl, **JoAnn Loulan** said, "They're the people who have always said exactly how it is. And they don't mince words, and they don't care who doesn't like it. So I always think of them as the true protective mothers of our movement." **Miriam Ben-Shalom** waxed eloquent about how *Lesbian/Woman* changed her life: "*Lesbian/Woman* was one of the first things I read that said something positive about who and what I was. . . . And I will sing the praises of Del Martin and Phyllis Lyon forever simply because, without them, I would have been rootless. I would have not understood how to begin the process of being me, and what I am." All of their male contemporaries recognized their efforts (even if many felt lesbians didn't suffer the same kinds of societal problems and discrimination male homosexuals faced), but **José Sarria** probably spoke best for them all when he told me, "You had other women, but they're the ones that, for what reason, put their necks on the chopping block." **Jack Nichols** spoke for the next generation: "I always felt very respectfully towards those two women. They were like sentinels out on the West

Coast, beacons that stood up high, all the way across the States. We felt good and confident that they were there." And I speak for my generation, who may otherwise take their valuable work for granted. May we never disdain—or forget—their life-altering efforts.

Notes

1. However, questions of Lyon and Martin's butch-femme identities never quite disappeared. As Barbara Grier exclaimed to me, "Del is as close to a pit bull, in a woman, as anybody I've ever run across. I mean, she is absolutely—she *could* be, when she was younger, terrifying." In *Stitching a Revolution*, Cleve Jones wrote that "Del and Phyllis were the classic butch/femme couple. Del had the guy's name and was butch, and Phyllis looked an awful lot like my mom." Another interviewee alluded that Del and Phyl were the quintessential butch-femme couple, even if they themselves didn't see it that way.

2. *Lesbian/Woman* explains that these offshoots became "Quatrefoil, a group comprised largely of working class mothers and their partners, with a sprinkling of singles," and "Hale Aikane, which had all the pomp, circumstance and ritual of a secret sorority."

3. In the October 1957 *Ladder*, Martin acknowledged that Mattachine and ONE, Inc. "have favored us with encouragement, advice, and publicity, without which the DOB would not have been able to proceed as rapidly as it has."

4. While DOB permitted only women to become members, many men attended its public meetings and supported the group's aims. Indeed, the women eventually chose several men to become honorary Sons of Bilitis (or SOBs), a tongue-in-cheek designation they wore proudly.

5. Several years ago, however, Grier's published views regarding Del, at least, were considerably softer. In the December 1968/January 1969 *Ladder*, writing under her pen name "Gene Damon," Grier wrote: "Del Martin is one of the leading figures of the homophile movement. . . . She has been instrumental in the dialogue between church organizations and the homophile movement in the San Francisco area, has been prominent in politics in that community, and is known, and quite sincerely loved, throughout the movement. More importantly, she has individually motivated uncounted dozens of others to follow in this cause. It is, I think, in this last respect, that she is most to be loved and lauded."

6. In *Making History*, Nancy May, the only woman arrested during the festivities, recalled that there were "probably 200 to 250" attendees. In contrast, Del believes over five hundred people attended; she counted the tickets after the ball.

7. Del and Phyl became the first lesbian couple to receive a "couples discount" in NOW.

8. Other works refer to their connections to Bay Area politician John Burton and the "Burton Machine," but Lyon and Martin counter, "the Burton Machine is a myth of disgruntled folk."

9. *Battered Wives* noted that Martin "has authored and co-authored eight books."

7

BARBARA GITTINGS/ KAY TOBIN LAHUSEN

> **I've been thirty-six years a gay activist. I wasn't in on the beginning of the movement; I missed the first ten years. But I certainly hope it isn't going to take another thirty-six years of activity to accomplish [justice]. I really would like to see the gay rights movement go out of business as a social change movement in my lifetime. And I'm sixty-two. And I think that could happen, if everybody would pitch in who feels that they can pitch in.**
>
> —Barbara Gittings, 1994

Since its inception around 1950, the gay movement has never lacked self-anointed leaders, most of whom have dedicated themselves to one or two particular organizations or causes. However, it has lacked dedicated followers, foot soldiers willing to do the scut work necessary anywhere they could identify a need. Two East Coast lesbians, together now over forty years, have left an indelible imprint on the movement, one with her words and pictures, the other with her public speaking abilities, unfailing good humor, and seemingly inexhaustible energy. Among American women, only the equally indefatigable **Del Martin** and **Phyllis Lyon** have influenced the gay and lesbian movement as long or as much as Barbara Gittings and Kay Tobin Lahusen. It was my great and good fortune to interview Barbara and Kay at their home in

Wilmington, Delaware, the week after New York's Stonewall 25 celebration in June 1994.

Barbara Katherine Brooks Gittings was born on July 31, 1932, in Vienna, Austria, where her father was a secretary in the American diplomatic service. Barbara lived in Austria, North Carolina, and Maryland. Like her older brother and sister, Barbara received a Catholic boarding school education in Montreal, Canada, for three years. World War II brought her family back to the United States, and they settled in Wilmington.

Following her high school graduation, Barbara attended Northwestern University in Evanston, Illinois, ostensibly to study drama. Instead, she cut classes (except for her beloved Glee Club) to scour every library on campus and in nearby Chicago, attempting to gain an understanding of her lesbianism. Despite her best efforts, she found little helpful material. After one year, Barbara returned home in academic disgrace, with a report card full of "Fs" and an unslakable thirst to understand her attraction to women.

In Jonathan Ned Katz's *Gay American History*, Gittings recalled,

> I went to a psychiatrist in Chicago and told her about myself, and she said, "Yes, you are a homosexual." . . . I think she did me an enormous service, because once I said, "Yes, that's me, that's what I am," I was able to work with it. I had been living throughout my high school years and first few months of college with this hazy feeling: "I don't quite know what's happening to me." It was a fog of confusion. Now I had something clear-cut I could come to grips with.

Her initial salvation lay in lesbian-themed fiction: Barbara told Kay in *The Gay Crusaders*,

> I started finding the novels of homosexuality, books like *Nightwood*, *The Well of Loneliness*, *The Unlit Lamp*, *Extraordinary Women*. At last here were lesbians shown as real people! They didn't exactly have lives of bliss, but at least they were functioning people and had their happinesses. They had more realism than all the case histories I'd read put together! I still feel enormous gratitude and affection for those early lesbian novels. Finding the fiction literature of my people was a godsend to me.

Years later, Gittings would find a way to bring her healing experience to other questioning lesbians and gays. But in her youth, when Barbara's father discovered *The Well of Loneliness* in her room, he actually mailed a letter to her (despite their living in the same house!), labeling it "a depraved and obscene book" which she should burn immediately. (Her response? "I hid it better.") Soon afterward, Barbara ran away from home and went to Philadelphia, where she could investigate homosexuality without restriction. Still, Barbara struggled, telling Tommi Avicolli in a 1981 *Advocate* article, "I was really frightened because I had nobody to turn to and I had nothing except what I could pull out of my own head."

In the early '50s, Gittings experienced her first tenuous relationships with other lesbians, and she discovered the gay bar subculture of the time, which epitomized a butch-femme dichotomy. In *Making History*, Gittings explained, "I'm not really the kind for skirts and high heels and hair piled up on my head. So I looked at this division and said, 'Well, I must be the other kind.' So that's how I dressed because I thought that's what you had to do to fit in. It was as silly as that and as simple as that. And it really meant absolutely nothing."

Barbara found her way out of the bars when she contacted Donald Webster Cory, author of the groundbreaking 1951 book *The Homosexual in America*. When they met in New York in 1955, Cory shared information with Gittings about existing homophile organizations: "I don't think he mentioned Mattachine, but he told me about ONE. And I determined that the next opportunity, I would go to the West Coast and visit ONE, Inc. Because the idea that there might be groups of people of my own kind was very appealing to me." In the summer of 1956, Gittings flew to Los Angeles, where she met with members of ONE, Inc. They in turn told her about Mattachine in San Francisco, so she flew there, meeting **Hal Call** and others. Almost forty years later, Call vividly remembered Barbara's initial visit: "She was a vivacious and energetic and very outgoing girl. She was a grown-up tomboy from the word 'go.' She was a lot of fun. . . . And she was in the middle of it all. She was the central conversationalist, and she had everybody rapping and going."

San Francisco Mattachine connected Gittings to the organization to which she would devote her energies for nearly a decade. The Daughters of Bilitis, the nation's first lesbian organization, had existed for less than a year when Gittings attended a 1956 meeting where she met, among several other lesbians, Phyllis Lyon and Del Martin. As Lyon remembers it,

> We went out to the airport to meet her. And she got off the plane, and she had this little sleeveless dress on, and backpack. And Birkenstocks. . . . And then we went back to New York in 1958. And one of the things that we did was to meet with her. She got a group of people together, and started DOB [back East].

Despite their differences through the years (Lyon told me, "It's true that we haven't always gotten along with Barbara, but then, hell,

[Del and I] don't always get along with each other!"), all three worked closely together through the mid-'60s.

On September 20, 1958, Gittings was elected president of DOB's fledgling chapter in New York,[1] a position she held until 1961. Barbara made financial sacrifices for her cause; by the mid-'60s she quit her regular job to work solely on behalf of the gay and lesbian movement. In *Unspeakable*, she told Rodger Streitmatter, "I survived on a small trust fund and by living very frugally. I was so committed to the movement that I saw no alternative to giving it all of my time. Gaining equal rights for homosexuals was my number one priority. I simply couldn't manage a full-time job in addition. Making a living was entirely secondary." At a 1961 DOB picnic, Barbara's life changed as a new romance blossomed.

Kay Lahusen, born on January 5, 1930, was raised by grandparents in Cincinnati, Ohio. Her grandmother was a Christian Scientist. In a September 1993 interview with Marc Stein, Kay discussed her childhood: "I was always what was called a tomboy. And even though I wasn't physically strong or big, I did play football . . . . I was very fearless. I got blue ribbons in horseback and riflery and archery and things like that. And I liked boxing at camp. . . . But [my grandparents] were pretty forbearing. They told me I could do whatever I wanted to do." Her first intimate relationship with a woman occurred in 1948, shortly after she graduated from high school, but it took a year before Kay could accurately name her emotion. As she told Eric Marcus,

> I finally faced the fact that this was more than friendship. This was desire and sex and lust and love, just like straight people feel. I have to tell you, I had a breakdown over this revelation. I literally had to go to bed and lie down. I was totally weak. It was like a hammer was pounding my head. This went on for two weeks.

Finally, Kay "just decided that I was right and the world was wrong and that there couldn't be anything wrong with this kind of love." The relationship lasted six years. After both graduated from a state university, Kay's lover succumbed to family and societal expectations and married a man. Devastated, Kay moved to Boston in 1956, where she worked as a reference librarian for *The Christian Science Monitor*. She checked the newspaper's clipping files under "Homosexuality," and she was shocked to be referred to the listings for "Vice." The few clippings under "Vice" were about arrests and spy cases. Eventually her persistent research led her to a New York author and psychoanalyst, who handed her a copy of *The Ladder*, DOB's magazine. Kay contacted the New York chapter in 1961 and continued her search for a life partner and a life work.

Barbara and Kay met at a DOB picnic shortly thereafter. They hit it off immediately, and they began a long-distance relationship. As Kay described their courtship in *City of Sisterly and Brotherly Loves*, "We traveled back and forth between Philadelphia and Boston for the better part of a year. And then she proposed I come live with her in Philadelphia. I was very tired of Boston winters by then. And she said, 'Philadelphia is just like Boston, only warmer.'" It was a good line, and Kay fell for it; after all, she had fallen for Barbara.

Unlike many others, finding their hearts' desire did not cause them to abandon DOB. Instead, Barbara, with Kay's help, began editing *The Ladder* in February 1963, and she continued until the summer of 1966. In a 1983 forum, Barbara acknowledged, "Actually, at least sixty percent of the credit for the work on the magazine goes to my lover, Kay." Kay began calling herself Kay Tobin, not for concealment, but because her given name Lahusen is hard to spell, pronounce, and remember. Barbara steered *The Ladder* in a much more aggressive and confrontational direction, reflecting her own exposure to the more radical ideas (such as picketing) of gay men like **Randy Wicker** and **Frank Kameny**. Indeed, she nearly changed the magazine's title: *CSBL* reports, "Early in 1964, Gittings began using the subtitle *A Lesbian Review* on the *Ladder*'s covers. She recalls that she and [Kay] did not like the magazine's name because it was not identifiably lesbian: 'We made the letters for *The Ladder* smaller and smaller and the letters for *A Lesbian Review* larger and larger, until they were about the same size. . . . We couldn't get rid of the name, *The Ladder*, but at least we could pale it into insignificance.'"

Barbara and Kay also sought and found lesbians willing to grace its cover beginning in 1964: "We wanted to show lesbians and others who might be reading the magazine that lesbians are happy, healthy, wholesome, nice-looking people." Persuading lesbians to appear on *The Ladder*'s covers was a victory over the pervasive invisibility of gay people at the time. Kay and Barbara played a major role in bringing lesbians out of the closet.

Barbara and Kay marched in the White House picket demonstration in October 1965 as well as at a Pentagon picket that July and at pickets at Independence Hall in Philadelphia every Fourth of July from 1965 through 1969. These were the earliest instances of well-organized militancy for gay civil rights, and the pair was thrilled to participate. Yet Barbara acknowledges, "It was risky and we were scared. And our protests seemed outlandish even to most gay people." Kay photographed these early pickets as well as other gay rights events for more than a decade; she was in fact the movement's first openly gay photojournalist. Kay also wrote reports under various names, to make it seem the small movement had more writers than it really did.

Meanwhile, Barbara and Kay chafed at the conservatism of DOB's governing board, whose stance they disdained as "up *The Ladder*, into skirts, and into society." Both felt DOB scolded a mythical laggard lesbian to become acceptable to society instead of demanding major social changes. But when Martin and Lyon yanked Gittings from *The Ladder*'s editorship in 1966, it was probably not due to differences in philosophy or over tactics such as picketing. Del and Phyl told me that Barbara's inability to meet the magazine's deadlines (a failing Barbara admits) necessitated the change. Regardless, both Barbara and Kay stepped into a host of projects where gay women and men worked together.

Between 1967 and 1974, Barbara was active in Philadelphia's Homophile Action League and the North American Conference of Homophile Organizations; worked closely with Frank Kameny on legal battles against the federal government; hosted a pathbreaking radio show, "Homosexual News and Reviews," on New York's public radio station WBAI; appeared with six other lesbians on David Susskind's nationally aired TV talk show; served as co-keynote speaker (with Morris Kight) at the 1973 Gay Pride March in New York; and served on the first board of directors of the National Gay Task Force. In the award-winning 1998 documentary film *Out of the Past*, Barbara detailed her gradual process of taking risks to press movement concerns and personal liberation forward:

> All along, I think I felt that I was in a situation where I was probably less likely to lose something important than a lot of the other people in the movement. So every time a decision had to be made—shall I appear on this radio talk show, and if so, shall I use my real name? Shall I agree to be interviewed for this newspaper story, and if so, shall I give my real name? And should I let them have a picture of me if they want it?—Every time a little decision had to be made, I decided that I would take the chance.

Gittings's most influential actions impacted the American Psychiatric Association and the American Library Association. Although never a librarian, Gittings was a bibliophile, and she remembered the days when she could not find library materials to help her understand her sexual orientation. She explained in *The Gay Academic*, "What we found was strange to us (I'm the kind of person they're writing about but I'm not like that!) and cruelly clinical (there's nothing about love) and always bad (being this way seems grim and hopeless)." When she joined the ALA's Task Force on Gay Liberation in late 1970, she compiled its first gay-positive bibliography. The handful of positive materials fit onto a single sheet of paper. But it was a start. Barbara felt at home in ALA's gay group, and in 1971 she became its coordinator, a position she held for fifteen years. Later she wrote a short history of the group's first sixteen years, "Gays in Library Land," published in 1990.

In the American Psychiatric Association, Barbara's activity included speaking at APA's 1972 meeting on a panel challenging antigay attitudes (where she presented a masked gay psychiatrist who told about having to stay hidden as a homosexual in his own profession); producing and running gay exhibits at annual APA meetings in 1972, 1976, and 1978; and being fairy godmother to the emerging caucus of lesbian and gay psychiatrists. As a result of gay activists' efforts to remove homosexuality per se from the APA's classification of mental illness, Gittings and others ultimately emerged victorious. (The APA's board of trustees cast no dissenting votes against the progay stance on December 15, 1973; in a resulting referendum launched by antigay APA members, the APA's general membership ratified that decision on April 9, 1974.) Barbara recalled in *Out of the Past*, "With a stroke of the pen, and an announcement in public, you could cure people who were formerly considered to be sick, just by saying, 'We've been wrong.'"

Meanwhile, Barbara and Kay endured stresses in their personal lives. The devoted pair lived apart from 1969-1972; Kay went to New York and Barbara stayed in Philadelphia, but they saw each other often. **Jack Nichols** told me that what brought them back together was "time, and continuing perseverance on Barbara's part, and Kay sort of realizing that this is the way to go. And loving Barbara too. They both loved each other; there's no doubt about that."

Kay's activism while she lived in New York differed from Barbara's. Kay attended Gay Liberation Front meetings in New York in September 1969, but, as she told Marcus, "GLF was always chaotic." By December 1969, Kay cofounded Gay Activists Alliance with twelve other activists[2]: "We wanted a structured group. . . . We decided to have officers, elections, and all those standard things. . . . We did plenty of things, and I covered it all for the *GAY* newspaper," a weekly that was the gay newspaper of record at that time in New York City. Kay later described GAA as "an exciting place for a range of us who weren't out-and-out revolutionaries" and "really beautiful. It's very Spartan, and everybody leaves his other grievances at the door."

Kay was *GAY*'s first news editor as well as a reporter and photojournalist (working closely with Jack Nichols). In 1972 she also produced a delightful paperback, *The Gay Crusaders*, in which she interviewed and profiled fifteen lesbian and gay activists. It was the first book of its kind, and it included a photo section. (*The Gay Crusaders* also credits Randy Wicker as its coauthor, but he freely admitted to me, "Kay Tobin had put together the idea for the book. . . . And the publisher said, 'Well, we like the idea, but we need a well-known male author before we'll sign the contract.' . . . I think I wrote one page in that book, of which one paragraph was not changed. So this book is Kay Tobin's book.")

Also in the '70s, Kay cofounded Gay Women's Alternative, a popular discussion forum in New York City; worked in the Oscar Wilde Memorial Bookshop; and encouraged longtime activist Craig Rodwell in his 1978 organizing of Gay People in Christian Science. All through the '70s until 1986, Kay helped Barbara and the gay librarians' group in their campaign to tackle gay issues in libraries.

But during the late '60s/early '70s, Barbara and Kay found themselves caught in some of the political cross-currents of that era. Many of the younger, newer activists brought New Left ideas with them, to the chagrin of many of the old-timers: As Gittings recalled in *CSBL*, "Suddenly, here were all these people with absolutely no track record in the movement who were telling us, in effect, not only what we should do, but what we should think. The arrogance of it was what really upset me." And some lesbians in the '70s subjected Barbara and Kay to considerable pressure because they refused to operate under the separatist theory that dominated lesbian political thought at that time. **Jim Kepner** shared with me that "the first wave of radical feminists hated [Barbara]. She was driven off the platform at a number of speaking engagements by them." Why? "Because she would work with men." Gittings denied that charge, telling me, "I don't remember that. . . . [I was] never driven off a platform." Despite criticism, Barbara and Kay continued charting their own paths: Gittings said in *The Gay Crusaders*, "I want to deal with gay issues—first and foremost! . . . I have more in common with homosexual men than with heterosexual women." More than twenty years later she remarked in *CSBL*, "I have always characterized the '70s in our movement as the time of greatest separation, which I never took part in and always opposed." In *Our Right to Love*, Kay and Barbara wrote,

> with so much work to be done, . . . the movement needs diversity but can ill afford divisiveness. . . . Gay women and men have a long social history as friends and allies that far antedates today's organized gay movement, and we doubt that the general amity between them will ever be shaken.

From the late '70s through the '80s and '90s, each continued making her mark. Kay went into real estate, organized a gay realtors' group, and launched one of the first gay realtor ads in a gay paper. She also began planning gay history photo exhibits, such as "Standing Tall Before Stonewall: The First Gay Pickets." Barbara helped start the Gay Nurses Alliance; sat on the first board of the Gay Rights National Lobby (forerunner to the Human Rights Campaign); served on the Pennsylvania Governor's Council for Sexual Minorities; and lent her name to the International Gay & Lesbian Archives. During these years she was in demand to give speeches and workshops as well as interviews for books and documentary films.

One of my favorite memories of Stonewall 25 in 1994 was seeing Gittings at two events: lecturing with **Martin Duberman** and **Troy Perry**, and enjoying **Holly Near**'s open-air concert at Lincoln Center (backed by the Gay Games IV Festival Choir, including my husband).

When I asked how they had managed to transition more effectively than most from the '50s through the '70s and beyond, Kay joked,

> Well, you could say our minds were so open, our brains fell out. But that wasn't really it. [Laughs] You could say we didn't want to be left behind, and be a couple of old dinosaurs. No, that really wasn't it, either. I think it was true love of gay people. . . . We always liked to see the next wave, and what they were going to do that was more audacious than the previous wave!

If the individuals I interviewed could elect a "Miss Congeniality" from among their peers, Barbara would win hands down. Randy Wicker described Gittings as "selfless"; **Dick Leitsch** as "sweet"; Martin Duberman as "a wonderfully warm, generous spirit"; Frank Kameny as "a longtime, cherished colleague for whom it understates the case to say I have the deepest of affection." (Only **Barbara Grier** sounded a discordant note: "Barbara Gittings is the only person, actually, from the early movement with whom I really did not get along.") Despite Kay's remark to me that "I have a bad disposition. And I say dumb things," Phyllis Lyon called Barbara and Kay "really special people," while Jack Nichols, who practiced yoga with Kay, noted that "I felt warm tones a lot of times in Kay's voice, colorful, warm tones . . . . [Kay] understood that life and the movement went together. . . . I often felt Barbara came to life much better in a public situation." Nichols and Lige Clarke also wrote in *I Have More Fun with You than Anybody*, "What we like most about Kay is a personal value: her thoughtfulness." I concur; Kay sent me several warm notes and cards, encouraging me to complete my work.

Barbara credited Kay in part for her own movement longevity: "The wonderful work that she's done, the inspiration that she's been, the driving power behind our work together in the movement, that's been marvelous. And she hasn't flagged, so I haven't flagged. We both have a very strong sense of mission, and we do see that things get changed!" Kay told Eric Marcus why she remained active:

> The driving force and the reason I am so passionate about this [movement] is because it's so wrong that a good gay relationship had to break up because it was felt at the time that this was no kind of life to be lived. I just want to turn that around in this world. This is what drove me then and still drives me now.

Wicker summed up Gittings's contribution best: "Barbara Gittings is that rare thing in any political movement, and the most important block. She's a builder. She's like the worker bee. She's the one that really makes things change. Because how many thousands of books did she put into how many hundreds of libraries, that really changed lives?" Gittings summarized her goal in *Out of the Past*:

> I don't want to see people go through what I went through as a young person, groping all by myself to find information, and to find my way to gay people—and absolutely dead silence, and no visibility anywhere! I want to make sure that every child growing up in the future who is going to be gay, can grow up learning that being gay is happy, and healthy, and normal, and they can be themselves.

What work possibly remains for these two dynamos? Barbara closed the 1999 documentary *After Stonewall* by saying,

> My partner Kay and I have talked about the need for gay retirement homes for older gay people. We know the time is coming. I guess I would call it the Lavender Light-Years Retirement Home. And I will be able to rock, and say, "Do you remember when we picketed the White House in 1965?" [Chuckles]

In *The Gay Crusaders*, Barbara told Kay, "I've always been a joiner. Some people just like to get in there and pitch." If Barbara Gittings, aided by Kay Tobin Lahusen, had done nothing but her library work, she would have bestowed a precious gift to the movement. While her pitching couldn't "shut out" the opposition, she never feared to step to the plate and hit home runs for all who followed.

Notes

1. New York and Rhode Island became DOB's first chapters outside San Francisco.

2. According to Edward Alwood's *Straight News*, Kay's GAA co-founders included Steve Adams, Arthur Bell, Fred Cabellero, Tom Doerr, Gary Dutton, Arthur Evans, Richard Flynn, Leo Martello, Fred Orlansky, Jim Owles, Marty Robinson, and Donn Teal.

PART II

BUILDING ON A FIRM FOUNDATION

8

RANDY WICKER

Sometimes I feel like the wallflower at the historical ball. I usually get a little attention, but only in passing. Meanwhile, by chance, some of the most obscure people get catapulted into the limelight and others who are far more worthy of attention than myself are totally ignored.

—Randy Wicker, personal newsletter, December 1993

When I interviewed **Barbara Gittings** in 1994, a few days after I interviewed Randy, she brightened at the mention of Wicker's name, saying, "Well, he was certainly a pioneer, and he has not got the recognition that he's deserved." A year later, **Dick Leitsch** told me, "Randy was *always* a total asshole. We spent all of our time fighting. He's totally mad, bizarre, a walking egomaniac." The homophile movement's first picketer, a successful entrepreneur and gadfly, the most conservative radical (or radical conservative?), Wicker, I believe, merits these characterizations in earning his place to date in gay history. This colorful and controversial character deserves a fuller delineation.

Randy Wicker was born Charles Gervin Hayden, Jr. in Baltimore, Maryland, on February 3, 1938. While very little has been written about Wicker's early days, he seems to have bounced around the East Coast during his childhood, moving to Florida at age twelve and graduating from high school in New Jersey. Randy videotaped a rare comment about his mother, Iris, during the Stonewall 25 march: "[My father] thought I was gay because my mother was taken away. She had TB when I was five years old. And I came in the bathroom crying,

'Daddy, why did Mommy run off and leave me in the middle of the night?'"

After two years of college at Virginia's Washington & Lee University, Wicker left the East Coast to attend the University of Texas (Austin) in 1958. Along with running for student body president (which he narrowly lost), he also became involved in the Negro civil rights movement there, joining a "sit-in" to integrate Austin's lunch counters in 1960.

In the late '50s, because of his self-identification with the homophile community, Wicker changed his name at the request of his father, a "Taft Republican" who

> knew I was gay from reading my diary. And was very progressive, in a sense. He said, "Look, I just want you to be the best-adjusted homosexual you can be, 'cause I'm not always gonna be here to take care of you." . . . I showed him some Mattachine stuff and told him about some of the stuff I was doing. And he sort of smiled, and he looked at it, and said, "Well, it's your life." He said, "I really don't think you're gonna get very far with this. Just do me one favor, will you?" And I said, "What is that?" He said, "Just don't involve my good name." Well, I was Charles Gervin Hayden, Jr. And he was Charles Gervin Hayden, Sr. . . . This was corporate, bureaucratic-pressure America. So how could I not respect the wishes of my father? Who had wore dollar ties and fifty-dollar suits to put me through college?

He chose the pseudonym "Randolfe Wicker" ("If I get a pseudonym, I want to have one that stands out. 'Twyla Tharp' hadn't come along yet, or I would have taken Twyla Tharp"), which eventually abbreviated itself to Randy; after several years of use, he legally changed his name in 1968. He described to me his "split personality" during that era: "By day, I went to work, selling business machines in slacks, suit and tie, Underwood-Olivetti. By night, I was Randolfe Wicker, fighter for rights of gay people. . . . I almost felt like, kind of, Superman, popping into the booth and taking off the coat at night."

In the meantime, until he graduated from college in 1960 with a psychology degree (the University of Texas would not permit a homosexual to attend its law school, or Wicker would have pursued a legal career there), Randy spent his summers in New York City, becoming Mattachine New York's youngest member at age twenty. "You were supposed to be twenty-one. I had to lie. The national chairman said, 'Just tell 'em you're twenty-one.'" Randy recalls Mattachine New York, circa 1958:

> They had gotten this little ratty hall in a fifth floor walk-up at Sixth Avenue and Forty-eighth Street for like $50 a month rent. And they could seat maybe forty or fifty people. It was just a small little hall, right? And they would have a monthly lecture. If it was a big success, they might have thirty, thirty-five, forty people sometimes! 'Cause the membership of the organization was only sixteen. Most people were afraid to join. I was the sixteenth member. So I came in, and they were gonna have a lawyer discuss homosexuality and the law. I said, "Let's promote this. Why don't you promote these things? Get people to come?" So anyway, it cost five cents apiece for three hundred posters, black on yellow paper, and it said, "Citizens! A lawyer discusses homosexuality and the law. Free admission. Questions answered. Mattachine Society." . . . So what happened was, the night of the talk, where they usually had thirty or forty gays, they had three hundred. Mainly women, mainly college students in bobby sox.

Unfortunately, the police also saw Wicker's posters; since the space Mattachine rented was situated above a bar, and at the time New York law forbade taverns to serve alcohol to homosexuals, the landlord terminated Mattachine's lease.

> So at that point, in the [Mattachine] Society, half of the people were saying, "Well, this is what we've been trying to do; educate the public, have successful meetings." You know, "This is fantastic!" But the others said, "Fantastic? That little troublemaker! He got us evicted! He's no end of trouble! We got kicked out after slaving away on that office!"

Not atypically, Randy's publicity efforts garnered both praise and criticism. In *Straight News*, early MSNY president Curtis Dewees related,

> Randy was very young and wild-eyed. He was very radical and did things that the rest of us didn't have the guts to do. Many of the people in our group were professionals, and I think they thought Randy was moving too fast. We weren't sure things were ready for someone like him yet. But he certainly made us sit up and take notice.

In the late '50s/early '60s, Wicker tried to mobilize New York gay bar patrons, but encountered little success:

> When I would try to recruit people in those bars—they called me "Miss Mattachine." I was derisively referred to—"Oh, there's Miss Mattachine!" Because I was always trying to get people to meetings. And they would say things like, "Don't you think the subterranean atmosphere is a large tradition? Don't you think it would be boring if

> we were accepted, just like everybody else? I mean, we'd lose this feeling of intrigue." . . . So those were the perceptions, and that's what fueled me to go into the movement.

Wicker often found Mattachine bureaucracy aggravating; as a pro-active young turk,

> I got tired of trying to push a wagon uphill. So I formed the Homosexual League of New York, which was myself and whatever friends I could help. 'Cause then, if I wanted to do something, I didn't have to go and get approval. I'd say, "I don't care what you people are doing, but the Homosexual League of New York—" . . . I wasn't gonna have to get approval. I was gonna do what I thought needed to be done. There was enough work to do without sitting around trying to get their approval.

Or, as the summer 1964 *Mattachine Review* reported, "Wicker's organization . . . got mention more than once because of the sheer audacity of its spokesman who knew no doors too formidable to enter." DOB's *Ladder* announced in August 1962 that Wicker "addressed a group of 60 heterosexuals at the Hall of Issues in Judson Memorial Church . . . placed an exhibit of homosexual publications at the Hall of Issues," and reported:

> The *Village Voice* weekly newspaper, which has refused Mattachine advertising in the past, now claims ads will be accepted or rejected on their own merit and no blackout of the word or subject of homosexuality will be pursued. For a newcomer to the homophile movement, The Homosexual League of New York seems to have embarked on an impressive public relations program.

In *Before Stonewall*, Barbara Gittings pointed out, "One of the major successes of the gay movement in the 1960's was our breakthrough into mainstream publicity. As much publicity as possible, that was the whole idea, to crack that shield of invisibility that had always made it difficult to get our message across." Wicker deserves credit as one of the first to put that idea into action.[1] Randy related, "There'd been homosexuals behind potted palms and whatnot, but no one who was willing to just stand up and say, 'I am a homosexual, and the attitudes on sexuality by society are absolutely crazy.'" **Martin Duberman** referred to Wicker in *Stonewall* as "something of a genius in media manipulation." Why does Wicker believe his efforts proved successful?

> I saw what I thought were the pressure points. The pressure point was to break down the media door. My real thing was, the way to go, is we have to change public perception. And to do that, we have to get radio and TV and the press telling the truth about us gay people. What they're like, and what their lives are like. In other words, a public education campaign. I don't know why—I don't think this is so insightful—but I knew that when I heard those doctors talking on [New York radio station] WBAI, I [went] up there and I said, "This is ridiculous! These yo-yos don't know nothing about homosexuality! We're the authorities on homosexuality!" . . . It was time for us to speak out for ourselves, and not let these guys that say we have regressive fathers and dominant mothers talk about us.

Wicker also took what many then considered a radical approach in presenting information about gay men and lesbians. The conventional homophiles attempted to present homosexuals in the best possible light, as "the boy/girl-next-door" types. In contrast, *The Ladder* revealed that in an October 6, 1962, panel discussion Wicker "stated that *all* types of homosexuals should be presented to the public from the most respectable to the most flamboyantly disrespectful. In short, the homosexual should be shown simply as he is."[2] Or, as John Loughery commented in 1998's *The Other Side of Silence*, "The Mattachine policy had been to avoid airing dirty laundry in public; the Wicker policy was bluntness in everything at all times." A tactic still seldom employed by gay community leaders, I believe it remains the most effective method to reach the segment of straight society either misinformed or unaware of the range of the gay experience.

Toward that end, Wicker assembled an eight-homosexual panel (himself included) for a discussion of homosexuality entitled "Live and Let Live," broadcast on WBAI on July 15, 1962. (Shortly before his appearance, Wicker wrote his mother that the moment was "the greatest chance I have ever had in my life to do something *really important*, *really noble*, and *really satisfying*.") Jack Gould, in the *New York Times*, reported the next day that

> Last night's discussion of homosexuality was handled with candor and tact. . . . The ninety-minute program was by far the most extensive consideration of the subject to be heard on American radio, and it succeeded, one would think, in encouraging a wider understanding of the homosexual's attitudes and problems.

In contrast, the week before the program aired, Jack O'Brian of the *New York Journal-American* told his readers that "We've heard of silly situations in broadcasting, but FM station WBAI wins our top prize for scraping the sickly barrel-bottom. . . . (Change those call-letters to

WSICK)." The broadcast caused some listeners to file charges against WBAI with the Federal Communications Commission. In a precedent-setting move, the FCC declined to hear their grievance. As Edward Alwood reported in 1996's *Straight News*,

> the agency told the disgruntled challengers that if it prevented provocative programs by denying broadcast licenses, then "only the wholly inoffensive, the bland, could gain access to the radio microphones or TV camera." In essence the decision sent a message to the rest of the radio and television industry that homosexuality was an acceptable topic for broadcast, at least as far as the FCC was concerned.

Wicker also appeared as part of a panel including **Frank Kameny** on a two-hour Chicago television program, "Off the Cuff," airing April 4, 1964, and more notably, a January 31, 1964, episode of New York's *The Les Crane Show*, where, according to *Gay Militants*' Donn Teal, Wicker "was the first homosexual to appear as such on New York television, in behalf of homosexuals." Randy told me what happened in those first radio and television shows:

> Well, you'd get all these stupid questions. Like, "Do you want to be a woman? Do you want to wear a dress? I mean, how about homosexuals, aren't they all like Communist Party [members]? How about blackmail? Aren't you afraid you're going to be blackmailed? I mean, you're a security risk. Mentally ill." You know what I mean. "Don't you want to be cured?" I mean, all these questions, which today would be absolutely ludicrous! People today wouldn't—we've come a long, long way. I mean, they would not begin to ask some of the questions today that they naïvely asked in those days.

Taking a page from the Negro civil rights movement, Wicker organized the first picket for gay and lesbian concerns, when the tactic was still somewhat new and certainly controversial. On September 19, 1964, Wicker and others picketed the Whitehall Army Induction Center in Manhattan to protest its treatment of homosexuals. "The first [gay picket] in America was down on Whitehall Street, on the Army. 'Cause the Army not only didn't let you in, it was mainly when they discharged you, they gave you a dishonorable discharge, which just followed you for the rest of your life." With less than a dozen participants,[3] Wicker said, "We didn't get any big reaction. But what we had done is we had done it. It's sort of like a toe in the water. And an alligator didn't bite off our toe. . . . Nobody came and [said], 'What do you mean, you goddamn queers! This is outrageous! You commie freaks!' We thought we were really taking a risk."

Wicker also participated in another major picket at New York's United Nations building, protesting Cuban dictator Fidel Castro's imprisoning homosexuals in work camps. *The Ladder* reported that at Dag Hammarskjöld Plaza "29 persons picketed on Sunday, April 18 [1965]." The same article reported that the day before, ten people representing Mattachine Society of Washington picketed the White House "in regard both to Cuba's campaign against homosexuals and to American homosexuals' grievances against their own government."

Randy was (and is) a curious amalgam of conservative and radical philosophies. **Jack Nichols** recalled that "in 1964, Lige [Clarke] and I went to visit him, and we became friends with Randy and Peter [Ogren, then Randy's lover] together. We would go up there and smoke dope with them, and then go back to straight Washington [D.C.]. And Wicker turned me on to the first poppers I ever had." But given his strong capitalist streak, many homophiles considered Wicker a conservative. Wicker and Ogren opened a successful button shop in Greenwich Village. According to Barbara Gittings, their first two buttons consisted of "a lavender equal sign on a white background. The second said 'Equality for Homosexuals' and had black letters on a white background." Barbara's partner **Kay Tobin Lahusen** related,

> Randy said to me recently he never liked that ["Gay Is Good"] button [one of the earliest homophile slogans, credited to Frank Kameny]. . . . He didn't like it because it was bland and namby-pamby. He wanted something with more pizzazz, oomph to it. . . . He wanted things that were a little bit offbeat and cute and sassy.[4]

Nichols recalled, "Early on, when he and Peter first opened the button business, Wicker told me, 'No relationship has a chance in hell without this big almighty dollar as its solid foundation.'" Yet their financial acumen failed to guarantee "wedded" bliss: A couple for several years, Wicker and Ogren ended their relationship in 1971.

While he stayed involved on the fringes of the movement (as he does to this day), Randy told me, "I got burned out in '65 and gave up on homosexuals ever seeing the light. And I just went on to fight the antiwar movement, and legalized abortion, and all these other things." Randy described his frustration in a letter to *The Advocate*, published in April 1968:

> For many years I gave a great deal of my time and energy to the homophile movement. As a matter of fact, I worked like a fanatic, full-time, for nearly ten years, trying to get homosexuals to work together to better their overall position in society. Then I just got exhausted, tired, fed up and I decided it was time to stop trying to do

> good works and save the world; that it was time for me to save myself and a single homosexual individual instead.

But he feels he and the other homophiles never received their due from the movement that followed afterward. He told Harry Hay at Stonewall 25 in 1994,

> We created the airplane, and all they did was get in it and fly off. And we answered all the questions. "Are we sick? Are we sinners? What do we want?" We laid out the agenda. And it was all ready to go! All they had to do was run over and pick it up. We'd been trying to get them to pick it up for twenty years!

When the Stonewall riots occurred in the Village in June 1969, Randy had left the cutting edge of the movement. Consequently, he told me,

> when I heard this description of drag queens kicking their heels up at the cops—I mean, chorus lines of drag queens, when I had spent ten years of my life running around telling people that homosexuals were not drag queens—I said, "Oh, God! This is my stereotype come back to haunt me!" And then on top of that, they were putting fires in trash bins. I thought, one little Italian lady or one baby burns up in some tenement fire over there, and we're gonna be the boogeymen of the '70s!

As one of the gay liberation pioneers, he was asked to speak at a community meeting the Monday after the riots. "I said, 'Rocks through windows don't open doors! We don't get acceptance by going out and breaking windows, and setting bonfires in trashcans that could cause a public disorder. This is a mistake!'" While Randy caught hell for his words at the time, he now provides his mea culpa: "I was a fool. I did not see that the revolution had finally arrived."

What changes did Randy see after Stonewall?

> Suddenly, where we'd had a lot of middle-aged people [in the movement], . . . there were all these young, young—I was about thirty-one years old. And, I mean, these were *kids* that were out raising hell! I was—at thirty-one, I was an old man. . . . Now, suddenly, you had a movement that was just burgeoning, but it was all young, fresh—and they were screaming things like "Gay Power," a whole new concept. You know, and it was fabulous.

But Randy experienced frustration as well: "After Stonewall, you had a whole change in the movement, in the sense that I found out that when the movement greatly exploded, I really didn't fit in anymore, on all sorts of levels."

Romantically, Randy and David Combs, together for nearly two decades, wed on January 28, 1990, as David lay dying of AIDS.[5] Randy wrote about the experience in the winter 1994 edition of *QWER Quarterly*: "[T]he world is positively overrun with religious folks. I should know. I even got trapped into marrying one. . . . David's happiness meant more to me than ideology."

When I visited Wicker the week before Stonewall 25 in 1994, he owned and operated an art deco lamp shop on Hudson Street, which he continues to run. Amid the chaos, Randy squeezed our interview in between one for a National Public Radio team and one for another journalist visiting from Florida. Nearly a quarter-century from the forefront of the movement, I originally expected to find a bitter old man. Instead, the youthful-looking Wicker possesses a great zest for life.

In 1997, Randy made headlines as a proponent of cloning, founding an organization called Clone Rights United Front, demonstrating on its behalf in Greenwich Village, and making such provocative pronouncements as, "I realize my clone would be my identical twin, and my identical twin has a right to be born." In his 1997 newsletter he admitted,

> It's true I've closed early, tossed a few customers seriously looking at $500 sconces and thousand-dollar chandaliers [*sic*] out of the shop in order to get some of our events underway. Even some of those friends helping me think I've lost my perspective. Well, ideas and ideals are sometimes more important than money. I've worked hard and saved all my life just so I could finally afford to do what I really wanted to do in life.

In his 1998 newsletter he shared that in February he "was one of only 18 witnesses to testify to the U.S. House Committee on proposed anti-cloning legislation." Wicker continued as one of human cloning's most visible and vocal adherents through the end of 2000 and beyond. In his otherwise undistributed "Xmas Letter December 2000," he lamented,

> For this fleeting and passing moment in time I "am" the voice of the pro-human-cloning movement. It is like the early 1960s when I was the voice of gay liberation. But, I know, from the experiences of the past, that once this movement reaches "maturity" I will be discarded. . . . What a glorious and wonderful opportunity I have had, this late in my life, to "once again" catch the breaking wave of history. I am so fortunate.

Asked whether the gay movement to date has been a success or a failure, Randy replied, "I think that's why the gay movement has succeeded. Because American society is basically tolerant, wants to be tolerant, whether we basically are or not, and I think strives to learn more about everything, and strives to adapt their viewpoint to new information."

Jack Nichols, still one of Randy's best friends, shared a poem with me that he wrote about Randy, which reads in part:

I recall a vision.
It is R.W.,
"an arrogant, card-carrying swish,"
riding the subway.
I follow him through the corridors.
His, a swift gait.
His, a loud mouth.
An American voter, he,
persevering, whining, enjoying a good cackle,
holding tight
to skepticism and his purse,
generous to the undeserving,
Odd revolutionary:
praising Calvin Coolidge.

I see, spread from coast to coast
a myriad of buttons
speaking the unspeakable
in keeping with R.W.,

Giving body to anarchism's era.

Nichols also added, "I enjoyed [Wicker's] outrageousness and his honesty and fairness. . . . One of the reasons I always trusted him as an editor, as a writer for *GAY* on news stories and everything else, was because I knew he would never say anything negative about anybody without being scrupulously fair."

Despite your recent cloning publicity, Randy, I hope I've given you an opportunity to dust off your tuxedo and enjoy at least one "spotlight dance" all by yourself. To date, we both agree that history has not treated you kindly; I hope I have portrayed you as fairly as Jack said you portrayed others, and that history can better judge you on your merits and your drive to set matters in motion when so few dared take any action whatsoever.

Notes

1. However, *Straight News* reported that Los Angeles television station KTTV broadcast a meeting of Los Angeles's Mattachine Society in April 1954, including an interview with its secretary, "Curtis White," who acknowledged his homosexuality. **Hal Call** and Tony Segura also participated in local radio and TV shows as members of San Francisco and New York Mattachines, respectively (if not as avowed homosexuals), as early as 1958.

2. In this regard, Wicker seems to have taken his approach from Donald Webster Cory's *The Homosexual in America*.

3. And, according to another participant, no onlookers: "We had no spectators, actually. There was nobody there! It was a Saturday!"

4. Kay also added, "He's a very good entrepreneur. He's always made money. Which is why the movement heretofore didn't really like him or give him a lot of credit." Barbara too chimed in, "It's better to be poor and noble than rich and effective."

5. After seventeen years together (and despite Wicker's atheism), they were the only couple married by Rev. Robert Williams [later defrocked], the controversial gay Episcopalian minister.

9

FRANK KAMENY

I've always been perfectly willing to challenge society's values. . . . If society and I differ on something, I will give it a second look. And I'll give society a second chance to prove that it's right. If we still differ, then I am right and they are wrong, and that is that. They can go on being wrong, as long as they don't get in my way. If they do get in my way, there is going to be a fight. And I tend not to lose my wars. . . . On those issues on which I have chosen to fight, I have chosen not to adjust myself to society, but with considerable success, to adjust society to me. And society is much the better off for the adjustments that I have administered.

—Frank Kameny, 1994

Among the many distinguished contributors to the gay and lesbian civil rights/liberation movement in the United States during the second half of the twentieth century, I consider Frank Kameny the single most influential figure. Why? Timing: Kameny played a seminal role in the '60s, providing the transition necessary for the gay/lesbian movement's post-Stonewall flourishing. Effectiveness: Frank's considerable intellect, powers of persuasion, and formidable ego ensured others would hear his message. Beneath these admirable traits lie an unquenchable thirst for justice and four decades worth of unwavering determination.

Franklin Edward Kameny was born on May 21, 1925, in New York City, the son of European Jews, and he grew up with his parents and sister in Queens. Theirs was a modest household. As he told **Kay Tobin Lahusen** in *The Gay Crusaders*, "Pennies had to be watched. Always there was talk of the mortgage, and the mortgage on the mortgage." His mother Rae, one of his staunchest supporters, was only a month shy of her ninety-eighth birthday when I interviewed Frank at his D.C. home in the summer of 1994. In Howard Brown's *Familiar Faces, Hidden Lives*, Rae spoke of her journey toward acceptance of her son's homosexuality (which Frank revealed to her shortly before his appearance in CBS's 1967 documentary *The Homosexuals*). She advised other parents of homosexuals to "accept them. Love them. *Show* them that you love them. And above all, don't blame yourselves." Frank spoke to me proudly of both his parents (his father, an electrical engineer, died in 1958): "My parents were both very, very intelligent, bright people. Tolerant of diversity. In all ways. There was never any prejudice in any of a variety of different ways."

A precocious child, Frank became an active reader at age four; by age six, he decided upon a career in astronomy. Despite a bar mitzvah, by age fifteen he embraced atheism. That same year, Kameny also began attending Queens College, majoring in physics with an emphasis in optics. World War II intervened, and Frank served in the U.S. Army in Germany and the Netherlands as a lowly private first class (telling Tobin, "I was known as a nonconformist") before returning to complete his undergraduate degree with honors in 1948. He followed up his B.S. with a masters and Ph.D. in astronomy from Harvard by 1956, but first Frank spent a "golden summer" in Tucson, Arizona, in 1954.

By the time he reached puberty Kameny suspected he might be homosexual, but he largely accepted the conventional wisdom of the time that one might outgrow such feelings, like adolescent acne. (Frank also acknowledged to me that "with people, I was not the most socially latched on to others in those days.") At Tucson's University of Arizona, while studying the heavens from its observatory, he told me

> there was one person there who was gay, and he sort of sounded me out a little bit. And eventually told me that he was gay. And I indicated that I had at least some feelings in those directions. . . . Through him, I met someone else. . . . [Keith] was seventeen. He was in high school. At that point, he had had more gay experience than I had in the next five years. And he was very strongly attracted to me, and very much took the initiative, to which I responded, without any resistance whatever. And so, actually, on my twenty-ninth birthday, we first got together.

Later that summer in Tucson, Frank recalled in *The Other Side of Silence*, he visited his first gay bar:

> I well remember the first time I went there, I stood outside for three-quarters of an hour, afraid to go in. Finally I realized that all these people were going in looking happy and coming out looking happier. I didn't see the roof falling in on anybody or anybody getting carried out dead, and this was just plain silly. So I walked in, took one look around, and said to myself, "This is for you. You've come home."

Kameny's relationship with Keith faded when Frank moved to Ireland to continue his studies, but now Kameny had identified his sexual orientation, "and I took to it like a duck to water." He also told me, "Ultimately, I came to terms with it, and proceeded to spend the next several years making up for lost time. Very conscious of the dynamic that was going on, when that happened." Kay Tobin Lahusen informed me that "before Frank got in the movement, he was organizing little commuter flights from Washington to Fire Island on weekends. He was a party animal! [Laughs] Very few people know that." (Kay's comments pleasantly surprised Frank: "You know, I had completely forgotten that!") Kay and her lover, **Barbara Gittings**, who later figured prominently in Kameny's life and work, also pointed out Kameny's fine dancing skills, especially waltzes and polkas. (Kameny once even made dancing a political statement: At the May 1972 American Psychiatric Association convention in Dallas, Frank "liberated" the dance floor at the banquet with longtime gay activist Phil Johnson, to many psychiatrists' chagrin.)

Degree in hand, Kameny relocated to Washington, D.C., where a promising future in his chosen field lay before him. He began teaching at Georgetown University in 1956, and he accepted a position with the U.S. Army Map Service on July 15, 1957. By the end of the year, his life changed inalterably and forever.

On December 20, 1957, the army summarily dismissed Kameny from its employ. As Frank described it in the 1986 documentary *Before Stonewall*,

> Your first year is a probationary year, and there's normally an investigation during that year. And I was called in, and they said, "We have information that leads us to believe that you're a homosexual. Do you have any comment?" And I said, "What's the information?" And they said, "We can't tell you; that would reveal our sources."

A lewd conduct charge he received in California a few years earlier cost him his job.[1]

Kameny was not the first civil servant to lose his job on grounds of homosexuality—even in the '50s in America, at the height of Red-baiting, it may have been considered worse to be a homosexual than a communist. But Frank's dreams of space exploration abruptly ended:

> NASA was just being formed. I would have transferred over to NASA. That was already in the cards. I *know* that if I had stayed with NASA, I would have volunteered as one of the early astronauts. I like to think, in my dreams of what might have been, that I might have been one of the early astronauts. That's one of those little things that I've always regretted.

But the government erred badly when it challenged Dr. Franklin E. Kameny, who refused to go gentle into that good night, like so many others before him. **Troy Perry** said it succinctly when he told me, "When the government fired him, they just didn't know the monster they had created. And he's been the good monster for us." Instead of studying stars, in his own way he would become one.

As Frank continued in *Before Stonewall*,

> I proceeded to appeal administratively through the formal appeals procedure, which went up a few steps. And then I always follow avenues to their end, so I appealed it ultimately into the White House, and got nowhere there. I attempted to appeal it to the House and Senate Civil Service Committees, which were not terribly sympathetic.

With lawyer Byron Scott's assistance, Kameny sued without success through the appellate courts. When Scott declined further representation, Kameny drafted his own brief to the Supreme Court; on March 20, 1961, it declined to hear his case. Having now exhausted all legal channels, Kameny turned his energies to the small homophile movement then extant.

As a result of Kameny's unsuccessful suit, Bruce Scott, similarly fired under the government's unfairly discriminatory policy, contacted Frank. Having lost his own battle, an even more determined Kameny vowed not to lose the war. Bruce Scott became the first of many aggrieved plaintiffs Kameny (and later Barbara Gittings) successfully assisted in preparing legal arguments against the federal government, including several cases against the U.S. Armed Forces.[2] In *Profiles in Gay and Lesbian Courage*, Gittings recalled that at those hearings

> I wore a dress, and heels and hose, and Frank always had on a suit, white shirt and tie. We looked great. But there was one jarring note we employed to unsettle the hearing examiners. We wore one or two slogan buttons with blatant messages, that were completely out of step with the rest of our conventional attire. The little buttons made

> statements like "Cheers for Queers," "Gay Is Good," and one of the most deliberate eyepoppers of all time, "Pray for Sodomy."

Kameny continues to pursue such cases with characteristic vigor. When I asked whether, given his decades of experience and obvious competence in the field, he had ever considered attending law school, his answer revealed the thoroughness of his thought processes: "Most of the legal work I've done has . . . been at the administrative level, where I can do anything that an attorney can, as a court well knows. Furthermore, it gives me an additional element of freedom," as Kameny (unlike a practicing attorney) can eschew rules of ethical conduct with impunity. (As Frank says, "Having never been 'embarred,' I cannot be disbarred.")

Kameny founded the Mattachine Society of Washington (MSW) in November 1961, claiming to be America's first "civil-liberties, social-action organization dedicated to improving the status of the homosexual citizen through a vigorous program of action." His decision almost immediately thrust him onto center stage within the fledgling movement. From the beginning, Kameny never feared taking a stand, and his dogmatic style turned nearly everyone's genteel attitudes about education, information, and research into the life of the sexual variant topsy-turvy. As *Out for Good* described him,

> Frank Kameny had the confidence of an intellectual autocrat, the manner of a snapping turtle, a voice like a foghorn, and the habit of expressing himself in thunderous bursts of precise and formal language. He talked in italics and exclamation points, and he cultivated the self-righteous arrogance of a visionary who knew his cause was just when no one else did. He was General Patton as gay activist: a brilliant, indomitable man, a general without an army, alone against everyone else.

(A few years earlier, Kameny told Eric Marcus in *Making History*, "Looking back, if anyone told me years ago that I would be a political activist, I would have thought he was insane.")

The movement's first wave of leaders well remembered their interactions with Kameny, whether pro or con. **Hal Call** admired Kameny because "when something happened, he can step right in and be a real shit-stirrer, and get things going. . . . He's well read, and he knows what he's doing, and he's fearless. And he makes sense!" **Jim Kepner** told me

> Kameny is almost incapable of realizing that there can be two sides to any question. That there could be two approaches, or fifty approaches, to any problem. That people who have a different goal or

> different strategies are not fools. The first time I met him . . . I got an angry, sharp lecture from him—I didn't get a word in edgeways—informing me that we out on the West Coast, ONE particularly, were just wasting all of our time.

Dick Leitsch said Kameny "had no sense of humor. And he was a boring speaker. And not an effective spokesperson for the movement. I mean, he was just negative. He wasn't attractive; he made no effort to be charming. He was just a big old bore!"[3] In forty years of activism, Frank's style has never really changed; as he told me,

> I have a great deal of faith in the validity of the products of my own intellectual processes. And if I've thought something through extremely carefully, and come to a conclusion, my general operative principle is that I'm right, and those who differ are—whether innocently, malevolently, it depends on who they are and where they're coming from—are wrong!

Of those whose activism simultaneously sparked the movement, probably his most noteworthy protégés were Gittings and **Jack Nichols**. Jack flatly stated, "Frank is one of the mentors of my life. . . . I am grateful to Frank for having helped me at an earlier time in my life hone and develop my own perspective." Similarly, Barbara added, "I remember feeling a great sea change of attitude after hearing about Frank's work . . . I still think of Frank as my mentor, and someone who really helped me define my goals in the movement, and crystallized my thinking about what we could do, and why it should be done." During the '60s and '70s, Kameny developed dynamic relationships with Bob Martin aka Stephen Donaldson (founder of the first gay student organization, Columbia University's Student Homophile League), openly gay soldier Leonard Matlovich, Lilli Vincenz, and Dick Leitsch (which later went awry), and he participated in legendary feuds with Donald Webster Cory and Arthur Warner aka Austin Wade, among others.[4]

In a movement desperate for mainstream publicity, Kameny's bold stroke in mid-1962 to send a news release of MSW's formation and statement of purposes to almost every important member of the federal government ("We feel that the Government's approach [regarding its prejudice against homosexuals] is archaic, unrealistic, and inconsistent with basic American principles. We feel, in addition, that it is inexcusably and unnecessarily wasteful of trained manpower and of the taxpayers' money") resulted in one congressman's heated denunciation of MSW and its aims. As Kameny related in *Making History*, "Thanks to that congressman, Representative John Dowdy from eastern Texas, everybody in the world knew what we were up to. This was a welcome bounty." (Frank later proclaimed that Dowdy was arguably "the man who contributed most to the homophile movement in 1963.") As a result, Kameny testified on Capitol Hill, the first openly gay person to do so. Even negative-appearing publicity beat no publicity; as Kameny and others made a forum, they presented their case and began influencing those empathetic to the movement's goals.

Kameny continued to take the lead through the '60s, making such bold statements (for the time) as, "in the continuing absence of valid scientific evidence to the contrary, homosexuality per se cannot properly be considered a sickness, illness, disturbance, disorder, or pathology of any kind, nor a symptom of any of these, but must be considered as a preference, orientation, or propensity, not different in kind from heterosexuality, and fully on par with it," "I take the stand that not only is homosexuality . . . not immoral, but that homosexual acts engaged in by consenting adults are moral, in a positive and real sense, and are right, good, and desirable, both for the individual participants and for the society in which they live," and "We ARE right; those who oppose us are both factually and morally wrong. We are the true authorities on homosexuality, whether we are accepted as such or not. We must DEMAND our rights, boldly, not beg cringingly for mere privileges, and not be satisfied with crumbs tossed to us."

In 1965, in response to a news article that Cuban dictator Fidel Castro's government was sending its gay citizens into labor camps, Kameny decided both to challenge U.S. policy and to gain mainstream attention to human rights violations against lesbians and gays by picketing national institutions. While not the first to picket on behalf of gay/lesbian concerns (see **Randy Wicker**), Kameny persistently and effectively organized pickets in the '60s. Frank left nothing to chance: "These demonstrations were very tightly organized. Not merely closed. We agreed in advance on our signs. Got a list of the slogans, and had a sign-making party. Not only on the signs carried, but on the order in which the signs were carried!"

First, on April 17, 1965, Kameny picketed the White House. This new technique of airing grievances against the U.S. government worried most participants, including Frank: "We didn't know what reaction we would get. If we expected rocks thrown at us." But the event electrified participants:

> We felt a strong sense of accomplishment and success. And realized immediately that we weren't gonna make any impact at all if we didn't publicize. So we made the decision immediately to redo it. And we had our second demonstration a little over a month later, on May 28. . . . June [26] was the Civil Service Commission; Fourth of July was the first at Independence Hall; later in July was the Penta-

> gon; August 20, I think, was the State Department, and then finally, a big wind-up demonstration, in which we had all of sixty-five people, with a big contingent from Chicago, from the newly formed Mattachine Midwest, in October.

Years later Kameny received criticism for the picketers' very formal dress code, yet he forcefully defended his stance to me:

> "The '60s" really were the late '60s and early '70s. And things had only begun in '65. And among the things that had *not* yet happened was the dress revolution. . . . We had just barely come out and gotten past the hat revolution. . . . I've been *accused* of imposing this on people. Quite to the contrary. This was voted *unanimously*. Very possibly by '68, and certainly by '69, we might very well now, in retrospect, have relaxed that significantly. But in the earlier years, no.

Kameny also encouraged coalition among lesbian and gay leaders in the '60s, particularly in ECHO and NACHO (pronounced "NAY-ko"). (In contrast, according to **Martin Duberman**'s *Stonewall*, Dick Leitsch wrote that Kameny's "roles in NACHO and ERCHO are well-known as divisive. His power plays have shocked and amused all of us. His egocentricity has aroused the sympathy of those of us who are soft-hearted, and the anger of those who are not," and **Dorr Legg** described Kameny as "somewhat fanatic and doctrinaire.")

In 1968, inspired by the Negro movement's slogan "Black Is Beautiful," Kameny

> realized *precisely* what the psychodynamic was. And how much we needed the same thing. And so I toyed around for about a month, playing with words very, very carefully. And ultimately I decided not to focus on just one of the issues—the medical, the legal, or the moral. And "good," while it's certainly more bland than "great," at the same time covered all the waterfront.

Participants at the '68 NACHO convention in Chicago endorsed his slogan, "Gay Is Good." That same year, Kameny also proudly proclaimed in *The Same Sex*,

> it is time to open the closet door and let in the fresh air and the sunshine; it is time to doff and to discard the secrecy, the disguise, and the camouflage; it is time to hold up your heads and to look the world squarely in the eye as the homosexuals that you are, confident of your equality, confident in the knowledge that as objects of prejudice and victims of discrimination you are right and they are wrong, and confident of the rightness of what you are and of the goodness of what you do; it is time to live your homosexuality fully, joyously, openly,

> and proudly, assured that morally, socially, physically, psychologically, emotionally, and in every other way: *Gay is good.* It is.

But Frank drew a permanent line in the sand where no one else had yet dared regarding whether homosexuality per se constituted mental illness. Kameny categorically and emphatically refused that designation, stating, "The entire homophile movement is going to stand or fall upon the question of whether homosexuality is a sickness, and upon our taking a firm stand on it." Despite the towering obstacles of court and church, Kameny realized "we were not going to win the criminality argument, and we were certainly not going to win the sin argument, as long as we were sick. . . . In general, as long as we were mentally ill, or perceived as that, we were not going to get anywhere with anything else at all." Accordingly, through MSW Kameny stated that "in the absence of valid evidence to the contrary, homosexuality is not a sickness, disturbance, or other pathology in any sense, but is merely a preference, orientation, or propensity, on par with, and not different in kind from, heterosexuality." (Jack Nichols laughingly recalled that "the one thing that will bring either [Kameny or Gittings] to absolute light under the spotlight—and you can just see their eyes glow, Barbara in particular—is the whole sickness question.")

Gittings asserted in *Making History* that Kameny "believed that we should be standing up on our hind legs and demanding our full equality. Our full rights, and to hell with the sickness issue. *They* put that label on us! *They* were the ones that needed to justify it! Let *them* do their justification! We were not going to help them!" Largely due to Frank's dogmatism, on April 9, 1974, the voting membership of the American Psychiatric Association removed homosexuality from its list of psychiatric disorders. (In May 1994, the APA duly honored both Kameny and Gittings for their contributions to psychiatry.)

Unlike many pre-Stonewall activists, Kameny didn't lose steam or influence as the '70s dawned. Instead, in 1971 he ran to secure a seat as a nonvoting member of the House of Representatives in the District of Columbia's first twentieth-century congressional race. On March 23, 1971, following a spirited campaign (dissected in detail in *Out for Good*), Frank finished fourth in a six-person field, garnering only 1.6 percent of the vote, yet he achieved his objective. In *Out for Office* Kameny explained,

> as a candidate formally placed on the ballot by the Board of Elections and Ethics, I was required to be included on an equal basis in all public debates and public forums, including radio and television appearances. This provided me with an invaluable opportunity to make my pitch for gay rights. I utilized it to the fullest.

Kameny's run earned substantial political benefits: D.C. gays (the nucleus of Kameny's Congressional Campaign Committee) founded GAA of Washington, and in early 1975 D.C.'s mayor appointed Kameny to the city's Commission on Human Rights, thus becoming the first openly gay person in the country to receive such an appointment. (After serving the maximum time mandated by law in that position, Kameny was appointed to D.C.'s Board of Appeals and Review around 1983, where he served until 1989.) Kameny was also elected a delegate to the D.C. Statehood Constitutional Convention in 1982. ("We wrote a foresighted, modern, progressive constitution, with a superb bill of rights, which explicitly included us. I saw to that.")

In the '70s, Frank received greater recognition for his influence on the movement: In 1973 he cofounded NGTF, and he discussed security clearance and organizational non-profit tax status issues at the historic White House meeting with President Jimmy Carter's staff on March 26, 1977. (As Troy Perry related in *Don't Be Afraid Anymore*, "We were determined Frank should be with us. Kameny, a thorn in the side of many administrations, was almost single-handedly responsible for initiating changes in some of the federal government's antigay bias . . . [Assistant to the President Midge Costanza] said to Kameny, 'Frank, I've read all the reports about you—and I'm still going to let you stay!'") *Brave Journeys* reported that during the meeting, Kameny leaned over to then-Massachusetts representative Elaine Noble and whispered, "This is such a wonderful moment for me."

And who but Kameny among the "Old Guard" would publicly invite D.C.'s police chief, federal prosecutor, and corporation counsel to engage in sodomy with him ("I hereby invite, suggest, and propose to, solicit, encourage, and urge you to engage with me in an act or acts of oral and/or anal sodomy of your choice, in the role or roles of your choice, in a mutually agreeable, indisputably private place in the District of Columbia, at an early time of our mutual convenience"), attempting to create a test case to repeal D.C.'s sodomy law? Before that law was repealed in September 1993 "as the culmination of an effort of thirty years, one month, five days, and approximately eleven hours," Kameny drafted the text inserted into D.C.'s sodomy laws at Section 22-3502: "No act engaged in only by consenting persons sixteen years of age or older shall constitute an offense under this Section."

Finally, after eighteen years in the trenches, Kameny won his "war" against the federal government: On July 3, 1975, the Civil Service Commission ceased its officially sanctioned discrimination against gay men and lesbians. Despite the victory (Kameny recalled in *Family* that "they called me up in advance to tell me"), it came too late to impact Kameny's own employment situation positively: "Science moves fast. And in the time that I had been out of astronomy, the total body of astronomical knowledge had *at least* doubled. And I would have had to go back to graduate school. . . . Secondly, by then, I was so deeply involved in the gay movement, it wouldn't have worked."

A long-term romantic relationship with another person also never worked for Kameny; I suspect Frank's lover has been, in fact, the movement itself. He has not apologized for his single status (nor need he); indeed, *Newsweek* quoted Kameny in an August 1983 article as saying, "I have never looked upon 'promiscuity' as a dirty word. It is a natural and normal style of living, while monogamy is [a] deeply entrenched cultural overlay," and, as he wrote in the introduction to 1991's *Gay Midlife and Maturity*,

> it might be immature and even psychologically unhealthy to compulsively seek a partner on whom to lean dependently for as long as possible. I remain a staunch believer in the emotional maturity of the self-reliant, and in the joyful promiscuity of the contented single—albeit *careful*—promiscuity for the nonce.

High-profile leaders seldom escape criticism. In 1983, *Advocate* publisher David Goodstein editorialized that Kameny, who had "pleaded poverty and sought contributions toward his house payment, was in fact quite well off. Kameny is the director of GRNL who said the role of directors is to direct, not fund-raise." (In response, Frank stated that his mother provided him some stocks in the '80s, and he lived on the dividends as his sole income.) And although later admitting his error, in 1979 Frank criticized efforts to put together the first March on Washington. Additionally, Kameny did not approach the gay/lesbian movement from a feminist perspective, to the chagrin of many movement women. Frank explained to me,

> Now, I recognized *fully* that there was a separate movement, and a separate set of issues, of very great importance, for women as women, heterosexual or homosexual. I never derogated those issues. They were crucially important. Once I was very much aware of them. But they were not *our* issues. . . . Feminism, gay rights, anti-Semitism, are *big* categories. And you can't take on everything. Within the gay issue, it was gender-neutral, at least in my view. And it remained so! And does!

Considering his many accomplishments, I asked Frank for what he thought he would be remembered. After laughing at the question, his exhaustive reply was vintage Kameny:

> Oh, boy. At this point, it's hard to answer that, other than subjectively. Because you only think in terms of what you consider important, that doesn't necessarily mean what other people consider. I think probably, for a number of individual victories, or at least for individual fights, put it that way. Because most of the victories were accomplished with a lot of other people. But they were fights that I initiated, or pushed very hard, like the Civil Service, and the American Psychiatric Association. Here in the District, among District people, sodomy law repeal. Things of that kind. Plus, in general, having given impetus and life and direction to the gay movement, in a way that I think has carried on, and continues, and still does, and wouldn't be the same if I hadn't. Plus, specifically and pointedly, 'Gay Is Good.'

Frank shared with Eric Marcus that "my life has been more exciting and stimulating and interesting and satisfying and rewarding and fulfilling than I ever could possibly have dreamed it would be."

In the '90s, despite many of his movement colleagues' disappearance from the sociopolitical map, Kameny could no sooner voluntarily retire to the sidelines than cease breathing. Those testifying to his contributions include **John D'Emilio** ("I think Kameny is a really interesting and in some ways one of the most important figures of that era. . . . He provided, I think, a determination and a ferocity that was needed in the '60s, to move things along"), Randy Wicker ("Kameny is a brilliant theoretician. He's a tireless worker. And he's the man, I think, probably that the gay community should honor more"), and Troy Perry ("Frank is, honest to God, a person I so admire. Because he never gave up. . . . He's really the elder statesman in the lesbian and gay rights movement in this country").

The last words on Kameny go to Jack Nichols, who wrote in 1972 in *I Have More Fun with You than Anybody*,

> We knew that Franklin Kameny for ten years had been the only bright, persistent voice of assurance and counsel for Washington homosexuals. Distressed men and women, the guilt-ridden, those fearful of job loss, young people and Armed Forces personnel had been able to call him late at night and even into the early hours of the morning to get precise, detailed instructions and advice. He'd tracked down blackmailers, fought bigoted employers and the government, and relieved hundreds of silly guilts. Now a devoted staff worked diligently at his side. He'd earned their devotion: not only was he "eloquent and erudite" as the *Post* had put it, but a kind and thoughtful gentleman as well.

Nichols reiterated to me two decades later, "A lot of people do see Frank as a person who is too much of an automaton, and not nearly enough of a person with feelings. I have seen other sides of Frank, and

I have also seen the other nurturant, helping side of Frank, where individual problems and people's concerns are involved." More than any other person, Kameny shaped the American lesbian and gay rights movement into its present state today.

Notes

1. Kameny explained to me, "That was when I was still utterly inexperienced in everything. . . . I'd taken a bus somewhere. And I was at the bus terminal. And somebody approached. And I didn't do anything. But he groped me. . . . There was some sort of one of these cop-out pleas. . . . And upon application, if there had been no further arrests, under California law, the arrest was expunged. . . . I applied for the expungement, and received that consistent with their law. And I assumed an expungement is an expungement is an expungement, by definition. And normal usage of expungement—that which is expunged no longer exists. So when I applied for my job, with the Civil Service, there was a question about arrests. . . . And I answered the question consistent with all of that, including my interpretation of 'expungement' as being wiped from the record. And I was then accused of falsification. . . . And that started the whole battle."

2. In the '60s, Frank authored a pamphlet, "What to Do in Case of a Federal Interrogation." It contained eleven points, which Kameny neatly summed up as "say nothing; sign nothing; get counsel; fight back."

3. Kameny might have surprised Leitsch had he crossed the country to attend Jim Kepner's memorial tribute in 1998. There, the day after his seventy-third birthday, Frank delivered a sparkling speech reminding his audience of the transformation of American society since the dawning of the homophile movement: "We started with nothing, and look at what we have wrought! [Applause] Who would have imagined upwards of a million gay people marching in Washington and filling the Mall? Who would have imagined, not merely a fading of antigay discrimination, but laws affirmatively prohibiting such discrimination? Who would have imagined personal appearances by the president and the vice president of the United States at major gay events, and congratulatory statements by the president supportive of gay pride festivals? In fact, who then would have imagined gay pride, much less public celebrations of it? In an era when the government was our enemy, and was out to get us—and they did—who would have imagined organizations of gay federal employees, supported by government agencies and departments and secretaries? Even the FBI. And who would have imagined that the front-burner social issue of the day, taken seriously by all, would be same-sex marriage? [Applause]"

4. Frank characterized his disagreements with Cory as "civil," and his feud with Warner as "one-sided (by Warner)."

10

JACK NICHOLS

> **If [people] don't know me, then they don't know that it's possible to have lived a long and happy life as an openly gay man. That's one thing that would be very helpful to them, I think, if they knew that it's possible, if you get in touch with yourself at a relatively early age—which is hard when you're young. I think youth is the hardest time of all. [Laughs] You overcomplicate everything; I was so glad when I reached thirty, and realized things weren't as complicated as I thought they were. But I would like people to know that happiness exists, and that you should reach for it.**
>
> —Jack Nichols, 1994

The genius and imagination of Walter Elias Disney, Jr. has influenced American children since the '20s. Of Disney's many screen translations, one of the more effective was 1941's *Pinocchio*, the story of a wooden puppet who wanted nothing more than to become "a real boy." In his as-yet unpublished memoirs, Jack Nichols writes of his first viewing of the classic in 1944:

> *When You Wish upon a Star* helped shape my philosophy of life and Pinocchio's adventures affected me in a way that Bible tales didn't. I noticed that on Pinocchio's jaunt to Pleasure Isle, in company with macho boy Lampwick, he smoked cigars and played pool, trying to act tough. He looked ridiculous because he was wooden. In front of his eyes Lampwick turned into a jackass. It was a particularly horri-

> fying scene. Pinocchio himself sprouted donkey's ears and a tail. Searching for the good, he found the ever-hungry Monstro who'd swallowed his dad. Building a fire in Monstro's belly he caused the great whale to sneeze its prey to safety. In the rescue attempt the puppet was killed, but resurrected to fleshly reality by the Blue Fairy. The fable, no doubt, was a Sun God myth, like the story of Jesus. The central character sacrificed himself for others and, though killed, was resurrected.

John Richard Nichols, Jr. was born on March 16, 1938, in Washington, D.C., the only child of John and Mary Haliday Finlayson Nichols (later Southwick and Lund). The couple separated when "Jackie" was three years old, but Jack writes of his "memorable shock" upon discovering at age eight that "my parents had been long divorced." Jack's father played a peripheral role in his life; a man whose new wife "tried to wean him away from old ties, and who spent time trying to impose his awkward concepts of masculine deportment on me: How to be, if possible, as much like him as training would allow. His concern was extreme. He feared I might become one of the *unthinkables*, which, not surprisingly, I did." Both severed their tenuous connection after Jack picketed the White House on April 17, 1965; his father, an FBI agent, threatened Jack's life for putting his job in jeopardy.

Jack learned his value system from his mother and her parents, first-generation Scottish immigrants Murdoch and Euphemia, as they all lived in Chevy Chase, Maryland, a D.C. suburb. Nichols's first of two great literary mentors, Robert Burns, left an indelible mark as the result of Jack's grandfather:

> He wielded Burns like some unobtrusive patriarch who was satisfied to leave advice-giving to others if only he could first quote the poet aloud. . . . From Poppop I learned that the constant repetition of themes laden with *values* turns those values into one's marrow. One becomes what one absorbs. From his love of Burns I absorbed a disdain for hierarchy and status. Burns's songs laughed at lords and nobles, celebrating instead the life of the common person, insisting that an honest man is preferable to a rich one.

Great gay American poet Walt Whitman later augmented Jack's life in similar ways. As Jack shared with me, "I am a child of the poet Walt Whitman, and have been for many years . . . . So I'm sort of a combo of Burns-Whitman, but more of Whitman, certainly in terms of my world-view."

Jack discovered his same-sex attraction early on, engaging in an all-boy "mini-orgy" at the tender age of six. At age twelve, Jack disclosed his predilections to his mother. As Jack recalls in his memoirs,

"She knew nothing more than what the doctor told her. 'He's a healthy boy. Leave him alone.' These words didn't soothe me. I'd become aware of the full horror of what it meant to be homosexual in America. I'd never be able to be truly myself." Fortunately, Jack's dilemma eventually passed, as he could not help but fall for attractive men. By the mid-'50s, Nichols frequented the gay bar scene in D.C., where he met many friends and short-term lovers.[1]

A chance meeting at the end of 1960 forever changed Nichols's life when Jack overheard **Frank Kameny** discussing Donald Webster Cory's *The Homosexual in America*, a book Jack knew intimately. Together Nichols and Kameny founded the Mattachine Society of Washington on November 15, 1961. As Kameny shared with me, he and Jack "struck it off to some considerable degree. He ended up being a close friend and coworker. . . . [H]e was figuratively, even if not perhaps literally, the second charter member after me. And was always an officer of the group. And we worked well on quite a number of things." The two men quickly became a most effective team, particularly in the area of challenging the mental health profession on its unthinking assumption that homosexuality per se constituted mental illness. As Jack averred to Jim Sears in *Lonely Hunters*, "Kameny and I agreed we must plan challenges to the psychiatric establishment. This singular aspect of our cause united the two of us, perhaps, more than did any other issue."

In 1965, Nichols convinced Kameny of the efficacy of picketing the White House to protest reports of dictator Fidel Castro's imprisonment of Cuban gays (complaining that U.S. conditions were little better). Three women and seven men grabbed signs and "respectable" outfits and picketed the White House. Nichols was chosen to lead the picketers because he "was tall and an all-American sort. Also, I suppose, because I'd conceived the event. . . . During the remainder of the year I was placed at the head of each line. Thus, in future accounts, I should hope my name will be linked to the practice of direct action." The most visible picture of Nichols's demonstrating resides on the cover of Eric Marcus's *Making History*: Frank Kameny, directly behind Nichols, looks combative, while Jack appears clearly terrified. When I asked what thoughts might have been going through his mind at the time, he told me, "I was never nervous when we did that. [But] Frank Kameny was goose-stepping right behind me [Laughs]." Jack also led the picketing of the State Department later that year, as demonstrated in the 1986 documentary *Before Stonewall*.

In the mid-'60s Nichols attended several homophile conferences, chaired MSW's Council on Religion and the Homosexual, and worked with Richard Inman[2] on the logistics of the Mattachine Society of Florida. Although Nichols remained on the MSW Executive Board until 1967, he had already fallen quite seriously in love in one of the two most significant romantic relationships of his life.

Jack met Elijah Hadynn Clarke, born February 22, 1942, in a D.C. gay bar on July 8, 1964. "Lige," as friends knew Clarke, hailed from the Appalachian hills of Cave Branch near Hindman, Kentucky, and served in the U.S. Army when he and Jack met. While they came to love each other deeply, at the beginning of the relationship movement politics competed with Lige for Jack's attention, and Lige often lost. After less than two years of what Jack believed idyllic bliss, Lige announced his dissatisfaction and moved out, both men crying as they parted. It took a year for Jack to learn to reprioritize his time to permit their relationship to flourish, which it did afterward.

While Jack was separated from Lige, Mike Wallace interviewed a pleasant, smiling Nichols in an hour-long March 7, 1967, CBS documentary entitled *The Homosexuals* (while shadows and potted plants obscured all but one other gay interviewee). There, appearing as "Warren Adkins," Nichols proclaimed that he felt no guilt about being homosexual, and stated, "I can't imagine myself giving this up, and I don't think most other people who are sure of their sexuality, whether they're homosexuals or heterosexuals, could imagine giving that up, either." (The day after the program aired, Nichols's bosses fired him.)

After a wide variety of jobs early in his career, including assisting the Washington bureau chief of the *New York Post* in 1961, Nichols eventually found his niche as a writer in 1968 when he and Lige teamed with publisher Al Goldstein to write an uncensored weekly column, *The Homosexual Citizen*, for *SCREW* newspaper, "an otherwise rampantly straight journal." Their column began, "Lige and Jack are male lovers who dig life together and think it's a groove. They poke fun at those who would make love a crime, and hope for the day when homosexuals and heterosexuals are happily integrated." And poke fun they did: As **Kay Tobin Lahusen** recalled with me,

> in the pages of *GAY* newspaper, Jack was very caught up in rebutting the psychiatrists. Now, he didn't do it in just a scholarly, academic way. But he would try to do it in a flip way. A putdown way. And so, the GAA thought he was totally out of date, because he talked to them. He talked *at* them. He talked *down* to them. He sassed them. You know. He made fun of them. GAA, these little purists, thought you shouldn't even talk to them.

Jack agreed, telling me, "A good joke is one of the best ways in which to unsettle the opposition. And the opposition *was* stuffy, so why not call attention to their stuffiness, their pompousness?"

Before long, *SCREW*'s circulation reached one hundred fifty thousand. In *Gay Insider USA*, John Francis Hunter editorialized that, "Lige and Jack wrote an upbeat, no-nonsense, unapologetic, vibrant, sexy, and liberated weekly message that was gobbled up by thousands like me, rendering the authors overnight the most celebrated and recognizable homosexuals in America. They were witty, wise, straightforward and *pretty*." A silhouetted photo montage of Lige and Jack making love to one another graced the pages of an early issue.

Goldstein and his business partner Jim Buckley later teamed with Lige and Jack to create *GAY* newspaper, which debuted on November 15, 1969. A quarter-century later, Nichols said of *GAY*,

> We did want to be representative of all different parts of the community. We were *very* representative of the counterculture flavor of the times. We made sure that many, many of our headlines were absolutely funny and humorous, and that the pictures were humorous to go with it, so that there was a sense of lightness and light. . . . [F]or the most part, *GAY* was a very happy family of excitable and excited and happy-go-lucky writers.

GAY ran 110 provocative issues. Jack ruefully recounted choosing to cease printing nude frontal photographs about a year into publication: "That was one of the compromises I made with reality. . . . The advertising people would come in and say, 'You know, we're never going to get any ads if they're afraid they're going to be placed next to somebody's dick.'" After almost four years as a biweekly paper (weekly from April 1970 to October 1971), and second in American targeted gay community publications only to *The Advocate*, Nichols and Clarke withdrew in the summer of 1973.

By this time, Jack and Lige had already written two books together (1972's *I Have More Fun with You than Anybody* and 1974's *Roommates Can't Always Be Lovers*), and Jack would write two others in the '70s (1975's *Men's Liberation*, his most serious work from that period, and 1976's lighthearted *Welcome to Fire Island*). In *Roommates*, both wrote, "A loving union assures that each member is self-regulating so that if one partner or the other withdraws or dies, the other will be equipped with his own strengths." Jack utilized all of that strength when Lige died suddenly from gunshot wounds on February 10, 1975, near Tuxpam, Mexico. To this day, Jack remains uncertain of the circumstances surrounding Lige's death, not fully able to believe the version related by a mutual friend who accompanied Lige to Mexico and then quickly faded from view. Jack knew only that after a decade as closest companions, Lige lay dead just before his thirty-third birthday, any possible provocation cloaked in mystery. As Jack told Cory Jo

Lancaster in a 1987 *Orlando Sentinel* article, "I don't think the truth will ever be known about Lige's death." Jack gratefully shared with me, "After Lige was shot, I got such an outpouring of affection from the gay community. As very few people do."

Jack and Lige had moved from New York to Florida in 1973; a few hopscotches to Manhattan and San Francisco aside, Jack would spend most of the rest of his life in the Sunshine State at Cocoa Beach. But on an interlude to New York in the fall of 1975, Nichols met again a handsome entertainer named Robert Logan Carter (having originally met in Orlando in 1973). Carter, who performed as "Roxanne Russell," had become "Miss Florida Female Impersonator" in 1974. Carter and Nichols swiftly fell in love and moved among Florida, New York, and San Francisco in search of Logan's big break into mainstream entertainment (albeit as a female illusionist, makeup artist, and clothing model for both genders). An extremely talented entertainer, Logan performed in onstage reviews and several times on national television. (In the meantime, despite their frequent moves, Jack edited *Sexology* magazine for a year in New York City, and he reported for the *San Francisco Sentinel*.) Unfortunately, Quaaludes and similar drugs powerfully attracted Logan, who attempted suicide early in their relationship. When Jack left San Francisco at the end of 1981 to return to Florida he left Logan behind, but the two remained close until Logan died from AIDS in Hollywood in June 1988. In a November 1996 *Watermark* article describing both Logan and Lige, Jack said, "first, I would say they were kind; second, they were honest; and third, they were bold. . . . I've been very lucky in life because I was loved twice. And they're both dead now."

Only a few years before, in 1984, doctors diagnosed Jack with Waldenstrom's macroglobulinemia, a rare blood cancer, and they gave him not more than ten years to live. Indeed, the disease nearly killed him before he received a peripheral blood stem cell transplant at Tampa's Moffitt Cancer Center and Research Institute. The first such treatment ever performed on a Waldenstrom's patient worked effectively, pulling Nichols from the brink of death and, in so doing, adding a small chapter to medical history in the process. At this writing, a flourishing Nichols is senior editor of the World Wide Web site GayToday.badpuppy.com.

When I visited Jack in Cocoa Beach for Thanksgiving 1994, he personified kindness and thoughtfulness. Nursing a slight cold, he insisted on putting us up for three nights at the Holiday Inn where he worked. When I sat to interview him, we spent over five hours recounting his life and his comrades along the way. Perhaps a histojournalist shouldn't reveal such personal reflections, but I confess I fell in love with Jack, whom I now consider both a role model and the dearest of friends. But I'm in good company: almost a year after I interviewed Jack, **Mark Thompson** told me that Nichols "is a genuinely kind man. And, again, he's in pursuit of what I would call the great mystery of what is this thing that we call gay, really. So he's a role model." **Randy Wicker** called him "my best friend in life."

Lest anyone nominate Jack for canonization, however, **Dick Leitsch** shared an anecdote designed to prevent Nichols from assuming any unwarranted pedestals: On one occasion, Jack smoked "about four joints in the morning. And then [Nichols was] driving down this stupid highway, with the biggest joint hanging out of his mouth. And he was in every lane but our own, on both sides of the lane. Everybody blowing their horns. I'm sitting there like [mimics], 'Oh, God! My car!'"

Jack's beloved toy Pinocchio wanted nothing more than to become "real." Nichols, still strikingly handsome ("I was always seen in those earlier years as a macho boy. I was tall and relatively low-key"), easily could have settled for being, in today's parlance, a "boy toy," concerned with parties, sugar daddies, and other vanities. Instead, Jack chose the road less traveled to stand with integrity in the vanguard of the gay liberation movement, where he remains as a writer (with his most recently released book, 1996's provocative *The Gay Agenda*), journalist, and critic. Now having entered his sixties, he retains a teenager's infectious enthusiasm. While in his mid-thirties, in *Roommates*, Jack (with Lige) unknowingly described himself today:

> [T]here are men in their forties, fifties and upward who have a high sense of adventure and whose manner indicates curiosity and humor. They say "yes" to life and are open, generous and optimistic as a result. They have cared for their bodies, and this care has paid off in high spirits, zest and gracefulness. In short they are beautiful.

I take the wand of the Blue Fairy to pronounce: "Jack, you have become a real man."

Notes

1. Jack's educational background is a bit muddled. Despite proudly telling me, "I'm a sixth-grade graduate. I graduated, deservedly, from Somerset Elementary School," he also spent some time (according to his memoirs and **Kay Tobin**'s *Gay Crusaders*) at Ardmore (Pennsylvania) Junior High, Alice Deal Junior High, and Bethesda-Chevy Chase High School. Despite a spotty academic track record, Nichols read and studied independently and voraciously, and eventually he received a G.E.D.

2. For more information regarding Inman, see Jim Sears's thorough and fascinating account in *Lonely Hunters*.

11

DICK LEITSCH

> **[M]ost people in the damn movement are so asexual, or anti-sexual. And sex is the middle name of homosexuality. I mean, you can't talk about it! What unites us, what makes us homosexuals? Sex! Sex! Sex! Sex! It's not because we all like to [read] eclectic writings of Gore Vidal and Truman Capote. And it's not all because we like Judy Garland's music. It has to do with sex. S-E-X! It's what you do in bed. Or the bushes, or baths. [Laughs]**
>
> —Dick Leitsch, 1995

As I began my journey, I assumed an interview with Dick Leitsch, president of the Mattachine Society of New York (MSNY) whose tenure spanned the pre- and post-Stonewall eras, would be unobtainable. Except for an occasional letter to the editor in the gay press, Leitsch dropped out of the gay movement over two decades earlier. While **Frank Kameny** believed Dick had moved to Florida, I had no luck finding him there. Knowing his affinity for New York, I tried the Manhattan telephone directory; there I found his name, phone number, and address. I wrote to him, but received no reply; later I discovered his reticence resulted from his natural shyness with strangers (his opening quote notwithstanding). As he told me, "Nobody understands I'm the shyest person you'll ever meet. I am very shy. And I have trouble talking to strangers. If I don't have a role to play, I don't say anything." After **Jack Nichols**, whom I interviewed in November 1994, spoke favorably to Dick on my behalf, Leitsch called me to arrange for an interview the following summer in Manhattan. How had the years treated him? I wondered. And why did historians such as **Martin Duberman** and **John D'Emilio** write so negatively about this most militant moderate (or moderate militant) who played a leading role for half a dozen years as one of the most visible (and verbal) proponents of the gay movement?

Richard Valentine Leitsch ("My name was supposed to be Valentine Richard, but my mother said, 'It will *not* be!' [Laughs] The family always named the oldest son Valentine") was born on May 11, 1935, at St. Mary Elizabeth's Hospital in Louisville, Kentucky ("But they tore the sonufabitch down! Everything connected with my childhood, they have torn down. . . . If I'm ever famous, there's no place to put a plaque"). Given the time and place, his parents' status among the first white NAACP members in Louisville made them liberals. Dick also shared that his great-grandmother began a retail tobacco business, and "turned it into a huge empire, which is the source of the family money that we lived on for like two generations. The generation before mine pissed away a lot of it, and my generation pissed away the rest of it. The old American story of rags to riches to rags in three generations." An unconventional woman raised in a Catholic orphans' home after the death of her parents, Dick's mother

> was the right age to become a flapper! And she turned my daddy into a sheik. And they had a wonderful time during the '20s! . . . She was Zelda Fitzgerald. . . . But I had this old-maid aunt who desperately wanted children, and didn't have any husband or anything. So she kind of adopted me. So I hung out with her most of the time, and [she] was a surrogate mother.

Dick's unconventional parents raised at least one unconventional child, in addition to Dick's brother and two sisters: "My family was—I hate to say 'sophisticated,' but they were, kind of. I mean, I was ten years old, and I was reading Dorothy Parker."

The sophistication carried over into matters sexual. Unlike so many of his era who grew up believing themselves "the only one in the world," Dick recounted,

> My mother had gay friends. So I grew up knowing gay people and all that kind of stuff. So it was no big deal. . . . [My parents] insisted that I bring my boyfriends home, because they wanted to meet them. After I moved to New York, when I got a new boyfriend, my father would call me and say, "Well, looks like y'all have been together for a while. When you gonna bring him down to meet us?" And I'd say, "Well, I don't have any money." "Well, I'll send you two plane tick-

> ets. I don't want you up there messin' around with nobody we don't know!"

Dick identified his homosexuality at age ten, and had sex for the first time with a male when he was in his mid-teens, but even he admitted "when I first figured out that I was [gay], I didn't quite know how to tell." Finding a partner proved an even tougher challenge: "It was not easy. I thought I'd never get laid. Everybody used to warn us about child molesters. I thought, 'Where are they? How ugly am I? Nobody wants to molest me.' I'd go into bad neighborhoods, and nothing would happen." Eventually that problem resolved itself. But greater matters affecting society at large remained frustratingly intransigent.

Once firmly entrenched in Manhattan (Leitsch disdainfully referred to others during our interview who lived in such places as Brooklyn or Queens as "out in the 'burbs"), Dick encountered longtime gay activist Craig Rodwell. Through their relationship, Rodwell's youthful enthusiasm for the slowly burgeoning gay movement seems to have led Leitsch in that direction by early 1964. Leitsch joined MSNY, and soon found himself captivated by a Frank Kameny speech in July 1964. Spurred to political activity for the first time in his life, Leitsch quickly became editor of MSNY's newsletter, and combined it with Mattachine Society of Washington's newsletter to form *Eastern Mattachine Magazine*. By November 1965, after Leitsch served as President Julian Hodges's assistant, other "gay progressives" drafted Dick to run for president on a slate with Hodges, Kameny, and Dr. Hendrick Ruitenbeek against a "gay moderate" slate, which included Donald Webster Cory for president. Cory, in many ways the East Coast "father" of the gay movement, had continued to take ever more moderate positions since the 1951 publication of his *The Homosexual in America*. In explaining Cory's position to MSNY's voting members, Leitsch shrewdly quoted Cory's introduction to Dr. Albert Ellis's *Homosexuality: Its Causes and Cures*, in which Cory stated that

> Homosexuals in this society, if they are exclusive or near exclusive in their erotic interests in their own sex, are disturbed individuals . . . they are compulsive, neurotic . . . tend to be goofers, to be self-destructive, to make poor relationships with fellow human beings, and in fact, they are frequently borderline psychotics.

Conclusively rejecting these views, MSNY members elected Leitsch and the rest of the progressive slate (including **Randy Wicker**, who ran for secretary independently).

Two months earlier, in September 1965, Leitsch also appeared on the 11:00 P.M. news, beginning an impressive run of media appearances lasting several years in New York City. *The Ladder* reported that Leitsch "summed up the purposes of the homophile movement, giving them their first airing by a major television network during prime time." Dick also appeared on the David Susskind show in 1967 and the Dick Cavett show in November 1970, and he was featured in *Esquire*, *Playboy*, and *Time* magazine articles. Leitsch spoke modestly about these appearances:

> It wasn't that I was necessarily the best and brightest spokesman the movement could ever have had. It's just that I was the one that everybody knew. Because anytime you went to the office, I was there. I was at every meeting. I'd go do Dick Cavett's television show, and then go back to the Mattachine office to scrub the toilets . . . . Everybody else was running out, trying to gain tenure at schools, or build their psychiatric practices, or whatever. And I was the only one that was there.

Despite the media attention, Leitsch intended to concentrate on effecting tangible changes in the ways society discriminated against homosexuals. (An admirable goal, his tactic became futile after Stonewall, when the newly emerging movement sought liberation instead of civil rights.) During the last half of the '60s and into the very early '70s, Leitsch fought and won several issues in New York, including homosexual entrapment by vice officers, employment discrimination, and the practice that forbade a bar to serve an acknowledged homosexual at the risk of losing its liquor license.

Leitsch accomplished the latter through a "Sip-In" staged on April 21, 1966, when he and his lover John Timmons brought along Craig Rodwell, Randy Wicker, and several members of the press to witness a bartender's refusal to serve acknowledged homosexuals. At each stop, they presented a written statement:

> We, the undersigned, are homosexuals. We believe that a place of public accommodation has an obligation to serve an orderly person, and that we are entitled to service as long as we are orderly. We therefore ask to be served on your premises. Should you refuse to serve us, we will be obligated to file a complaint against you with the State Liquor Authority.

However, as bartenders chose to disregard the law, the frustrated activists visited several bars before Julius', which catered to a mixed gay/straight crowd, refused to serve them. After several near-misses, they sighed with relief when the action succeeded (Timmons reportedly said, "Another bourbon and water and I would have been under the table"). While the State Liquor Authority refused to take action against Julius', New York City's Commission on Human Rights chairman took up the cause; after Leitsch appealed a trial court's adverse decision, in 1967 an appellate court ruled in Leitsch's favor.

As the '60s progressed, however, Leitsch increasingly found himself doing much of his work alone. He avoided attending NACHO conventions for years, finally appearing only in 1970, after Stonewall changed the face of gay activism forever. He also chose to avoid the internecine fighting (as well as the cooperation) among his era's organized gay groups, which he believed rankled Frank Kameny:

> Kameny and I were very competitive. Kameny was more competitive than I. I mean, I just sat here in New York, minding my own business. I didn't care what they did in Washington, what they did in Philadelphia. I was just determined that I was going to work for the city authorities, and I was going to clean up New York City. I was going to stop entrapment; was going to end the harassment in the bars; I was gonna . . . make everybody take responsibility for themselves.

(Of his relationship with Leitsch, Kameny told me, "There were some ideological differences, which he made more of than I did. But which ultimately created a certain level of animosity from his side; never from mine, really, except perhaps responsively to a minor degree.") Then, too, Kameny was hardly the only movement leader who struck a nerve with Leitsch; in correspondence to Denver Mattachine homophile stalwart Elver Barker, Dick wrote that

> the so-called "homophile movement" is not an effective movement, but too often an albatross around the necks of those who are trying to be effective in the cause for which we are all supposedly working. Richard Inman, Clark Polak, **Hal Call**, and Shirley Willer are the obstructionists, who frequently have to be worked against more diligently than the recognized opposition!

Leitsch, too, worked a few nerves: GLF member Martha Shelley, for one, was repulsed by Leitsch's habit of asking "Who opened the tuna fish?" whenever a woman entered a room full of men.

I wondered how in less than half a decade Leitsch went from being perceived a militant to being perceived a moderate. Perhaps the fairest reporting about this supposed metamorphosis came from Toby Marotta's 1981 book *The Politics of Homosexuality*:

> The truth is that for all of the publicity generated by its season of militancy, toward the end of the 1960s MSNY could boast fewer than a dozen members willing to participate in activities that required them both to reveal that they were homosexuals and to endure the attendant embarrassment, risks, and costs. . . . It was partly this lack of support that forced Leitsch to invest more and more time in educational and negotiating ventures which he could pursue by himself or with the help of a few discreet professional associates. And soon he began to think as well as to act like a moderate. He came increasingly to believe that the issues raised by homosexuality were complicated. He contended that long-term efforts to gather and disseminate information, to win the support of mental health and social welfare professionals, and to help troubled individuals were more important than dramatic crusades to reform policies. And he maintained that consultations and court tests that resulted in concrete improvements were more important than bold public initiatives that made headlines but alienated influential supporters.

Dick told me,

> I don't think the perception of me changed at the time. I think the perception of me has been gone back and changed, from more recent times. . . . Once Stonewall was over, I decided that was it. You know, that *was* the homosexual revolution. And after that, all the fighting and backbiting and competing and everything started. . . . I really basically lost interest. And I stayed around a lot longer than I should have.

Here even Marotta disagrees with Leitsch; while agreeing that Dick likely stayed too long at the fair, I sense he only reluctantly turned the movement over to wild-eyed radicals like Martha Shelley and Jim Fouratt. But this didn't mean the battles had ceased, as a more personal skirmish ensued.

Leitsch and his then-lover of three years, Bob Amsel (MSNY president in 1970), filed joint income tax statements for two years; Leitsch tells me the IRS never questioned them. The truth regarding Leitsch's departure from MSNY in 1971 seems difficult to ascertain: *The Advocate* reported that MSNY accused Leitsch of diverting MSNY funds to a secret bank account for a defunct Mattachine branch in Syracuse, New York, and the group terminated his employ as executive director. Leitsch countered that he had resigned in April 1971 before embarking on a European trip for a few years following his father's demise, while admitting, "The financial records of every gay organization are, at best, haphazard. . . . In my eight years in the movement I have seen every prominent figure accused of financial wrongdoing at least once." One may be tempted to recall the adage "no smoke without fire," but Leitsch's abrasive personality and dogmatic approach left him vulnerable to political enemies of all stripes.

His only remaining movement activity was writing for *GAY* magazine, which he did with Jack Nichols. Nichols presented a side of Dick few others acknowledged:

> He was, in many ways, a much more cultured and interesting person in his own right [than the GLF-type radicals], and [had a] knowledge of literature and all kinds of things that those young upstarts didn't even come close to. . . . There were things about Dick as a leader that none of these other people ever came close to. His comfort with various segments of the gay community, comfort that even in those days I didn't have. . . . That easy kind of familiarity that he had, which all of those other people lacked in terms of the gay community's cultural development at that time.

Randy Wicker also praised Leitsch:

> Dick Leitsch worked for years in Mattachine, going in everyday, keeping that organization going before Stonewall, doing Herculean work. . . . I think that he's probably one of the most tragic figures in the gay movement. 'Cause he kept the gay movement alive in New York City. . . . And he has no defenders. Because the people that would defend him are basically responsible, quiet, you know, middle-class types. . . . Of the writers for *GAY* newspaper, Gore Vidal said the only one he'd like to meet is Dick Leitsch. Dick Leitsch could have been one of the great gay writers this country ever had. . . . Dick Leitsch is a brilliant writer. And it's a shame he never really pursued that.

Indeed, Nichols wrote that Leitsch may have written "the first and most thorough account of the [Stonewall] uprising, appearing in the New York Mattachine Newsletter," as well as a very early interview with Bette Midler before she became "The Divine Miss M." But eventually Dick ceased writing regularly as well, and he dropped out of sight from the movement he had led, writing in an August 1971 letter to the editor in *The Advocate*, "I have left the organized homosexual movement because of disgust at this game playing. I certainly have no intention of joining the power game on a national scale."

Instead, Dick pursued his version of "La Dolce Vita," working only when it suited him. (As Nichols told me, "Dick I would describe as a man who, as he once put it, happy on a Monday afternoon, having a mint julep, when everybody else is off working, makes him feel a little superior.") He continued to write freelance articles (and one unpublished book) for fifteen years, and he worked as a bartender and manager. In 1989, when a later lover died, leaving Leitsch $125,000, Dick "stopped working until I ran out of money."

In the history of the lesbian/gay movement, many people's contributions have been either overlooked or ignored. Since no one could erase his fingerprints, it seems someone smudged the surface to malign Leitsch unfairly. Dick (who told me he had not read *Stonewall* but heard reports from former activists) believed he knew why he had been relegated to the historical dustbin:

> I think Rodwell poisoned the well . . .[1] I mean, I don't want to sound paranoid, but that's the only thing I can think of. I mean, why else aren't any of these people calling me? . . . I left a paper trail six miles wide and ten feet deep. And you would think that if anybody was doing any research, they would certainly call me, because my name was all over the place!

I think I understand why, to some degree—Dick is flip, and glib, and likely to say the politically incorrect thing no matter where one stands on the political spectrum. (Oh, the stories Leitsch told me that I haven't shared here!) But his heart is guileless and his spirit willing, and he retains a virtual treasure trove of information about the movement during the Stonewall era. With all due respect to movement historians of the past three decades, I believe their omission to interview Dick Leitsch has been a grave oversight in assessing this movement's history. Even if he arguably represented the last dying gasp of the accommodationist wing of the homophile civil rights movement, only his peers seemed accurately to grasp his pivotal role along the road to liberation.

Note

1. In *Stonewall*, Martin Duberman presented Rodwell's version of events, including reports that Leitsch "fixed" a MSNY election in 1965, stole money from the MSNY treasury, and that within a few years "if Leitsch had once been a militant, he was now, in Craig's view, interested solely in the advancement of Leitsch. He had become a mere politician, concerned more with protecting and inflating his own role as the broker between gays and the city administration than with empowering gays themselves, through confrontational action, to build a proud, assertive movement."

12

TROY PERRY

I think [the gay movement has] done a tremendous job! And unlike the other prophets of doom, I'm the eternal optimist. And I believe with all my heart that we have done an incredible job. And we shouldn't be beating up on ourselves on that. I think we can do a fantastic, *better* job. If we can get beyond the fights internally, of being so politically correct that we destroy the movement, that we can't make any kind of move because we're going to offend someone. You've got to get over that. And you've got to move on, and say, look. We're gonna move together. And at least on these issues, we can all agree on. There may be others we can't. But let's move on what we can. The one issue we can agree on is, we're not gonna be persecuted in this culture, or any other one. If we can agree on that, then we can get things done.

—Troy Perry, 1994

Given their shabby treatment at the hands of many homophobic mainline churches, many lesbians and gays abandoned faiths that abandoned them solely on the basis of their sexual orientation, and certainly they do not subscribe to such religious phenomena as miracles. Yet ironically, the largest umbrella organization serving the gay community is a Christian denomination. That someone began such a church (pre-Stonewall, no less!) is not the miracle—Mattachine cofounder Chuck Rowland conceived a "gay church" more than a dozen years earlier in southern California, New York's Church of the Beloved Disciple formed before Troy's first church took root, and San Francisco flirted with at least one gay church in the late '60s. The miracle has been the growth from one church into a denomination (the Universal Fellowship of Metropolitan Community Churches, or UFMCC), its continuity for over thirty years, and the important role UFMCC still plays in gay liberation outside America's big cities. (For example, *Unspeakable* noted of the four hundred marching contingents at the 1987 March on Washington that "The Metropolitan Community Church had the strongest presence, with some twenty separate congregations marching down Pennsylvania Avenue.")

I'll admit my prejudice up front—I've been actively affiliated with UFMCC since 1984. Therefore, an opportunity to meet the denomination's moderator and founder in the summer of 1994 was, as my husband said, tantamount to "an audience with the Pope!" But more than simple hero worship earns Troy Perry his place in this book. Troy's vision for UFMCC has always included social action for gays and lesbians, and on that count Troy practices what he preaches.

Troy D. Perry, Jr. was born on July 27, 1940, in Tallahassee, Florida, the firstborn of Troy, Sr. and Edith Perry's five boys. Given their modest surroundings, the Perrys were upper middle class, and Troy described to me an idyllic early childhood: "I cannot ever remember not having anything I didn't want. Christmases at our house when my dad was alive were every child's fantasy." In addition to several legitimate businesses, Troy, Sr. supplemented his family's income as northern Florida's most successful bootlegger. In June 1952, a car chase with the long arm of the law resulted in a fiery crash, taking the lives of Troy's father and a cousin. Shortly before his twelfth birthday, Troy's life changed radically.

Within six months of Troy, Sr.'s death, Edith married the third of her five husbands. Bob Martin, Troy's new stepfather, made their lives miserable. Much as Troy loved his mother (calling her "my best friend" and the most influential person in his life), he feared his cruel and abusive stepfather still more. He ran from home to live with relatives, first in southern Georgia and later in El Paso, Texas, before returning to his Florida roots (and later moving to Mobile, Alabama) after Edith separated from Martin.

In the interim, Troy discovered two passions: preaching and sex. In Perry and Thomas Swicegood's 1990 book, *Don't Be Afraid Anymore*, Troy spoke of his first sexual encounter at age nine with another boy several years his senior. Simultaneously, religion and preaching drew Troy. With a background in both Baptist and Pentecostal churches,

Troy began to preach publicly at age thirteen, and he received his Baptist preacher's license at age fifteen.

Having found his calling, school held little appeal for Troy ("By that time I had become the most fanatical human being with which any scholastic institution has ever had to contend"). He did not complete high school, but he earned his G.E.D. and attended Moody Bible Institute and a nonaccredited Bible college, where he performed well. Only one stumbling block remained to Troy's budding preaching career: congregations and church leaders expected pastors to be married. Troy and a bright, young, piano-playing Pentecostal minister's daughter, Pearl Pinion, both just eighteen years old, wed in the summer of 1958.

For the next five years, Troy pastored Pentecostal churches (first in Joliet, Illinois, then in Santa Ana, California) and fathered two sons, Troy III and James Michael. A spurned male lover in Joliet reported his sexual trysts with Troy to Perry's spiritual overseer, who ran Perry out of town. In Santa Ana, Troy faced up to his homosexuality as a result of reading Donald Webster Cory's *The Homosexual in America*, which "let me know I didn't have to be mentally ill to have the feelings that I had." In 1963, Troy and Pearl separated, and Troy gradually began to explore the gay life (such as it was) in Los Angeles, leaving preaching behind him.

In 1965, the U.S. Army drafted Troy, despite his acknowledged homosexuality; he obtained a high security clearance and transcribed coded messages in Germany for a year and a half before earning an honorable discharge. Returning to Los Angeles in 1967, he fell madly in love with a young man, but after six months the object of Troy's infatuation left him. Troy responded with a suicide attempt, slashing his wrists with a razor blade. Chastened by his action, Troy rededicated his life to God, but he still struggled to reconcile his homosexuality with his spirituality.

In the summer of 1968, police arrested a friend of Troy's in a gay bar on bogus charges. When the friend told Troy that God didn't love homosexuals, Troy received God's answer to his fervent prayer to comfort gays effectively isolated from God: Start your own church, ministering to the gay community.[1] Twelve people attended the first Metropolitan Community Church service on October 6, 1968, at Troy's Huntington Park home, where Troy presented a three-pronged gospel message of Christian salvation, community, and social action. When I asked Troy if he believed MCC's survival was a quirk of fate, he responded,

> No. I don't think so. I think it was divine providence. [Laughs] I believe God wanted the gospel carried to our community. And I believe with all my heart that it wasn't any kind of quirk. God was trying to

> reach our community. God was trying to push through all the lies that had been told to us. And God pushed through.

In a November 1969 sermon, responding to some early criticism about his commitment to Christian social action, Perry told his growing congregation, "I feel like there are some things I must do. I'll promise you this, though: I'll never bring a reproach on this church. I will only do those things that are right, aboveboard, and out in the open." Troy faithfully kept that promise. And the church grew, despite many bumps in the road. (In fact, Troy's Board of Directors once fired him while he was publicly fasting to obtain gay civil rights!)

From the first MCC in Los Angeles sprang churches in other cities, beginning in 1970, and the denomination of the Universal Fellowship of Metropolitan Community Churches arose. Troy modestly told me, "If I have a genius, my genius is that I surround myself with people who are a lot more intelligent than I am in certain areas, who have expertise and gifts that I don't possess. And they don't frighten me." He also shared with me, "I am, I think, a good, wonderful, emotional but intelligent preacher. . . . I know that I have a real gift to be able to motivate people. And I don't lie about that. I'm a good speaker."

The early days were punctuated with trials by fire: the "Mother Church" in Los Angeles was destroyed by fires on January 27 and April 6, 1973, and several members of the New Orleans church died in a barroom arson fire that summer. UFMCC also experienced internal strife, as some pastors and congregations chafed against either the denomination's Christian salvation aspect or the church's mission to perform social action. Troy himself became one of the most visible and active leaders for gay and lesbian social justice, first in the Los Angeles area and later nationally from the late '60s through the beginning of the twenty-first century. In the tradition of Martin Luther King (with whom he has often been favorably compared), Perry publicly fasted and prayed on several occasions to effect social change for his community; Los Angeles police arrested Troy in 1970 during a spiritual fast for obstructing a sidewalk. Perry also picketed companies that discriminated against gays in their hiring practices, fought gay bar owners who desired to discriminate against African Americans, challenged prejudicial laws against lesbians and gays (especially regarding holy unions, or "gay marriages"), took a leadership role in L.A.'s first Christopher Street West parade in 1970, received an appointment to serve on L.A. County's Human Relations Commission in 1975 (only months after East Coaster **Frank Kameny** became the first openly gay person to serve on such a commission), participated in the historic White House meeting on March 26, 1977,[2] cofounded Concerned Voters of California (organized to fight the antigay Briggs initiative) earlier that year, and participated at all four Marches on Washington (in 1979, 1987, 1993, and 2000), telling the *Washington Blade*, "I'm going to continue marching until we win our rights." Publishers also originally released his autobiography, *The Lord Is My Shepherd and He Knows I'm Gay*, in 1972.

And can he preach! While visually he presents a mild-mannered appearance (whether in Roman collar or clerical robes), the Pentecostal influence remains dominant in Troy's sermons. (Because UFMCC draws pastors and congregants from virtually every Christian faith, the "flavor" of each MCC's service can differ widely from "high church" to "low church," depending on the pastor's or congregation's desired worship style. But somehow each always feels like an MCC church.) Troy also claims no faultless divinity: "In MCC we've got some real saints, I used to say, but I'm not one of 'em. I'm very human."

Along with **Ginny Apuzzo**, Troy Perry is the consensus candidate for the gay community's "most charismatic" award, as Apuzzo herself freely acknowledged. When Troy and I talked about charisma, he told me,

> I think, for me, my deliverance again was that I am not afraid of emotions. To be charismatic, I believe with all my heart, means that when your people suffer, you're able to articulate that and suffer right along with 'em. And not be phony about it. I mean, you're suffering with everybody else. When there's joy, being able to articulate that. When there's discouragement, being able to remind them they can make it.

For many years, UFMCC struggled with women's role in the church and inclusive language issues. While Perry had attended Pentecostal churches that permitted women to preach, most of the Fellowship's earliest pastors came from denominations that forbade women preachers. UFMCC licensed its first female minister, Rev. Freda Smith, in September 1972; a year later, she fought to change the (perhaps unconscious) sexism expressed in the Fellowship's bylaws. (Ironically, largely as a result of her principled stance, the male-dominated Fellowship elected her its first female elder, the church's highest leadership position save Troy's position as moderator.)

The fierce inclusive language battle raged within the denomination for at least a decade, as male and female feminists attempted to broaden images of God and God's creation beyond the exclusively masculine ones most learned from their earliest church training. **Phyllis Lyon** and **Del Martin** perceived Troy a male chauvinist into the '70s: Lyon told me Perry "was dragged, kicking and screaming, into changing the [sexist] words," while Martin spoke of a mid-'70s Texas tour she embarked on with Troy, Sgt. Leonard Matlovich, and **Dave Kopay**, where a condescending Perry told her afterward, "Gee, Del, I didn't know you could speak!"

Troy conceded that UFMCC was

> like every group. We have struggled with what does it mean to be a feminist, what are the boundaries of that, if there are boundaries. . . . But we're much more conscious, and it's something we fight with. . . . I think [inclusive language is] a sticking point because there will always be discussion on language. Not only in MCC. I mean, it's not unique to us. Every church on earth is going through this.

At this writing, the denomination has largely resolved both issues; more than forty percent of UFMCC's clergy are women, and clergy and congregations understand the purpose of inclusive language. Troy proudly acknowledged that "one gay historian said to me that Metropolitan Community Church gets first prize for men and women together in an organization. . . . He said, 'Yours truly reflects, is reflective of what's happened with the gay and lesbian community in America.'"

Perry paid the price for his visibility in the earlier days of his ministry with a somewhat unstable personal life. Relationships with his first two lovers, Steve Jordan and Ramon Garcia, each lasted approximately five years, but "Steven had a love-hate relationship with the church. So did Ramon. . . . It was almost as though that was the wife, and they were the mistress." In the spring of 1981, Troy met Greg Cutts, a Canadian gay activist, in a Vancouver bar; an instant attraction occurred. When Greg moved to the United States to live with Troy, he experienced no immigration problems, but he could not obtain legal employment. After Troy chose Greg, an experienced TV producer, to produce an hour-long video for UFMCC, entitled *God, Gays, and the Gospel*, he later learned that some in church circles regarded Cutts as Troy's "$55,000 screw." As the result of a toxic reaction to a prescription drug and an over-the-counter medication combination, Cutts died in Vancouver on May 24, 1983; Perry was understandably devastated.

Two years later, Troy met twenty-year-old Phillip Ray DeBlieck in a leather bar. Troy said of the encounter, "We exchanged phone numbers, and two weeks later we had our first date and he never went home." When I interviewed Troy, the incredibly handsome, intelligent, HIV-positive DeBlieck was attending exotic animal management training courses at Moorpark College (quite near my alma mater, California Lutheran University in Thousand Oaks), maintaining a perfect 4.0 average. Their secret for a happy marriage? Troy says, "for the first six years that we were together, I was on the road seventy percent of the time. And it always kept our relationship very fresh. . . . [Phillip said] 'Not only do we have our own interests in each other, but we have interests outside of our relationship.'"

Only two months after meeting Phillip, Troy experienced a long-desired reunion with his younger son. While stationed with the navy in San Diego, Mike, born around 1962, located Troy in Los Angeles in July 1985. Following their emotional reunion after nineteen years' separation, Troy described their interactions as "the best relationship a father and son could have." However, when I visited Troy in 1994, his elder son Troy III, an air force man then stationed in South Carolina, still did not want to see his father. As Troy told me, "in the meantime, he is missing knowing me as a person instead of a label."

More recently, Troy crusaded to obtain new headquarters for the Fellowship and a new home for the mother church, destroyed by earthquake in 1994. After locating a property on Santa Monica Boulevard in downtown West Hollywood, the multimillion dollar deal closed in 1996 after Perry raised the $1 million down payment. Troy hasn't stopped believing in miracles, so God keeps providing them. Perry also visited Anglican archbishop Desmond Tutu in South Africa (where UFMCC churches have recently flourished) in December 1997 to discuss religious issues. By the end of 1997, UFMCC could boast of 42,000 members in over three hundred congregations in fifteen countries worldwide—not bad for a denomination less than thirty years old!

Troy also possesses a keen sense of humor; **Jack Campbell** recalled that Troy nicknamed the orgy room at the Club Baths in Cleveland the "Helen Keller Memorial Room." **Jean O'Leary** added, "I just love Troy. He's coming from the right place. He's always got his eye on the ball. He's out there. And he doesn't get caught up in a lot of bullshit." **Robin Tyler** noted his leadership qualities: "I think that Troy Perry is probably one of the greatest leaders we've ever had. . . . A lot of executive directors of organizations come and go, and Troy Perry will always be here." At the opening of 1982's Gay Games I in San Francisco, **Rita Mae Brown** praised Troy: "He was really, in a sense, the beginning of our spiritual rebirth, as well as our political rebirth. Now, I know Reverend Perry does not walk on water, but in my book, he comes awfully close." Perhaps only **Dorr Legg** maintained control over a gay organization as effectively as Troy, but while ONE, Inc.'s days of greatest influence lay behind it with the advent of Stonewall, UFMCC continues to grow and thrive, carving out a community niche many would have believed impossible to achieve—or maintain.

Notes

1. Some viewed Troy's motives with a jaundiced eye. In *A Few Doors West of Hope*, Joseph Hansen described Perry as "a tall, handsome, drawling young evangelical preacher, lately defrocked, who saw his mission as making the church accepting, comforting, safe, for homosexuals. . . . [T]he desire for the comfort of a belief in a strong and caring deity is as insistent a component of some people's makeup as is sexuality, and just as mysterious and confusing. Troy Perry understood this, and how to cater to it." And recalling L.A.'s first gay pride parade in June 1970, longtime lesbian activist Karla Jay sniped in *Tales of the Lavender Menace*, "Reverend Troy Perry was never at a loss for something to do. Like Morris Kight, he was a master at grabbing attention. . . . Many whispered that Troy aspired to be our Martin Luther Queen."

2. As Perry described UFMCC's struggles at that meeting, Carter aide Midge Costanza recalled in *Out for Good* that Troy "was the kind of preacher she had met from time to time who made her want to forget everything, drop to her knees, and pledge devotion."

13

GINNY BERSON

The part of [my old "fuck you"] stance that was directed towards everybody who was not as politically pure as [The Furies] were, I'm not sorry it's gone. The part of it that was directed towards the patriarchy—I am sorry that it's gone. . . . I guess what I'm more sorry about is that there isn't that kind of activism, really, anywhere right now. It certainly is needed. But personally, that's not where I am. Why? 'Cause I'm older? Or, I did that, and I need to do something else, I don't know. But in terms of how self-righteous and arrogant we were, and how judgmental of everybody else, and how demanding—I am not sorry that that's gone.

—Ginny Berson, 1995

Collective living was a product of the late '60s that extended into the '70s. Great in theory, an attempt to practice and live in a collective seems to have discouraged many from making a second attempt. Not only did Ginny Berson "survive" two collectives, they probably constituted the two highest-profile lesbian collectives in contemporary history: The Furies and the "mothers" of Olivia Records. An integral part of both groups, Ginny contributed considerably to the movement, even if most gay men and lesbians have never heard of this pioneer's accomplishments.

Born on April 25, 1946, in Hartford, Connecticut, Virginia Sima Berson (who became Ginny Z. Berson) was the middle child of three girls. While she first identified her same-sex attraction around age ten, she did not embrace it for more than another decade. As she explained to me,

> I don't think I knew anything at all about lesbians. Except I guess I knew that I was one. On some level I knew something, because I knew that what I felt was wrong. . . . When I was in high school, I knew there was something wrong with me. I'm not sure I knew what it was. When I was in college, I kept feeling the same way. I kept going out with boys; I didn't like it; I kept feeling attracted to women. I didn't like it.

After two years in the Peace Corps, Berson capitulated to her feelings in 1969 with a welcome assist from the resurgent women's movement: "The minute I went to my first women's liberation meeting, the first thing I thought was, 'Oh, thank God! I don't have to go out with men anymore!'"

The Peace Corps, the women's movement, gay liberation, and the spirit of the '60s melded to imbue Berson's activist persona. In *Daring to Be Bad*, Alice Echols described a young Berson as someone "from Mount Holyoke who wrote occasionally for the leftist periodical *Hard Times*." **Charlotte Bunch**, who worked with Ginny in The Furies, described Ginny vis-à-vis herself: "Ginny came to Washington [D.C.] from the left, much more distinctly even than somebody like me, who was sort of more soft left. And I think that Ginny is a much more quiet, committed political person, much more behind-the-scenes person."

However, in 1971 Berson stood in the thick of things when it came to American lesbian political activism. She joined a collective called Amazing Grace; after six months of planning, it lasted all of one week before disintegrating. As Berson recalled in *Daring to Be Bad*, the situation presented

> an extreme case of class conflict. . . . Here were these two Mount Holyoke girls and a Swarthmore girl who stayed home and didn't hold wage jobs and these three other women from South Boston who went to straight jobs every day and worried about money while the middle-class women just assumed our financial needs would always be taken care of by a generous world.

But there were several similar groups fomenting, and the most memorable became The Furies (first known as "Those Women").[1]

In May 1971, ten women[2] formed The Furies in Washington, D.C.[3] As Berson told me, "There were straight women who had come from the left; there were straight women who had come from women's liberation; Joan [Biren] and Sharon [Deevey] were really lesbians who had come from women's liberation, and then there were lesbians who had come from sort of a more 'old gay' culture." When I asked Ginny to describe The Furies's agenda, she lapsed into parody: "The agenda was to develop a revolutionary cadre of hm-hm-hm. I don't know what the agenda of 'Those Women' was. To play softball. . . . We made trouble for straight women wherever they went." As **Rita Mae Brown** described Berson to me, "Ginny was real kind of laid back. Kind of hard to describe. But she always could see the humor in a situation. She never took things as seriously as some of the others."

But The Furies suffered both internal and external problems. Internally, while class issues played a significant role in the tensions, Ginny thinks that

> The Furies's greatest problem was unacknowledged power struggles. . . . I feel like I learned more about class. I grew up as a middle-class woman, but I feel like I learned more about class oppression from living with some of the other middle-class women than from anything else I did.

Externally, The Furies generated considerable antipathy from all corners, including other D.C. lesbians. (Given Berson's dogmatic declarations in The Furies such as "Lesbianism is not a matter of sexual preference, but rather one of political choice which every woman must make if she is to become woman-identified and thereby end male supremacy" and "[l]esbians must get out of the straight women's movement and form their own movement in order to be taken seriously, to stop straight women from oppressing us, and to force straight women to deal with their own lesbianism," could anyone truly feign surprise?) Berson recalls, "We were incredibly self-righteous. We had a tremendous influence on lesbians around the country. But in our own town, we were—nobody wanted anything—we were such snobs!" Is that why a prophet isn't honored in her hometown? "I don't know. If so, it's because the prophet is really obnoxious."

The collective lasted about a year and experienced mixed success. However, as a whole, Berson described that time as "a tremendous learning experience for me. It was extremely difficult. It was very exciting. . . . It was scary. It was very challenging. It was great! It was awful. It was all of those things."

Through The Furies, Berson met and fell in love with singer-songwriter Meg Christian. According to **Holly Near**'s *Fire in the Rain . . . Singer in the Storm*, Berson was the inspiration behind Christian's "Valentine Song." As her relationship with Meg blossomed, Ginny began to produce Meg's concerts at several East Coast venues. Although Ginny and Meg's primary relationship ended after four years when Christian and Near fell in love, a chance remark on a radio show in 1973 provided Berson with her next great adventure:

> In the course of this interview, we were talking to Cris [Williamson] about her recording experience. She had had a record out on Ampex. And she was making jokes about, you should—I don't know. We were all sitting around, joking. And she was saying, "You should start a women's tap dance team." Blah-blah. And then she said, "You should start a women's record company." And the light bulb went off for me. Because I had been looking for something. I knew the elements of it, but I didn't know what it was. And I said, "That's it! That's it!" So I did.

From a purely practical business standpoint, the venture appeared a fool's errand. To begin with, it was woefully undercapitalized. When I asked Ginny if the reports of Olivia Records beginning with $12,000 were correct, she told me, "Actually, we started with less. Started with a lot less. I say now if I knew then what I know now, I never would have done it. But we didn't *know* what we didn't know. It was doable." Olivia Records wasn't the first attempt to bring lesbian music to a wider audience: Maxine Feldman's *Angry Atthis* and Alix Dobkin's *Lavender Jane Loves Women* sought lesbian audiences earlier, but had neither the quantity of artistic styles Olivia developed nor (fortuitously for Olivia) the right timing. Berson told me,

> You couldn't do that today. You could say timing was a factor why it was so successful. You could also say Olivia created the timing that made it successful. Lesbians were really starting to create a separate movement that was not the women's movement; it was not the gay movement; it was the lesbian movement. Feminists were starting to be less afraid of lesbians. And networks were starting to be created around the country. . . . So yeah, it was the right thing at the right time. And it also helped create the time.

Creating Olivia also appealed to Berson's politics:

> I did not want to entertain people. I wanted to make radical lesbian feminists. I still wanted a revolution. And to me, the way to do that was to create an alternative economic institution. . . . Part of what was important to me—part of why I wanted an economic institution—was I wanted women to have jobs where they were not drained; where they were not oppressed; where they were treated well. Partly so that they would then have time to be active radical political people, and partly because I believed that the best way to make somebody a feminist is to show them how wonderful feminism is! . . .

> Before we had a clue about how to make a record, we had a document called "The Rights of the Workers."

Such grandiose, if well-meaning, visions also tend to work much better in theory than in practice; Olivia never achieved Berson's dream of transforming large numbers of women into feminists. Ginny never intended to run Olivia as an end unto itself, but rather as a means to an end: By 1980,

> It was very clear to me that Olivia . . . had to succeed as a business in order to do everything else that it needed to do. . . . And the choices that we made as business choices were not the choices that I wanted to make as political choices. And I understood that Olivia needed to do that. That was fine. I didn't want to do that. So I left.

What are Ginny's thoughts about collectives in general?

> The process of making the collective work has to be one of your major goals. . . . But it almost has to be an equal goal, with what you've come to be a collective for. It's incredibly difficult! I mean, can you create a nonracist, nonsexist, nonclassist, nonoppressive mini-society? . . . I think that the only way that a collective can work is if you spend all your time making it work. And then why bother being collective?

For a few years, beginning in 1980, Ginny ran her own production company called Heart's Desire, but as time went on she found it neither fun nor profitable. While she continued producing concerts until about 1983, radio station KPFA in Pacifica, California, hired Berson in 1981, first as women's programming director until 1987, then as station program director through 1990. After producing live radio events for KPFA's parent foundation, Pacifica National Programming, for three years, Berson returned to KPFA as program director in 1993. When I met with her in her Oakland home in November 1995, she had just completed a massive station format change; whereas in the past, "If it's the third Wednesday of the month, at 1:00, it's Hawaiian music, but if it's the second Wednesday, and it rained on Tuesday, it's Bulgarian music," now "it's much more organized. . . . You actually cannot tell what day of the week it is when you turn on KPFA."

In the late '80s, Berson developed a passion for scuba diving, which continues to this day. Sadly, her hobby also resulted in great personal pain when her partner of thirteen years, Raye Amour, developed a cerebral embolism in a freak diving accident, and died in 1994. But she also began a new relationship shortly after I met her, writing, "I fell in love . . . She fell in love . . . Now we're in love."

During my interview with Ginny, an incident occurred that still embarrasses me. The batteries in my trusty pocket-sized tape recorder went dead in the middle of the interview. By the time I realized it, I had lost about half an hour's worth of our conversation. When it dawned on me, I was mortified to explain what had happened. Experienced radio pro that she is, Ginny, bless her heart, pulled two fresh batteries from her freezer, and we set about reconstructing our discussion. (I've never been so grateful to see two fresh batteries in my life!)

When I asked Ginny how she would like to be remembered, the tape ran out. She would later write me, "[W]hat I would like people to know about me is that I try to operate from my heart; that I care deeply about justice; and that I am basically a very kind and compassionate person." Noble sentiments indeed, but ones that seem fairly attributable to her. Charlotte Bunch agreed: "I think that she's one of the unsung stalwarts of the lesbian and gay movement." So did Rita Mae Brown: "She was really a special soul."

Berson unquestionably served as an agent for social change in the last quarter-century. Although she has moved into relative obscurity in recent years, her willingness to create and participate in both The Furies and the Olivia collective changed the lesbian community for the better.

Notes

1. In *Daring to Be Bad*, Echols notes, "They decided to call themselves 'Those Women' because heterosexual feminists were forever referring to them as 'those women' apparently because they could not yet bring themselves to say the word 'lesbian.'"

2. Berson, Joan E. Biren ("JEB"), Rita Mae Brown, Bunch, Sharon Deevey, Helaine Harris, Susan Hathaway, Tasha Peterson, Coletta Reid, and Lee Schwing initially comprised the group; Nancy Myron and Jennifer Woodul later joined them.

3. As Ginny wrote in January 1972, "The story of the Furies is the story of strong, powerful women, the 'Angry Ones,' the avengers of matricide, the protectors of women. Three Greek Goddesses, they were described (by men) as having snakes for hair, bloodshot eyes, and bats' wings; like Lesbians today, they were cursed and feared. They were born when Heaven (the male symbol) was castrated by his son at the urging of Earth (the female symbol). The blood from the wound fell on Earth and fertilized her, and the Furies were born. Their names were Alecto (Never-ceasing), Tisiphone (Avenger of Blood), and Magaera (Grudger). Once extremely powerful, they represented the supremacy of women and the primacy of mother right.

"Their most famous exploit (famous because in it they lost much of their power) involved Orestes in the last episode connected with the cycle of the

Trojan War. Orestes, acting on the orders of the Sun God Apollo, killed his mother Clytemnestra, because she had killed his father. Clytemnestra had killed the father because he had sacrificed their daughter Iphigenia, in order to get favorable winds so his fleet could sail to Troy. The Furies tormented Orestes: they literally drove him crazy, putting him under a spell where for days he could not eat or wash his blood-stained hands. He bit off his finger to try to appease them, but to no avail. Finally, in desperation, Orestes went before the court of Athena to plead his case.

"The point at issue was whether matricide was justifiable to avenge your father's murder, or in other words, whether men or women were to dominate. Apollo defended Orestes and totally denied the importance of motherhood, claiming that women were no more than sperm receptacles for men, and that the father was the only parent worthy of the name. One might have thought that Athena, Goddess of Wisdom, would have condemned Orestes, but Athena was the creation of the male God, Zeus, sprung full-grown from his head, the first token woman. Athena decided for Orestes. Some mythologists say that Zeus, Athena, and Apollo had conspired from the beginning, ordering Orestes to kill his mother in order to put an end, once and for all, to the religious belief that motherhood was more divine than fatherhood. In any case, that was the result.

"The Furies were, of course, furious, and threatened to lay waste to the city of Athens. But Athena had a direct line to Zeus, King of the Gods; she told the Furies to accept the new male supremacist order or lose everything. Some of the Furies and their followers relented, the rest pursued Orestes until his death.

"We call our paper *The Furies* because we are also angry. We are angry because we are oppressed by male supremacy. We have been fucked over all our lives by a system which is based on the domination of men over women, which defines male as good and female as only as good as the man you are with. It is a system in which heterosexuality is rigidly enforced and Lesbianism rigidly suppressed. It is a system which has further divided us by class, race, and nationality."

14

ROBIN TYLER

The reason "straight" people don't want us to come out has nothing to do with what we do in bed. Ours is not a movement from the waist down! Sex is not the main part of our existence. We are fighting for the right to love. If I never had sex with a woman again, I would still be a lesbian. That is why I do not refer to being gay as a lifestyle. It is more than a lifestyle—it is our life.

—Robin Tyler, *Don't Be Afraid Anymore*, **Troy Perry**, 1990

"Outrageous." What other word could describe a woman arrested in a nightclub for "female impersonation," who explained "feminism" to Jane Fonda, performed an antiwar USO tour *in* Vietnam, did the first naked radio show, and has made lesbians (and everyone else) laugh around the globe for decades? How about "softie"? That's how Robin says she sees herself, and is in many ways how I perceived her when we met. But I also saw the anger and the passion—and loved those parts, too.

Recovering alcoholic Canadian Jewish feminist lesbian producer/director/comic Robin Tyler carries more than enough labels to fill a "Hello, My Name Is" sticker. Robin was born Arlene Maxine Chernick, one of three children of a hatchery owner and a manic-depressive housewife, on April 8, 1942, in Winnipeg, Manitoba, Canada. (As Robin says, to her Minneapolis was the Deep South.) She recognized her performing gifts early, acting professionally at the Manitoba Theater Center beginning at age eleven, and later studying at the

Banff School of Fine Arts. She also identified her lesbianism in the dark days before gay/lesbian liberation emerged. In 1959, Robin displayed a sign that read "Gay Is Good" on a Winnipeg street corner; as she recounted it, "People thought 'gay' meant merry and they gave me a dollar." She also stumbled upon a copy of DOB's *Ladder*, and read **Del Martin**'s suggestion that lesbians move to big cities. Robin heeded that advice and moved in 1962 to New York, where she studied at the American Musical and Dramatic Academy. At that time, Robin said,

> I came out to everybody. Not because of being brave; I was just stupid. But that just shows. A lot of times, we write things, or we do things, and we don't understand the influence or the impact it's going to have. And [from] that one piece of paper [Martin's article], I went from being Arlene Chernick to Robin Tyler, an activist.

For years Robin said that a salary increase of $16 a night transformed her from singer to comic. In reality, after a "stupid little fight" with three women musicians with whom she worked, Robin simply decided, "I will never work where I will need anybody with me again." The gay men Robin met in the early '60s (and with whom she performed as female impersonator Stacy Morgan) radicalized her, and they taught her camp humor. As Robin's comedy persona evolved, one evening fashion model Pat Harrison spontaneously heckled Robin during a performance; audiences enjoyed the interchange so much that Robin and Patti formed a comedy team exhibiting a feminist consciousness. Audiences learned to love them, beginning with college kids and gay men before lesbians embraced Robin and Patti's humor, but much of the establishment and the counterculture had difficulty comprehending their act; while *Newsweek* applauded Harrison and Tyler, *Ms.* magazine condemned them. ABC launched them in four comedy pilots, but the network failed to capitalize on their strengths as intelligent, funny women. Robin says, "We were writing 'Saturday Night Live' stuff, and they tried to make us Donny and Marie Osmond. [On] one of the shows, Patti and I were banana splits. We weren't even women; we were banana splits." Somehow, Robin persevered. She and Patti were both lovers and a comedy team from 1969 to 1978; while no longer lovers, when I interviewed Robin in 1994 they still lived together on the same property in the northern Los Angeles hills, and they had been friends for over thirty years in what Robin describes as "probably one of the most important relationships of my life." Tyler now lives happily with Diane Olson, her lover since 1993.

Robin differed from other women comics (*not* comediennes, thank you) at that time because she dared to make herself (and, by extension, other women) the subject, rather than the object, of humor. Robin explained it to me: "When women were the object of humor, [men] did 'Take my wife—,' 'She's so ugly—,' 'My mother-in-law—' jokes. It objectified women." In contrast, as the subject of humor, Robin talked about her life without putting herself (or anyone else) down. In the mid- to late-'60s, "women weren't even allowed to be assertive, let alone aggressive. The only way women were allowed to be aggressive was if they turned it on themselves. So they became self-deprecating, and objectified themselves. Like Phyllis Diller: 'I'm ugly.' Or Joan Rivers: 'I'm fat.' So you had brilliant women having to be self-deprecating."

Robin's openness regarding her lesbianism only complicated matters. "It was very, very difficult from the beginning, because nobody had been on stage to tell their stories. Nobody was that open, as a gay or lesbian. Here I was not only open about it, I was funny about the pain. So what doesn't seem very radical now, in 2001, that everybody's doing their coming out stories—" proved no small feat in the early '70s.

So Robin made mainstream audiences laugh until she altered her focus upon attending the Michigan Women's Music Festival in 1978. In *Eden Built by Eves*, long-time "Michigan" coproducer Boo (Barbara) Price (with whom Tyler was "having a little fling" at the time) shared that "Although [Tyler] had all the best feminist politics in her act, I had to help her get over her feeling that the women's music scene was just kids in basements. And she was so fascinated by what she saw, by the huge audiences we had even then, that she went home and began to think about creating her own festival." Robin concurred in the *New Our Right to Love*:

> After I'd been to Michigan that year, I knew that I could no longer continue in establishment show business. Women's music, no matter whether folk or jazz or rock or classical, was about the changing lives of women, of lesbians—and listening to it, being immersed in the huge dynamic lesbian village out in the woods was a totally transformative experience.

After performing her comedy act there that year, Robin acknowledged in *Eden*,

> I was very controversial because I wore a tux, said I was a butch—remember when butch/femme was politically incorrect?—and I was considered "too Hollywood" because I came out of show business. I also made fun of vegetarianism and declared the stage a "crystal-free zone." The majority of the audience loved the material; a small minority did not. Since 80% of stand-up monologuists [*sic*] had been Jewish, I felt badly; I was just too polished, slick, butch, Jewish for Michigan.

Interestingly, Robin told me, "I didn't start out to be a performer. I started out writing. And I started out always wanting to direct. I always wanted to be [P.T.] Barnum, and never the elephant." Tyler chose as role models male producers such as Barnum, Michael Todd, and Mack Sennett: "I always thought I could just do anything I wanted, because of these guys. Because I had their attitude, nothing's impossible." But her producing career ignited as the result of—what else?—her own joke.

In St. Paul during an April 1978 performance, Robin originally planned to tell her audience, "I think we should march on Washington. We'll set up tents. We know how gay men love camping." Once Robin delivered the first sentence, the audience spontaneously supported the idea with wild cheers; Robin wisely cut the punch line and went with the flow of the moment. Eighteen months later, on October 14, 1979, organizers held the first lesbian/gay March on Washington, D.C. ("MOW") over many gay activists' objections that it would show the community's weakness rather than its strength. More than one hundred thousand attendees effectively silenced the march's critics.

Robin loved and admired charismatic gay leader Rev. Troy Perry, and knew his style would perfectly complement hers on the road (or railroad tracks) to the first MOW in 1979. As Robin tells the story,

> I got to know [Troy], and I invited him to dinner. And I served him turkey, 'cause it has tryptophane in it. And it makes people very passive. And then after turkey dinner, I said, "Troy, they're having a Freedom Train to Washington." I said, "Let's speak on the train." And so, he thought it was a great idea. And we did it. We had two or three hundred gay men, and two women who wouldn't talk to them.

As the Freedom Train traveled across the country, Robin and Troy spoke about gay and lesbian civil rights at every stop (envisioning themselves the gay equivalent of Franklin and Eleanor Roosevelt). The Freedom Train began its journey in San Francisco, and it reached its D.C. destination four days later. Along the way, Robin, Troy, and the other gay passengers opened many minds and hearts to the lives of open lesbians and gays. Troy says of Robin, "If we were in a pitch battle together, and I had to be in a foxhole with somebody, I would want somebody like Robin Tyler watching my back."

As the mainstage emcee at the 1979 MOW, Robin made the first of her several controversial decisions there and at subsequent MOWs in 1987 and 1993. March organizers scheduled Troy Perry to speak thirty-seventh on the mainstage, by which time Robin knew the crowds (and the media) would long have disappeared. When she discovered Troy's position among the speakers, Robin told him, "Don't worry. You will not be speaker number thirty-seven. You will be first! I'm the emcee, and I'll do what I think is right, once I get up on the stand." At the 1993 MOW, longtime activist (and former lover) Torie Osborn reported to Robin that ACT-UP members intended to storm the stage if organizers refused to permit controversial gay activist Larry Kramer (absent from the mainstage schedule) to speak. Robin thought quickly: "Now, I'm political. I'm a producer. And so I thought, 'OK. The cameras are out there from the world. What do I want to do? Take the chance that ACT-UP could charge the stage, or let Larry Kramer speak?' I said, 'By all means, have Mr. Kramer come to the stage.'" Angered by Robin's decision, a member of the MOW Executive Committee grabbed Robin's arm and twisted it; she says it's the only time she's ever been injured in a demonstration. At the 1993 MOW, Robin also decided that AIDS activist and singer Michael Callen, who would die eight months later, should sing not only with his group The Flirtations, but should also perform his solo "Love Don't Need a Reason" against the wishes of the Executive Committee. Robin defended her decisions to me:

> In 1993, to be afraid of Larry Kramer's radicalism when [it] jump-started the entire AIDS movement, and he is absolutely right—for us to be afraid of that kind of anger, just like they were afraid of Troy being a Christian, this fear permeates. And you get a group of people deciding that, no, the Christian minister shouldn't speak, or the radical guy like Kramer with AIDS, or no, Michael Callen shouldn't sing his song, 'cause every group gets one song. So you get this small group of people together that usually have never had power, and it can become very fascist. So I have been so controversial because I get in these positions where they're always scared I'll do something. But right is right.

Not everyone has seen things Robin's way, however. **Charlotte Bunch** related that initially, "I was a little suspicious of her, because she was sort of a bit too capitalist; a bit too self-promoting; and certainly never made any pretension of being remotely collective in her approach to anything. . . . Her politics in the world and her politics in her life are not very much in sync."

After being the first to call for, and then producing the 1979 MOW main stage, and with only an $18,000 settlement from a car accident, Tyler kicked into high gear, producing the West Coast Women's Music and Comedy Festival every year from 1980-95, and the Southern Women's Music and Comedy Festival from 1983-92. But these also proved often contentious events. Robin's festival philosophy ("What some women saw as 'rules and regulations for women's space,' I saw as the equivalent of fundamentalism. Intolerance of others' choices was not acceptable. I was a feminist, and to me feminism meant the right to choose") curiously rankled many.[1] Tyler also faced criticism for daring to call her venture a woman-owned small business ("We were supposed to embrace downward mobility. . . . Any of us—myself included—coming from poverty did not see the nobility of remaining poor"). Author Bonnie Morris provided perspective in *Eden*:

> Ironically, when festival producers begin to make money, they sometimes lose the trust of their own community—a community so accustomed to the volunteer ethic and female poverty that lesbians with money to invest (and lose) become class enemies. Robin Tyler has experienced such suspicion. Some women are baffled by the festival community's ambivalence toward profit. Throughout 25 years of women's music and culture, few topics have invoked a more confused political response than the concept of lesbian artists actually making money. For so long in radical communities, wealth has been equated with selling out.

After producing a successful 1980 West Coast Festival, Robin painfully recounted in *Eden* that just before the 1981 Festival,

> a small group of women of color came to me and said that I had to give one third of the festival to women of color, as I was a rich Jew, and Jews were responsible for slavery. I couldn't believe what I was hearing! . . . [If I didn't,] they would organize a march against the festival. And I said no, that I wouldn't give in to this form of extortion. That night, over 200 women marched on me while I was on the main stage. A group of women even came with torches—Yosemite had a "no fire" rule because the fire hazard was enormous—and they threatened to burn down the cabin I was in. I was in shock.

Robin spoke not metaphorically, but literally. As a result of the confrontation, she continued, "I had a nervous breakdown. Actually, for the next 12 years I not only disassociated, but to ease my anxieties and nightmares, I also became a periodic alcoholic. The next year the West Coast festival was boycotted, and I lost $50,000—that I didn't have." Despite the perfidy, years later Robin could still somehow opine, "I will always be grateful for the festivals. . . . Our sense of community and family is something that we as a generation of women loving women were privileged to experience. Our culture, our commitment, our growth, and our love for each other will sustain me throughout the rest of my years."

In the meantime, although she shunned live performances, Tyler produced several comedy albums, including her own *Always a Bridesmaid, Never a Groom* and *Just Kidding*, and several comedy albums with Patti Harrison. After all these years, does Robin have a secret to her comedy?

> It's easy to get a laugh out of validating stereotypes. What's not easy—humor should be used as a tool that illuminates the truth. . . . If people laugh at [humor], they think it's the truth. . . . When you use this weapon—humor—it's very powerful. To illuminate what you want them to believe. To just use it as a tool for understanding, it becomes very powerful. Because somehow you get them to sympathize with you, on your side. . . . I think I was more of a visionary than other people. Because I did feminist comedy before it happened—before anybody was doing non-self-deprecating stuff, Patti and I were doing it. And I came out as a lesbian comic ten years before other people came out. And so I actually was about fifteen years ahead. So it wasn't just the ability to be funny, but it was the ability to take risks. And most performers, when you live in a television world, where you're selling commercials and whole wheat, they don't want you to take risks. And the one wonderful thing about being a lesbian—because they didn't want an open lesbian comic on television anyway, I had nothing to lose by taking a risk. It would be like Richard Pryor doing comedy but not saying he's black.

Robin is also not enamored of political correctness ("P.C."). When I asked her if she had a problem with P.C. language, she replied:

> Yes. I hate it. I used to do this thing, [Sings], "Let's put the 'E' back into 'women'!" I have a problem with politically correct anything. Because I don't want our own Moral Majority. And that's what happens. These people who think they're just right, and there's just one way. . . . Part of politically correct [is] to be a vegetarian. It's politically correct to be a lipstick lesbian. Whatever it is, it becomes a fad thing, in which everybody should be no different from anybody else. It's all peer pressure. . . . Although I was extremely political, I was always at odds with purism.

I asked Robin about the changes she's seen in the movement in her lifetime:

> In the beginning, when most of us came out because we had such trouble meeting each other, the differences didn't matter as much. The first wave of people I met—**Troy Perry**, and **[Jean] O'Leary**—no matter what our backgrounds or our differences were, because we were all activists, you know, and outlaws, somehow there was a camaraderie. Now, with the different organizations raising millions of dollars, competing for donors and corporate sponsors, I don't think that it's the same closeness as when we were outlaws. Which is not to

> say I want to remain outlaws, but there's something about being on the cutting edge that you must go through together.

Robin also has her own take on the movement's evolution regarding visibility:

> We are mistaking "liberation" for "civil rights." In 1979 we got together [for the first March on Washington]. We would have been happy if ten thousand people had come, and one hundred thousand came. In 1987, [the MOW] was the biggest civil rights demonstration in the history of the United States, and a lot of the anger focused on the government's inaction around AIDS. And yet, not one major magazine even mentioned it! The mainstream press covered it. The gay press covered it. But *Time* magazine claimed they had never heard about the March! What happened since 1987 is we became visible. Which means that now we're on Oprah, and we're on all the talk shows. But it also means that we went from being a movement to an industry. Because in becoming visible, we also became visible as consumers. And so gay industry started up. And I'm not saying there's anything wrong with this. . . . But, when I went to Stonewall [25 in June 1994 in New York]—I've got to tell you, I was very disappointed. The freedom to walk down Fifth Avenue in leather and feathers, to wear high heels, to go in drag, is terrific, but we still do not have civil rights.

Robin continued her theme when in 1998 she called for the Millennium March on Washington for Equal Rights ("MMOW") for 2000, enlisting primary support from HRC's Elizabeth Birch and UFMCC's Troy Perry. Despite her best intentions, an Ad Hoc Committee for an Open Process criticized Tyler and other organizers, initially alleging "that the march was being organized in a 'top-down' manner," then claiming, among other things, that corporate sponsorship of such an event could "corrupt" participating national organizations. With additional support from other national groups, such as P-FLAG, NGLTF, and GLAAD, and emphasizing Robin's belief that a board comprised of other community organizations' executive directors would best assure fiscal and ethical accountability, in November 1998 Tyler told attendees at NGLTF's annual Creating Change Conference in Philadelphia, "To focus all the attention at this conference on a group called 'sex panic' is not productive. We do not have one right we asked for in '79. We need to focus on civil rights, and not on 'crotch politics' and sexual addiction. We need to go back to Washington."

Tyler's battle against her critics, who accused her of insensitivity to minority concerns, continued through 1999, as several organizations either refused to endorse MMOW or withdrew their support. (At the same time, other groups signed on.[2]) Three days later, Robin sent an open letter to the gay media, stating in part,

> [F]or once, a small group of extremists is not dominating the March or imposing their views on the grassroots. . . . As an activist for thirty years and as someone who has been involved in all of the national LGBT marches . . . I have seen enormous abuse in this movement . . . . But I have never before seen the level of character assassination and distortion that March opponents have heaped on good, committed activists.

Because of constant conflict over what Robin perceived as a lack of financial ethics, despite no allegations of wrongdoing by Tyler, the MMOW Board demoted her in the fall of 1999, citing "conceptual and creative differences"; on November 5, she resigned. At that board meeting, Robin read a long statement about what she perceived to be the unethical, and at times illegal, actions of a number of board members with regard to their personally profiting from the march. After the march, as Robin had warned, hundreds of thousands of dollars were missing, and the FBI was called in to investigate. In the face of such scapegoating, Robin admirably chose the high road at her departure, saying, "I wish only good things for the Millennium March. I still believe passionately in this march's ability to move our national agenda forward and to empower our community. . . . [But] this march is not dependent upon one person or one group of people. To me, this is the greatest legacy."

While MMOW continued its activities without Robin's presence, she quickly turned her attention to derailing the then-forthcoming Paramount television talk show of antigay radio personality Dr. (of *physiology*, not psychology) Laura Schlessinger. For her part, Robin traveled across the country to rally supporters, and with other nonpaid volunteers cofounded the StopDrLaura.com website to disseminate Schlessinger's hateful opinions and elicit support. Tyler and her allies also simultaneously encouraged potential commercial sponsors to reconsider spending their advertising dollars on a woman whose homophobia sprang from the Neanderthal era. Robin became the national protest coordinator of StopDrLaura.com, and she helped to organize and participate in local protests all over the country. Ultimately, Dr. Laura's program landed on the airwaves in September 2000 virtually dead on arrival (finally expiring in early 2001).

If one sees only the humor and the anger in Robin Tyler, then one overlooks a crucial component. What do people not know about Robin that she wished they did?

> Well, they see me, and they think I'm very tough, and very hard, and they see me producing, or they see me on stage, and basically—I don't know if I want them to know it. I feel like a big teddy bear. You know, I love my animals, and I run around, and I kiss them, and I'm very soft, and I cry at things. I think I'm probably a lot softer than my outside image. Very, very sensitive, and very, very soft.

I believed her. She also described her ongoing battle as a recovering alcoholic: "That's the hardest struggle. It's harder than getting up on stage every day in front of a million people."

During the '90s, gay comedy became a thriving industry. In *A Funny Time to Be Gay*, Tyler theorized why: "Comedy follows the civil rights movements. When the focus was on blacks in the 1960s, a lot of black comics came up. When the focus was on feminism in the 1970s, a lot more women comics came up. Now, the focus is on us. . . ." She also added, "We, as a community, are beginning to not be dysfunctional—we're no longer keeping secrets. And the comedy of gay and lesbian comics is a reflection of what's happening in our community—the pride, and the truth, and the guts to come out." While I was tempted to include current gay comics such as Suzanne Westenhoefer or Lea DeLaria for this book, Robin's work in large part made their careers possible. Is Robin bitter about other gay comics' success in relation to her struggles?

> You can't do things for other people's approval. I sit here, very content, with knowing that I made history. And knowing that I changed things, and I helped change things. And in the end, when you're old, all you have is your memories. . . . No one can ever take away the memories. So you basically have to do it for yourself. And you know what? I did it. Just the thrill of being first up on the front lines, and being able to do whatever we dared to do, is probably reward enough. Because in my head, I know. I know I was first.

Even Tyler's critics respect her role in gay history. As Charlotte Bunch acknowledged,

> She was one of the few people running music festivals who made a strong commitment to bring political writers and speakers. She brought me to a couple of festivals, which no one else had ever done before or since, in terms of the music/cultural festival world. . . . So I began to realize that she genuinely wanted the political things to happen as well. And that that wasn't a contradiction to her also wanting to make money, and wanting to be successful.

Despite criticism, Tyler has learned life's most important lesson: "Sheer anger does not sustain me as an activist. I will always keep on fighting, but fighting for and with love, and always going toward the light." Not only has Tyler gone toward the light, she has been a light for a community struggling to find its way out of darkness.

Notes

1. As fellow producer Michelle Crone shared in *Eden*, "Working for Robin, I had no illusions about being in a 'cooperative.' She was up-front and honest—if you didn't like the rules, you didn't have to be there. But it was different from sisterhood."

2. It angers me that skeptics apparently believed Robin had not yet banked sufficient goodwill to demonstrate her commitment to her community, despite twenty years at the helm of all three successful marches and numerous other productions.

PART III

THE WRITTEN WORD

15

BARBARA GRIER

The basic goal of Naiad Press . . . is to make sure that someday, any woman, any place, can recognize her lesbianism and be able to walk into a bookstore and pick up a book that says to her: "Yes, you are a lesbian and you are wonderful!"

—Barbara Grier

"Unique: 1. Being the only one of its kind; solitary; sole. 2. Being without an equal or equivalent; unparalleled" (*American Heritage Dictionary*).

"Unique" receives frequent overuse by people whose word usage possesses little or no sense of precision. Accordingly, I hesitate to describe a person with that adjective. In my travels while interviewing subjects for this book, I met people from all walks of life, in all kinds of settings, and with all sorts of philosophies. But in rural north Florida, in a breathtakingly beautiful beach home on Alligator Point, I interviewed a woman unlike anyone I have ever met, with a personality so singular as to justify my use of the word to describe her. By vocation the owner of the world's most successful publishing house distributing books and other materials specifically targeting a lesbian audience, she has engaged in lesbian/gay movement activism in one guise or another since the '50s. Her dry wit and great timing would give even comic **Robin Tyler** a run for her money. She is a coherent jumble of contradictions: brusque and gracious, brutally honest and generous, biting and good-hearted.

Barbara Glycine Grier ("Glycine is the botanical name for the flower 'wisteria.' I lived in Florida before I realized that the 'clinging vine' I so loathed as a name is actually rather formidable, and can tear down any building") was born in Cincinnati, Ohio, on November 4, 1933, the daughter of a physician and a secretary, and the eldest of three girls. (Grier also has two older half-brothers.) During her childhood, Barbara lived in several midwestern cities, including Chicago, Detroit, and Kansas City, Kansas.

To begin to appreciate the way Barbara Grier interacts with life, witness the way she dealt with her lesbianism when she came out during her adolescence in the mid-'40s:

> When I was about ten years old, living in Chicago, I realized that I was a superior being. Now—I mean literally. I knew that I was a superior being, and that I was different from other people. And that I was different from all the people around me in my school, as well as the adults around me. But I didn't have any idea why. And I did spend some time thinking about it. And of course, I seem to be painting the portrait of a young psychotic. But I didn't reflect on it as being something that meant that I should, say, burn down buildings, or attack and murder people. It was just—I was different! And I was superior. But I had no concept as to why. When I was twelve, and living in Detroit, I went to the public library, and that's where I found out I was a, quote, homo-sexual. Came home on the streetcar, and told my mother. And my mother threw back her head and laughed, and said, "Well. If you are, you're a lesbian, because you're a woman. But you're very young, and I think we should wait at least six months before we tell the newspapers." . . . But at twelve, when I discovered I was a lesbian, I remember clearly thinking to myself, "Well, this is why. I'm superior because of this thing. I'm a lesbian, and this is what *makes* me superior to everybody else." So you see, I started out with this super self-confidence as a result of that.

Barbara developed a love of literature early in her life; "My family was a reading family." As she says, "I have spent my entire life determined to bring people to books and books to people." That determination colored the remainder of Barbara's life, from meeting her life partners to her hobbies to her vocation. In November 1951, after graduating from high school that May, Grier met Helen Bennett, sixteen and one-half years her senior, in the Literature Department of the Kansas City, Missouri, public library; beginning in October 1952, they lived together as a couple for just under twenty years. She shared the circumstances of their meeting with *Ladder* readers in the February/March 1965 issue:

> Once when I was 18, and full of the brashness bred by lack of confidence, I went into a library to kill time. Inspired by a whim, I asked the attractive librarian on duty if they had THE WELL OF LONELINESS (shich [*sic*] I already owned). I was hoping for a shocked reaction. Instead, she coolly assured me they had not only this book but others in the same line, and she reeled off several titles. That was thirteen years ago. Now I have hundreds of other books—and I still have the same "reader's advisor."

When they met, Helen was married to a man, but as Barbara says, "We soon put a stop to that." Helen and Barbara moved to Denver, where Helen obtained a graduate degree in library science; upon completion, they returned to Kansas City.

There they lived happily until 1972, both working for the public library when Barbara met Donna McBride in the same literature department where Barbara met Helen two decades earlier. After twenty years together, Barbara chose to leave Helen and begin life with Donna. Barbara identified that day as the most traumatic of her life:

> That probably [was] the only thing in my life I've ever done that I really was agonized about. Because there was no real reason. In other words, I could not say, "After twenty years of serious abuse, I've run off with another person." I can't even claim that I was unhappy or that anything was really wrong with the relationship. Which nobody will believe, but is true.

Barbara describes Donna as "one of these people who was raised as her mother's daughter and her father's son, so therefore, she bakes wonderful bread and pies [Author's Note: I can attest to both!], but can also build houses, and does everything mechanical known to humankind." Barbara and Donna remain together in a busy, happy, loving relationship.

Barbara began participating in the Daughters of Bilitis (DOB) in 1957, shortly after she first saw an issue of its publication *The Ladder*. Devoid of interest in creating a lesbian political organization ("I was *never* a political animal. I was never interested in the politics"), Grier wanted to improve the quality of DOB's magazine. In *Unspeakable*, Grier related,

> Our most needful readers were the isolated lesbians who, for one reason or another, lived in areas where they had no personal contact with anyone else like themselves. Through our writing, we strived to become a lifeline for those women. We were a loyal friend who arrived every month for a chatty visit.

She told Kate Brandt in a May 1990 interview published in *Happy Endings*, "I felt that my duty, my function, was to find every scrap of anything relevant to lesbians and to report on it. I took that as a life function." She began as a correspondent, submitted several crisp essays, contributed most of the book reviews in a column entitled "Lesbiana," wrote under several pen names (including Marilyn Barrow, Gene Damon, Vern Niven, and Lennox Strong), and eventually became *The Ladder*'s last editor in 1968 "by default. No one else would take the job."

From 1968 until *The Ladder*'s demise in 1972, she and then-DOB president Rita Laporte took both the magazine and the organization in a direction different from their predecessors. Barbara interpreted the change as a philosophical difference:

> It was much more important to [DOB cofounders **Del Martin** and **Phyllis Lyon**] to run a little kingdom of five or six hundred lesbians in San Francisco than it was to produce *The Ladder*. *The Ladder* was always the tail of the dog to them. And to those of us outlying, quite obviously, *The Ladder* was the dog, not the tail. The organization was the tail.

When Grier took over the magazine in 1968, it counted perhaps three hundred paying subscribers; when it finally ceased publication in 1972, Barbara stated that the number of subscriptions had risen to 3,800. Unfortunately, due to a lack of appropriate advertisers ("In those days, the only ads a magazine like *The Ladder* could get were the kinds of things that it would not have wanted. The women would have run screaming into the night"), *The Ladder* folded for lack of funds; without advertising, more subscribers meant only more publication costs, which could not be borne by subscriptions alone. In *Lesbian/Woman*, Martin and Lyon described *The Ladder*'s demise: "Grier and Laporte learned the hard way that the magazine could not be sustained without the financial support of the organization that had spawned it. After almost 16 years of continuous publication *The Ladder* went defunct in 1972."[1] Barbara praised *The Ladder*'s loyal volunteers in 1976: "No woman ever made a dime for her work, and some worked themselves into a state of mental and physical decline on behalf of the magazine. I believe that most of them believed that they were moving the world with their labors, and I believe that they were right."

In fairly short succession, DOB chapters sprung up in several cities in 1969 and 1970, Grier and Laporte "stole" *The Ladder* from DOB, the chapters failed to prosper, the national organization disbanded, and the magazine dissolved. Like "The Heist" in 1965 when Don Slater "stole" materials from the ONE Institute library, Grier and Laporte perpetrated what I think of as "The Second Heist." **Barbara Gittings**, also a former *Ladder* editor and DOB president, provided her version of the story to me: "I feel that [Grier] did steal *The Ladder*. She certainly stole it from the organization that had been publishing it. And made it her own property. And out of that, she built the Naiad Press. . . . There was a time when she did not like it, that I was telling people about this. And now, I think, she's come around." Grier tells the tale somewhat differently. In 1970, with Grier's foreknowledge, Laporte and her lover

> picked up the magazine, and moved from San Francisco to outside greater Sparks, Nevada. We "stole" the magazine, but there was nothing to steal! We took the mailing list and the corporate seal. There was no bank account. [Laporte] left $160 or something in the bank account. And just abandoned the place. Because by that time, DOB was nothing but the magazine. And when we went away, DOB died. Literally.

The Daughters of Bilitis retains a presence in Boston, but nothing else remains today aside from issues of *The Ladder* and the memories of the women who participated during its seventeen-year existence.

For someone whose life has revolved around literature, and whose spare writing style delights me, I surprisingly discovered that Barbara dislikes her own efforts:

> I write, I think, piss-poorly. And I'm not modest. I can write a decent essay. . . . I usually wrote out of anger. I must say, I hadn't thought about that, until this minute. Most of my essays were flavored with the fact that I was pissed at all my peers. Primarily because they were so God-damned busy socializing, that they weren't *doing* the social activism that I thought was important. And so I wrote a lot of things that were very political, very politic-driven. . . . I just wanted people to get up and move. I was really trying to inspire. I'm not religious at all; I'm really kind of antireligion. But I would try to proselytize people into doing what I thought they should do.

Despite Grier's displeasure with her own writing, she wrote prodigiously, not only for *The Ladder* but for *ONE Magazine*, as well as more than thirty-five books under various pen names. Since Grier desired to connect lesbians and gay men with self-affirming materials but didn't intend to create them herself, she entered the distribution business. As Barbara puts it, "Instead of [becoming] a better writer, which I knew I couldn't be, I instead decided to own a lot of writers."

When Barbara and Donna began Naiad Press in 1973, they partnered with an older, retired lesbian couple, Anyda Marchant (who wrote fiction under the pen name "Sarah Aldridge") and Muriel Crawford. In a 1983 *Advocate* interview with Joyce Bright, Barbara mused, "We started Naiad with $2,000. It might take $6,000 today, but you can't start a damn chicken franchise for that." Grier recalls that Naiad was in reality only a vanity press for Aldridge during its first few years (the older couple provided the seed money to begin Naiad, but otherwise remained silent partners). Barbara and Donna thought in larger terms, envisioning a "real publishing company." After nine years as a part-time effort (while Grier and McBride also worked "day jobs"), and after their move to Tallahassee, Florida, in 1980, Barbara began working full time for Naiad in January 1982. The gamble paid off handsomely; when I visited Barbara and Donna in November 1994, Grier predicted that Naiad, whose income supports fourteen women, would sell $1.8 million worth of materials that year. Both worked full-time for Naiad until they decided to scale back their duties in 2000, and they thoroughly enjoy their duties. (In an October 2000 *Advocate* article, Grier confessed, "I have reached the age where I now can occasionally get tired. My goal is to work a 40-hour week, like everybody else, instead of 70 to 80 hours.") **Sasha Alyson**, former publisher of Alyson Publications, summed up Grier's work nicely: "I think [Barbara] gets a lot of the credit for the expansion of the small press, and the influence of the small press. And for making it clear that bookstores can carry gay and lesbian fiction successfully." At this writing, Naiad remains the oldest and largest lesbian publishing house in the world.

Like most businesses, Naiad's path to success contained a few potholes. Barbara found herself embroiled in controversy in 1985 after Naiad sold excerpts of Rosemary Curb and Nancy Manahan's book *Lesbian Nuns: Breaking Silence* to *Forum* magazine, a *Penthouse* publication. At the time, many in the lesbian press vilified Grier for what they perceived to be lesbian exploitation before a straight male audience. When I discussed it with her, Grier laughed, and remarked,

> Oh, I haven't even thought about that in years. That was a big deal. But it was such a silly deal, when you think about it today. . . . The *Lesbian Nuns* thing was a matter of innocence on my part. We're talking, now, *major* innocence. I will say this. I am a First Amendment person. I think that [Andrea] Dworkin and [Catharine] MacKinnon [two leaders in the antipornography movement] are assholes of the worst order. These are people who want to take our civil liberties away from us. We are talking about people who want to stop what makes this country good! . . . I would do it again. But I

> would do it in a different way. What I did was innocent. I sold excerpts to anyone who wanted them. It never *occurred* to me that people would say this is sinful, because [*Forum*] is a dirty magazine. . . . I always assumed that with the *Lesbian Nuns* things that what I was doing was simply making material available. And that there are lesbians everywhere: walking on the beach; riding down the road; in the churches; in the schools; everywhere. And that there wasn't a little box that said, "Oh! Lesbians can be in here, but nobody else can be in here." It made people very angry at me. In those days, pornography was a big argument. The idea that it was objectifying women. And of course, that's—forgive me—bullshit.

Did Grier smooth things over with Curb and Manahan?

> Nancy Manahan in recent years has called to, in effect, beg forgiveness. And my approach to both of them is, "Do *not* approach me in the desert, dying for lack of a glass of water, when I'm in charge of the water tower." I actually have not made any effort to make any kind of [rapprochement]. They *did* make our lives hell for a while. . . . The interesting fallout from that is, to this day, we have women who will come up and say, "I really didn't approve of your doing that. But I'm so glad you're here, and I'm so glad nothing happened to Naiad Press." . . . That was an unpleasant six months in our lives. But those things happen.

(Amusingly, in 1985 the Gay Academic Union presented Grier with its President's Award for Lifetime Service.)

Naiad critics have also groused regarding the mediocre quality of its romance novels. In *Alyson Almanac*, "columnist, critic, and curmudgeon" Rachel Pepper ranked Naiad romances among the worst lesbian books, opining that Naiad's "novels are notorious among discerning readers and booksellers for their poor cover design, lousy characterization, and weak plots." Barbara herself might agree, telling Brandt, "I myself find [romances] dreadfully boring, but I publish them because there are a lot of women out there who really like them. And they have a right to."

For all Grier's many accomplishments, perhaps her collection of lesbian and gay literary works and other gay miscellanea ranks most impressive. When Barbara Gittings met Barbara Grier in 1963, Gittings also collected gay and lesbian literature; after meeting Grier and seeing her collection's scope, Gittings stopped: "She lived amidst what seemed to me thousands and *thousands* of gay-themed books. And I was so depressed with this! I was just absolutely bowled over! . . . I decided, oh, I can't possibly compete with this! So I kind of gave up what little efforts I made to keep up my collection."

After many years of packratting, in October 1992 Grier sent a fully packed eighteen-wheeler of materials appraised at $400,000 to the James C. Hormel Gay and Lesbian Center at the San Francisco Public Library. (She had previously sent many of her periodicals to the June Mazer Lesbian Collection in West Hollywood.) Why did Barbara decide to send the bulk of her collection there, instead of to a major university or an established lesbian/gay archive?

> We picked it because we knew they were doing a lesbian and gay archive, and that it was a state-of-the-art thing. In other words, they were really doing the right stuff. [The head of the archiving project] did all the right things. In other words, she went to the National Endowment for the Humanities, and got a $220,000 grant. That grant enabled them to de-acidify the pages of the books, to give them extra life. She went to the Xerox Corporation, and got half a million dollars to commit the entire collection to CD-ROM, which means that a hundred years after you and I are dead, somebody in Zanzibar can push a button, and get the whole damn collection. Which means I've made for myself instant immortality. College and university libraries are always "other." And they're also forbidding. The average under-educated person is afraid of places like that. . . . Putting them into the public library, in a place where the second floor of the building is going to be this enormous gay and lesbian center—this is going to make it possible for kids from all over the country to never go through [such isolation] again. . . . There's nothing to protect the Lesbian Herstory Archives. It could be easily blown off the block tomorrow. And it has no financial underpinning. And this has the City of San Francisco. People say, "Well, what if the Gestapo become in charge of the City of San Francisco?" Which, I suppose, they could. But once the damn thing is on CD-ROM, it's gonna be shipped all to hell and gone all over the world. The problem solves itself. It's never going to be invisible after that. It's the closest I could come to protecting it. It's like sealing a child in a Lucite case.

Barbara also anticipates sending another eighteen-wheeler during her lifetime, and notes that "the librarian who's in charge of the collection [indicated that] something over seventy percent of [Grier's books] were uncatalogued in normal reference tools in the United States. Which means that we have literally rescued really obscure stuff." That kind of clear thinking may have led **Ann Bannon** to remark to me, "I think Barbara's a national treasure." And in a July 1998 *Curve* piece, cartoonist Alison Bechdel embellished, "I have nothing but respect for the work Barbara and Donna have done. . . . [T]heir impact on this community has been immeasurable."

Among all my interviewees, Barbara provided the best answer when I asked her what people don't know about her that she wishes they did: "The main thing is, because I am so dedicated to my business, and so busy in my business, people don't know things like: loves cats; collects shells; travels all over the world. And—nobody would believe this—could walk away tomorrow, and never look back. And I really could!" She also possesses an exceptional zest for life, belying her placid and somewhat acerbic demeanor:

> I have fun all the time! Everything is fun. . . . I've been lucky. And blessed. I've had an incredibly rich and full life. I've had most everything in the world I've wanted. I've been really a fortunate person. And I have everything! I don't have everything. I, *fortunately*, do not have everything. And have eagerness and ambition ahead. I can't live to begin to do all the things I want to do.

Barbara, I hope you live long enough to do most of the things you want, and take generously from a world to which you have given generously. Your efforts have made a profound difference.

Note

1. Time has not softened Del and Phyl's antipathy toward Grier. Lyon told me Barbara "talks about how she was 'out' before anybody else was ever out. And she was so deep in the closet in Kansas City you couldn't even find her! . . . Barbara never came to anything. She never came to any of the conferences—." Martin added that Grier and Laporte "thought that they had discovered feminism. And that none of [the previous generation of DOB leaders] were with it. And that we were all gay, but we were not lesbian feminists at that point. We were *way* ahead of her. . . . That's what they said when they stole *The Ladder*. That was their grounds."

16

ANN BANNON

[In 1961] I was invited by the Mattachine Society to come and talk to them. Which I did, and they were really darling to me. And my husband hated that! And I did have to find someone to sit with the children, which he disapproved of. And it began to be very painful. So every time I would start to reach out [to the lesbian/gay community], I would get struck down. . . . In my own life, I couldn't operationalize [my feeling that gays should end the secrecy and take more pride in themselves and their lives]. I couldn't find a way.

—Ann Bannon, 1995

Question: How many lesbian sexual experiences need one have had to write the best-selling (and arguably the best) lesbian novels of the '50s and '60s?
Answer: None.

On the surface, that answer seems rooted in a fiction more implausible than the works she produced. But often truth *is* stranger than fiction. In no other way could the product of a Victorian upbringing, a wife and mother of two young daughters, create characters and situations that resonated powerfully for as diverse a group of lesbian and gay writers as **Joan Nestle**, **Kate Millett**, Allen Ginsberg, and Audre Lorde when lesbianism was not only "the love that dared not speak its name," but the author herself acknowledged that "I don't think I knew the word 'lesbian' when I wrote *Odd Girl Out*. I had never heard it."

In the '50s, most people possessed less sexual sophistication than they do today. Ann Bannon's works, extraordinarily tame by today's standards, were then perceived as soft-core pornography, according to publisher and gay miscellanea collector **Barbara Grier**: "Specific erotica and soft pornography is readily available [for those] above the age of five everywhere in this country, in everything, including *women's* magazines! But in the '50s and '60s, that was not true. . . . And in those days, they were the soft porn equivalent." Bannon only knew that she loved to tell stories, and ultimately she received encouragement to write about what latently interested her. Bannon's books influenced an entire generation of guilt-ridden lesbians: When I asked Grier if I were to write about only one author in the lesbian paperback genre, without hesitation she declared,

> Ann Bannon. Without even a discussion. . . . You'd get that answer from everyone. *Everyone* would tell you Ann Bannon. . . . There was a triumvirate of Paula Christian, Valerie Taylor, and Ann Bannon. But in terms of actual influence, sales, everything, Bannon. . . . She literally sold hundreds of thousands of copies of her books. She was much more widely distributed than any of them.

Armed with that information and an address, I visited Bannon at her small but tasteful apartment in Sacramento, California, in November 1995.

Ann Bannon[1] was born in Joliet, Illinois, on September 15, 1932. She spoke little of her childhood, other than mentioning four younger half-brothers, but it seems marked by an obligation to do "the right thing," which certainly excluded lesbianism from her range of options. Only when Bannon attended college (as a Kappa Kappa Gamma) did she consciously begin to identify her own homoeroticism, but at that time it never evolved beyond fantasy. Unable to follow her heart into the lesbian community at that time, Bannon took a page from her background and followed her head instead, marrying in 1954 and raising two children. However, the subplot of two women exploring their feelings toward one another found its way into her first novel ("You kind of have to get [that first novel] out of your system, you know. . . . And it was *way* too long—it was something like six hundred pages!"). She shared her draft with a writer whose work she admired, novelist "Vin Packer," author of lesbian novel *Spring Fire* (and other books under the name "Ann Aldrich"). Packer introduced Bannon to her editor, Fawcett Gold Medal's Dick Carroll. He looked at Ann's voluminous work and suggested, "If you take this thing home and dump most of it, but hang on to that little bit you've got somewhere in the middle about the two young women sort of getting together, and getting interested in each other, that would help." Thus Carroll launched Bannon's career as a lesbian novelist. When I asked if it was hard for Ann to dump most of her novel and start afresh, she laughed, saying,

> I was so craven as to be willing to do just about anything, at that point, to get in print. . . . I was kind of shaken, because I didn't think I had been so obvious! . . . So I went home, and I sort of pulled up my socks, and threw out the rest of it. And I wrote about Beth and Laura. And I brought it back, and he didn't change a word.

The result, 1957's *Odd Girl Out*, surprisingly became Fawcett Gold Medal's second best-selling paperback original title that year. Bannon followed that success with five more published novels, *I Am a Woman, Women in the Shadows, Journey to a Woman, The Marriage,* and *Beebo Brinker.*[2]

Read today, Bannon's lesbian characters pale in comparison to literary cousin Molly Bolt in **Rita Mae Brown**'s *Rubyfruit Jungle* just a decade or so later. But for their time, her heroines dealt remarkably forthrightly with identifying their feelings and finding ways to resolve them. (Bannon's books also retained extraordinary durability: At the end of 1999, Jesse Monteagudo selected Bannon's series in the upper half of his "Top 100 Gay Books of the 20th Century.") While in her first book Bannon clearly equated lesbianism with emotional stuntedness ("It comes out of a cultural matrix that itself was, in this regard, kind of stunted . . . I think that did permeate my thinking. I had so little to go on!"), and her protagonist expiates her guilt by injuring herself with her own fingernails, plucky Laura nonetheless challenged society's lesbian stereotypes:

> She thought that homosexual women were great strong creatures in slacks with brush cuts and deep voices; unhappy things, standouts in the crowd. She looked back at herself hugging her bosom as if to comfort herself, and she thought, "I don't want to be a boy. I don't want to be like them. I'm a *girl*. I *am* a girl. That's what I want to be. But if I'm a girl why do I love a girl?"

With no physical experiences of her own upon which to draw, how did Bannon manage to captivate her lesbian audience so successfully? In the Canadian movie *Forbidden Love*, she explained how she absorbed the atmosphere in a gay milieu during her infrequent visits there:

> When I first started writing, I would travel from Philadelphia, where we were living, up to New York on the commuter train, and beeline right down to Greenwich Village. And sometimes I would spend long

> hours simply walking up and down the streets of the Village, to soak it up, to sort of make it mine. Because I could only have these little moments, these short periods of time. It was never more than a week at a time, and even a week was rare. It mattered to me, and therefore it was imprinted on all my senses, as something to take away with me and keep, and use, to mine it for my subsequent writing. It left me with a sort of magic place in my mind and imagination that's Greenwich Village in the '50s. My grandmother would have said it's a diamond in your pocket, you know. You carry that with you forever. And it feeds the stories.

She also ventured into lesbian bars during those Greenwich Village forays, recalling:

> It was a lot of fun. It was the social center. It was the one place where you could be yourself, dress yourself. *But* it made you terribly vulnerable, because the cops did, literally, stage those raids. The most terrifying thing I could think of was to have been in one. And to have been a respectable young housewife with little children. I would have lost my children! My home, my name.

So successfully did Bannon engineer this ruse that few could guess the disparity between her heroines (especially super-dyke Beebo Brinker) and the author's day-to-day existence. Her fictional characters proved therapeutic for her, probably never more so than when Beebo killed her own dog. Ann recounted in *Happy Endings*,

> Beebo had taken on all my own strength and energy and anger. I knew that maybe I couldn't take it—I couldn't stand some of what was happening to me—but Beebo could take it. Beebo really, in a way, had my nervous breakdown for me. . . . I think I was just overwhelmed with grief and anger that I was not able to express.

Then, too, one senses Bannon's internal conflict when, in *Women in the Shadows*, one of her gay characters tells Laura,

> do you want to grow *old* here in the Village? Have you seen the pitiful old women in their men's oxfords and chopped-off hair, stumping around like lost souls, wandering from bar to bar and staring at the pretty kids and weeping because they can't have them any more? Or living together, two of them, ugly and fat and wrinkled, with nothing to do and nothing to care about but the good old days that are no more? Is that what you want? Because if you stay here, that's what you'll get.

Much as she loved her children ("The reward for staying with a wretched marriage came many years later, when two children grew into lovely young women, rich with mature intelligence, beauty, academic success, and warm hearts"), in a 1983 *Advocate* article interview with Camilla Decarnin, Bannon described her marriage as "an emotional calamity." Why did she remain trapped in a joyless (to her) marriage for twenty-seven years?

> I married a man who desperately needed me to be deferential, supportive—he used to say to me, "I want you to be attuned to my every wish in such a way that you will know before I do—" . . . My children grew up in a stable, secure home. And the whole time, my heart was elsewhere. I guess I did the right thing for my children, and the wrong thing for myself. And it was desperately hard. And I don't know if, looking back, I would have made the same choice. It's hard. But this is my life; this is how I did it; it wasn't a dress rehearsal; it was the real thing. I produced two children, and by God, I had a sense of the stick-it-out, make-it-right, keep-everybody-happy. That's what the women's path is. That's how we do it!

How did she manage to continue writing lesbian-themed novels while married to such a domineering man? "I don't know whether to this day he quite ever got it. He didn't read them; he just gladly accepted the checks when they came in! And he encouraged me, because he saw that it was successful. And profitable."

Bannon somehow managed to maintain a scintilla of interaction with the lesbian and gay community for a time. She attended a couple of Daughters of Bilitis meetings in Los Angeles around 1960 ("There were some women there who became very obsessive. And they would find out where I lived, and follow me home, and all. I did get scared. Finally, I withdrew. It was too bad"), attended a meeting as a guest speaker of the Mattachine Society, and wrote in *ONE Magazine* her views of how lesbians and gays could gain acceptance in the larger society:

> Eventually, if we stick closer to the truth and everyday lives of homosexuals, without sacrificing dramatic interest, perhaps we can dispense with the old bromides burdening gay society; that is, that it is a world of shadows; a world in the twilight; a world full of oversexed half-men and half-women, all blundering around in the dusk without giving a damn for anything but who they'll spend the dark hours with.

(The events at Stonewall and afterward filled her with "this great sense of sort of motherly pride—[Laughs]—in what the younger generation has done. And the bravery they've exhibited.")

By 1962, Ann ceased her novel writing. Four relocations in as many years, ultimately bringing her to California, exhausted her. Then too, she recounted in *Forbidden Love*,

> I stopped writing in the early '60s at a time when my children were just of an age to start asking what I was doing at the typewriter for so many hours a day. And beginning to be able to read, and interested in what I was doing. And it made me uneasy. I wish I had been braver, because I think I was beginning to be a lot better writer.

In the meantime, Ann found a career avenue acceptable to her husband (and herself) when she began to explore teaching. By 1966, she enrolled at Sacramento (California) State University to obtain a teaching credential,

> thinking I would teach French and English in high school. But at the same time, in order to get the credential, I went back and took some additional coursework in literature and language. And discovered I could finish an M.A. if I just stuck around one or two more semesters. And that went so well that I applied for doctoral programs at Berkeley and Stanford. And Stanford accepted me.

Around 1974, she returned to Sac State as a linguistics professor, and eventually became department chair. But while her academic career soared, her home life soured.

Once her daughters left the nest, Bannon finally felt she could claim her personal life for herself. To do so, she had to obtain a divorce from her husband, a tortuously difficult process she knew would take all her emotional strength: "When I left, he was thunderstruck! That a), I would do such a thing, and b), there were any problems. He said, 'But we're happy!' . . . Joe turned every screw he could get his hands on, of guilt and misery. And that went on for four years before the divorce was final!" The day she left her husband she recalled as the most terrifying of her life: Knowing Joe would be out of town for a few days, Ann made arrangements with a moving company to move her larger pieces of furniture to an apartment of her own. After accepting the job, the company stalled for several days; on the day Joe planned to return, the new owner explained the company had just declared bankruptcy. "And I thought, 'If he comes home, and he finds me here, he'll either kill me or he'll kill himself.'" Unable to find another mover on such short notice, she panicked until the owner of the bankrupted firm showed up to move her belongings himself. "I remember to this day the terror and anguish I felt, having to stand there surrounded by everything packed up, and say to Joe, 'I'm leaving you.' . . . I've had some scary times, but I think that was the time I really thought my life was on the line."

After Ann finally freed herself from her emotional prison, Barbara Grier sought Bannon out, and she proposed reissuing her paperbacks through Naiad Press, a wonderful opportunity to share her work with a new generation. Bannon agreed, and life once again began to hold promise. However, on the verge of a breakthrough, Ann's body rebelled:

> Even when Barbara was there, and I suddenly saw the world starting to open up in a wonderful way, and I was running with arms wide open, at the same time it was like having a ghost, a monster hanging onto you, pulling you down. And then, you suddenly have that scary feeling, that here's the hill and the sunshine. "If I could just get up that hill!" And something is hanging on, and pulling you down. And for a little while there, you're out of balance, and you don't know if you've got the strength to make it. Finally, the divorce was final. And within two months, the chronic fatigue [syndrome] hit me. And so—you've got to think it's connected [to the years of suppression], somehow. At the time I denied it fiercely, but I really think I beat myself up horribly, in ways I'll never know. . . . I was just paralyzed with exhaustion. I couldn't lift a soup spoon. I dropped twenty pounds, and I didn't weigh very much to begin with.

The illness first caused her to take a sabbatical from work; when she returned, she accepted a less taxing position as an associate dean. Her CFS also impacted a budding relationship:

> I did briefly connect with a very accomplished young woman, shortly after Joe and I separated, and shortly after the books came out. And we had a brief affair of a little over a year. She was in the military, and has long since moved on. It was a mismatch; I think I was just so eager to get out and do something. And I regret that, because I think it made her unhappy. But it didn't last. . . . I'm not partnered, and I sometimes feel sad about that. But partly, that was the chronic fatigue. . . . In my case, I can do my job; earn a living. [But emotionally] I spend everything I've got. By the end of the day, it is gone!

While she still must conserve her energy, she retired in 1997, and she intends to turn her attention to her manuscript, *Applehood and Mother Pie*. Bannon prematurely submitted it to Barbara Grier, who bluntly told her, "I hate this book! I don't want the book, but I want to publish it when you rewrite it." Even Ann agreed with Grier's assessment:

> I know what's wrong with it. I simply shouldn't have sent it to her while it was hatching! [Laughs] . . . I think it's a funny book! And I think what's missing is that Beebo was not as erotic as she needs to be, because she didn't have that edge that we were talking about. She was a heller.

While life has thrown Bannon many difficult curves, she remains a survivor, retaining a delightful sense of humor and an indomitable determination. When I asked Ann what she thought she would be remembered for, she thoughtfully answered,

> I hope it's for having a voice when so few had one, and for using it to say that your life can reach a happy ending. . . . In my books, people didn't die, and they weren't punished for being gay. And I would hope that mine was an early voice that was experimental in several good ways. In the friendship between gay men and lesbians; in the hope that people could connect, and find joy with each other, and give joy to each other, and not be punished for it. In the recognition you could live an honorable, productive life, and be a gay man or lesbian.

While hardly revolutionary today, such sentiments found precious little exposure half a century ago. Paradoxically, it took a young woman suffocating her lesbian identity in a conventional marriage to illuminate those beliefs for the lesbians who read her novels, providing them an opportunity to recognize the fresh air dispersing the requisite gloom many believed endemic to lesbianism in a hostile society. Bannon's half-dozen little novels afforded a paradigmatic switch for a generation of lesbians, replacing self-hatred with self-acceptance.

Notes

1. "Ann Bannon" and "Joe" are pseudonyms. While she disclosed to me her birth name and the names of her ex-husband and children, before I submitted my manuscript she explained that she would "much prefer not to have my actual name and those of my family members in print. For one thing, I have no right to reveal the identities of my kids and their father to a reading public which has no legitimate interest in them. For another, I've been stalked a few times by overeager and even unbalanced fans." Maybe a tougher histojournalist would disregard her preferences. Unfortunately, I can't bring myself to do it, so I accede to her wishes.

2. Ann didn't originally intend to create a series: As she explained in a 1991 interview printed in *Happy Endings*, "I did write a second book that nobody wanted. . . . So I set it aside, and I thought, I'm going to go back and follow Laura to New York; I didn't *finish* that story! So I started writing about Laura going to New York to try and get her life together, and somewhere in the first fourth of the book, Beebo walked into the story, and walked up to Laura, and that book just took off! There was a tremendous amount of energy there; I was hooked."

17

KATE MILLETT

What if we were free to be sexual beings? Even bisexuals, rather than just join the hetero or the homo team. What if you could just be sexual? This is a terrifying possibility. Freedom is really scary stuff.

—Kate Millett, 1995

"This can't be happening," I thought. After hours of frantic searching to find The Farm, Kate Millett's women's art colony in Poughkeepsie, New York, a resident tells me she is not here. "She went into the City today, and I don't know what time she'll be back. Shall I have her call you when she gets in?" Sure, why not; have her call me at my inlaws' home (conveniently located in Hopewell Junction, on the outskirts of Poughkeepsie). But I am quite distressed. After her nice letter to me, did she forget our appointment? Blow me off? Change her mind? Did I unwittingly offend her? I ponder these questions until 9:00 that evening. Kate calls, and apologizes for forgetting our appointment. "Would you like to come over now?" she asks. This option is not feasible; I have another interview scheduled in New York City at noon, and I'm exhausted from all the travel of the past few days. Yet she persists: "What about tomorrow morning?" It'll have to be awfully early, say 7:00 A.M.? That sounds good to her. I agree to return to The Farm the next morning.

After half an hour's drive, I arrive just shy of our appointed meeting time. At this hour The Farm is beautiful, and wondrously silent. Too silent. Not a creature is stirring, and I don't want to waken any of the other artists in residence at this hour. So I wander about the grounds, anxiously waiting for any sign of human life. Finally, at 7:25, I spy a woman walking from one building to another. I explain my purpose, and ask if she can help me find Kate. She tells me Kate is waking up; would I like a cup of coffee? Gratefully I accept while waiting for Kate's arrival. She appears in the kitchen at 7:50, as I mentally refigure my new departure time. After Kate has a smoke and a few sips of coffee, my "Type A" anxiety level at fever pitch, we settle in for a disjointed, rambling, fascinating two hours of conversation.

Katherine Murray Millett was born on September 14, 1934, in St. Paul, Minnesota, flanked by elder sister Sally and younger sister Mallory (*nee* Mary). Kate's Irish Catholic heritage remained central in her life long after she renounced her faith as a teenager, the rituals and the mysticism of both identities coursing through her veins evermore. In 1948, her father, James Albert Millett, left his wife and daughters for another woman; to sustain Kate's family, her mother Helen Feely Millett, an English literature graduate from the University of Minnesota, became "one of the most successful women in insurance in the country." But Kate certainly wasn't unhappy to leave St. Paul; in her 1974 book *Flying*, she tells her mother, "All your life you have been run by that small-town narrow-ass provincial opinion and the Catholic Church. . . . Respectability is death, Mother."

Kate's attraction to women manifested itself early in her life, as she told me, "I was in love with Aunt Dorothy from the time I was conscious. I'd say that I was aware of that around age five. And then I had a grand affair, adventure in love, when I was in high school, that lasted from freshman to senior year." But her love for women did not require her to exclude men. Indeed, it is a great and peculiar irony that a woman whose behaviors ought to have classified her technically as bisexual was identified—and in some circles vilified—as a lesbian.

Academically, after graduating Phi Beta Kappa and magna cum laude from the University of Minnesota in 1956, she crossed the Atlantic to attend Oxford University; under its dreaming spires, she achieved an academic "first" in English literature in 1958, an honorific that identified her as a scholar of the highest order.

In 1961 she moved to Japan, where she exhibited her sculpture in Tokyo, and met fellow artist Fumio Yoshimura near the beginning of 1965; later that year, both moved to the United States and wed. While they loved one another, the marriage was also designed to keep U.S. Immigration from harassing or deporting Fumio.

Despite Millett's primary reputation as a writer, she practices several artistic disciplines, including sculpting, painting, and photography.[1] Kate displayed her multidisciplinary talents at the Great American Lesbian Art Show, held in Los Angeles in August 1979. Is it difficult for Millett to receive so much acclaim for her writing, yet comparatively so much less for her other work? Yes, but with a caveat: "If I'd gone on, you know, being professor of women's studies, producing the correct line on criticism and all that, I never would get a chance to sculpt. And if I had an academic job, I sure as hell couldn't write the books I do. So I guess it kind of worked out."

Ginny Berson told me that Millett also merited a small footnote in lesbian history: "I believe the first women's music festival was actually in Sacramento, and it was organized by Kate Millett in 1973. I don't know that she even remembers. When I mentioned it to her, she looked at me like, 'Oh, yeah, I kind of vaguely remember that.'" But Kate mentions it in passing in *The Loony-Bin Trip*; perhaps it receded in her memory in light of other events that fateful summer. Millett also taught literature and philosophy, among other subjects, during the '60s at Bryn Mawr and Barnard (whose powers-that-be fired her twice). Despite all this, Millett gained renown—and notoriety—with, of all things, her doctoral thesis.

Sexual Politics, a tome which challenged men's subjugation of women in (male) literature, was the kind of polemic the women's movement sought; upon its 1970 release, it became a best-seller. As Millett told *Time* that year, "I was really afraid to write this book so much. I used to go crazy with terror about it. . . . In eight months, I had 2-1/2 days off." As she wrote it, her work days sometimes lasted eighteen hours. "Success," however, brought its own problems. As Susan Brownmiller described Millett's summer of 1970 in *In Our Time*,

> Kate, the avant-garde sculptor and reluctant academic, was on a merry-go-round that was spinning out of control. Her dark hair no longer confined in a braid or the prim bun she'd worn to her Doubleday meetings, the author of *Sexual Politics* was vomiting before public appearances and gulping bourbon to quiet her nerves. [Kate objected to that characterization, telling me, "I never drink bourbon and I never throw up. But those were stressful times."] If the media needed one personality to stand for the movement, Kate Millett resolved to fulfill that obligation. If a group at a college somewhere needed a public figure to rally the troops, Kate Millett would get on a plane. By September she began to think she was going crazy.

While Millett's remark about her mental state would prove uncannily prescient, by the end of 1970 she dealt with more immediately pressing concerns.

Having joined New York NOW immediately upon hearing of its existence in the late '60s, Millett flung herself into action, serving as

NOW's education director and participating in nearly every picket line and demonstration NOW proposed. When journalists interviewed Kate regarding *Sexual Politics*, she acknowledged her participation in women's groups spanning the gamut from NOW to Radicalesbians. *Time* attempted to spotlight women's liberation vis-à-vis Millett's book, and graced its August 31 cover with a bold representation of Millett the Theorist (much to Kate's chagrin; she would have preferred a crowd of women, or failing that, NOW president Betty Friedan). Now irrevocably branded a "leader" (albeit unwitting) in a supposedly "leaderless" movement, Millett received harsh criticism for months from her activist sisters. Yet her newfound visibility and her belief in the cause made the movement Millett's Holy Grail all the more; anything she could do—from contributing funds to lecturing—she would.

Millett had not been particularly reticent about acknowledging her bisexuality as a professor at Columbia University, where she co-founded Columbia Women's Liberation. But when the patriarchal mainstream press heard about a panel at Columbia where Kate intended to represent the bisexual view on a panel with gays and straights, it attempted to use her sexuality to rebuke her into silence. As Millett recalled in *Flying*,

> Teresa Juarez's voice loud butches me from a floor mike center of the room, a bully for all the correct political reasons. Five hundred people looking at me. Are you a Lesbian? Everything pauses, faces look up in terrible silence. I hear them not breathe. That word in public, the word I waited half a lifetime to hear. Finally I am accused. "Say it! Say you are a Lesbian!" Yes I said. Yes. Because I know what she means. The line goes, inflexible as a fascist edict, that bisexuality is a cop-out. Yes I said yes I am a Lesbian. It was the last strength I had.

Soon afterward, a December 1970 *Time* editorial pronounced,

> Ironically, Kate Millett herself contributed to the growing skepticism about the movement by acknowledging at a recent meeting that she is bisexual. The disclosure is bound to discredit her as a spokeswoman for her cause, cast further doubt on her theories, and reinforce the views of those skeptics who routinely dismiss all liberationists as lesbians.

As she told David Galligan in a 1977 *Advocate* interview, "I thought, 'They are going to present this in such a way that it will harm the women's movement—but what choice do I have? Betray gay people?' No, I was not about to. So I finally had come to the confrontation. It was about time that women's liberation took a stand for gay people."

Briefly it seemed women's lib would banish Millett for the heresy of acknowledging her love for women; NOW leader Betty Friedan allegedly told Millett, "Kate, drop the issue of homosexuality and turn off your followers or you will destroy the movement." *In Our Time* reports Kate recounting, "It was as if I was standing on a huge platform and suddenly this wind tore off all my clothes and the multitudes were looking up at me and laughing." Ultimately, as Kate told Galligan, "The women's movement pulled itself together. We took eighteen hours and stayed up all night hammering out a press statement endorsing gay liberation. They turned it away from 'we're going to protect little Kate because somebody beat her up.'" At the press conference, Kate stated,

> Women's liberation and homosexual liberation are both struggling towards a common goal: a society free from defining and categorizing people by virtue of gender and/or sexual preference. "Lesbian" is a label used as a psychic weapon to keep women locked into their male-defined "feminine role." The essence of that role is that a woman is defined in terms of her relationship to men. A woman is called a lesbian when she functions autonomously. Women's autonomy is what women's liberation is all about.

Kate continued to Galligan, "We'd all done the correct political thing, but at the same time it was much harder to work out at the individual emotional level. It's very easy to give a correct political answer, but how to deal with families and jobs and ourselves is another thing altogether."

As a result of the publicity, Millett became one of the most visible lesbians in the United States, and she spoke out frequently. As John Francis Hunter reported in *Gay Insider USA*, on March 14, 1971, Kate proclaimed from a bully pulpit before as many as three thousand demonstrators at a state capitol rally for gay civil rights in Albany, New York,

> The [first] Christopher Street march in June [1970], that blew my mind. . . . That made me feel freer than any place I've been. Like, to be together, to be out in the streets, finally to be public, to feel—it seems so crazy—Gay Pride. All we've ever known was shame. We were feeling proud and we liked ourselves and we were free, and we were beginning to show them that we meant to stay that way. And they've got to know that now.

Kate wrote about her experiences, and sex, and coming to terms with celebrity,[2] and much, much more, in *Flying*, which she claimed in the 1990 reissue (and reiterated to me) her favorite among her works.

Flying's greatest strength lies in its unblinking, unvarnished, and unsparing honesty, yet much of it consists of things no reader particularly wants to know. Passages meander interminably, followed by terse, clipped sentences. Millett's feelings, from ennui to anxiety to terror to tenderness, jump off the page, while love seems elusive and illusory. For the most part, *Flying* was not well received; following its publication, Kate told me, "I went on writing my books, but they didn't sell."

Toward the end of the '70s, she seemed to turn her focus to espousing difficult causes, including her unsuccessful attempts to save the life of civil rights activist and accused murderer Michael Malik (aka Michael X) of Trinidad, and flying to Iran, where she was invited to speak and hoped in vain to witness women's liberation, but found instead the Ayatollah Khomeini's fiercely repressive regime. Then she was said to manifest symptoms of bipolar disorder (manic depression).

Of course, it wasn't that simple. As she chronicles in *The Loony-Bin Trip*, perhaps her best work, a large part of receiving a manic diagnosis is the subjective belief of others. After two involuntary hospitalizations at her family's hands in the summer of 1973 (her second release came as the result of a civil verdict), Millett ingested lithium, an anti-manic treatment, for several years. When she chose in 1980 to experiment with not taking her medication, she began exhibiting behaviors her companion, Sophie Keir (who was aware of Kate's experiment), interpreted as manic. Soon, Millett's husband, family, and friends implored her to return to lithium; when she declined, they attempted once again to commit her involuntarily. Barely eluding their clutches in New York, Kate flew to Ireland to back the work of Irish hunger strikers. Soon after her arrival, since she was advocating for the hunger strikers, the Irish justice and mental health bureaucracies detained Millett for about two weeks, while Irish friends worked feverishly to secure her release. (Kate told me of that episode, "I seem to have an unkillable little body. No matter how discouraged my heart and soul got." Good thing—in *The Sisterhood*, Marcia Cohen reported that Kate considered suicide several times.)

Millett wrote *The Loony-Bin Trip* in a style similar to *Flying*, but unlike the more self-indulgent, disjointed earlier work, this later, cautionary tale draws a reader in, watching and feeling in amusement, amazement, and horror while Kate bravely battles for acknowledgment of her sanity against her well-meaning relations and an indifferent, calcified mental health system. (Millett's other written works include *Sita*, a depressing, obsessive read of Millett's failed love affair with another woman; *The Basement*, a fictionalized account based on the true story of sixteen-year-old Sylvia Likens's vicious murder; *Going to Iran*, chronicling her ill-fated 1979 trip; and *A.D.*, a memoir of her beloved paternal aunt and mentor, Dorothy Millett Hill Lindeke, released in 1995.)

For years, Kate also envisioned what seemed an impossible dream: to create and sustain a women's art colony. She purchased property in Poughkeepsie, and thereafter she split her time between earning a living in New York City and restoring the property. With the help of several women, she realized her vision. The Farm, a beautiful, peaceful, and functional place, has served as an oasis for many women.

Throughout her life, Millett has participated in many and sundry love affairs; when I asked if she currently had a "significant other," she exclaimed, "Gee. Lots and lots! Including everyone I was ever close to! I really maintain relationships." But those relationships often transmogrify, as people switch from acquaintances to lovers to friends (in her books she writes of so many primary relationships it becomes absolutely vertiginous). Perhaps Kate developed her longest, and seemingly healthiest, relationship with her husband, an artist and sculptor. An open relationship, Kate described it as the best within their circle of friends. Although separated for several years, they had remained comrades and colleagues; it therefore shocked Kate when Fumio asked her for a divorce, which a court granted in 1985. Given her often agonizing writing about the loss of love, I asked if she thought love had been more difficult for her than for most people, or whether she simply wrote about it with more honesty. She laughed, and admitted she didn't know. Yet in *Flying* she wrote, "I turned out to be not a Millett, but Mother—the one who gets hurt."

She knows *Sexual Politics* is her legacy; for what would she like to be remembered? "Hmm. For The Farm. For the archives we're making there. For my sculpture. For my books. . . . I'd *love* to be remembered as an American writer. [Laughs]" I believe she'll be remembered for uniting women's liberation and gay liberation when she refused to disavow either identity, at great personal cost.

As I drove away from The Farm, I feared I would arrive late for my noon appointment (indeed I did). Then it dawned on me. Having forgotten our appointment, Millett could have cancelled our appointment completely. Instead, she accommodated a wandering minstrel, come to explore her psyche. Given her experiences at the hands of journalists, it was a magnanimous gesture. She also kindly inscribed in the copy of *A.D.* she thoughtfully asked her publisher to mail me, "For Paul with gratitude for *hearing* me." It was the least I could do—and the least she deserved.

Notes

1. My then-adopted hometown of Phoenix sampled Millett's artistic vision: In a 1996 exhibition on the American flag, a re-creation of Kate's 1970 assemblage, "The American Dream Goes to Pot" (featuring the Stars and Stripes, a toilet bowl, and a cage), earned her the ire of many veterans, who protested its inclusion in the exhibition. As a result of the controversy, the exhibition became the best-attended event to that time in Phoenix Art Museum history.

2. Kate became a lesbian "celebrity" at an especially unfortunate time, when such a designation became an epithet that smacked of "star-tripping" in the then politically-correcter-than-thou lesbian movement; some lesbians considered Kate's signing her own book an elitist gesture!

18

MARTIN DUBERMAN

I'm a social historian, and change is something that is an ongoing struggle. You don't get it overnight. What you look for is some improvement. Well, you know, impatient adolescents want it overnight, and that's always been the trouble with the American left, because it's been full of adolescents. Because Americans are adolescents—they don't understand that the revolution isn't going to happen tomorrow, that you can only see a little piece of it in your own lifetime, and the torch has to be passed and carried, and all you can do is what you can do at this moment, at this place, and you have the obligation to do it. But most people don't have the patience. I mean, Americans are into instant gratification.

—Martin Duberman, 1995

By the time I arrived for my interview with Martin Duberman, I had been traveling alone on the East Coast for several days, had already interviewed **Charlotte Bunch** that morning, and had managed to negotiate the unfamiliar streets of Manhattan to find the West Side brownstone Duberman shares with his lover, Eli Zal. Yet I encountered one more test: Marty's building had no elevator. I would have to drag my tired body and asthmatic lungs up four flights of stairs. As I started the trek upward, I heard a friendly voice calling down the stairwell, encouraging me: "C'mon, you can make it. Just one more floor. OK, you're almost there!" Finally I reached the last turn, and viewed a beaming Duberman. While it remains a mystery to me how (and why) anyone would choose such a challenge every day, at the end I was gratified to have made the trip. We developed an instant rapport, and Marty was—and has been since—kindness itself to me.

Martin Bauml Duberman ("I no longer use the Bauml, though I used it on two books") was born August 6, 1930, in New York City, four years after his only sibling Lucile. As he wrote in his 1991 book *Cures: A Gay Man's Odyssey*, "Despite the odds, and although our relationship would always have tumultuous interludes, she and I became close friends." Indeed, when we visited, Lucile was in the hospital, and Marty's devotion and concern for her health touched me. In his 1996 book describing his experience of the '70s, *Midlife Queer*, he spoke of his relationship with his mother Josephine: "Growing up, I never had reason to doubt her love for me; she had been my rock, the omnipotent guardian angel who could magically make everything come right." Almost two decades after her passing in 1977, Duberman chronicled, "Her death had a deep and lingering effect on me, not the least, I suspect, because our entangled relationship had never gotten worked through; the emotional bond remained powerful but subterranean, felt but avoided."

While he remained more distant from his father Joseph (the classic configuration destined to make a boy gay, or so it was widely and erroneously theorized in the '50s and '60s), Marty nevertheless grew up as a much-doted-upon Jewish prince. He excelled in academics and athletics, a strategy which caused fellow students both in public school and at the Horace Mann School for Boys to like him. During his teens he toured in theatrical summer stock, and he also suffered a bout of polio. At that time Duberman chose not to disclose his sexual feelings. As he told George Whitmore in a *Gay Sunshine* interview, "I was very busy denying what I sensed inside: That I wasn't really part of the 'in' crowd, that I *was* different—and I hated being different." Some adolescent fun and games with other boys at summer camp aside ("a ritual we called 'fussing'"), as he summarized in *Cures*,

> Except for a single clouded experience in New York City—where I met someone in Grand Central Station, but then, in the hotel where we went, felt too uneasy to go through with it—that was about the sum of my sex life until age twenty-one. Two blow jobs, two panic attacks.

In the classroom, Duberman continued to shine: He matriculated at Yale in 1948, and he graduated Phi Beta Kappa in 1952. Playing by the book, "good boy" Martin followed his undergraduate degree by continuing his studies at Harvard, earning a masters and a Ph.D. in history in 1953 and 1957, respectively. Again, in *Cures*, Duberman explained,

> It was clear where I was going to find applause and the self-esteem that purportedly follows in train. I had all the important traits for a successful life in scholarship: a huge capacity for isolation (to endure all those mandated hours alone in the archives), a deeply compulsive and perfectionist nature (to persevere in tracking down every last fact), and a well-developed sense of fairness (to prevent me from reducing complex evidence to cartoon heroes and villains).

He also began tiptoeing into the community, visiting gay bars and even taking a lover for five years. However, his personal liberation remained a distant goal. During the latter half of the relationship, Duberman went into therapy (de rigueur for affluent gay men in the '50s); his counselor encouraged Marty to terminate his "unhealthy" union with his lover. As Duberman left Harvard to teach at Yale in the fall of 1957, the relationship shriveled and died. Duberman spent most of the remainder of the '50s and '60s in individual and group therapy, painstakingly detailed in *Cures*.

In the meantime, he entered into and disengaged from relationships with other men, even as he fought acknowledging his true sexual nature: During the '50s and '60s many psychologists considered it abhorrent and self-sabotaging for an externally successful person to accept and integrate his homosexuality into his life. As Duberman confessed to Whitmore, "At one point in the mid-sixties I didn't have sex for fifteen months. And I see myself as a very sexual person. You can imagine the will power that took—and the depth of self-loathing." While busily practicing sexual self-sacrifice, Duberman focused on work and career.

After the success of his first book, a biography of Charles Francis Adams, Martin was awarded the coveted Bancroft Prize in 1962, and Princeton University offered him a better (and better-paying) position, which he readily accepted. There he spent nearly a decade as writer/scholar/liberal gadfly, tweaking the conscience of the academic *cognoscenti*, and even abandoning grading systems for his students. He also began dabbling in playwriting: His first play, *In White America*, portraying the Negro experience in the United States, received critical acclaim and ran over five hundred performances off-Broadway in 1963. In retrospect, the play's success to some degree exemplified beginner's luck; his later works, many featuring gay male characters, garnered decidedly mixed reviews and considerably less attention.

While Duberman had spent nearly two decades edging out of the closet, the events at the Stonewall Inn during the summer of 1969 and their aftermath considerably hastened the process. For people like Duberman, the post-Stonewall world resembled nothing they had previously known. Despite the unintentional teasing his plays like *Payments* provided its audience, Duberman did not publicly reveal his homosexuality until 1972, in one sentence of *Black Mountain: An Exploration in Community*.

In *Black Mountain*, Duberman yet again experimented with historical presentation, telling Robert Buttry in a February 1975 *Advocate* article,

> The whole point of this book is that the historian was to show himself, instead of hiding behind the mask of objectivity; he was to show the process by which he interacted with the evidence and influenced the evidence. You have to show your bias so people can understand your point of view and make their own judgments accordingly.

Discussing the dismissal of Black Mountain's gay theater director in 1945, Duberman found himself "choked with anger," writing, "It's hard to think well of a place that could cooperate as fully as Black Mountain did in an individual's self-destruction—indeed to have assumed it as foreclosed. But perhaps I exaggerate—a function of my own indignation as a homosexual, a potential victim." Some reviewers harshly criticized this new way of declaiming history, but the self-revelation ultimately freed Duberman. Like Merle Miller, Howard Brown, **Kate Millett**, and **Dave Kopay**, Duberman's coming out in the early '70s as a minor celebrity made him a de facto leader and hero to many in a movement desirous of respectable types to correct the public perception of gay inferiority. As Tom Stoddard commented in a 1996 *Advocate* review of *Midlife Queer*, Duberman "had much to lose by putting on the mantle of a 'gay activist' at a time when the word *gay* (at least in its modern sense) still connoted 'freak.' He came out, he stayed out, and he spoke out."

After publicly revealing his homosexuality, Duberman brought his talents to NGTF from 1973 to 1977, and to the Gay Academic Union ("GAU") from 1973 to 1975, serving on both boards. Neither organization proved wholly satisfying to Marty, as feminism, racism, classism, and "integrationism" clashed with gay liberation, a recurring problem in many gay groups in the '70s and '80s. Indeed, Duberman admitted in a 1978 *Advocate* article that upon founding NGTF in 1973, he worried the organization "might be a superstructure without a constituency. It seemed like it might be viewed as a group of self-anointed leaders. That caused a lot of hard feelings at first."

Since then, Duberman has turned his primary efforts to researching/teaching and writing about lesbian and gay history. After leaving

Princeton in 1973, he went to Lehman College, City University of New York (CUNY). There he struggled for five years to develop the Center for Lesbian and Gay Studies (CLAGS), becoming its first executive director in April 1991. CLAGS held Duberman's primary focus until he stepped down as director of the organization in mid-1996. After coming out, much of his work emphasized gay history (including his own), with books like *About Time*, *Hidden from History* (as coeditor), and *Stonewall*, as well as the autobiographical *Cures* and *Midlife Queer*. Duberman also edited two Chelsea House series: biographies of famous lesbians and gay men, and issues of gay and lesbian life. While Chelsea House originally planned to publish fifty-five biographies, at this writing less than a quarter of them have reached the public. In 1995, Marty told me of his peculiar struggle with the series: Originally designed for teens, "The books are such high quality that there are lots of marketing problems. They're too good."

During our two-hour interview, after discussing his movement colleagues of two decades we spoke mostly in the present tense. I wondered why he felt guilty for being a privileged, middle-class white male, asking, "Being gay and Jewish isn't enough oppression for you?" Marty laughed, and replied,

> Listen, believe it or not, I'm back in therapy dealing with exactly these issues. . . . What I'm beginning belatedly to understand is as long as you try to use your privilege in constructive ways rather than simply for your own further advancement, then that's the best you can do, that it's not my fault that I was born privileged.

We discussed changes in the African-American community in the United States since Duberman wrote *In White America*:

> The way I view it, there has been undeniable, significant progress, but it's for a limited segment of the African-American population. I think a strong argument can be made that for the majority of African-Americans the daily conditions of life are today worse than they were before the onset of the civil rights movement.

He drew a parallel to the gay movement: "When I go around the country to tour, I'm constantly startled. It's like reentering a time warp often, in which gays and lesbians are living in the kind of secrecy and fear that we were in the '50s." We discussed the historic struggle of national gay service agencies:

> All of our organizations are understaffed and underfunded. . . . It's very hard to raise money for anything that relates to gay and lesbian, unless it is AIDS. . . . It's still essentially just a handful of wealthy

> gay men and lesbians who are giving the donations to a wide variety of groups. . . . And the dominant attitude still is, "I'm all right, Jack." I don't want my lifestyle bothered, I don't want my cover blown, I will give my money instead to the Cancer Society, or the Metropolitan Museum of Art, because that's where I want to be acknowledged . . . .

And because he has spoken and written about it so candidly, we discussed sex and monogamy. Personally, despite suffering a heart attack in 1979, Marty entered a happy domestic relationship in 1987 that continues at this writing. I wondered whether, ensconced in a long-term relationship, he still agreed with a 1975 *Advocate* quote attributed to him:

> We keep thinking that as long as we have a lover and maintain a reasonably monogamous sex life, we are showing the straight world that we are healthy, when all we're really doing is adopting their standards of what health is. In other words, we have to start setting our own standards as to what is healthy for us as individuals.

While he acknowledged (and values) his own monogamous relationship, he also realized,

> to this day, I think we tend to privilege coupledom. And we tend to think that these are the healthiest people in our community, the ones who have successfully navigated through a relationship, and are settled down. And I think those judgments are a reflection of standard heterosexist norms in our culture. That doesn't mean they're without validity, but there are plenty of people, I'm sure, who are perfectly healthy, whatever that means, whose preferred lifestyle is being single, or celibate, or adventuresome, or monog- — There are different strokes for different folks.

The comments I heard regarding Duberman demonstrated the chasm between the "academics" who knew the person, and the gay activists who knew only his work product. The latter criticized him mercilessly, perhaps in light of Duberman's portrayals of them in *Stonewall*, still very fresh in their memories. (Although, to Marty's credit, he disclaimed the film version to such an extent that he picketed it when it arrived in the United States from Britain.) **Randy Wicker**, photographed with Duberman during that picket, called him "a slipshod historian, and his book was filled with inaccuracies. A very moving, well-written, good book, but an historical novel, not a real report on what happened at Stonewall." **Jack Nichols** went even further, describing Duberman in various magazine articles as a "nit-picking, guilty, self-flagellating, fork-tongued dimwit" performing "slipshod scholarship," and writing me, "We'd all be much wiser and better off—if Mr. Duberman had stuck to play writing instead of history writing." In *We Must Love One Another or Die*, Larry Kramer told Larry Mass, "Marty's review of *Faggots* was one of the most unkind, ungenerous, hateful reviews that any writer has ever received, that any gay person has ever given to another gay person. And I didn't even know the man then." (In a 1998 letter to me responding to these criticisms, Duberman stated of "the tainted, self-serving Messrs. Wicker, Nichols and Kramer" that "in Wicker and Nichols' cases, the real source of their animus is my treatment of them in the book; though I describe their very real contributions to the movement, I did not portray them in the grandiose terms in which they view themselves. . . . As for Larry Kramer, you need to know the complex background of our relationship before you can responsibly contextualize and understand the particular comments he made about my review of *Faggots*.")

The mixed comments would not change in 2000: In the spring 2000 *Gay & Lesbian Review*, reviewing Duberman's 1999 collection of political essays, *Left Out*, Michael Schwartz wrote that

> where the failures of the left cause me to oscillate between sarcasm and despair, Duberman exudes generosity and optimism. The generosity reveals itself in its effort to be nonjudgmental about almost everyone; his optimism, in his ability to see the revolutionary potential in the world around him.

Yet in his 1999 book *Gay Lives*, Chris Robinson (a former Duberman student) flung several jibes at Duberman, unfairly viewing Duberman's psychiatric experiences before his coming out from a contemporary perspective, rather than in its proper societal and historical context.

In contrast, Charlotte Bunch recalled Marty as one of those "gay men in the '70s who I think were also very supportive [of feminism] and very strong allies." **Joan Nestle** told me, "My view of Marty is as a very dedicated man, to his vision of what he can contribute to the gay/lesbian future, which is CLAGS. . . . He's really a very generous and committed man, to leaving a legacy of gay and lesbian thinking." Of those who personally knew Duberman, only **Frank Kameny** (who served with Marty on NGTF's board) allied himself with the activists, criticizing *Stonewall* on the bases of technique and the characters Duberman chose through which to tell the story. But I feel **John D'Emilio** summarized Duberman best:

> Marty also is a person who I think has made a tremendous difference. I mean, there are very few people of his generation who came out as early as he did. And, I mean, in a certain sense, he was almost standing alone, for really a long time, as a certain intellectual, academic of the first rank, with a certain status and all, who had put not only the academic community but in the world of culture and art. And the work that he's done at CUNY, in terms of starting CLAGS, and keeping CLAGS going, has been very important.

I was especially pleased when Marty told me,

> I feel lucky to be where I currently am. It's probably the happiest, most productive time of my life. And at various early points—not just in the '50s or '60s, but as recently as the early '80s—it was touch and go for me. . . . [The '90s] has been the most stable decade of my life. I'm very grateful for it.

Given his prodigious output over the course of his life, I was glad Duberman managed to incorporate a measure of personal happiness and satisfaction as well. Given his willingness to tell us who we have been, and his honesty in telling us who he is, it seems a hard-fought but well-deserved reward.

19

RITA MAE BROWN

> **[I]f my back is up against the wall, I will pick the movement before any individual. Including myself, which really shocks me. Because I am not, by nature, a martyr. But we've worked too hard to let people tear it apart. . . . And that movement just has to come first.**
>
> —Rita Mae Brown, 1995

Over the course of a two-year journey in which one interviews more than two score people, one is bound to experience disappointment when meeting some of them in person. However, if there was anyone for whom the anticipation paled in relation to the actual experience, it was Rita Mae Brown. A personal phone call from this gifted writer and lesbian icon two weeks before my 1995 East Coast marathon trip literally snatched the breath from my lungs on a hot Monday morning, and the encounters only intensified from there. At her bucolic, nearly 500-acre spread in rural Charlottesville, Virginia (where fictional writer John-Boy Walton first put pen to paper), I ate a cheeseburger accompanied by more than a dozen assorted (yet delightful) cats and dogs, Rita Mae, and her lover since 1993, golf pro Betsy Sinsel. (Rita Mae insists that one cannot write without a cat; "preferably two.") Between bites, I switched my trusty tape recorder to "on," and recorded an hour and a half of shimmering vibrancy, scathing wit, and undeniable brilliance.

Before she managed to make the entire world sit up and take notice of her, she began life as Sue Kristin Young, the only daughter of Juliann Young and James Gordon Venable, born on the Hanover Shoe

Farm in Hanover, Pennsylvania on November 28, 1944. Rita Mae was adopted by Ralph Clifford ("Butch") and Julia Ellen Buckingham ("Juts") Brown, a butcher and his wife. Despite a family "mixed up worse than a dog's breakfast," including half-brothers and sisters she has never met, her extraordinary parents guided but did not spoil her. As she wrote in her 1997 memoir, *Rita Will*,

> Mother was wound tighter than a piano wire; Dad was relaxed. Mother possessed a rapier wit; Dad, good humor. Mother had to be the center of attention; Dad was content to bask in her glow. Mother owned a ferocious temper; Dad barely raised his voice. Mother was highly and combatively intelligent; Dad had only average intelligence but profound insight into people's hearts. Mother could be cruel; Dad didn't have a mean bone in his body. Mother planned ahead; Dad lived in the moment. Mother was fanatical about time; Dad was habitually late. Mother devoutly believed in the Lutheran Church and its dogma; Dad believed God was in the trees, in the sunrise, inside each of us. And most important for me, Mother loved the idea of a daughter, while Dad loved me.

Despite her mother's insistence that she attend cotillion to instill proper southern social graces, Rita Mae was raised in a working-class rather than a middle-class family; when applying for college scholarships in the mid-'60s, Rita Mae and her parents' combined income totaled approximately $2,000 (as she told me, "We had great bloodlines, but we were poor as paupers"). Next to the library (she began reading at age three; "The day I found *Bulfinch's Mythology* at age five in the Martin Memorial Library was the day my life truly began"), her other favorite locale was the tennis court (an irony that substantially influenced her later years). When she moved from Pennsylvania to Fort Lauderdale, Florida, at age ten, the weather there provided her the opportunity to become the number one player on her high school and college tennis teams. Around the same time, a young blond player on the same Holiday Park courts dreamed of playing as well as Rita Mae. The child's name was Christine Marie Evert, who grew up to be tennis's version of America's Sweetheart (or the Ice Princess, depending on your viewpoint).

Upon her graduation from Fort Lauderdale High in 1962, Rita Mae attended college at the University of Florida at Gainesville. After two years, her penchant for fighting bigotry and hypocrisy led her to a losing showdown with the school's administration; her scholarships were summarily (one might say ceremoniously) yanked from under her. By the summer of 1965, after attending Broward Junior College, she moved to New York City to continue her education and hone her writing skills. This also seems to be about the time when Rita Mae began having sexual encounters with other women. In *Rita Will*, Brown explained that until she arrived at the University of Florida, "I simply did not know what I was sexually. Nor was I eager to find out." However, in an earlier article, "Take a Lesbian to Lunch," Brown described love letters she had written to a female friend when she was sixteen, stating, "I did love the girl, and if that was lesbianism I was damn glad of it." Her mother's response to Rita Mae's revelation?

> I offended my mother heartily. My dad was dead by now. What offended her was not that I was homosexual; not remotely. She could have cared less! But it was that I wasn't gonna marry, and produce an heir! I mean, she said over and over again, "Marriage is a business. You just do it!" . . . And I was simply to play my part! And the fact that I didn't want to do that was what made her furious. Not the sex; she could have cared!

Brown enrolled at New York University, where in 1967 she and Gay Liberation Front (GLF) radical Martha Shelley were the driving forces behind NYU's chapter of the Student Homophile League, the nation's first gay student group (headed by Bob Martin aka Stephen Donaldson at Columbia University). However, few women participated in the group; as Brown described it to me,

> The focus for the men was almost exclusively sex, at that point. There was not yet a political analysis of oppression. There certainly was for people of color. And there was the beginnings of one for women. But there was none at all for lesbians, or gay men. And those meetings were really, to most women, very frivolous.

During the late '60s/early '70s, Rita Mae began earning her activist stripes, becoming involved for short periods of time in groups such as Redstockings (a consciousness-raising feminist group which Brown found unprepared to deal with lesbian issues), Radicalesbians, The Feminists, the Gay Liberation Front (where lesbian concerns were again drowned out by gay men's worldviews), and the National Organization for Women (where she served as New York NOW's newsletter editor). As Brown recounted in *After Stonewall*, NOW's participants really annoyed her:

> God forbid you should have a sense of humor about [your oppression], you know. You were supposed to just weep and wail, and just immediately become a victim. And the more victimized you were, of course, the more of a woman you were. And I'm like, "What are you talking about? The women I came from weren't victims. They kicked

> butt! So I'm gonna kick some too, little Yankee girls. Let me show you how this works!"

As Alice Echols wrote in *Daring to Be Bad*, "The charismatic Rita Mae Brown probably did more than any other individual to raise feminists' consciousness about lesbianism." In 1971, University Press published Brown's first major work, a collection of poems entitled *The Hand that Cradles the Rock.* Around that time, she also wrote articles for publications such as *Rat*, *Come Out!*, DOB's *The Ladder*, *Off Our Backs*, and *Women: A Journal of Liberation*, and later for *Amazon Quarterly*, *Lesbian Feminist*, *Lesbian Tide*, *Sisters*, and *So's Your Old Lady*. NYU awarded Brown a bachelor of arts in English and the classics in 1968, and in 1976 she received a Ph.D. in political science from the Institute for Policy Studies in Washington, D.C. Rita Mae dedicated *A Plain Brown Rapper*, her marvelously radical book of personal and political essays published by Diana Press in 1976, to the Furies collective, a group critical in her personal transformation.

The Furies, a group of twelve lesbian-feminists ranging in age from eighteen to thirty based in Washington, D.C., wanted to explore lesbian-feminism in an environment consisting exclusively of radical lesbian feminists. (See **Charlotte Bunch** and **Ginny Berson** chapters for more information.) The Furies flourished as an entity for less than a year (spring 1971 - spring 1972). Brown, Bunch, Berson, and photographer Joan Biren were widely perceived to have taken leadership roles in the collective. Berson illuminated Rita Mae's style for me:

> I was doing a lot of drugs when I met Rita. You know, a lot of smoking dope, and a lot of psychedelics. And she basically said to me, "If you want to work with me, you have to stop doing drugs. I don't want to work with anybody on drugs." And I did. Rita's a very single-minded woman. She was another of those very important to me. She really taught me a lot about writing. And she's always known what she's wanted, and she always seems to know how to get it.

Bunch described Brown to me as follows:

> She's very charismatic; she's very funny; she's very bright. And she's also very single-minded, in terms of—her truth is the only truth! . . . Working with her as a political organizer was very difficult, because I don't believe you can be a political organizer if you think you have the only truth.

The collective created its own publication, *The Furies*, that began in 1972 and ran through 1973. Despite the liberating ideas the group spawned, The Furies became cannibalistic, excising its own members when leadership, class, and power issues became stultifying. Brown was quoted in a 1995 *Washington Blade* article by Sue Fox as remembering most "a suffocating sense of togetherness." As she recalled in *Rita Will*, "That I was willing to try [communal living], introvert that I am, illustrates the passion of the time, the raw excitement of ideas exploding out of an emerging generation. . . . Here I was stuck with a bunch of women in sticky, hot Washington: Of Humid Bondage."

The most contentious issue became the struggle regarding raising the three children in the collective (one belonging to Coletta Reid, the others in the care of Biren and lover Sharon Deevey). Bunch recalled that "the issue of the children was probably one of the main mistakes the group made—a very painful mistake," and she told me, "I would say that Rita Mae was clearly the key person here, and it's probably the one decision that I feel guilty for allowing her to dominate us." (In *Rita Will*, Brown claimed concern for the children's physical safety, given the volatile political climate.) Not only did the collective choose to "outsource" the children, it ultimately banished Biren and Deevey from the group. Several months later, on March 6, 1972, the collective asked Rita Mae to take her considerable talents elsewhere. Brown was quoted in the *Blade* article as saying, "My rap or sin—since no one wanted to be emotionally direct so everything was couched in ideological script . . . was that I'd grown too big for my britches. In other words, I was a leader; I'd put myself before the group." For Rita Mae, this likely proved an example of a syndrome she described when she penned, "Time and again I would need to be the whipping girl to give other people the room to succeed." In contrast, Bunch told me that Brown

> definitely saw herself as the leader of the group. And she was in many ways. . . . [S]he was the most dominant leader. And her style of leadership was such that that created a lot of conflict. And at the same time, her drive was a lot of what got us going, and got us to write and get [The Furies's] newspaper out in the first place. And that was the positive part of it. But it was very intense. . . . When she realized the group was going to confront her about her leadership style, she simply turned it around and came to the meeting wearing one of her military jackets . . . ready for a fight. And that's when I realized—I had been actually prepared to fight to keep her in the group. But that's when I realized that it was a losing battle.

In *A Plain Brown Rapper*, Brown wrote, "The Furies taught me I have two talents, organizing and writing. Given the state of feminism I am in no danger of exercising the former." Yet to their credit, Alice Echols noted, "The Furies, and Rita Mae Brown in particular, deserve a great deal of credit for analyzing class dynamics within the women's liberation movement." Rita Mae told Fox in the *Blade* article,

> What I took from the Furies was a resolution never to be involved with people who are pure, never to live in a nunnery, and never to listen to bad music. . . . The good I took from the Furies was knowing that a small number of people, clearly focused on a political task, can move mountains. It was an incredible gift, that knowledge.

Through her experience with The Furies, Charlotte Bunch became the first (but not the last) of Rita Mae's high-profile lovers. (After The Furies collective disbanded, Rita Mae also wrote for Bunch's magazine, *Quest*; for her part, Charlotte arranged the grant that resulted in Brown's breakthrough literary triumph.) **Jean O'Leary** (who described Brown to me as "one of the most linear, most directed people that I've ever met") told me that she and Rita Mae lived together (although not in a relationship) for about six months in New York (and that, according to Jean, "It was a sexual thing"); when I asked her, Rita Mae's comment was, "I don't remember living with Jean. But if we did, I hope it was good." Shortly after The Furies disbanded, Brown became the lover of Massachusetts House of Representatives member Elaine Noble. In a WGBH-TV interview with both women, they described their first meeting at a party in New York: After Rita Mae greeted Noble, she decided that "the more I saw of Elaine the more I thought, this is one of the most delightful human beings I've ever met in my life. So I called her up and said, this is an indecent proposal, and we took off from there. . . . She said, do you want to come and live with me?" Rita Mae did—briefly. Yet, as Brown shared in *Rita Will*, "While my romance with Elaine was short-lived, I wasn't upset. I rarely was, because I neither understood romantic love nor wished to understand it. It looked like neurosis shared by two. So when the bloom was off the rose, I was fine."

Meanwhile, Brown had completed the Great American Novel (lesbian variety), and quickly attained celebrityhood. Whether she desired it or not, such status suited her magnificently. Tongue-in-cheek, Brown told me,

> You have to remember, for almost thirty of my fifty years, I've been the only lesbian in America. It's really only been the last five years that I can take a break! [Laughs] . . . I've been accused of having affairs with everybody under the sun, which I think is very funny. I would have never gotten any books written. On the other hand, I'd be insulted if I *weren't* accused of them! . . . [B]y virtue of being, quote, the only lesbian in America, I have paid a very high price that I didn't even know I was paying. 'Cause nobody wanted to be around me, for

> fear that light would shine on them. . . . So there were no women, during daylight hours. It was like being, you know, *Chronicle of a Vampire*. There were no women near me. At night, they came out of the woodwork!

Rita Mae elaborated in her memoir that by the late '80s, "I was also bored to the point of dementia with being America's leading lesbian. How ironic to be known for something I considered superficial in terms of my character and which, furthermore, was not entirely accurate." Later she elucidated, "I don't want to spend my life focusing on what is least interesting about me. And I'm not even a good lesbian. I'm much more bisexual." In a December 2000 *Advocate* interview, columnist Liz Smith recounted Brown telling her in the mid-'80s, "I'm just sick of being described as a lesbian writer. I'm a writer who happens to be a lesbian." Smith further observed that Brown "had real regrets, I think, that she outed herself and outed other people—whom she made very unhappy. And she feels, I think, that maybe she limited her own career and limited theirs."

Begun in 1971, *Rubyfruit Jungle* is Brown's largely autobiographical tale of nonconformist lesbian protagonist Molly Bolt, a lass even more buoyant than the unsinkable Molly Brown. Again she shared in *After Stonewall*, "And so, I sat down to write my first novel. And, you know, you're supposed to suffer? [Pause] I loved it! I didn't suffer for one minute! I thought, this is the most fun thing I have ever done in my life!" Even Rita Mae had no particular expectations of her first novel; turned down by every major hardcover publisher, the small feminist press Daughters, Inc., accepted it in 1973. Daughters, Inc., initially printed two thousand copies; without any advertising, readers purchased seventy thousand copies. Bantam Books picked it up in 1977, selling millions of copies worldwide. *Rubyfruit*'s success brought Rita Mae "a ton of hate mail, numerous threats on my life including two bomb threats, increased outrage from the conservative wing of the feminist movement and scorn from the radical dykes. Straight people were mad because I was gay. The dykes were mad because I wasn't gay enough." Historically, it has held up quite well, ranking seventh on Jesse Monteagudo's "Top 100 Gay Books of the 20th Century" at the end of 1999. While optioned several times to become a movie (like Patricia Nell Warren's *The Front Runner*, it would make a fine screenplay), Brown believes "unless I do it, it won't be done." Like Jacob selling his birthright for a mess of pottage, Rita Mae sold the film rights for a pittance before she knew better; at a price tag of over $200,000, she can't afford to buy them back.

As often happens in the writing world, she has continued to write better (and more profitably) for over two decades since penning *Ruby-*

fruit Jungle, including such works as *In Her Day*, *Six of One*, *Southern Discomfort*, *Sudden Death*, *Bingo*, *High Hearts*, *Venus Envy*, *Dolley*, and a series of Sneaky Pie Brown mysteries (Sneaky Pie is one of the many cats that own Rita Mae), but she has never received acclaim from reviewers to compare with *Rubyfruit Jungle*. In her marvelous, highly autobiographical book for writers, *Starting from Scratch*, I believe she speaks to herself as well as others when she says, "So if you are a lesbian, be prepared. They'll take you seriously as an artist when you're dead. Then you can join the ranks of the angels like [Gertrude] Stein, [Willa] Cather, and Colette." When I asked her whether she was taken seriously, Brown told me,

> No. Not as a literary figure. Some people do. People that have studied classics, they know their Latin and Greek; they'll take me seriously, because they really know what I'm doing. And they see the structure underneath the stories. . . . But to the average English professor, he's gonna take John Irving seriously, not me. . . . And I knew that going in. I will be disregarded as an entertaining writer.

Following her establishment as a popular novelist and lesbian icon,[1] Rita Mae entered a relationship with a tempestuous serve-and-volley Czech expatriate in 1979. Martina Navratilova became the other top woman tennis player of her generation (along with the aforementioned Evert). (Perhaps no one experienced more internal conflict than Rita Mae watching her lover play the girl who had idolized Brown as a player; she wrote, "Those close matches between Chris and Martina tortured me.") In our conversation, Brown spoke lovingly yet critically of Navratilova:

> When the career started to come to an end, and there was nothing left to lose, she came forward [as a lesbian spokesperson], because she loves the applause. She still does not have a political understanding of gay oppression, how gay oppression relates to every other form of oppression . . . But the fact that she has come forward now, when there's nothing left to lose, still doesn't mean it isn't genuine. And still doesn't mean that some twelve-year-old girl sitting in Omaha, Nebraska, won't see her first, and it'll be that child's first step toward liberation. So she's doin' her damned job. That's how I look at it.

They terminated the relationship in 1981 (Brown revealed in a November 1982 *People* profile that Navratilova "was probably my first real love," yet told Lori Medigovich in a 1994 *Lesbian News* interview that "Martina never was the love of my life"),[2] but Brown would later play an instrumental role in a future Navratilova divorce.

Brown moved to California in 1981 to work with Norman Lear on a TV special, *I Love Liberty*, for which she received an Emmy nomination. (In 1985, she was again nominated, this time for *The Long Hot Summer*.) In 1982, she returned to Charlottesville and purchased a "farm" (she now owns approximately 500 acres of gorgeous land, complete with stables and a field for polo, a sport at which she is an accomplished competitor). She was also the perfect choice, given her background in the arts and as an athlete, to emcee the first two Gay Games, both held in San Francisco, in 1982 and 1986. (But the Federation of Gay Games has never since expressed interest in her participation, which has hurt her feelings.) Given her history as an activist and a noted public figure, she was also the perfect narrator for the 1986 film *Before Stonewall*, documenting gay history in the United States from 1900 to 1970.

In 1991, when Navratilova broke up with Judy Nelson, her lover of seven years, Rita Mae attempted to mediate for the couple, telling me,

> I worked for over a year to keep those two out of court. I've never worked so hard on anything so unrewarding in my life! [Laughs] . . . And unfortunately, I was in the position [where] there was no way I could win with either one. I knew I would jeopardize my relationship with both of them. And I did. So I've lost them.

After the breakup, Rita Mae and Judy paired briefly in 1992-93. In a 1995 *Advocate* article, Navratilova told Suzanne Westenhoefer, "Well, it just figured. I thought, 'they deserve each other.' [Laughs] Then I got a letter from Rita Mae saying, 'I don't know how you stayed with her for seven years. I lasted for six months.'" In 1994, Brown postmortemed her relationship with Nelson, explaining to Medigovich that the relationship "didn't happen for very long because I don't like sleeping with friends."

Rita Mae suffers no shortage of wit and wisdom, but two excerpts from *Rita Will* give considerable insight into her character:

> I never wanted to be a child even when I was one. I wanted to be grown, in full command of my body and mind, earning my keep. And I never wanted to be beholden to anyone. . . . I've learned I can't change anyone. I can't overcome homophobia. I can't overcome misunderstandings if the other people aren't willing to learn and reach out, too. I can only forgive, hope for the best and keep going. I decided a long time ago to emulate the best of Juts and Ralph. If there's good in life, I'm going to find it. If there isn't good, then I'll look for a party.

Rita Mae Brown remains a controversial and challenging presence in the lesbian and literary movements. In 1999's *Tales of the Lavender Menace*, Karla Jay wrote that in the '70s she "found in Rita an unsettling mirror of all that I could be and all that I feared it was." On later reflection, Jay contemplated that

> Rita was [the lesbian] Jay Gantry, someone who had totally reinvented herself once she landed on New York's shores. It was part of her charm, and also part of her failure, that she could always articulate the politics of the movement—demanding radical behavior and separatism when this ideology suited her ends and dropping these feminist goals when she wanted to sell novels and screenplays to a mainstream audience.

In a 1994 *Advocate* article, **Barbara Grier** said of Brown, "Lesbians feel that Rita Mae Brown belongs to them. But as an icon she slipped a little from grace and glory because her career seemed to go off in other directions." When I asked Rita Mae about that comment, she replied,

> First of all, I'm not here to be an icon for anybody. I have a true literary mission. And I will follow that mission until I'm dead. Along the way, I also have a responsibility as an American citizen. My struggle for our people is not about being gay. It's about being a full-fledged American citizen. That's why I've fought in the movement for racial equality; that's why I've fought against a war in Vietnam; that's why I'll fight whatever is before me. . . . I'm here to address the world in my lifetime. And I was prevented from that—and still am, to some extent—by the virtue of falling into a despised category. But I'm not gonna let it stop me.

You'd better believe she won't be stopped, and I would advise those desiring to cross her to stay out of her path. For sheer determination, few people can match the intensity and power of Rita Mae Brown.

Notes

1. Although not without repercussions, as *Odd Girls and Twilight Lovers* summarized of Brown's rise to prominence in the '70s: "When the mass media focused attention on one woman, the group often became concerned about 'star tripping' and support for her sometimes fell away; this happened to Rita Mae Brown, who had been a great hero in the lesbian-feminist community before her popular success, but became the target of strong criticism after."

2. Instead, according to Brown's memoir, that honorific seems to belong to actress and *Fried Green Tomatoes* writer Fannie Flagg.

20

MALCOLM BOYD/ MARK THOMPSON

I am Malcolm.
This is my baptismal name.
I am male and a Christian and someone growing old.
I am an American and white and a person who is gay.
Essentially, I am a person created in God's image.
I am also a sojourner, a pilgrim, a runner,
and one who wants to be free but still belong
to a community.

—Malcolm Boyd,
Edges, Boundaries, and Connections, 1992

The attempt to unify seemingly irreconcilable differences has been a constant motif in my life. And nowhere has this rift been more acutely felt than in my feelings as a practitioner of leather-sex-magic and as a Faerie-identified man. Not that my life—or any life, for that matter—can be so easily reduced to expedient labels. We all experience lives of many dimensions and are versed in the putting on and removing of appropriate masks. But being a faerie with "black leather wings" presents a unique challenge.

—Mark Thompson, *Leatherfolk*, 1991

I

The other couples profiled in this book came to prominence through some kind of joint project. Malcolm Boyd and Mark Thompson do not fit this pattern, yet they fascinate me as a marvelous meshing of two distinctly individual souls. Both have substantially contributed to the gay community, yet they have also synthesized to create a most harmonious relationship worthy of emulation.

II

Malcolm Boyd was born on June 8, 1923, in New York City, the only child of Melville and Beatrice Boyd. Malcolm grew up in the lap of luxury (his father was a pre-Depression financier), but he hungered for affection. Raised by governesses, he always felt the lonely outsider. At age ten, Malcolm's parents divorced, and he moved with his mother first to Colorado Springs and later to Denver. As he wrote for a series entitled *Contemporary Authors*, his childhood constituted "odd years because I was, in the classic sense of the word, a sissy. I knew nothing of sports. My friends comprised one or two adult women. Lonely and isolated, I could not identify with anyone of my own age."

But not for lack of trying. Soon after his parents' separation, while staying at a mountain resort in the Adirondacks, three teenage boys attempted to accost Malcolm, who fled in terror. As he recalled in his 1978 biography, *Take Off the Masks*,

> That night I cried myself to sleep. Why had the boys done that? Why had they scared me so? Why hadn't they just taken me camping with them, high in the mountains? I'd have done anything just to be with them. . . . Barely touching my body, they had raped my psyche, thrusting their presence into vitals of mine that both yearned for them and repelled their claims. Fearing them, I feared myself. Hoping for them, I feared myself even more.

Before the vacation ended, he engaged in mutual sex with a boy about his age, but this too was abruptly terminated. Again, Malcolm wrote, "Our lost playful innocence was a grim specter of the complexity of the adult world that awaited us. How did we know even then as two small boys that it was considered very, very wrong to show natural affection to one another?"

Boyd found his first avenue toward personal liberation in Colorado Springs, where "the junior high school newspaper became a salvific force in my life when I began to write for it." Despite some success interviewing several prominent artists, he remained lonely, despairing:

> [M]y life was utter hell. I felt an alien in a strange place. No one, I was sure, understood me at all. Any serious attempt to communicate with another human being seemed hopeless. I was "different." How could I cope with forever being The Outsider? I looked at easygoing, popular, handsome athletes and knew I was totally shut out of their world of acceptance, glamour, achievement (in my eyes), and fun. Girls either ignored me or found me a eunuchlike jester, someone to laugh with and confide in.

Even church, which he attended regularly, provided no solace; as a teenager, he realized "the prophetic Jesus whom they talked about all the time wouldn't be allowed three feet up the center aisle if he happened to pay a visit." He wrote in his 1986 biography *Half Laughing/Half Crying*, "Partially it was erroneous images of Jesus conveyed to me as a child in a plethora of Sunday school classes that led to my being a cynical and sometimes angry atheist in college."

From Denver, he headed to Tucson, graduating from the University of Arizona in 1944. Afterward, he moved to Hollywood, and soon he participated in the infancy of the now-ubiquitous presence known as television. He joined one of the nation's largest advertising agencies, Foote, Cone and Belding, where he wrote, produced, and at one point even hosted an interview show before he cast his lot with America's Sweetheart, Mary Pickford, and her husband Buddy Rogers. The three created a production company, and in many ways Boyd became Pickford's "adopted son." Boyd also became president of the Television Producers Association of Hollywood. Much of it was great fun: As he wrote in *Edges, Boundaries, and Connections*,

> I can hardly believe myself as I was then. Funny, self-important and glamorous people were all around me, we were making movies, and there was an innocence about it. We had no idea we were actually influencing the world in complex ways and making social history. We simply went to our jobs, laughed uproariously about life in the studios and the stars' intimate antics, made more money than other people, dined in the fanciest hotels and restaurants, gave little thought to the future, and put existential meaning on hold.

Despite the power and the enviable job, Malcolm soon realized the shallowness of it all, writing in *Take Off the Masks*,

> I never had truly good times. I drove myself too hard, simply wanting symbols of success to compensate in some measure for the growing vacuum of unhappiness and incompleteness that lay at the center of my life. I was in Babylon, attending all the parties, self-consciously enacting the role of a rising young golden boy—alone. My image of

> homosexuality remained distasteful beyond redemption, so I utterly repressed my sex.

In 1951, Malcolm exchanged closets—from Hollywood to a Berkeley seminary, where he studied to become an Episcopal priest.

On its face, it seemed a quixotic choice for Hollywood's golden boy, but Boyd sincerely desired to serve God. As he explained to me,

> I was in a room one night with some of the most powerful people in the world. And I realized that in twenty or forty years, I didn't want to be like that. . . . I wanted to open some windows in my life; let some air in; look out; see the views, perspective—what was life all about? And, to my surprise, that seemed to mean the Episcopal priesthood.

He would also write in his 1969 autobiography, *As I Live and Breathe*, "When I came into the church, I meant it. I was not playing games, establishing a successful career, running for bishop, looking for financial security, or shallowly seeking a new activism to replace an old. Active I had always been. I sought a commitment which would drive my life."

Following his graduation from seminary and his ordination in 1954, he continued additional religious studies until 1957, when he took his first parish in a run-down Indianapolis neighborhood. After two years, Boyd accepted a position as Episcopal chaplain at Colorado State University in Fort Collins. There he attempted a dynamic ministry that dared to reach outside the boundaries of the church's traditional four walls. Malcolm's success alienated his bishop, however, and Boyd was forced to resign. As he wrote in *As I Live and Breathe*, "At this moment I ceased to be an organization man. Henceforth I would place Christianity ahead of institutional loyalty; I would honor Jesus more than I would a bishop."

Malcolm's restlessness during the '60s accurately mirrored the times. During the first half of the decade he served as chaplain at Detroit's Wayne State University, *Life* magazine named him one of the "100 Most Important Young Men and Women in the United States" in 1962, and he combated racism by marching with Martin Luther King, Jr. and others in the Deep South. (Later in life, Boyd spent several hours in jail for anti-Vietnam War and AIDS protests.) Suddenly, in the middle of the decade, he became a national celebrity.

Are You Running with Me, Jesus?, a slim volume of earthy prayers/poems, was Boyd's seventh book.[1] Through his writing, Boyd learned "that real prayer or meditation is not so much talking to God as just sharing God's presence, generally in the most ordinary of situations." Neither author nor publisher harbored great expectations; after fighting to keep its title, Malcolm told me he "actually saw a memo, at the publishers. And it said, in a sense, 'This goddamn book isn't gonna sell more than four thousand copies, max! So let him call it whatever he wants!'" Not an immediate success, with the help of a *New York Times* review it began to find its audience about a year after its initial publication. Malcolm's "overnight" success forced him to face a series of new challenges. Fortunately, his civil rights work and his time in Hollywood left him better prepared than most to deal with celebrity. As he described that period in *Half Laughing/Half Crying*, "I cooperated happily with the developing media blitz, enjoying the excitement of recognition, and even believing this was a truly marvelous way to communicate. I was sincere. I believed. I played it straight."

Given a unique public forum, Boyd made the most of it, appearing by request at San Francisco's hungry i nightclub in the fall of 1966. In *As I Live and Breathe* he explained his reasoning:

> It is akin to why I went on the freedom ride in 1961. In each case I was invited to put my body where my words were. When I was asked to take part in the freedom ride, I sat up one night, trying to weigh all the factors which seemed to be involved and make a decision. I decided that if I didn't go I should shut up on the subject of racial justice. When I was asked to appear for a month at the hungry i, I felt that if I didn't accept I should have the decency to shut up forever concerning the church's involvement with the world. I decided to complement rhetoric with action.

He continues to write books (at least twenty-five at this writing, not including several plays and other works he has edited), but he found another way in the '70s to make national headlines.

Boyd had long ago developed a well-deserved reputation for talking to the universal Christian church bluntly, setting aside platitudes and demanding honest, loving answers to hard questions. (Who else would state in *Mademoiselle*—in the '60s no less—"many persons remain inside, as well as outside, the church *for the wrong reasons*. It is a wrong reason to remain outside because one has never faced the reality of the meaning of the church, as it is to remain inside a conveniently private club with economic, ethnic or racial qualifications for membership, along with a plaster Jesus"?) Yet he wrestled with his own conundrum for more than half a century; what repercussions would materialize if he openly acknowledged his homosexuality?[2] He believed he already knew: As he wrote in *Take Off the Masks*, "Hide. Hide inside a dark closet, and never step outside unless you wear a socially acceptable mask that obscures your truth and is therefore a lie." By the mid-

'70s some mainstream role models had developed, but precious few from within the recesses of the Christian church; most resembled Lazarus, firmly entrenched in their tomb-like closets.[3] During 1976, through a series of self-revelations (including his acknowledgment at a gay interfaith service in Chicago, an *Advocate* interview, an Integrity (Episcopal) conference, and a *Chicago Sun-Times* article), Malcolm Boyd became the highest-ranking openly gay Protestant clergy in mainstream Christendom.

Originally I planned to ask Malcolm if he regretted how much time it took him to come out; after concluding my initial research, I marveled he had ever found the courage to do so. He shared with me,

> I realize now that I had to get my self-esteem up to a certain level in order to come out. And I think what a lot of people have a hard time understanding is that someone that well known, who had achieved that much, who was a celebrity, didn't have self-esteem. A lot of people, even now, would shake their heads at that, and just not be able to understand it. . . . But this was all linked, of course, to the closetedness, and the social and religious view of homosexuality. . . . As a writer, and as a priest, it was essential to be honest, to come out, and to get on with my life. . . . I gave up a certain persona, and moved into another. And gave up, perhaps, a lot of money. And that's fine. . . . I did choose wholeness over love, at that point. I chose to be rawly naked in the name of love.

After years of hiding in the shadows, Boyd determined to bring sunshine into his relationships. In 1977, he began his first very public intimate relationship with John Due, eighteen years his junior. In Malcolm's 1986 book *Gay Priest*, he wrote of the termination of a relationship (which I believe was this one):

> A day came when imminent separation was a heartbreaking reality. I shall never forget the mutuality of such heartbreak. I heard my lover weep loudly, his cries tearing my soul and flesh. Both of us knew the utter sadness of our shattered life. I lay there listening to him cry, more fearful of the coming loneliness than anything else in the world, and loving him so much.

While they remain friends to this day, Malcolm told me they parted amicably after five years: "We were very different. And it was time to go our own ways."

After several years away from the pulpit, in 1980 Malcolm accepted the duties of writer/poet in residence at St. Augustine by-the-Sea Episcopal Church in Santa Monica, California, where he remained until his official retirement in 1996. Immediately he received (and accepted) an invitation to serve as poet/writer-in-residence at the Episcopal Cathedral Center of St. Paul in Los Angeles. Despite his continuing work within the organized church, we agreed that the Christian church has made relatively little progress in eradicating its hypocrisy regarding homosexuality since he's been out: "When you think of how many gay people are in the church universal, and in prominent roles—they've given us crumbs." He also served three consecutive terms in the mid-'80s as president of PEN Center/USA West, described in *The Advocate* as "the international association of poets, playwrights, essayists, editors, novelists, historians, critics, translators and journalists."

Malcolm freely admitted to me, "I've always wanted to be loved. And I think one of the nicest things about my life is that I have been loved extravagantly. And I have loved extravagantly." After an already rich and rewarding life, even Boyd might not have guessed what surprise lay in wait for him in 1984.

III

Mark Howard Thompson was born on August 19, 1952, in Monterey, California, the eldest of Howard and Patricia Thompson's children (followed by Kirk, Gail, and John). Until he left for San Francisco State University in 1973, he grew up on the Monterey Peninsula, one of the most beautiful places on earth, but his family dynamic did not reflect the idyllic physical surroundings. As Mark described it to me, "My family probably was the mother of all dysfunctional families. It was like literally growing up in a nightmare. There were always angry words in the air. My mother was particularly unhappy with her life." Of his father, he wrote in *Gay Soul*, "we were distant and apart, strangers in the same house. One of the predominate [*sic*] story lines of my adult life has been the recovery of his love—an epic search that meant forging my own self-acceptance." Mark elaborated in John Preston's *Hometowns*, "my father was a man's man. . . . Even his nickname was 'Butch.' And although I was born in the same place as my father and, so far as I know, his father too, I was never, for the slightest moment, ever destined to be called 'Butch.'" Thompson satisfied his desire for physical closeness with another male, his brother Kirk. The relationship provided Mark with his first sexual experience, and it saved both boys' emotional lives.

In his childhood and adolescence, like many other gay men, Mark retreated into theatrical productions and life at the movies (telling me, "I *really* wanted to be a filmmaker"). Mark also identified his sexuality around this time, writing in *Hometowns* that after visiting the grown-ups' locker room at a local pool his "curiosity about myself—and other men—came out of hiding. From that afternoon on, I knew that vicarious living would never satisfy this prickly appetite for knowing."

Such an appetite for questioning ran deep in Mark's blood—his maternal grandfather wrote for a small-town Nebraska newspaper. Mark was blessed by knowing early what he planned to make his life's work—journalism. As he told me, "I started in junior high, typing, making the student paper. And then I went on to high school, and I was the editor of the high school paper two years in a row. And then, from high school, I went to junior college there, at Monterey Peninsula College, for a couple of years." The junior high experience "hooked" him on his avocation: "The other kids might have thought me a nerd, but there was power to be had in the press: not only by learning how to mechanically manipulate it, but in deciding who and what got covered within its pages."

Despite Mark's difficult relationship with his father, and both men's discomfort with Mark's nonverbalized homosexuality, Butch ultimately did right by his eldest son when he sent the shy seventeen-year-old to apprentice with a local, highly respected gay couple who had made their lives in theatrical production. In contrast to Mark's surroundings (noting in a 1987 *Advocate* interview that Carmel was "an artsy-craftsy California town, and at that time the gay community consisted mainly of upper-class homosexuals in expensive sweaters who inwardly felt poor about themselves"), in *Hometowns* he lovingly penned that the Tantamount Theatre

> was where my true and lasting romance with self began. Ralph and Francois were the first great teachers I had in life. Indeed, they offered the best lessons any young gay man could wish to have. . . . Some evenings after the show they would take me on a tour of the theater and its adjoining studio. Fine prints, Oriental antiques, and shelves of books were carefully displayed. A loom, carving blades, paintbrushes, and other well-worn tools littered their private quarters. They were the creators of a special universe—especially of their own lives—and who they were, and what they said, was at odds with what I had previously observed about gay men. . . . [T]oday, long after words have failed, [my father and I] know this to be his lasting gift to me.

In 1975 Thompson graduated with a journalism degree from SFSU (where he helped lead the Gay Students Coalition), and he promptly hied to Europe. While there, at publisher David Goodstein's behest, he wrote several freelance articles for *The Advocate*, then unquestionably the nation's primary gay news magazine. Upon Thompson's return to the States, he began working in the company of fellow writer Randy

Shilts and others. Not that he received strong encouragement to write about the gay community; Thompson told me,

> Even my journalism professors said, "Whatever you do, don't take the job at *The Advocate*. It'll be the end of your career. You're too talented. You can go to work for *The* [San Francisco] *Chronicle*, or something else. Don't do this, Mark!" And I said, "No! This is my community." I specialized in community journalism. This is what I wanted to do. I wanted to write, you know, for my people. And I wanted to write about the issues that seemed most important to me.

Mark ultimately outlasted all of his well-known contemporaries, officially joining the *Advocate* staff as a part-time assistant art director in January 1976 and staying with the magazine for an unprecedented eighteen-and-one-half years, ultimately becoming senior editor in 1990 before his departure in June 1994.

While at *The Advocate*, in addition to his contributions in journalism, editing, layout, and photography, he also wrote incisive articles regarding the direction of the gay movement, most notably during the "Castro-clone" late '70s; while others busily noticed the surface glitter, Thompson looked within, writing articles about such issues as aging, androgyny, and spirituality. "At that time, the articles I was writing were basically saying, 'I'm sorry, but this can't be all there is to being gay, because the culture we're making for ourselves is sort of dysfunctional in many ways! Let's open the hood of the thing we're driving, as it were, and take another look at it!'" Or, as he told Vito Russo in a December 1987 *Advocate* interview, "I am encouraged by all the young people coming out, but what are they coming out to? The coming out process should be a beginning, not a goal. It is *not* the goal to have the condo in Munchkin City. We should be going to Oz."

Mark was one of the first (if not *the* first) to explore self-esteem issues in the gay mass media, realizing

> you can come out, and say that I'm gay, and I'm proud, and come out to your parents and all that. That still doesn't deal with the inner material. I think that the number one problem that we face as a community is internalized homophobia. Self-esteem injury is vast in us! . . . [W]e have to be doing this inner work. And we have to be pushing it, and advocating it, just as much as we are pushing and advocating notions of gay pride. Gay pride is from inside out.[4]

It was not the first time Mark Thompson found himself ahead of the curve insofar as gay male thinking had evolved, nor would it be the last. But not everyone delighted in Thompson's soul-searching journey: "From my professional peers, I was getting shit because I was writing about, quote, flaky New Age-y kind of things. . . . I was just doing what my inner voice was telling me I should do." That voice also led him into the Arizona desert where a new movement was beginning—the Radical Faerie Movement.

How does one describe the Faeries? Thompson described them in *Leatherfolk* as "gay men seeking spiritual alternatives to questions that had long echoed inside them." The Faerie Movement seemed tailor-made for spiritual seekers like Thompson, willing to do the "inner work" necessary to achieve personal wholeness and integrate all aspects of their being. Mark attended the first Faerie circle in September 1979, about which he wrote in *Gay Soul*, "under a hot Southwest sky, bodies and souls were bared in a brave attempt to shed a lifetime of hetero-imitative habits. The day was naked, in every way." Thompson participated with the Faerie Movement and its leaders (including Mitch Walker and Harry Hay) through the '80s and into the '90s. But when I attempted to speak with Mark about his experiences with the "Faerie Wars," for the most part the wounds remained too fresh for him to elaborate.

With the advent of the AIDS generation and the popularization of the men's movement, by the mid-'80s Thompson's efforts editing two books helped him find a much wider audience. 1987's *Gay Spirit: Myth and Meaning* and 1994's *Gay Soul* provided interviews, commentaries, and photographs with noted writers, teachers, and visionaries, including James Broughton, Don Kilhefner, Christopher Isherwood, Ram Dass, and Paul Monette, as well as Malcolm Boyd and Harry Hay. Mark also edited 1991's *Leatherfolk*, one of the first comprehensive books on the gay leather community, and 1994's *Long Road to Freedom*, an exceptional work which reflected on twenty-five years of *The Advocate*.

Shortly after that extraordinary book went to press, Thompson experienced a corporate callousness surrounding his departure from that journal in June 1994. As he bitterly recounted,

> Most people who've left *The Advocate* have either been fired or they'd slammed the door. I did not do that. I did it, I think, as graciously as possible. And it was four o'clock in the afternoon. And I had my last little effects from my desk in a cardboard box. And I waited. And I thought, "Well, certainly, they are going to, you know, maybe have a little ceremony, or a cake. Or just something." 'Cause not only, you know, nineteen years at *The Advocate*, but that's the longest run anyone's ever had in the gay press, period! My whole professional life. And you know what I'm going to tell you. Four o'clock in the afternoon. Not one person. So I finally picked up the cardboard box, went to my car, put it in the trunk, and drove away. . . . After two decades of blood, sweat, and tears, not even a handshake, or a gold watch at the door.

Even if *The Advocate* could not graciously acknowledge Thompson's contribution, his body of work would cause **Jack Nichols**, an early men's movement proponent who spans years of activism with years of journalism, to remark, "Mark Thompson is a gay spirit. He is honest and warm and empathetic and intuitive—one of my favorite, all-time favorite gay journalists."

IV

Malcolm and Mark met in February 1984 when they stayed in the same Los Angeles hotel. A mutual friend suggested that Mark drop in and say hello to Malcolm. As Mark remembered in *Gay Soul*,

> We were polite, yet we found each other engaging. What was meant to be a brief encounter stretched into a couple of hours. Though we never expected it, those two hours have become a relationship that has endured for the past ten years and, as far as we can see, to the end of our days.

Despite their instant rapport, Mark lived in the Bay Area, while Malcolm was ensconced in Los Angeles. Fortuitously, *The Advocate* relocated shortly thereafter to southern California, and the two men spent more time together. Later, Malcolm wrote in *Look Back in Joy*, at a "boring, anachronistic, sedate and uptight" Pasadena restaurant, he asked Mark to dance.

> I wore my white suit, you were in black, and we engaged in Astaire-Rogers cheek-to-cheek dancing. Did I hear a plate drop from a waiter's hand, a knife hit the floor, a spoon brush a cup? The self-consciously respectable room came to life. We did a deep dip, paid the check, and left. But then we couldn't find the car. A magical state of euphoria had apparently taken over our senses. We did the only sensible thing by going directly home and to bed. Ours was an explosive, passionate, but also tender coming together.

After a two-year courtship, Malcolm presented Mark with a ring, and he proposed coupledom to him on bended knee. The rest, of course, is history.

Like any other couple, they have overcome obstacles together. Perhaps the most challenging has been Mark's HIV-positive diagnosis. As Malcolm wrote in *Lambda Gray*,

> The big ship seemed to shudder after hitting an iceberg. Everything was changed in a moment. I felt chilled, wary. Were years dropping away like cards in a deck? . . . You had always wanted to grow old,

> you said. Become one of those wonderful old men who are wise and beautiful and caring, and whom people love.

Mark has lived with HIV for many years, telling me, "The more I walk in balance, the more I know that my walk is going to be longer. So I absolutely know I'm going to see the year 2000 and beyond." I believed him then, and his promise was fulfilled.

Their exemplary relationship still thrives at this writing. For those who believe like must attract like to attain happiness, it would appear a recipe for disaster: Three decades' difference in age (as Mark shared in a 1995 *Frontiers* article, "It's my observation that intergenerational bonds are in many ways the most enduring relationships we have in the gay community. Malcolm and I don't compete"); disparate religious systems (speaking about their approaches to "organized religion," Malcolm bluntly stated, "I often say that Mark's more Christian than I am. The point is, there was no problem fusing anything about spirituality. . . . Neither of us buys 'the package' under any circumstances. And so, we're very similar in the way we regard this. We see many paths to God; not one fucking goddamn path to God"); primary careers in the same field (Malcolm replied, "We help each other. . . . I always copy-edit Mark's stuff. And Mark helps me enormously. I need him to read what I've done, and then he kind of gets to the heart of it"); and sero-discordance (as Mark told me, "We had sex this morning, and it was safe. . . . From the day we met, I have insisted on [safe sex], absolutely"). But their relationship works, seemingly effortlessly to this outsider. As Mark wrote in *Gay Body*, a memoir published in 1997 and nominated for a Lambda Literary Award in 1998, "we share our lives as spiritual seekers, fellow writers, and soul mates who care passionately about the same things, not the least each other."

When I asked Malcolm what people didn't know about him that he wished they did, he replied,

> I feel totally misunderstood by a number of people. But it doesn't even matter to me anymore. It's the gay people who can't deal with the fact that I'm religious, or spiritual, and then it's the religious or spiritual people who can't deal with the fact that I'm gay. I am a human being; I have lived my life, in my opinion, very well, honestly. With deliberation. And fortunately, I'm not running for mayor; I don't have to be popular, or liked.

Mark's response was different yet similar:

> People try to peg you, or categorize you. So I'm either a flaky faerie, [or] a rabid gay activist, [or] some kind of pervert, you know, depending upon whatever anyone wants to choose. . . . The universe is a

> big place. And it's all about weaving, and blending, all of the elements of a life into one course. People just try to pick out one thing. And I'm not a card-carrying member of any group, any organization, any faction. But I just try to go where the spirit of my life [leads], and try to integrate and blend, because I think that is the ultimate truth.

Summing up their relationship, Mark told another interviewer, "A good relationship can help you maintain a healthy attitude about all aspects of life. You just can't go through—you shouldn't—you can't go through life alone. Malcolm and I are a family, and we're very committed, and we'll be together for as long as we are both kicking." As Malcolm shared with me, "We have a very relaxed life, but one open to intensity and experimenting and change. We're here for each other; we love each other deeply; we have our home; this is our sanctuary. Why invent dozens of problems that really aren't very important?" Malcolm and Mark have made the complex simple. They not only talk a good game, they live it.

Notes

1. The book's introduction demonstrates Boyd's unconventionality: "It has been asked by some persons why this book is not entitled *Am I Running with You, Jesus?* The query overlooks the fact that my prayer life, as the state of my spirituality, is neither very respectable nor quite correct. . . . [The book] more accurately reflects the grounding, motivation, and style of my prayer life and spirituality as I grapple with imperfections and ambiguities in myself and my society."

2. As early as *Are You Running with Me, Jesus?*, Boyd had evinced a noteworthy tolerance of homosexuals, writing a prayer for a gay bar, "This isn't very much like a church, Lord, but many members of the church are also here in this bar. Quite a few of the men here belong to the church as well as to this bar. If they knew how, a number of them would ask you to be with them in both places. Some of them wouldn't, but won't you be with them, too, Jesus?"

3. Malcolm described to me his personal experience with a literal closet: "As a child, someone locked me into a dark, dank closet, and said a white rat in there would eat me alive. And left me in there screaming, until my hands were bloody, beating against the door." Through repetition and trivialization the force of the closet metaphor has dimmed, but for Malcolm and countless others the images remain terrifyingly vivid.

4. Not content to settle for a fine journalistic career, Mark obtained a graduate degree in clinical psychology from Antioch University in September 1998.

21

JOAN NESTLE

When I joined in founding the Lesbian Herstory Archives, it was not because I wanted power or money or fame, but because all the experiences of my different identities led me there: my Jewish self that knew memory was a holy thing, never to be bartered or sold; my old femme self that knew the sacredness of a scorned courage; my new feminist self that wanted the delight of a women-only creation; my socialist self that believed all resources must be shared; my teacher self that had been taught by First World students the burden of colonization and the pain of exile; my psychological self that called on me to carry my mother and her loneliness into my own conflicts about security and freedom. And, like a hemp rope binding the parts together, ran my sexual self, taking on all these forms of being and rearranging them in stunning new ways. Out of this came the Lesbian Herstory Archives and this book.

—Joan Nestle, *A Restricted Country*, 1987

Joan Nestle refuses to apologize for her erotic passion. In contrast to the "P.C. Police," who insisted that only they could define the appropriate ways and styles by which lesbians might demonstrate their lust toward one another, Nestle rebelled against such an ahistorical view of lesbian sexuality. Her desire to speak her truth about lesbian culture, including the butch-femme aspects that in the '70s became taboo (the result of what **JoAnn Loulan** calls "the Androgynous Imperative"), led her to cofound New York's Lesbian Herstory Archives. Her seemingly heretical speaking and writing about "nonmainstream" lesbian sex and sexuality became a crucial component of the lesbian "sex wars" in the early '80s. If any one woman deserves credit for helping her lesbian sisters claim (or reclaim) their sexual stylings in the face of heterosexual and lesbian oppression alike, it most likely would be Joan Nestle. I met this warm, kind, fascinating woman at the cabin (with the most fantastic view!) she shared with her lover, Lee Hudson,[1] in New York's Catskill Mountains in the summer of 1995.

Joan Nestle (named for her father, Jonas) was born on May 12, 1940, in New York City. In *A Restricted Country*, she writes achingly of her mother Regina Mayer in several essays. Unlike the many middle-class voices profiled herein, Joan and her family (including her older brother Elliot, whom she described as "a sad man," but excluding her father, who died before Joan's birth) lived "on the edge." With no man to support her, and only an eighth-grade education, Regina Nestle made her way as a bookkeeper in New York's garment district. (Joan herself began working at age thirteen.) Mother and daughter forged a strong bond, if not always a secure or even a safe one: At times, Regina turned tricks to survive financially, and Joan witnessed the physical and emotional scars left when some of the men finished with her mother. From her heterosexual mother, Joan also learned how to claim her sexual desires, a concept not widely accepted among women in the '40s and '50s. Joan writes, "My mother was not a goddess, not a matriarchal figure who looms over my life big-bellied with womyn rituals. She was a working woman who liked to fuck, who believed she had the right to have a penis inside of her if she liked it, and who sought deeply for love but knew that it was much harder to find."

Joan identified her erotic attraction to women "very early"; as a pre-adolescent she engaged in sex with a peer she coyly referred to as "R." (but whom she identifies in her other writings), telling me, "We became sexual explorers together, from age ten 'till I graduated from high school, pretty much. . . . I was a ten-year-old child, exploring the tastes and smells of being between a woman's legs. I think it's really important; I don't think women talk about this enough." Ironically, as one of the most visible lesbian literary femmes, Joan first identified as a "butchy fem" who "looked strong and square in my outside clothes." Nestle spoke to me of experiences in her teens and early twenties:

> I remember, it was the day [President John] Kennedy was killed [November 22, 1963], and I was walking in the park. And a group of teenagers came by . . . they said, "What should we feed it?" . . . In the '50s, you grew up with this. Getting on a bus, coming home from the

> Village, and having some teenager say, "Oh, don't sit down next to *it*." . . . I was sick to the pit of my stomach over the fear of it.

But Joan learned to swallow her feelings long enough to graduate from Martin Van Buren High School in Queens in 1957, and to obtain English degrees from Queens College (B.A.) and from New York University (M.A.).

Still, Nestle's hunger to interact with women-loving women in the '50s drove her into the dangerous environment that constituted New York's lesbian hangouts, places where "respectable" women dared not venture, and where the chance of finding love and affection tangoed nervously with the dangers of arrest and brutality. In *Lesbians at Midlife*, Joan stated that "Over the years, I have explored butch-femme sex, androgynous sex, intergenerational sex (where I lusted after much older women), S/M sex, group sex, back room sex, sex for money and, in a ten year relationship, domestic sex which included much of the above." Her writing often describes experiences people of my generation cannot fathom, such as the cruel indignities lesbian bars perpetrated:

> Because we were labeled deviants, our bathroom habits had to be watched. Only one woman at a time was allowed into the toilet because we could not be trusted. . . . Guarding the entrance to the toilet was a short, square, handsome butch woman, the same every night, whose job it was to twist around her hand our allotted amount of toilet paper. . . . But buried deep in our endurance was our fury. That line was practice and theory seared into one. We wove our freedoms, our culture, around their obstacles of hatred, but we also paid our price. Every time I took the fistful of toilet paper, I swore eventual liberation. It would be, however, liberation with a memory.

Joan's vision encompassed more than lesbian liberation. In 1965 she flew to Selma, Alabama, to register black voters, and she was one of only three hundred chosen to march from there to Montgomery immediately after the height of the racial battles. Prior to that, she recalled in "This Huge Light of Yours,"

> I had ridden freedom buses into Philadelphia and Baltimore, had hidden from thrown rocks, had washed spit from my face and hair, had sat with CORE comrades at soda fountains while the no-trespassing laws were read to us, and had been dragged out of restaurants that black CORE members could not even enter. . . . I have carried Selma with me all these years as well, not to prove my Civil Rights credentials, for I know more than anyone how little I had really done in the face of lives that were committed every day, but because Selma is to me the wonder of history marked on a people's face and on their soul.

When Joan discovered the Daughters of Bilitis, a haven for many middle-class lesbians, she quickly identified its inability to meet her needs. As she said in *The Question of Equality*,

> It seemed to me that they really would be ashamed of a woman like myself. They certainly would have been ashamed of the women I was with in the bars. I mean, no prostitute would have walked into DOB and felt comfortable. . . . Being a bar woman, I was exactly what DOB had come into being to provide an alternative to. DOB says in its charter, in its code, that we want "to educate the sexual variant," to provide an alternative to the bars. That's one of the sadnesses of how the movement developed. . . . There were whole generations of women, very strong, mostly working-class women, who could have added, and who never entered the movement via groups like DOB or the feminist organizations because of this sense of class judgment.

In March 1973 Joan cofounded Gay Academic Union (along with **Martin Duberman**, **John D'Emilio**, and others). Speaking of GAU, Nestle recalled in 1998's *A Fragile Union*, "Our goals were to challenge the homophobia and sexism that flourished on college campuses, to end the isolation of gay and lesbian students and teachers, to share our research and writing, and to inspire curriculum changes that would reflect the contributions of gays and lesbians to our culture." At GAU's first conference later that year, Nestle and other lesbian participants discussed the need for an archive devoting itself to the lesbian experience. In *Long Road to Freedom* she wrote, "The strongest reason for creating the Archives was to end the silence of patriarchal history about us—women who loved women. We wanted our story to be told by us, shared by us, and preserved by us." While Nestle took her leave from GAU around 1974 when its members split the group around left-wing and feminist issues ("I was part of the left caucus of GAU, but was overwhelmed by the gay male emphasis and some of the arrogance of the men"), she pressed forward with the idea of the Lesbian Herstory Archives. LHA, residing in the Manhattan apartment Nestle shared with her lover of twelve years, Deborah Edel, opened to the public in 1975. Nestle again recounts in *A Fragile Union*,

> One of the first cultural goals of the archives project was to salvage secrets, to stop the destruction of letters and photographs, to rescue the documents of our desire from family and cultural devaluation. . . . In the early years of the archives, Deborah Edel and I scoured small-town library and church book-sale tables, often finding a rare lesbian novel that had been selected for throwaway; in the mail, we would often get posters and other memorabilia that had been saved from trash heaps. So many times did this reversal of cultural fortune hap-

> pen that we publicly spoke about transforming what this society considered garbage into a people's history.

Martin Duberman credited this effort as a "major accomplishment."

In December 1991, LHA's members and friends moved over ten thousand books and a treasure trove of various lesbian miscellanea to a three-story limestone building in the Park Slope section of Brooklyn. As part of LHA's mission to make lesbian history accessible to all lesbians, its three-story limestone home was retrofitted with a wheelchair-accessible elevator and bathroom. As Nestle explained to Victoria Brownworth in 1994, "We wanted a space where women from all over could be in a place that is just about our history as lesbians, not a revisionist version, but the history of lesbians as they experienced it, wrote it, lived it." This desire not only shaped Nestle's writings but also it explained how she could get into so much trouble within the lesbian-feminist community.

Even as Joan's separatist politics caused discomfort within GAU as she became involved with GAA's Lesbian Liberation Committee (later Lesbian Feminist Liberation), Nestle grieved when butch-femme identification fell from grace in the politically charged lesbian feminist culture of the '70s. Because LLC/LFL's feminist politic moved and empowered Nestle, she stayed. Yet, as she recounted in "Stone Butch, Drag Butch, Baby Butch,"

> Pretty young women form a circle to form a group called the Lesbian Liberation Committee. Two old-time lesbians arrive, grey-haired, short DAs. They stay on the outskirts. . . . Two of the young women stand in front of me. 'Why do they have to look like men? I hope they don't come back.' When I returned upstairs, the grey-haired women were gone. They never returned. **Jean [O'Leary]** and **Ginny [Apuzzo]** told the world who we were and what we wanted. . . . Shame is the first betrayer.

Nestle expounded to me,

> I didn't say, at that moment, "You're making a big mistake. They're why we're here." 'Cause they were my community. But I learned. I listened. I said, "OK, Joan. If you're gonna be part of the lesbian-feminist world, you have to learn to pass. You have to say goodbye to that history." . . . Basically, it took me ten years to work out the quandary of how do I keep the wonder of lesbian-feminism, and bring back a historical community, and living community? How do I create a politic that isn't exclusive of a group of women, and of a

> past, and of a sexual present that, in fact, were the pioneers of this movement?

Nestle, who felt no shame expressing her erotic language, dared to talk and write about her life experiences. Her works pained some lesbian-feminists, who perceived such statements as a traitorous attempt to re-create "the bad old days." As she penned in *A Restricted Country*, "Butch-femme relationships, as I experienced them, were complex erotic statements, not phony heterosexual replicas. They were filled with a deeply Lesbian language of stance, dress, gesture, loving, courage, and autonomy." I spoke with Joan of her battles to explore and discuss openly her sexual activities and fantasies; given the then-prevailing attitudes, her courage amazes me:

> What came out of those early [discussions] is a lot of anger, when I became targeted as a sort of public criminal figure for raising the issues of butch-femme. But why I enlarged it to sexual is that there were a lot of issues about sex for the lesbian-feminist community, which culminated in the "sex wars" at Barnard College [in 1982]. . . . It started with discussion of butch-femme, but it was connected to S&M. It was the whole split about, as feminists, how do we talk about sex? And how do you talk about pleasure and desire and fantasy? You know, there are two schools. There's one who say—like Andrea Dworkin, Catharine MacKinnon, the whole group—that sex is a tool to abuse and maim women. . . . And then there was a group of us who said, yes, you know, but we would like to explore publicly—which was the problem—with images and words, a more complex lesbian desire, that could include fantasies of submission. That could include butch-femme energies. It was explosive.

In 1966, Joan had returned to Queens College "as a teacher of writing in SEEK (Search for Elevated and Enlightened Knowledge), an educational opportunity program born out of the social anger of young Black and Puerto Rican women and men who believed higher education had turned its back on them." (She held that position until the project was defunded in 1995.) In 1982, Nestle recalled in "My History with Censorship," she

> was visited by a member of Women Against Pornography who saw it as her duty to warn a group of students and professors about me. "Don't you know she is a lesbian? Don't you know she practices S&M? Don't you know she engages in unequal patriarchal power sex?" (Butch and femme is what is meant here, I think.) I was told this when I was called to the Women's Center on campus and asked by the group of women students gathered there whether the accusations were correct. Only those of you who remember the cadence of

> those McCarthy words—"Are you now or have you ever been . . ."—can know the rage that grew in me at this moment. These young women, so earnest in their feminism, were so set up for this sad moment. "I cannot answer you," I said, "because to do so would bring back a world I have worked my whole life to see never come again."

In a 1985 *Bad Attitude* article, Nestle delineated the painful struggle: "Little by little we are being rounded up. First we are distanced and told we are not feminists—even though many of us have spent years building the movement. Then we are told we are patriarchal, that we are the voices of submission and dominance, that we are heterosexual lesbians." By the end of the '80s, lesbians no longer elicited the services of the sex police to determine what sexual words or pictures they could find appealing, thanks in large part to the tireless efforts of pioneers such as Nestle. Nearly two decades later, tens of thousands of younger lesbians who may never even have heard of her likely take Nestle's expansive position for granted. In 1995, Joan told me the issue "really has been resolved now, in the sense that such important work has been done about sexuality and desire by queer theorists, and other women." No lesbian's passion should be circumscribed by the dominant male culture, nor—worse yet—by the lesbian community. But a similar issue cropped up again after our interaction.

At a State University of New York (New Paltz) conference on the issue of women and sex in 1997, Nestle again confronted "sex police" (this time representatives of the state) who attempted to bully women who dared discuss sex into a muted submission. Joan refused to silence her lesbian tongue, again writing in *A Fragile Union*,

> Lesbians are still fighting for the right to just talk about sex and culture without the surveillance of the state or others who want to tell us what is "natural" for women. . . . I know now that the eyes of the watchers are cold stones even when the sun of their conviction is riding high in the political sky. I know now that surveillance is the weapon of the insecure, the frightened, the pinched. I still fear, however, the human art of policing thought or speech, of hands holding pens to take down our words, never allowing themselves to enter into the messy world of debate.

Joan's struggle against such adversity produced *A Restrictive Country* in 1987 (winner of a 1988 American Library Association book award), and *The Persistent Desire: A Femme-Butch Reader* (a collection of essays she edited) in 1992. In a 1991 interview published in *Happy Endings*, Joan explained, "When I wrote [about butch-femme relationships] in 1981, I was very careful, and I was still trying to placate lesbian-feminist gods. I didn't take the risks I should have taken. In this book [*Persistent Desire*], all the risks are there." Nestle also edited the Women on Women series (with Naomi Holoch), winning at least two Lambda Literary Awards, and *Sister & Brother* (with John Preston, who called Joan "my hero"). Additionally, Nestle received the first David R. Kessler Award from CLAGS, the Sappho Award of Distinction from the Astraea National Lesbian Action Foundation in 1994, and the Bill Whitehead Award for Lifetime Achievement from The Publishing Triangle in 1996.

Not only Preston appreciated Nestle's gifts. Neil Miller, in his fine work *In Search of Gay America*, wrote: "There is a poetic intensity about Joan Nestle. When she speaks, her voice is suffused with deep feeling. She is a survivor, the woman who has come through." Ginny Apuzzo remarked to me, "Joan will walk into a room, and like a sponge, absorb the pain that's in that room! . . . Joan marks that moment. And it has a purpose, because she petrifies that moment in a piece that she writes. And it is there for people to draw upon." JoAnn Loulan exclaimed, "I love Joan Nestle! She's another one that just says it like it is, and has this vision . . . . She's absolutely unbelievable!"

While few things could hold Joan Nestle back, chronic fatigue syndrome (CFS), which she began experiencing in 1978, severely curtailed her activities for a time. Ironically, without CFS, she might never have begun her sexual writings:

> The first sex story I wrote, which was a memory story, came out of a little writing group that a group of friends formed. Because my first year [with CFS], I was literally housebound. . . . Every time I'd have a bad flare-up, I'd write a sex story. So these sexual writings really came out as a response to illness. . . . The stories were a way of reorganizing my body, a way of re-celebrating touch that wasn't medicinal, that wasn't numb.

A different kind of body betrayal awaited Joan when doctors diagnosed her with advanced colon cancer in 1995. In February 1997, surgeons removed four feet of her colon. Afterward she wrote,

> I turned and saw a palette on which lay scores of scalpels, all nestling into each other, all sharp and shining with the clarity of their purpose. I did not flinch from their sight. If I can look upon the coldness of knives that will slit my skin and not ask anyone to intercede, I will never again betray myself. This is the kind of fem you are, I said to myself, and don't ever forget it.

Following the cancer and the loss of her primary relationship with Hudson, Nestle took a new lover. Acknowledging in *A Fragile Union* that "the wonder of life is change," she wrote, "Dianne Otto, a new friend and lover from Melbourne, Australia, has brought me a fuller understanding of love between women and an entryway into the world beyond my own country." Otto, she added, "braves life's dangers and brings me hope." I assume Nestle's selection as co-Grand Marshal for New York City's 1999 Gay Pride Parade must have also provided her some measure of hope, as she remarked beforehand, "It'll be a very special moment. I see it as the largest grass-roots demonstration in the world."

Unlike most of those profiled, who hold utopian visions for gays and lesbians, Nestle waxed pessimistic about the short-term future:

> As we speak, we're in a very shifting time. Because of the fundamentalist movements, and the political movements in this country: the right wing, the Christian, skinhead—you know, I mean, I think these are very scary times. And though on the surface it looks very good . . . there's a big cloud on the horizon. . . . I think within the protection of a movement it's easier. But there are real premonitions of difficulty.

Yet three years later in *A Fragile Union*, she expressed a more optimistic viewpoint:

> I am stunned when I think of the road I have traveled in the last forty years: from a pervert, policed and contained, to a queer lesbian fem woman who writes of sex and history. Decade by decade we suffered and fought our way to sense. This journey was made possible by lovers—lovers of the body and the mind. I have often thanked those who touched my breasts and spread my thighs, but now at the end of this century, I am honored by the touch of another kind of lover—the thinkers who tell me that perhaps it didn't have to be that way at all, perhaps we can understand things differently. These words are as exciting and as necessary as kisses.

When I asked Joan Nestle how she would like to be remembered, she said, "I hope the Archives. And I hope sex." I hope she's right.

Note

1. Hudson served as New York City Mayor Ed Koch's liaison to the lesbian/gay community from 1984 to 1988, and she became the first director of the Mayor's Office for the Lesbian and Gay Community in 1989. After ten years together, Nestle and Hudson went their separate ways in the mid-'90s.

22

JOHN D'EMILIO

I think [the movement has] been a tremendous success, actually. It's not as successful as everybody would want it to be. When I interviewed the people for *Sexual Politics, Sexual Communities* in the mid-'70s . . . almost all of them, in one form or another, said something like, "Never in my wildest dreams did I think so much would change." . . . And now, I have been involved in gay things for as long as they were involved, or longer, when I interviewed them. And I can also say I don't think I ever believed that this much would change. You know, the world is really different from what I was even able to imagine.

—John D'Emilio, 1995

Without **Jim Kepner**, I would never have found the people I needed to interview to make this book a reality. But without John D'Emilio's *Sexual Politics, Sexual Communities*, I would never have known where to start. *SPSC* remains the best and most comprehensive book regarding the first two decades of the American lesbian/gay movement. D'Emilio's primary contribution to the lesbian and gay movement has been his ability to document and capture the stories and the passions from which the organized gay movement we know today evolved.

John D'Emilio was born in the East Bronx on September 21, 1948, the firstborn of Sophie and Vincent D'Emilio, working-class, conservative Italians (John's brother Jim came along eight years later). The first turning point in young John's life came through academia, as he earned a tuition-free Manhattan Jesuit High School education. (In his entertaining book of essays, *Making Trouble*, D'Emilio wrote, "My mother had been grooming me for [Regis's entrance] exam almost from the moment I learned to read; the day I received my acceptance letter was one of great joy for my family. . . . I don't know what my life would have been like if I had followed my friends to a neighborhood high school in the Bronx.")

Despite his earnest desire to be a good Catholic boy, his forays into the heart of New York City provided what good Catholics would call "near occasions to sin," of which D'Emilio guiltily partook. While before puberty John had sexual experiences with both boys and girls, he told me that around eighth grade he engaged in

> explicit sex play with one or two boys, where we definitely saw it as secret. . . . I think the point at which I not only felt it, but I identified it, really came from James Baldwin's novel, *Another Country*, when I was a sophomore in high school. I think that was the point for me at which there were models and characters out there, who were a certain way, who were struggling with certain issues, about attraction and identity. . . . Really, it always comes from books for me—it's amazing.

John poignantly revealed in *Making Trouble* that "the encounters themselves ranged from gentle and generous to brutishly exploitative. But worse was the fact that I had no sense of an alternative. Desire drove me forward and I headed toward the only marked point on the map."

Seminary held an easy way out for D'Emilio, but although the Jesuits were prepared to accept him despite his "homosexual tendencies," he chose instead to attend college at Columbia University in 1966. There John "lost" his faith and became an agnostic, while his fear of what life held for him as a homosexual stubbornly refused to abate until a trick exposed him to Oscar Wilde's *De Profundis*. In *Making Trouble* D'Emilio wrote, "I think it fair to say that it saved my life"; when I asked how, he responded that Wilde "was providing me with a powerful emotional language that was rooted in spiritual tradition. . . . It spoke to me in my experience, but it was also saying in some way that this can be good, and this can be lofty."

After graduating from Columbia in 1970, D'Emilio eschewed postgraduate work for a year, choosing instead to pour his passion into his relationship with his Puerto Rican lover, to explore openly how being gay would impact his life and living, and to fall in love with U.S. history through a leftist perspective. In *Making Trouble* John recalled the catalyst that changed the course of his life: "Out of school, I happened upon William Appleman William's *The Great Evasion*. No other book had so stimulated my intellectual juices. It made me want to understand my country's history."

Simultaneously, D'Emilio cofounded New York's Gay Academic Union in March 1973, along with **Martin Duberman**, **Joan Nestle**, and others. Duberman described D'Emilio to me as a "good friend. Pioneering scholar. One of the few who has really managed successfully to combine the roles—to be a scholar-activist—and to be first-rate in both capacities." Nestle also remembered D'Emilio fondly from that era, calling him "wonderful," and placing him with Allen Bérubé and Jonathan Ned Katz among the early historians who were "very supportive, insightful, dedicated thinkers." Participating in GAU proved another turning point in John's life: "I had never been in a group of gay men where [we] were not there simply because we were gay, but because we were gay *and* we were something else. And it was not about sex; it was about politics and social change. And it was just tremendously exciting. I mean, it's a kind of excitement that you can't forever experience, because it becomes old hat after awhile. But then it was tremendous." While GAU made tremendous gains in the burgeoning field of gay history, internal struggles around gender and accommodationism divided its members. An ardent feminist (as well as a committed pacifist), D'Emilio agonized when many of the women and left-leaning men retreated from active participation by 1975, "which had the effect, of course, of leaving the Gay Academic Union in the hands of the most conservative male faction. And I don't think I would make that kind of mistake again. I would figure out how to drive them out."

Even as his participation in GAU tapered off, in 1974 D'Emilio expressed his desire to embark on what was then considered an extraordinary subject for one's dissertation: Homosexuality in America. When his professor sagely advised him to narrow his topic, John researched the American homophile movement from 1940 to 1970. At that time, the general public could access only precious few resources regarding gay American history, which required D'Emilio to track down and interview many movement founders. While our journeys were similar, I had the advantage of twenty years' experience before me and hundreds upon hundreds of volumes of reading material. In contrast, D'Emilio told me that armed with only a few books and the magazines produced by DOB, Mattachine, ONE, and SIR, he

> started with a name or two. And based on the contact with each of those individuals, there was a kind of snowball effect, where each person would turn me on to a few others, and they would turn me on to others. So that by the end of the process, I was interviewing people

> whom the original people I'd talked to had had no contact with for twenty years, or something like that.

Despite his important and historically groundbreaking work, it presented financial and, more important, emotional challenges. In a 1983 interview with Peter Freiberg in the *Washington Blade*, John recalled not only facing a "constant money crisis," but that

> kids who grew up in the East Bronx aren't supposed to write books. I had to work through real writing blocks. . . . I would sit at my typewriter some days and type pages and pages of expletives and curses at the people who I was angry at because of their choice of strategy.

While working a variety of odd jobs, "usually part-time or short-term and in what loosely could be called community organizing," D'Emilio and a roommate also developed a social experiment in 1976. They hosted an "open house" every Saturday night for several years (later occurring only monthly) to provide themselves and their gay friends (and friends of friends) an inexpensive, fun alternative to meet and socialize with others. The mix of attendees was eclectic, the food simple (spaghetti, chili, stew), the concept easy (no RSVPs or rules). Was John pleased with the results? "It was great! It was my home base in my community for many, many years. It was like family; it provided a kind of predictability and stability in my life. . . . I think it grounded me. It made the gay community very concrete, and tangible, rather than abstract." In 1981, John fell in love with Jim Oleson (a relationship that continues at this writing). But he also had an unfinished project to complete.

By fall 1980, D'Emilio recalls in *Making Trouble*,

> In the midst of a [counseling] session in which I was complaining about how stuck I felt, I realized that, once again, fear was shaping my choices. To finish my dissertation would put me face-to-face with several issues I preferred to avoid: Would anyone hire me as an openly gay historian? Could I deal with piles of rejection letters? Did I want the stress of coming out, year after year, to new cohorts of students? Could I combine a professional career with an activist's commitment to radical social change? Was I prepared to leave the security of my New York gay world? I determined to bite the bullet. Over the next year I finished and revised the manuscript, got a book contract, and began applying for teaching positions, wondering whether I would succeed and knowing that success would mean big changes in my life.

His assessment proved accurate, as the dissertation became a book in 1983. (D'Emilio told me that perhaps the most exhilarating day in his life "was when *Sexual Politics, Sexual Communities* arrived unexpectedly in the mail. And I saw the first copy. And I sat with it, and kind of laughed and cried and stroked it, and caressed it, and called everybody I knew, to tell them.") *SPSC* won the American Library Association's Gay/Lesbian Book Award in 1984, and it led John to a teaching position later that year at (of all places) the University of North Carolina at Greensboro, in the home state of antigay U.S. senator Jesse Helms. John told me that "not only was [UNCG] the only offer, it was the only academic job interview I got" from about fifty schools over a two-and-one-half year period. At UNCG, D'Emilio became a well-respected full professor and achieved tenure, but when I met with him, he had just begun a two-year sabbatical to pursue a new opportunity.

John had joined the NGLTF working board in 1988, and served as cochair from 1989 to 1991, working with a staff "of sterling quality," including **Urvashi Vaid** as executive director. On February 14, 1995, NGLTF chose D'Emilio to lead its Policy Institute, and he assumed his duties around the beginning of July. When I interviewed him barely six weeks later, the Policy Institute remained in its formative stages, but at that point D'Emilio envisioned its function "as mobilizing or marshalling the intellectual resources of the gay and lesbian community to have an impact on public policy and politics in this country." Toward that end, D'Emilio and the Policy Institute released a report in April 1996 which concluded through an exit poll of over fifteen thousand voters that self-identified gay, lesbian, and bisexual voters constituted 3.2% of the total voting population in the 1992 general election (and fully five percent of under-thirty voters). The report further indicated that the "gay vote" is likely as large as the Latino/Latina and Jewish votes, and it is a political force that a national candidate ignores at his/her peril. D'Emilio stepped down as director of the Policy Institute on March 28, 1997, succeeded by Vaid. D'Emilio remained at the institute as a senior fellow, and the National Endowment for the Humanities and the Guggenheim Foundation awarded John fellowships to pen a biography of gay black civil rights activist Bayard Rustin.[1] In 1999, the University of Illinois at Chicago hired D'Emilio to serve as a full professor in women's studies and in history. John was also slated to teach three classes on gay and lesbian topics there beginning in January 2000.

It both surprised and comforted me to discover John believes his greatest personal weakness to be timidity: "I'm timid, in the sense that conflict still scares me. And in ways that I'm often not aware, I structure my life and my activities so that I avoid conflict." When I asked him how he would like to be remembered, his answer charmed me:

> I would like to be remembered for ending oppression. I'd love to be eighty-eight years old, sitting on a rocking chair, on a front porch, and sort of interesting enough that the young people in the neighborhood are kind of flocked around, asking me to tell them what it was like when this funny thing called oppression existed.

D'Emilio also has the most wonderful laugh; if laughter can truly be described as infectious, I caught the bug just from the mirth in his voice.

By their very nature, academic historians run a great risk of being misunderstood. After all, who else could actually *enjoy* all that dry, boring research, tediously digging for tiny nuggets of valuable information scattered amidst the dross? Even D'Emilio alluded to this struggle in a 1989 essay entitled, "Not a Simple Matter":

> As for me, past experience and my sense of what the immediate future holds lead me to expect that I will continue to work a double shift—as an academic historian in a university department and as an activist and a community-connected scholar. It would be nice to feel confident that someday I could simply teach my classes, write my books, and rest.

But like most of us involved in the struggle for fairness and justice for gay, lesbian, bisexual, and transgender rights, D'Emilio continues to wear two hats and burn the midnight oil to further a movement that has profoundly shaped his life, even as his past and current efforts shape that movement.

Note

1. Toward the end of my journey, I discovered to my surprise that *SPSC* was not D'Emilio's first book. In *The Civil Rights Struggle: Leaders in Profile*, published in 1979, D'Emilio profiled many of the movers and shakers in the Negro civil rights movement, including Rustin and gay writer James Baldwin. After *SPSC*, Harper & Row published John and lesbian historian Estelle Friedman's *Intimate Matters: A History of Sexuality in America* in 1988.

Dorr Legg, Los Angeles, CA, 1994 (*chapter 1*)

Lisa Ben, Burbank, CA, 1997 *(chapter 2)*

Jim Kepner, 1992 *(chapter 3)*

Hal Call *(chapter 4)*

José Sarria, Clearwater Oaks, CA, 1999 *(chapter 5)*

Del Martin (l.) and Phyllis Lyon (r.), San Francisco, CA, 1989 *(chapter 6)*

Barbara Gittings (l.) and Kay Tobin Lahusen (r.),
Wilmington, DE, 2001 *(chapter 7)*

Randy Wicker, New York, NY, 1991 *(chapter 8)*

Frank Kameny, 1980 *(chapter 9)*

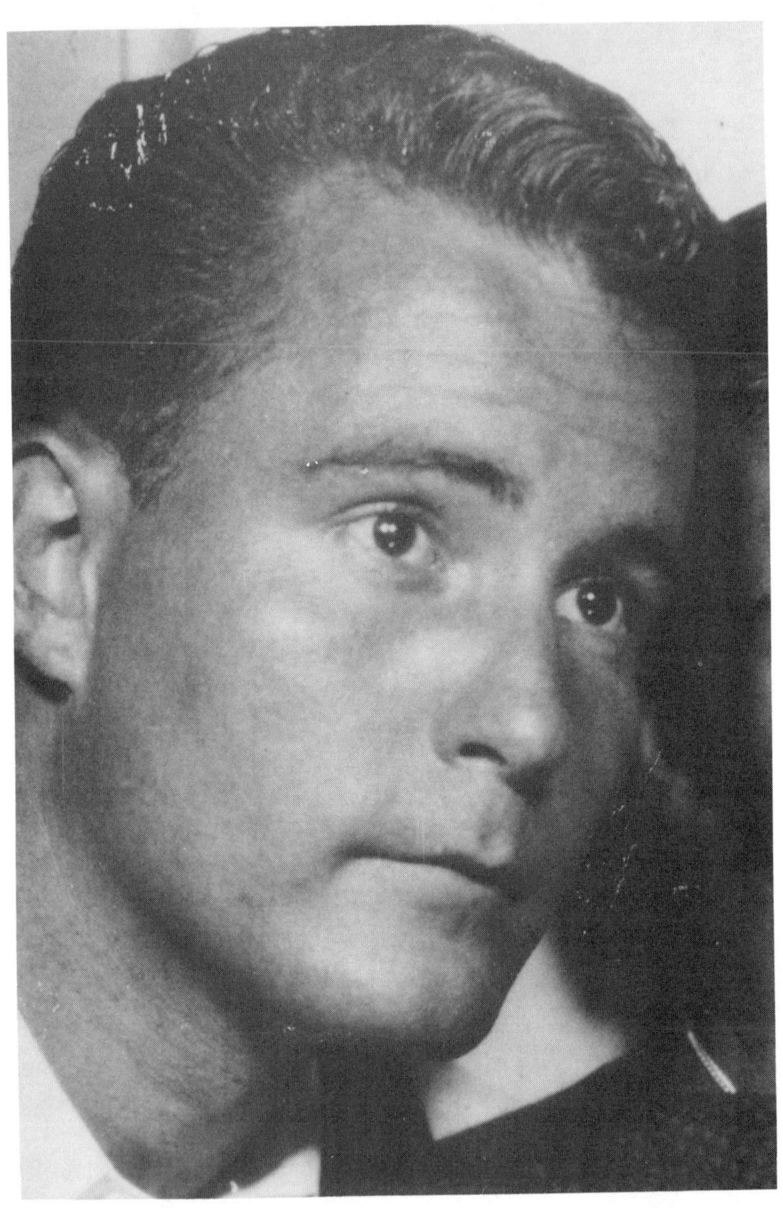

Jack Nichols, 1962 *(chapter 10)*

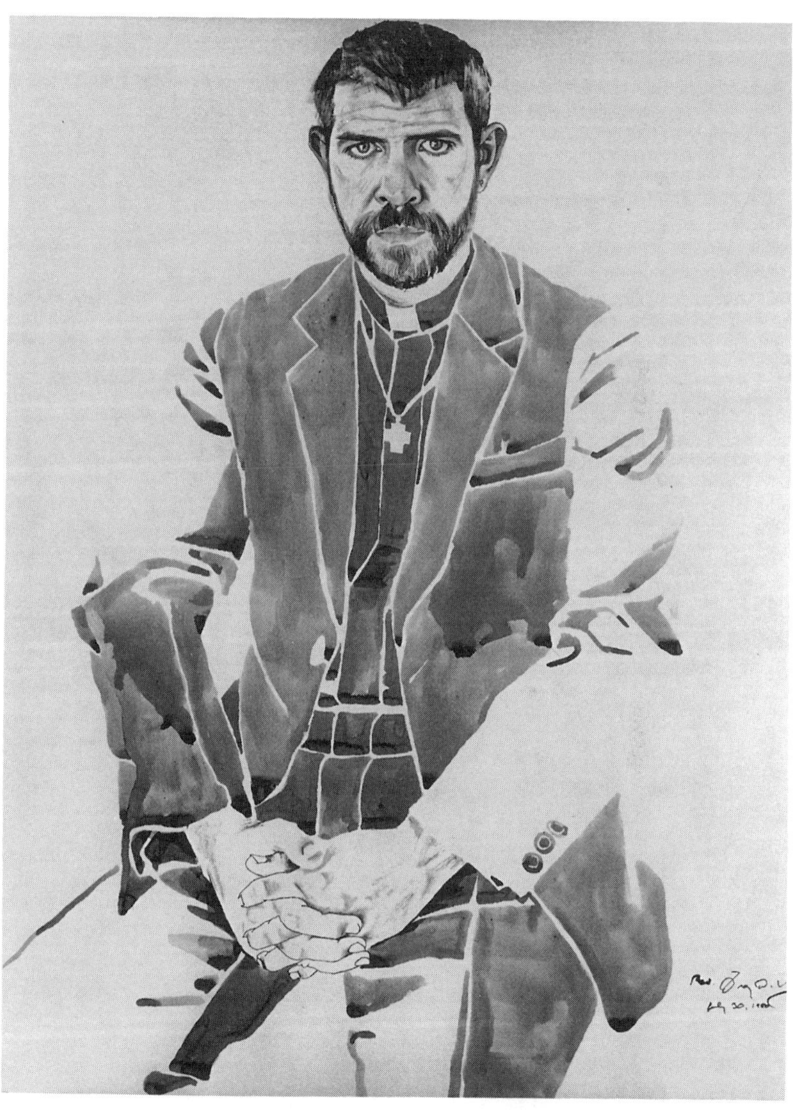

Troy Perry, 1980 *(chapter 12)*

Robin Tyler *(chapter 14)*

Barbara Grier (r.) *(chapter 15)* and Donna McBride (l.),
New York, NY, 1989

Ann Bannon, Sacramento, CA, 1989 *(chapter 16)*

Kate Millet, New York, NY, 1987 *(chapter 17)*

Martin Duberman, New York, NY, 1987 *(chapter 18)*

Malcolm Boyd (seated) and Mark Thompson,
Los Angeles, CA, 1989 *(chapter 20)*

Joan Nestle, New York, NY, 1987 *(chapter 21)*

John D'Emilio, Washington, D.C., 1993 *(chapter 22)*

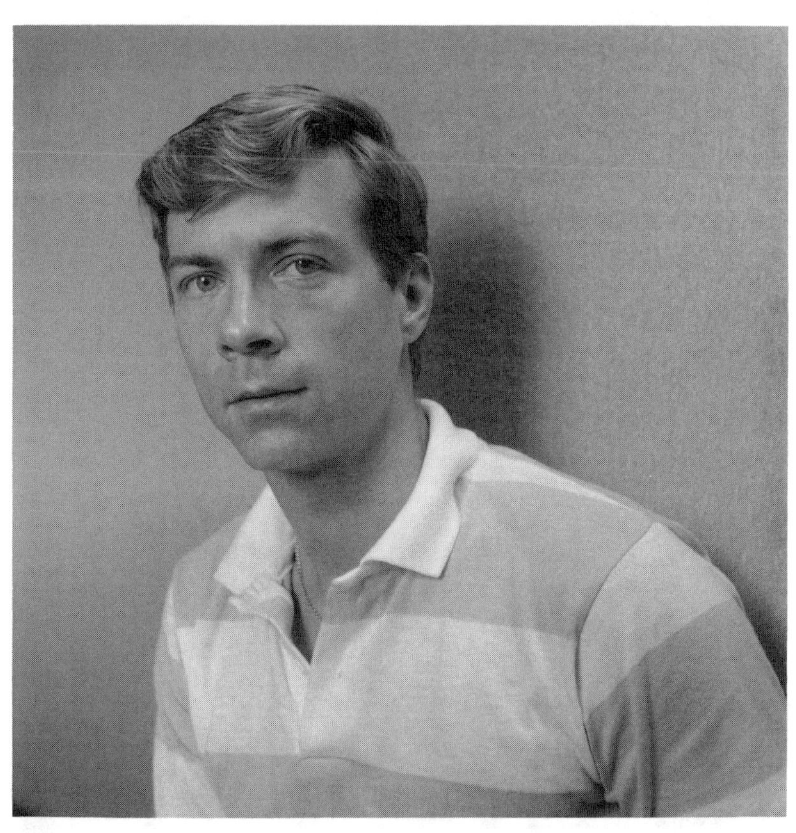

Sasha Alyson, Boston, MA, 1988 *(chapter 23)*

Jean O'Leary, 1980 *(chapter 25)*

Charlotte Bunch, Brooklyn, NY, 1990 *(chapter 26)*

Allan Spear, Minneapolis, MN, 1993 *(chapter 28)*

Cleve Jones, San Francisco, CA, 1988 *(chapter 29)*

David Kopay, 2001 *(chapter 34)*

Urvashi Vaid, Washington, D.C., 1991 *(chapter 39)*

23

SASHA ALYSON

> **Originally I didn't really have a focus. I was just going to do books that I thought were worth doing, really. And it very quickly, within a year or two, became clear that that was just spreading myself too thin, as a small press. That I would have to focus and specialize. And there was no question that [gay material] was what I was going to focus on.**
>
> —Sasha Alyson, 1995

Other than the love of my immediate family, I doubt if anything has influenced my life more than good books. They have taken me places I could never visit, introduced me to people I could never meet, and exposed me to ideas I could never alone conceive. No less important were the books that helped me name my feelings and showed me ways to live in this world. While it took writers like Mike Hippler, Patricia Nell Warren, Armistead Maupin, Randy Shilts, and **Rita Mae Brown** to write them, and **Barbara Gittings** to get them onto library shelves, too often the publishers who make and distribute the books others write stand in obscured shadows, like **Barbara Grier** and the man who published many of the important gay books of my generation, Sasha Alyson. I spoke with Sasha in August 1995 at the Alyson Publications office on 40 Plympton Street, located in a Boston warehouse district, as both the company and its founder underwent substantial transitions. There I found a restless spirit eager to experience the challenges before him, yet one who had learned to savor the successes already accomplished.

Sasha Alyson began life as John Schaller, the second-born of six children, on May 22, 1952, in Madison, Wisconsin. Why the name change? "Growing up in the Midwest, there are always about three Johns in every school class. I always sort of didn't like being one of many, in that sense. . . . I had several different [name] permutations going on. You know, these were just both names I'd picked up from who knows, who remembers where. And I sort of liked the ring of it; there's no rhyme or reason." Sasha discovered his attraction to men early: "Certainly by age eight or ten, I knew that I could feel some kind of special magic from certain good-looking men, but didn't have any real sense of what that really was."

His interest in publishing first developed in high school, when he and his friends began an underground newspaper. As he told James Saslow in a 1981 *Advocate* article, the school's official newspaper "wouldn't print anything about the issues that interested us." In this kind of milieu Alyson claimed his sexual orientation in his late teens: "Most of my friends were quite involved in political circles. None of them were gay, but they were all quite accepting of the fact that somebody might be. Nobody had problems with that." As a result, neither did Alyson, although he later found that many gay youth did not make as painless a transition as he. Alyson remembered and used that knowledge as he began his book publishing career.

In a 1992 *Booklist* interview, Alyson explained how and why he began Alyson Publications:

> I started it quite by accident—probably the best way you could start a small press. Most small presses start because somebody has a book they want to publish. They publish it, and pretty soon they discover themselves with the basement full of books they're not quite sure what to do with. I had been involved with small-press publishing for several years and decided there was a need for better distribution of mostly progressive and feminist and, to the extent that they existed, gay books. I started a company to distribute books called Carrier Pigeon. I did that for a couple of years [1977 to 1980], and only then did I start coming across manuscripts, also books that were out of print or had been published abroad that I felt would be good to have in print in the U.S. Only after I got the distribution network set up did I start publishing. It wasn't due to good planning. It was just coincidence, but it turned out that was a good way to do it.

On April 30, 1980, Alyson Publications's second title, *Young, Gay and Proud*, hit gay bookshelves nationwide.[1] In many ways, it typified the books Alyson Publications published for the next fifteen years: cutting edge, controversial, and committed to meeting needs in the community. It also demonstrated Sasha's desire to address issues faced by gay and lesbian youth, a leitmotif that continued throughout Sasha's tenure. Indeed, two innocuous works Alyson released about a decade later became among the most controversial books in the United States, capturing public attention in a way murder, famine, or political scandal could not.

While other publishers in the '80s chose to play it safe, Sasha, who did not fear risk taking, published significant gay writers like Michael Nava, Pat Califia, Leigh Rutledge, **Joan Nestle**, Essex Hemphill, Stuart Timmons, and John Preston. In 1983, while running his successful small press, Alyson began publishing *Bay Windows*. The newspaper challenged Boston's influential *Gay Community News*, again in response to an unfulfilled need: Sasha noted that *GCN* "wasn't really the Boston community newspaper; it was really more of a national newspaper. And it was very politicized. You never just got news; you got somebody's analysis of the news. And finally I decided I wanted something that gave the news. And that covered even the news that people didn't agree with." While Sasha sold *Bay Windows* to another publisher a few years later, it continues publication at this writing.

In 1988, Sasha edited a small volume, *You CAN Do Something about AIDS*. Distributed free of charge as a public-service project of more than a score of companies, the book included contributions by Surgeon General C. Everett Koop, Greg Louganis, **Cleve Jones**, Whoopi Goldberg, Dear Abby, Harvey Fierstein, and Michael Callen, among many others. Sasha told me that Alyson printed approximately 1,400,000 copies. It remains a work of which everyone involved can take pride.

In 1990, Alyson Publications increased its commitment to young readers by establishing Alyson Wonderland, a bookline designed for children of gay and lesbian parents. (In an earlier Alyson-published book, *One Teenager in Ten*, Sasha identified and met the need for a pen pal service for gay teens, the Alyson Teen Letter Exchange, despite his attorney's advice: "Actually, I learned a valid lesson there, which is that it's fine to get advice from lawyers, but you are paying lawyers to be cautious, and you don't always have to take it.") Sasha may have already experienced difficulty as an openly gay publisher, but the brouhaha over Alyson Wonderland's books made his previous adventures seem like child's play (pun intended).

Heather Has Two Mommies and *Daddy's Roommate* generated a firestorm of controversy when the New York Board of Education included them in its Children of the Rainbow first-grade curriculum. Suddenly, less enlightened parents and politicians dubbed these simple, age-appropriate, attractive books tools of Satan. Alyson shared with me that "for two years in a row, *Daddy's Roommate* was challenged more than any other book in public libraries. . . . I think Madonna's *Sex* was in second place once. . . . [*Daddy's Roommate*] has more all-time challenges than any other book." While Sasha didn't expect the controversy, "which may have just been naïve of me," he "was really largely impressed that there was very little actual censorship. . . . I don't know of any city where a public library took it off the shelf."

By 1992, Alyson's restless spirit drove him to explore other career arenas, and he attempted to sell Alyson Publications. The business, with annual sales around $1 million per year, sat on the market for nine months, but Sasha found no potential buyer with the right combination of finances, business acumen, and desire to continue the same kind of ideals under which the company operated. Not until May 31, 1995, did Sasha ink a deal with the owners of *The Advocate* to purchase Alyson Publications. Had that offer not materialized, Sasha admitted, "I would have wound it down. Because there was no doubt in my mind that I wanted to go and do other things."

One of Sasha's newer pursuits is Alyson Adventures, a travel company specializing in active vacations for the gay community. As with the publishing company, Sasha believes he identified an unmet business niche that interested him, so he decided, "There must be a lot of people like me out there who, if I provide it, will want it."

In comparison to so many of the others profiled for this book, Sasha Alyson does not exhibit the colorful, expansive personality that captivates journalists into unleashing their most expressive adjectives. Instead, despite admitting weaknesses of impatience and arrogance to me, I found a self-effacing, soft-spoken, humble man who earns descriptors like "earnest," "focused," and "determined." Perhaps these character traits ideally suit one who made it his job to bring others' work to the forefront. Alyson made an important contribution to the lesbian and gay community by daring to publish several bold authors' controversial ideas and concepts. Even those who disagree with some of the ideas contained in those books ought to admire the courage and foresight of the one who projected them before an ever-evolving community.

Note

1. Alyson first released *Energy, Jobs and the Economy* in September 1979.

24

JoANN LOULAN

I've written a third of the books on lesbian sex written since the beginning of time! That does not make me feel proud! . . . There were probably, you know, three books that came out last week on the long muscle of the rat!

—JoAnn Loulan, 1995

She is a psychotherapist, a sex researcher, a writer, and the mother of a teenaged son, who admits she looks like "J.Q. Mom from the burbs." By all rights, one could expect part Sigmund Freud, part Alfred Kinsey, part June Cleaver—kind of a drag. Well, park those preconceived notions on the margin; JoAnn Loulan is *the* funniest person I met on my journey. Despite recovery from a "people addiction" and a recent battle with breast cancer, Loulan is relentlessly upbeat and optimistic.

And did I mention she's *funny*?!

It certainly wasn't her childhood surroundings. JoAnn Marie Loulan was born on July 31, 1948, in Bath, Ohio. One might expect an openly lesbian writer/sex researcher to be the most notorious person of her generation to come from a small Midwestern town. But not Bath—even JoAnn couldn't compete with the infamous Jeffrey Dahmer. ("He lived on East Bath Road, and I lived on West Bath Road, two miles apart.")

While Loulan would not self-identify as a lesbian until 1975, in hindsight her first identification of same sex attraction came in

> fourth grade. Mary Simmer. Coming up the driveway, whistling at me. And me, completely wanting to faint. And my brother [Tim, two years her senior] and father standing there. And she gave me a wolf whistle! I remember what I had on: I had a pair of little white shorts and a white top that went with it, with little red piping. And she walked up the driveway and whistled at me, and I nearly came. I swear to God! And I knew, somehow, instantaneously, act like you did not hear that. . . . I immediately knew not to acknowledge it.

Since she knew to self-censor that experience, what did she then know of lesbianism? "I heard nothing. I never heard the words until I was in college. . . . I never heard 'lesbian'; I never heard 'homosexual'; I never heard 'gay' . . . . I was so naïve." But she was determined to lose her naiveté; after graduating from high school (where she was prom queen) and college, she left Bath for the San Francisco Bay Area in 1972, where she encountered a strange, brave new world.

Loulan married a man in 1971; they divorced in 1974. Like many women of that era, JoAnn had really never questioned her sexuality, and didn't recognize lesbianism as an option on her menu (definitely one from Column B). That is, not until the summer of 1975, when two lesbian legends changed her thinking. Attending a course for an organization called San Francisco Sex Information, she recalled,

> I had an all-day Saturday class. I was straight, or at least I thought I was. I was flirting and sitting with this guy in my class. . . . And this all-day workshop came. And it was [taught by] Pat Califia and Tee Corinne, and some gay men, I think. But Pat Califia and Tee Corinne *blew my mind*! . . . And I turned to this guy and said, "I think I'm a lesbian." . . . And he said, "What?" And I said, "I think I'm a lesbian. I mean, no one's ever said this out loud, in front of me before. I mean, this must be what is wrong!"

Armed with this new information, Loulan telephoned her sister-in-law to share the good news:

> [I] called her up, and I said, "I know what the problem is." And she said, "What?" I said, "We're lesbians." And then there was this like five-minute silence on the other end of the line. And she said, "Really?" [Laughs] . . . And within a year-and-a-half, I think, she came out. And she's been a lesbian ever since, too. So our mother-in-law is completely vindicated, that both her dear sons that are divorced were divorced by the lesbians.

JoAnn experienced great joy in "choosing" lesbianism, a construct in and of itself controversial in many circles. In 1995 she told me,

> I don't think there's anything wrong with choosing to be a lesbian. I don't know if I'm genetically a lesbian. I do know people that absolutely believe and know that they are genetically lesbian. . . . And I don't put myself in that category. And I don't think there's anything wrong with choosing to be a lesbian! It's a wonderful choice!

However, the lesbian community into which she emerged didn't quite know what to make of her. She recalled the bar crowd's reaction to her in Paris Poirier's delightful film *Last Call at Maud's*, as she waltzed in wearing

> Jewelry, lots of makeup. Scarves in my hair. Dresses. And I came in—of course, everyone thought I was straight. Because, at that time, when I came out in the mid-'70s, there was what I describe as the Androgynous Imperative. You know. If you came out looking like me, you were assumed to be straight. And so, when you came in the bar, the heads would turn. Not because people were looking at you. [Laughs] They were like, "How did *she* get in here?"

Many '70s lesbians considered ultra-femmes like Loulan an anathema, and even the ebullient Loulan temporarily succumbed to peer pressure:

> I tried androgyny. I really gave it a really, really, *really* big try. I dressed up in flannel shirts, and I cut my hair short, and I didn't wear makeup, and I didn't wear earrings, and I really tried hard. And it just never worked, you know? I was always a girl's girl. I was born with Mary Janes and little lace socks, you know. That is how it's always been for me. And I daresay it's how it always will be. But there was a lot of flak about butch-femme stuff. People would hiss; people would boo; people would flip out; people argued with me; people fought with me.

In *The Girls Next Door*, JoAnn said, "I identify totally as femme. And I love women who identify as butch. The more they identify as butch, the better." She also told (and showed) me, "People may think that because of the way I look that it's easy for me, because I can pass? Quote-unquote. But I work very hard at not passing. I tell anybody that'll listen that I'm a lesbian."

Simultaneously, she attempted to convince lesbians that, despite her appearance, she actually was (and is) a lesbian: "Every single one of us that has written a book on lesbian sex has been accused of [being straight]. Which always blew my mind. [Laughs] Why would we be writing books about lesbian sex if we were straight?" In part to counter this misperception, Loulan begins her live performances talking about sex and relationships before mostly lesbian audiences by saying, "Hi, my name is JoAnn Loulan, and I'm a lesbian. Are there any other lesbians here?"

But many lesbians excoriated Loulan in early 1997 when she publicly acknowledged violating a critical taboo: Lesbians may not have sex with men. JoAnn fell in love with Ronny Crawford, a professional drummer more than a dozen years her junior, yet she still identified as a lesbian (saying in a February 1997 *Advocate* interview with Katie Cotter, "I'm not into men. My culture is really lesbian- and woman-identified"). When, in an April 1998 *20/20* interview, Lynn Sherr asked Loulan why she initially hesitated to disclose her new relationship, she exclaimed, "Are you kidding?! Why? I thought, if I tell people this, they're gonna completely flip out." Sherr continued, "it was even worse than JoAnn had imagined. When she finally told her story publicly, many were shocked and resentful. She was viewed as a traitor, and her action—a lesbian leader with a man—was seen as a political and cultural insult to the lesbian and gay community."

In an essay in 1991's *Lesbians at Midlife*, Loulan may have dropped a hairpin or two when she wrote of the lesbian community's obsession with sexual rules: "We made rules about discussing sex, what kind of sex we could have and who we could have sex with. Any lesbian who had sex with men was out of the club without a second consideration by 'the committee.' Sex with men was the ultimate transgression against the 'lesbian national bylaws.'" Also, well before the furor ensued, she told me plainly, "I have always written and said lesbians can have sex with men. This does not make you *not* a lesbian! . . . You can even love a man, and have sex with a man that you love, and still identify as a lesbian." As Loulan tried to explain to Sherr, "They want me to say that I'm heterosexual, or that I'm bisexual." When Sherr asked, "And what's wrong with that?," JoAnn replied,

> I clearly am bisexually active, you know what I mean? But I think sexual orientation has to do with so much more than that. If this relationship ended, it's not like I'd say, "Well, whatever comes along next." I'd go right back to my lesbian community, and hang out with the women, and I'm sure I'd end up with a woman next.

For a time Loulan shouldered intense criticism (an *Advocate* reader responded, "If you're a dyke, you're a dyke, and if you're a breeder, then stop lying about it—and stop insulting my intelligence"), emotional and economic censure (Sherr reported, "Her icon status quickly disintegrated. For a time, her speaking engagements dried up. There were angry letters to the editor, hate mail sent to JoAnn's home"), and the abandonment of friends (telling Sherr while blinking back tears,

"It's hard that I've lost people, but I have a perspective of what's so! You know. And I just have to go with that. . . . I wasn't gonna not do what my heart wanted to do!"). But she also gained public support from **Robin Tyler** as well as **Phyllis Lyon** and **Del Martin**, who wrote, "We did not rebel against the heterosexual conformity of women's roles only to be saddled with conformist notions of what it is to be a lesbian. Over the years we have fought for choice, for individuality, and for being who we really are."

Loulan confessed to Cotter, "When I came out as a lesbian, I didn't have one ounce of trouble. But now I really get what agony people go through in terms of coming out because I feel like there isn't a place for me." By mid-1997, she retrospectively marveled at her own courage, stating, "I understand [some lesbians are] upset and don't want me to have the privileges of being a lesbian and having heterosexual privileges at the same time. But I'm proud of myself for telling the truth." (I was/am proud of her, too. When the news broke, I called and left a message to remind her that our community's struggle historically has been to love whom we choose without fear of reprisal, and that no matter the larger community's response, she would always have a friend in me.)

Perhaps the other part of the initial struggle for acceptance from her audience came because she chose to become a lesbian birth mother when the concept was practically oxymoronic. In Loulan's mind, it was all very simple: "I woke up one day, and went, 'Well, I have a uterus. I can have a baby. How do you have a baby? I need to get some sperm. How should I do that?'" Her first pregnancy, in 1980, ended in a miscarriage. On her second try, in 1981, she linked up with a gay man who desired a parenting experience: "It's sort of like, I feel like Mickey and Judy, you know. 'Hey! I've got a barn. Let's do the play in my garage!' It was sort of like, hello? I inseminated with a guy I don't even fuckin' know." While the "lesbian baby boom" began quietly in the late '80s and gathered momentum in the '90s, it made for stimulating lesbian conversation in 1982: "It was a big deal. Looking how I looked, and being pregnant—I'd go to lesbian things. And it'd be like, 'Now we *really* know she's not one of us!'" But she wouldn't trade the experience for anything: her son Gardner's birth made for the most exhilarating day of her life. Loulan has been Gardner's primary parent, but when JoAnn's schedule takes her away from home, he stays with his father Paul, with whom Loulan developed a very fluid sharing relationship: "We spend holidays together and everything. And so, my situation turned into a total dream."

Armed with her newfound self-knowledge and a therapist's degree from San Francisco's Lone Mountain College in 1977, Loulan tailored her practice to serve the lesbian community.

> I was one of the few "out" lesbian therapists. Because, you see, professionals at that time couldn't be out. So you had to find somebody, sort of a sneaky route. And so, I was out. I didn't know any better! I was out; I was young; I was full of myself . . . It never *occurred* to me not to be out! . . . And I found there are a lot of places for straight people to go to get therapy. So I really made my practice about lesbians.

She continues to practice out of a small office in Portola Valley, California (near Stanford University), and loves her work. But JoAnn's influence in the lesbian community has come from talking and writing about lesbian sex.

In 1979, Loulan, her then-lover Marcia Quackenbush, and Bonnie Lopez co-wrote *Period*, a book about menstruation for pre-menstrual girls, which they revised in 1981, but her next work explored radically different subject matter. In 1984, Loulan blatantly released her first solo book, *Lesbian Sex*, with a drawing of two women enjoying afterglow on a hot pink cover (no one ever accused JoAnn of subtlety). *Lesbian Sex* provided JoAnn a forum to showcase her talents as a writer (and later as a speaker), and she made the most of the opportunity.

> It was one of the first books about lesbian sex that somebody went out and promoted. So I went on a book tour. And I was a theater major in college. So, of course, what that developed into is me being on stage, and being with big audiences, and being able to speak out loud. And I'm a showperson, you know! The P. T. Barnum of lesbian sex.

Unlike her counterpart Susie Bright, whose work tends to focus on the sexual act, Loulan's "topics are around all kinds of areas. Around lesbian sociology, really. Self-esteem; self-worth; sexuality; coming out; all of the different things. And lesbian sex also." *Lesbian Sex* remains a delightful, humorous, well-written book that I heartily recommend to any sexual person—it is emphatically *not* for lesbians only! *Lesbian Sex* became a springboard for two other Loulan books, *Lesbian Passion* and *The Lesbian Erotic Dance*, and she became a "hot" lecturer on the women's festival circuit. A healthy child, a satisfying career, an opportunity both to educate and entertain her lesbian community—Loulan seemed to have it all. Until she discovered she also had something she *didn't* want—breast cancer.

The diagnosis did not surprise Loulan, whose maternal family tree demonstrated a high incidence of breast cancer, including her mother, aunt, and grandmother (although she admitted in 1995 that the day she received her diagnosis was probably the most traumatic of her life). Knowing her family history, however, Loulan had diligently sought regular testing. As a result, doctors spotted Loulan's breast cancer in its early stages, and treated her with radiation and surgery; at this writing, Loulan's cancer remains in remission. Choosing to see the glass as half-full, Loulan focused on the positive aspects resulting from her experience: "They started a breast cancer fund in my name in Atlanta. It's so great to have a fund named after someone who's alive, and who's gonna be alive. So my hope is that I'll be a spokesperson for breast cancer, period, but also especially for lesbians." When I interviewed her, she was writing a book about her breast cancer experience and facilitating a National Institutes of Health study at Stanford examining the needs of lesbians *vis-à-vis* heterosexual women in dealing with breast cancer.

In *Dyke Life*, Loulan described herself as a "femme bull dyke." While it may sound like a contradiction in terms, as Loulan explained to me, "I feel like bull dykes are often out; they're often visible; they're taking the hits for the community. I see myself as someone who can get out there, who is a cheerleader for the lesbian community. Who takes the hits. I take it, you know, right in the chops any time that needs to happen. I'm completely invested in that."

While everyone within earshot discovers Loulan's alternative sexuality, she told me she believed she had not experienced personal discrimination because of her greatest strength: "Being able to love all kinds of people. So it's like, you can see my neighbors here. I'm very involved in my community. I'm very involved in school. And they love me back." That they do. While we had lunch at her country club, I watched her interactions with her straight friends, male and female: being visible and vocal about her lesbianism doesn't keep her from being Gardner's mom, an active member of her community, and a lot of fun to be around. As she told Laura Post in a 1996 interview, "Someone was saying, 'Was JoAnn always like this?' She said, 'Yeah. This is just a bigger cafeteria.' I was always the talker, I was always the organizer, I was always the mover and the shaker. If I lived near where I grew up I'd be the one on the committee arranging all the reunions."

In the long run, I don't think her intimate relationship with Crawford will harm her reputation in the lesbian community—JoAnn seems always to position herself about five to ten years ahead of her peers. (Maybe "Lesbians Who Have Sex with Men" will be on the next *Oprah*!) It's noteworthy that when I asked how she would like to be remembered, she replied, "I would like to be remembered for challenging the lesbian community to think; to expose themselves; to try new things; to experiment, on all kinds of levels."

What aspiration has Loulan not yet achieved? Well, she's not Oprah—yet: "I want to be a talk show host. Just like one-third of America, or whatever. . . . Because I think it's about time that there was a talk show run by a lesbian that was a mainstream talk show, that everybody could be on. And was from this unique perspective, from a kind of big-mouthed lesbian." While the talk show craze now seems to have peaked, I still wouldn't put it past her. With apologies to Dr. Ruth, JoAnn Loulan could probably create the definitive talk show on sexuality and remind you of why people are sexual in the first place: because it's fun!

And did I mention she's *funny*?!

PART IV

POLITICAL CREATURES

25

JEAN O'LEARY

I believe strongly in doing whatever it takes to enhance public attitudes toward our community and our issues. We are making enormous strides toward an open and integrated society. The fact is, we have always been integrated—just not open. We are everywhere. We have the positions, we have the jobs, and we have our families. We just have to be able to keep them when people find out we are gay or lesbian. When we come out! That's why our slogan has never been "gay jobs." It's always been "Gay Pride!"

—Jean O'Leary, 1994

In some moments, everything comes together. While Jean O'Leary has suffered no shortage of accomplishments either before or since, she found the culmination of the National Commission on the Observance of International Women's Year (IWY) in Houston, Texas, in 1977 the most exhilarating day of her life.

> It's so rare, when you're a movement activist, or working within a system, that you can take a piece out and say, "I started it *here*, I ended it *here*. And it was successful." Instead of saying, "I was a part of this, with all these other people." I mean, that was true too, with all these other women! But knowing that you orchestrated it, from beginning to end—

Jean wanted the IWY conference to approve a platform supporting lesbianism; for a year and a half, she fought to make that desire a reality. As she tells the story, among the commissioners,

> I was always made to feel so much an outsider, always having to struggle. I was the *Lesbian*. And I really would have welcomed the opportunity to work shoulder-to-shoulder with my feminist peers on a women's conference, with lesbianism included, along with all the other issues. But no. Every time I spoke up, it had to be to, you know, bring up the issue. I was literally in tears after almost every meeting. And I hate to admit that. Because I was so alone.

Only two heterosexual women (Ruth Abrams and Ellie Smeal, president of NOW), and no other lesbians, supported Jean on the issue at the commission meetings, because "they didn't want to be labeled lesbians." Unable to get the issue on the agenda through the front door at the commission meetings, Jean went around to the back door, working with a woman she hired to get the issues passed on a state-by-state level. For an entire year she organized what was called the "lavender slate" (except in California, where it was known as the "orange slate"). Delegates in more than thirty-five states (more than the majority needed) ultimately passed the lavender slate to place a platform supporting lesbians on the agenda.

Next came the question of nomenclature, which demonstrated both the subtlety of politics and Jean's consummate skills.

> The next battle was, we would never get through this huge agenda, during the weekend that we had. And so, we only got to do it in alphabetical order. So then I fought to have it be called "lesbianism." And for the first time, these feminists [opposing the issue] were saying, "It *can't* be called lesbianism! It must be called 'sexual orientation.'" And usually, they never wanted to deal with the word "sexual." They wanted to make sure it was "lesbianism." They were contradicting themselves, tripping over themselves to get us to the end of the alphabet.

So Jean scaled a fence: "I created these buttons that said, 'Keep the Agenda Moving; Let Every Issue Be Heard.' That became the war cry for all the minorities. And it actually fostered a great spirit of cooperation among the minority issues, at the culminating convention in Houston. And everybody tried to keep the agenda going." When the issue finally arrived on the platform, a heated debate ensued for hours. But New York City feminist and long-time NOW activist Dolores Alexander, with Jean and **Charlotte Bunch**'s help, knocked down a huge wall: They spoke with Betty Friedan, who years earlier had called lesbians the "Lavender Menace" within NOW, and they convinced her to apologize for those remarks.

As a result of Jean's tenacity, the platform supporting lesbianism finally passed, although not unanimously: "We had delegations turn their back on us. Absolutely, just physically stand up and turn their back." Despite the minority's reaction, such a challenge demonstrated the kind of political work at which Jean excels. Clearly, Jean likes to win, as she did that day and so many others.

Jean Marie O'Leary was born on March 4, 1948, in Kingston, New York, the first-born of four in a close, supportive family. Jean believes that her parents most influenced her life: "My mother had a very soft, wonderful, human kind of way. And my dad was raised, 'There's nothing to fear but fear itself. And get out there.' And do it. And I think the combination really made me who I am. On the outside—the veneer, you know—it's like my dad. And on the inside, I'm a lot like my mother." Jean's mother Betty contracted polio when Jean was just six years old; O'Leary believes that experience drew her family even closer together, as they remain today. In 1976's *Our Right to Love*, Betty wrote, "It would be less than honest to say that hearing the news that my darling daughter is a lesbian made me jump for joy. I was heartsick. But when the initial shock was over, one thing I was sure of—my love for her never wavered one bit."

Her teachers considered young Jean a rebel, and mostly on merit; during her years at the all-girls Magnificat High School in Cleveland, Ohio, Jean received detention more often than any other student. Because of her "potential for creative disruption," the school would not permit Jean to run for class office; instead, she nominated her best friend, and found a different way to express her political aspirations. In the process, Jean discovered a knack for running campaigns, and she later put that skill to use not only on her own behalf but also to benefit the lesbian and gay community.

Jean discovered her attraction to the same sex around third grade. As time went on, her feelings bewildered her: "I thought homosexuality was a disease—it was a sickness; it was a perversion; it was definitely immoral. But despite what I thought about homosexuality, I loved girls, and that was very confusing." While in high school, Jean continued to struggle with ambivalence: "I wanted love, but I had no desire to do anything which would cause me to become an outcast. I wasn't ready to ignore social sanctions. The rest of my life might be in the balance if I made a mistake. Of only one thing was I definitely certain—that I wanted to love and be loved by women."

How could a good Catholic girl resolve this dilemma? O'Leary shocked everyone by announcing her intention to become a nun, and entering a Cleveland convent. Jean's lesbianism found a physical outlet in the convent, as she engaged in relationships with eight women. Jean remarks concerning that time, "When I went into the convent, I thought I was going in because I had a 'calling.' In retrospect, I know it was because I was a lesbian and wanted to be with women." She spent four and a half years as a postulant and took temporary vows before deciding to depart. Upon leaving, Jean even abandoned playing her precious drums, which she had taken into the convent with her ("I was a great drummer"). (The music world's loss became the movement's gain; otherwise, a determined O'Leary might have given Karen Carpenter a run for her money!) When I asked Jean what role spirituality now plays in her life, she reflected,

> It's influenced me, in how I live my life. And I tap back into it. It's an underlying strength. . . . This is the source from which I probably grew my first strength. . . . Knowing that with God behind me, I could do anything. It's not as clear as that anymore, but it was an initial foundation and a strong belief system.

While in the convent, O'Leary worked to obtain a bachelor of arts degree at Cleveland State University; upon receiving that degree in 1970, Jean left Ohio for New York, where she attended Yeshiva University. (While it seems an odd choice for an ex-nun just separated from the convent to attend a Jewish university, O'Leary explained it was one of the only universities in the country to have an Organizational Development curriculum, Jean's chosen discipline.) She also moved to the Big Apple "intending to find the lesbians" in Greenwich Village after reading a *Cosmopolitan* article that indicated they lived there. She moved into Brooklyn Heights with a former CSU dean of students; Jean discovered his homosexuality when she found a copy of *The Gay Militants* on his bookshelf, filled with news clippings and lists of places to meet other gays.

Together, they soon attended a GAA meeting, at which Jean saw that gay men vastly outnumbered lesbians: "Probably my only real distinction was being a woman, one of about a handful that showed up at every meeting." Due in part to her interest in organizational development, Jean chose to participate in GAA. Most of the men who ran GAA lacked feminist awareness, and Jean found herself fearlessly and tirelessly taking the lead on many issues pertaining to feminism and sexism. Like her political actions, her personal life reflected her increasing unorthodoxy; rather than simply embracing lesbianism theoretically (as many women did at that time), or establishing a single long-term monogamous relationship, Jean earned a reputation as one who enjoyed both casual sexual encounters and a multiplicity of relationships with women, something she did not deny during my conversation with her.[1]

Ultimately, Jean and the other GAA women began a new committee, Lesbian Liberation Committee (later known as Lesbian Feminist Liberation, or LFL), which increased O'Leary's interaction with Bruce Voeller, at that time GAA president. By December 1972, they clashed over a GAA constitutional provision that gave the president authority to attend all GAA committees' elections. Jean vehemently opposed the policy; as separatism between gay men and lesbians reached its apex, the women's committee separated from GAA to form its own organization under O'Leary's leadership. In time, Jean and Bruce resolved their differences, and in 1974 Jean joined Bruce to become the first co-Executive Directors for NGTF (now NGLTF). During O'Leary and Voeller's tenure, NGTF made great strides in media publicity, as Jean discussed homosexual issues on television's *Today*, and the American Psychiatric Association officially ceased classifying homosexuality a mental illness. **Marty Duberman** told me, "When I worked with [Jean] on the Task Force, I found her full of energy and enthusiasm, very charismatic and charming." O'Leary worked at NGTF until early 1979, when she sought—and found—other challenges.

In 1976, Jean became only the second open lesbian to attend a Democratic national convention. The process to get on a slate of supporters for a particular candidate in New York differed somewhat from most states. Three New York slates for Democratic presidential candidates (with six delegates per slate) existed when O'Leary began the process. As Jean had demonstrated fund-raising prowess and the ability to mobilize the gay/lesbian vote, Birch Bayh chose her to join his slate of New York delegates. However, as Bayh's campaign stalled, Jean realized she would have to shift to the Morris Udall slate. As eighteen people vied for six positions, Jean fought several high-powered politicians before securing a spot on the Udall ticket with the likes of Bella Abzug and David Dinkins. Nationally, Jimmy Carter became the Democrats' presidential front-runner in 1976; accordingly, Jean knew that to gain visibility and effectiveness within the Carter White House, she needed to switch her vote to support him. (Since Udall had already conceded to Carter, her vote for Udall would have been only symbolic.) Despite strong pressure from other Udall delegates, Jean crossed over to vote for Carter. O'Leary's strategy produced many long-term effects, and savvy Jean maximized the switch to full advantage.

Jean had become a good friend of Midge Costanza, a former vice-mayor of Rochester, New York, who became President Carter's liaison to minority groups. After American voters elected Carter president, O'Leary brought her political chits to Midge, who argued Jean's case before the president. As a result, Jean orchestrated the first White House meeting on lesbian/gay issues on March 26, 1977. As NGTF's executive directors, Jean and Bruce Voeller chose twelve gay/lesbian leaders from around the country[2] to join them in preparing position papers on issues of concern to the lesbian/gay community. How did Jean choose the speakers?

> I just picked them on the issues. What issues do we want to bring up? And then, what people can best represent those issues? And it was very simple, it seemed, at the time, because there were only so many issues. And then, who was the best in that area. And if there were two or three, I picked the one with whom I had the most experience.

Jean's DNC vote switch also enabled her to become one of forty-two nationally prominent feminists appointed by Carter to the IWY presidential commission.

In 1995's *Virtual Equality*, **Urvashi Vaid** reported that O'Leary and others actively participated in the Municipal Elections Committee of Los Angeles (MECLA) from the mid-'70s through the '80s, and that in the late '80s Jean and others "formed a small political network they called the Book Study Group. Members of this informal yet influential group met to discuss national gay political strategy; a number of its members went on to found ANGLE [Access Network for Gay & Lesbian Equality]." Vaid further wrote that ANGLE illustrated a situation "in which gay elites purport to represent a community to whom they are not at all accountable."

Perhaps it seems everything Jean touches turns to gold. Unfortunately, her Midas touch deserted her toward the end of the '80s as she became embroiled in a disastrous situation with the National Gay Rights Advocates (NGRA), the organization for which Jean served as executive director from 1981 to 1989. While Jean's tenure at NGRA provided her a national platform from which to operate, its resolution pained all concerned.

As Jean tells the story, San Francisco-based NGRA perched on the brink of dissolution due to financial stresses and internal problems when she joined its Board of Directors in 1981, shortly after O'Leary moved from New York to Los Angeles. Other NGRA board members asked O'Leary to take the reins as executive director, in essence telling her she could write her own ticket if she could save the organization. O'Leary found the challenge irresistible, and she accepted the position. At the beginning, Jean says, "I could do no wrong. Because I pulled NGRA out from nothing to a million-dollar organization within three years, and the largest [gay] organization in the country, at that time. Largest membership, largest budget, largest everything."

According to Jean, NGRA's Board of Directors never took the necessary steps to safeguard the organization's financial health: "*No one* else was raising money. I raised every penny for NGRA." Not a lawyer herself, and not desiring to immerse herself in NGRA's legal issues, by 1987 O'Leary began encountering friction from the organization's three staff attorneys (Leonard Graff, Benjamin Schatz, and Cynthia Goldstein). Jean's desire for a larger forum outside the legal arena through her involvement with the Democratic Party and later as co-founder of National Coming Out Day only added to the tension, as NGRA's budget increasingly allocated more money for nonlegal projects.

NGRA's Board of Directors resolved the untenable situation in November 1989 by firing Schatz and Goldstein (Graff had left earlier), while retaining Jean as executive director. San Francisco's gay press fanned the flames, promulgating various unsubstantiated allegations. Schatz and Goldstein notified several gay community organization leaders around the country; Vaid and others signed and distributed a letter criticizing the NGRA board (and O'Leary by extension) for mishandling the situation. Then Jean saw the writing on the wall: "When the letter came out, I realized the controversy was not going to stop. If NGRA was to have a chance to survive, I had to resign. The letter was the final straw." She resigned on December 4, 1989. Lacking a leader who could raise sufficient funds, NGRA closed its doors on May 17, 1991, more than $200,000 in debt. Jean summed up this nasty debacle for me: "There's nobody that is proud or self-justified or righteous about their role in what happened with NGRA. . . . People said it's probably the worst thing that's ever happened, organizationally speaking, in the history of this movement."[3]

Before NGRA collapsed, Jean played a crucial role in devising the first National Coming Out Day (NCOD), October 11, 1988. NCOD resulted from a February 1988 "War Conference," held in Virginia for lesbian and gay leaders around the country. The NCOD concept brought O'Leary's passion for gay and lesbian visibility to the forefront. Jean and Rob Eichberg, founder of the Experience Weekend, quickly discussed the proposal, and they agreed to work on it together. Jean asked Rob because she believed he "would be a perfect counterpart to me, and I knew we would make a wonderful team," combining O'Leary's political know-how with Eichberg's personal skills. They ultimately enlisted and received active support from over eight thousand gay and lesbian groups across the United States. But NCOD also suffered its critics; Jean recalled,

> It was so unpopular the first year. You would have thought I was resurrecting Hitler, or something. "Why do we need this? Why are you

> forcing people out of the closet? This is too slick." Coming up with all these marketing tools and promotional items like cups and notepapers and hats to promote 'National Coming Out Day.' I got so criticized for that. . . . And now it's probably our most popular national holiday, and I think it'll just grow and grow and grow. It's amazing what you can start, if you have belief and a vision. And you know where to tap in, because that's where we're going, and what's gonna last. And it's just amazing, how many people try to tear it down while you're doing it. Until it becomes untouchable. Or institutionalized.

Since stepping down from NGRA, Jean lives happily with her partner Lisa Phelps and Lisa's adopted daughter Vicki, born in 1990, in a gorgeous, post-Northridge-earthquake-renovated home in the San Fernando Valley. O'Leary also started PrinTec Industries, Inc., and she serves as president of the successful national telemarketing and computer supply business. Politically, she currently serves as the first open lesbian/gay appointment on the Democratic Party's Executive Committee, one of the party's highest honors, and in 2000 was elected co-chair of the DNC's newly recognized Gay and Lesbian Caucus. Despite these actions, friends like comic **Robin Tyler** commented on Jean's "semi-retirement" from the national gay/lesbian political scene:

> I think that her not being executive director of an organization is a great loss to this movement. . . . Those of us that came from the early movement, we didn't have any money. There was no million dollars. We ran off sheets of paper, and got someone to run it off for free, and we worked very frugally, because there was no money. The people coming up now can raise maybe hundreds of thousands of dollars, and something costs millions of dollars. But they don't know how to budget like we did. . . . So I miss a Jean O'Leary that was able to fundraise $3 million, and I look at Stonewall [25 in New York in 1994] that owes lots of money, and I look at [Gay Games IV] that lost money. And then I look at all the great expertise that somehow gets burned out or leaves the movement for a while.

Discussing gay/lesbian leadership today, Jean identified a restlessness in American culture generally:

> I think it's the same thing that affects the whole society today. "I want it, and I want it now. I deserve it." What is this anyway? Nobody wants to work for anything. And it would be nice to live in a perfect world, and people would bestow harmony and peace and equality upon everyone. But we don't. This whole society, this world struggles. It's a competitive environment we live in. We can't change that. What we need to attempt to do is deal with it the best we can. And learn how to get ourselves a place at the table. And learn how to

take power that we need to accomplish things. And this is an incremental process. And it is a compromising process.

When I asked O'Leary if one must adopt a pragmatic attitude to succeed in the movement, Jean said she saw herself as both a pragmatist and a visionary. While an unusual combination of traits, I believe both accurately describe her. Asked to describe her greatest personal strength, Jean replied: "I'm strong. I have a very great ego strength. I have a great sense of myself. I love myself. And I'm a very assured person. Like when I go out after something, I don't question myself. I don't question my motives. I don't question success or failure. I go do it. Very strong. Internal strength." That strength may explain her critics' disdain; **Ginny Apuzzo** guardedly shared with me, "Jean made an enormous contribution to the community early on, that we all have to respect. And we do, for the most part. You know, that's about it." **Joan Nestle** in particular mentioned incidents that indicated Jean's ill-suitedness for sainthood. Fortunately, sainthood doesn't seem a status to which she aspires.

O'Leary believes lesbian/gay history primarily will remember her role in instituting the White House meeting, but she would like to be remembered for her several accomplishments over the course of more than twenty-five years of activism. While Jean arguably has sat on the sidelines of the movement for the last few years, I can't envision her staying there for long. Her enthusiasm, her energy, her passion, and her youth convince me that we have not seen the last of Jean O'Leary's good works.

Notes

1. Curiously, even her mother voiced her concerns in 1976: "I worried, and still worry, about the lack of permanency in her relationships. First she'd be with one woman, then another, and in the meantime I would have heard four or five other names. I wondered if she was going to be a playgirl all her life."

2. Those attending the meeting included Pokey Anderson, Charles Brydon, Charlotte Bunch, **Frank Kameny**, Cookie Lutkefedder, Mary Mendola, Elaine Noble, **Troy Perry**, Betty Powell, George Raya, Myra Riddell, and Charlotte Spitzer.

3. I asked Urvashi Vaid to comment on her role in the NGRA experience. She admitted, "In retrospect, I really wish I had processed some of it more with Jean, but I probably still would have cosigned the letter. . . . But having the chance to think about it, I think the first thing I should have done was call Jean right away. And say, 'Jean, I'm gonna do this.'" O'Leary acknowledged that Vaid "called up to apologize to me, two days after I resigned. A lot of good that

does then. You know, I hung up on her." However, she and Vaid put the issue behind them a few years later.

26

CHARLOTTE BUNCH

> **[In 1975, when I said, "It is not OK to be queer under patriarchy, and the last thing we should be aiming to do is to make it OK,"] I was probably even more critical of people just seeking individual success than I am now. But it's hard to separate it sometimes, because how much do you sell out? I mean, we're all in that. You know, I have a nice apartment now, for the first time in my life. Am I sold out? I don't know; I don't think so. But, you know, it's a balance all the time, I think. . . . [A]s long as the getting of one's [possessions] is not at least explicitly at the expense of others. All of it is at the expense of others, since we all "get ours" in a system that creates that. But I think if you don't explicitly do it in a way that is offensive to others, and you continue to give back to the movement in whatever way you choose, to whatever organizations, through whatever methods, and you see that the problem still exists, that may be all you can do.**
>
> —Charlotte Bunch, 1995

As I embarked on my journey to create this book, I realized I would learn many things. One of the people I am particularly glad to have met who I inexplicably left off my original draft list was an extraordinary lesbian-feminist theoretician and activist, perhaps the most balanced fusion of both disciplines the lesbian community has ever produced. **Jean O'Leary** told me I "had" to interview Charlotte Bunch; as so often happens, Jean was right. While Charlotte has lived her life away from the forefront of the lesbian movement for more than a decade, her contribution to the lesbian, women's, and gay communities provided an opportunity for us all to view ourselves and our world differently.

Charlotte Anne Bunch was born in the mountains of North Carolina on Friday, October 13, 1944, the third of four children. Her family (parents, two sisters, and brother) moved to Artesia, New Mexico, when Charlotte was six weeks old, and they were once chosen New Mexico Methodist Family of the Year. What did she experience as a child?

> I didn't have a troubled childhood. I was not an abused child. I had a fairly successful and not difficult situation. I experienced my own family as very supportive of me intellectually, and very much into the life of the mind, and wanting us to be civic-minded and activist in those kinds of ways, so in that sense it was very supportive. . . . In a small town like that, it wasn't hard for me to flourish. . . . My primary thing, when I was a child, was keeping busy. 'Cause I was bored a lot. And so I joined every possible club: I was editor of the newspaper, editor of the yearbook, and then I joined the band even though I'm tone-deaf. [Laughs] I did everything, because it was a small town, and I had a lot of energy. And I didn't yet know where to go with it, except that I was a very public person.

In the meantime, this dutiful daughter obeyed society's rules. Curiously for that time, her femaleness seems never to have hindered her from any activities in which she desired to participate. Bunch acknowledged this to me, adding,

> I think it was an anomaly. I don't know for sure why. . . . It's not that I haven't encountered barriers, but when I encounter barriers, I don't believe the barriers are right. And I do whatever I can to get around them. . . . I think people just found what I did useful, and let me do it, and then it was sort of like, it was an exception: "So she's a woman."

Bunch began attending North Carolina's Duke University in 1962 as a religion major. While at Duke, she involved herself with the University Christian Movement, which she described to me as "sort of the Protestant version of the radical Catholic liberation theology types that were emerging" in the '60s. While an undergraduate, Bunch encountered "campus ministers who were very supportive of, and very involved in, the civil rights movement. They encouraged a lot of us in this Christian social gospel activism mode. And that was the channel through which I made the transition to politics." In *In Our Time*, Susan Brownmiller quoted Charlotte as saying, "My moral fervor went directly into the civil rights movement. My first protest was to hold a pray-in at the segregated Methodist church in Durham." Charlotte became the national organization's first president, but she believes the University Christian Movement ultimately "failed because we were too young; we didn't really know how to pull that off. There were those of us who, in many ways, were becoming more and more political, and less and less Christian, in our identity." That included Charlotte: "Part of my dilemma was that I thought it was an important organization, but I really was no longer very identified in a Christian religious way." Yet she remained "nice": As **Rita Mae Brown**, who figured prominently in her life, wrote of Bunch in her 1997 memoirs, "When I made her acquaintance . . . she was Goody Two-shoes. The years have given her a leavening cynicism but her basic impulse is still to overflow with the milk of human kindness. Initially, I thought this was a pose. It truly is Charlotte."

Bunch's self-acknowledgment of her lesbianism encountered complicating factors, primarily in the personages of her husband of four years and her first female lover. In the spring of 1967 Bunch married Jim Weeks, with whom she had a very respectful, supportive relationship: "I never lived in any of those oppressive modes, in terms of male-female roles." But as a feminist, she found herself working closely and living communally with lesbians, through whom she met the dynamic Rita Mae Brown before Brown achieved renown. A backrub from Rita Mae in the fall of 1970 ("I remember thinking, 'So *this* is how lesbians seduce people!'") led to Charlotte's first lesbian sexual experience. Charlotte addresses the widely held (mis)perception of that encounter:

> I realized that, to the world, [Rita Mae] sort of saw this women's liberation leader, and this Left-y relationship, and came in and seduced me. To introduce me [to lesbianism], and get me into a political alliance, which was a very critical alliance; we did create The Furies together, really. But I was not at all naïve. . . . I couldn't think of a better way to figure out whether I wanted to be a lesbian than to be seduced by Rita Mae and see what it was like.

To pursue a relationship with Brown and to learn to fully experience her nascent lesbianism, Bunch reevaluated her marriage and her commitment to Weeks. During a two- to three-month period, she says, "I had several conversations with him. At one point, I was talking about politically and intellectually why this was an important thing for me to do. And at one point he said, 'Look. If you want to leave me, you have to leave me. Because I'm not gonna give you permission.'" In retrospect, Charlotte believes Jim's approach constituted an extraordinary gift on his part; they remain friends today. Charlotte and Rita Mae's primary relationship lasted six months, but its conclusion hardly surprised or emotionally devastated Bunch: "You have to be stupid if you're seduced by Rita Mae and think that she's gonna stay with you for life, no matter what she says. So I wasn't that stupid; I knew that I was making a decision about a sexual lifestyle, and a political direction."

In February 1971, Bunch and Brown began what they called "the lesbian come-out c-r [consciousness-raising] group," mostly consisting of women in the process of emerging from their closets. Then, that May, Bunch helped create The Furies collective in Washington, D.C. (See **Ginny Berson**.) In *Daring to Be Bad*, Alice Echols neatly summed up the group's crucial historic role. She wrote that while

> The Furies was by far the most famous lesbian-feminist collective, it was perhaps not the most representative group. Other groups were less absolutist and zealous. But they were not nearly as influential as The Furies. . . . [W]hile The Furies failed to persuade most lesbian-feminists that they should form a separate lesbian-feminist movement, they nonetheless set the terms of the debate.

How does Charlotte remember that extraordinary experiment?

> When I look at my whole career now, of thirty years of political activism, it was my most extremist, my most dogmatic, my most separatist, my most sort of vanguardish moment. And I don't believe in those politics as the way to organize. . . . Although I am in no way an extremist in my political method, I have an appreciation for that being done by people. . . . I had my problems with it too, because I also think that if you don't keep a perspective on what you're doing when you do that, it can become very destructive.

Toward the time of The Furies's demise, "When most of the group wanted to ask [Rita Mae] to leave, and did, the rest of us decided that it was simply time to disband the group, that we were no longer functional, that it was cannibalistic, dysfunctional, and better to end it than to keep doing that."

Bunch briefly retreated with then-lover (and fellow Fury) Nancy Myron to process the experience, but she returned to movement work in 1973 by participating in the founding of *Quest: A Feminist Quarterly*, as well as working in the women's liberation movement to effect positive changes for lesbians. Bunch served on the board of NGTF beginning in 1974, organized a lesbian caucus (with Jean O'Leary) for Houston's International Women's Year conference in 1977, discussed anti-gay immigration policies at the 1977 White House meeting of gay leaders during President Jimmy Carter's administration, and spoke at the first March on Washington (D.C.) in 1979. Charlotte received high praise across the board as a fantastic collaborator. Ginny Berson described her as "a real leader, and a real pathfinder;" **Martin Duberman** once wrote, "She is as warm as she is wise;" Jean O'Leary told me, "I was the activist, she was the theorist. I really had so much respect for her. Talk about somebody who could really pull all the sides together." Rita Mae Brown remembered her as "a really good manager of people. . . . I've never met anyone I liked as much, to work with, and indeed loved. I think she's one of the best people the United States has ever produced."

In 1987, Charlotte turned a collection of her essays into *Passionate Politics: Feminist Theory in Action*, a book noteworthy for its intelligent political thought. Since 1990, she has served as director and founder of the Center for Women's Global Leadership at New Jersey's Douglass College, Rutgers University. In August 1995, when I interviewed her in the lovely Manhattan apartment she shares with her partner Roxanna Carrillo, Bunch was organizing caucuses for and planning a global tribunal on women's human rights for the U.N. World Women's Conference held in Beijing, China. In 1996, Charlotte was inducted to the National Women's Hall of Fame, a richly deserved honor.

While never leaving the lesbian movement, and continuously identifying herself as a lesbian since the early '70s, Charlotte addressed her concern that

> I know that some people feel that I've left the lesbian and gay movement because I don't work on the lesbian issue and the lesbian and gay movement as my focus. . . . I actually do view how lesbians and gay men trying to work in the mainstream and take political leadership and remain out, but also work on other issues, as an enormously important development of lesbian and gay life. . . . I feel very much a part of that movement. And I'm not always sure that movement claims me, or people like me, who do this.

If movement leaders discount Charlotte's wisdom and experience, it will discredit the movement rather than the individual. Bunch's quiet strength and dignity stand in sharp contrast to those who insist on screaming at the top of their lungs. Amid the cacophony of voices comprising our movement, the clarity of Charlotte's well-reasoned contributions and her fusion of theory with activism remains unmistakable—and arguably unparalleled.

27

GINNY APUZZO

You know, I'll probably have it put on my tombstone, seriously. Because I believe it. And I wrote the words, and I've said it a hundred times; I've said it in many different arenas. That this isn't a struggle of the lesbian and gay rights bill. This isn't a struggle that will end with the cure —treatment and cure—for AIDS. This isn't a struggle that will end with an antiviolence bill. This is a struggle in which we must be vigilant for as long as ignorance can bully, and as long as justice is frail.

—Virginia Apuzzo, 1995

Charisma: "A rare quality or power attributed to those persons who have demonstrated an exceptional ability for leadership and for securing the devotion of large numbers of people." One cannot buy or sell it; it exceeds or supersedes one's reputation. Almost every gay and lesbian community leader has coveted such a quality, but only a precious few have possessed it. While others have demonstrated it to varying degrees with different constituencies, over the course of the last half of the twentieth century consensus has bestowed it most definitively upon two community leaders, both of whom I was delighted/privileged/honored to interview. **Troy Perry**, a California-transplanted Floridian, through charisma built the largest community organization in the Universal Fellowship of Metropolitan Community Churches, while a Bronx-born woman parlayed charisma into a political career on behalf of the entire movement for more than a quarter-century.

Virginia Marie Apuzzo was born on June 26, 1941, the elder daughter of Adolph Apuzzo and Ivy Owen Apuzzo Jones. While her mother's background melded English, Irish, and possibly other cultures, her father's loving, extended Italian-Catholic family provided her primary cultural influence. Ginny clued into her sexual orientation at about age ten, telling me how she proposed to her best friend:

> I remember standing between flights of stairs with my bicycle—her name was Lucille—and I said, "When we grow up, will you marry me?" And she got very angry at me, and didn't talk to me. And that taught me not to tell another girl that I loved her, for a very long time.

Given the absence of gay role models in the '50s, Apuzzo wondered if her "problem" might be gender confusion, like fellow Bronx resident Christine Jorgensen: "When the newspaper stories came out in the [New York] *Daily News*, it said that she [had] lived on Zerega Avenue. And I used to walk by, because I thought that maybe that's what I was." She movingly recounted to Peter Freiberg in a January 1983 *Advocate* interview, "I remember not knowing there was another one of us in the world. That is a lonely feeling for a child to have." Soon Ginny identified that she didn't want to be a man, but that she did want to love a woman. That experience came in time, but first Ginny absorbed other lessons.

She graduated from a State University of New York college with a major in Afro-Asian studies while engaging in a few short-lived lesbian relationships. At that point, Ginny chose to assess her life's path; instead of picketing and rioting her way to social change, Apuzzo "dropped out" and joined a Catholic convent from 1966 to 1969. While she previously discussed that period of her life with journalists as a "time out," she shared with me that in addition to creating and teaching black studies classes, she "chose to study theology with one question in mind: Is it possible to be a homosexual and be saved? . . . The question for me was, is redemption possible? If the pursuit of the answer of that question had taken ten years, I would have been in the convent for ten years. And if it had taken forty years, I'd still be there." Fortunately, it took Apuzzo only three years to realize

> whatever I have been given in my life as making up who I am, a big piece of that is being a lesbian. . . . So I left, deciding not that it was OK that I could die as a lesbian and go to heaven, but that being a lesbian meant that I would celebrate being a lesbian, and that I would take this gift that I had, and bring it to its logical conclusion, which is liberation.

In *Our Right to Love*, Ginny also related a pivotal self-encounter when she and her lover spoke at a Gay Academic Union conference in the early '70s:

> We were sitting on a stage and I said something about being a lesbian and stopped. There were about 110 men and thirteen women in the audience, and I said, "I want you to know that is the first time I have ever heard myself say, 'I am a lesbian.'" I had a loving partner who helped me articulate and accept what took years to say, and having said it, I dove in in terms of celebrating it.

Along her life's journey, she would enjoy relationships with several high-profile lesbians, including a brief affair with NGTF cochair Lucia Valeska (whose ouster Ginny later called for in a *New York Native* article), and a lengthier relationship with NGTF board member Betty Powell.

Her religious convictions remain important to Ginny today:

> I am a spiritual person. I make no apologies for that, in a community that has certainly suffered, particularly at the hands of the Catholic Church. . . . It's a pivotal part of my life. There is no day that goes by in which I don't thank a higher power for the blessings I have in this life, which are tremendous. There is no time I don't thank that power for the gifts it's given me, which are legion. And there is no time that goes by that I don't ask it what it wants me to do with those gifts.

Before leaving the convent, Apuzzo took a teaching job in the School of Education at Brooklyn College, where she stayed until the mid-'80s. Teaching fit her ebullient personality marvelously, but other opportunities to influence her world simultaneously arose that she could not ignore.

Ginny participated in women's, gay, and Brooklyn politics for several years before she decided to seek a seat in the New York State Assembly (Fifty-Seventh District) in 1978. She spoke with Sasha Gregory-Lewis in a 1977 *Advocate* article about running as an avowed lesbian:

> I always wanted to go into politics to be a public person, and when I realized that . . . I was homosexual, I was heartbroken. When it became apparent to me that . . . someday I could be gay and in politics, I made up my mind that that would be the only obstacle that I would ever have to deal with.

After running a spirited campaign, Apuzzo finished with 15 percent of the vote in the September 12, 1978, four-person Democratic primary. (She was later quoted in Stephen Stewart's *Positive Image* as saying that openly gay candidates at that time faced three substantial obstacles: "We have no role models. Our community doesn't take its own candidates seriously enough. And the media refuse to look beyond our sexuality, as if that's all that mattered to us.") Nevertheless, the attention she attracted by putting her name before the electorate paid off handsomely down the road.

In the meantime, Ginny continued to influence national Democratic politics. In 1976, **Jean O'Leary** and Bruce Voeller, at that time national cochairs of NGTF,

> asked me to run that campaign to get a gay-rights plank from the offices of the National Gay Task Force. . . . Michael Barnes literally threw Jean O'Leary and I out of an open meeting of the Platform Committee! . . . [Jean said] "Let's go get chairs." I said, "Jean, if we leave this room, we're not gonna get back in!" And they *literally* barred the door from letting us get back in!

Little did they know it would take more than a locked door to stop Virginia Apuzzo.

In March 1977 she participated in the meeting of gay activists in the White House,[1] and by June 1980 Apuzzo, now a member of the Platform Committee, ensured that the official Democratic platform include the gay-rights plank. Despite criticism that the plank provided only a watered-down version of what the lesbian and gay community really needed, Apuzzo explained: "I can be pragmatic, if I'm in this arena. Because my goal in that arena is not to do a revolution! My goal in that arena is to get us two miles down the road!" She also described to me the difference at that time between New York and San Francisco gay politics: West Coast activists

> had that San Francisco view of the world, that we can do all things. Well, in 1980, with [President Jimmy] Carter, and Stu Eizenstat, and Joe Duffey—I knew these people! You couldn't do all things with them! They were limited! . . . So, you know, I'm sorry if we disappointed the community in San Francisco. But I was pleased that we were able to move that issue.

By 1984, the plank was strengthened to include opposition to discrimination based on sexual orientation in employment, immigration, and military service. Apuzzo called it a "giant step forward," and she commented, "I think they got the message that the gay and lesbian community would settle for nothing less than specific remedies in the platform. They were not going to get away with euphemisms this time."

While affecting national Democratic politics, she simultaneously redefined national gay and lesbian politics.

In the fall of 1981, the Fund for Human Dignity, NGTF's educational affiliate, appointed Apuzzo executive director; a year later, reeling from lack of effective leadership, NGTF chose Apuzzo as its executive director. For the next two-and-one-half years, Apuzzo served as the primary political leader of the lesbian and gay community. **Urvashi Vaid**, who was then still cutting her teeth in the gay movement, told me that one of Ginny's stump speeches "made me feel like I absolutely *had* to get involved in the gay civil rights movement; that I had a really important contribution to make. And she made it seem so emotional, moving. She's a very powerful speaker, and she connected to my heart." Vaid also wrote in *Virtual Equality* that Apuzzo's "eloquence made her one of the best national spokespersons that the gay movement has ever had." Asked to name her heroes in a 1993 *Advocate* interview, Roberta Achtenberg stated, "I really admire Ginny Apuzzo. She is a fabulous combination of wit and passion and pragmatism. She's tough, but she's also squishy and extremely lovable."

As executive director, Apuzzo decided to "hit the road," bringing the good news of NGTF and organizations around the country to the great expanse between the East and West Coasts:

> I was probably the first executive director who really took the mission of outreach to mainstream across the country seriously, and literally went to a hundred places. I went to every town that I could. I spent weekend after weekend going from one place to another, visiting people and talking. And it was the most remarkable time of my life. And I miss it! I think it's very important to meet people; I think it's very important to reach out; I think it's very important to engage the local communities. They are where this struggle will be won or lost! It will not be won or lost in Washington; it will not be won or lost in New York; and it will not be won or lost in San Francisco. It will be won or lost on Main Street in the million towns across this country.

However, despite her best efforts, the number of members and financial contributions remained relatively static during Apuzzo's years there, and she had difficulty delivering results from her good friend, New York governor Mario Cuomo, for whom she had actively campaigned in his successful 1982 gubernatorial race.

Suddenly, in November 1984, after two years of backbreakingly hard work, she discovered that her cousin, a heroin addict, had contracted AIDS;

> my lover of [approximately four] years announced that she was leaving; and the Sunday after Thanksgiving my father took a stroke. All that happened in one month. And, to me, who believes in grace and listening to what's happening in the world, the higher power and what it says to you, I said, I think it's calling me home to closer watch.

Within four months, she secured a job within the Cuomo administration as deputy director of the New York State Consumer Protection Board, and she resigned her executive directorships. She received generally good marks for her community service: After she announced her resignation, Paul Vandenberg, cochair of NGTF's board, said of her that "she brought credibility back to the National Gay Task Force. It went beyond that to bring credibility to the gay movement across the country. No other person in the history of our movement has had as much exposure as she has had, on the networks, in the gay press and in the straight press." Ginny takes credit for transforming NGTF from "just a lesbian/gay rights organization to, while I was there, *the* premier organization, in terms of the issue of violence against lesbians and gays. The first, and foremost, organization dealing nationally with AIDS." In retrospect, Ginny accepted the criticisms of her performance as an honor, telling me, "I felt that I was criticized because people expected more of me. And I think that's a compliment. If I say to somebody, 'I expected more of you,' then it means I see a great deal in you, and I want more from you!"

Apuzzo also talked about the challenge of leadership in the gay community:

> Leadership is something you have, or you develop. And then, you've got to be willing to walk out in front, and make mistakes! . . . You work hard; you do the best you can; then you stand up in front of these people and you say, "You know what? I fucked up. And I'm sorry." And then they look back at you and they say, "We love you; we know you tried." But if you say, "I didn't make any mistakes! Me? I'm perfect," then they look at you and say, "Drop dead! We're still struggling!" . . . The struggle will shape you; the fire will shape you. And it will magnify what is in you that has the potential to do good. And it will also magnify your deficiencies. . . . It's the nature of being out in front.

Curiously, in a 1992 *Advocate* article, Larry Kramer spoke of Ginny as "one of the best speakers I ever heard and one of the smartest political minds in terms of knowing how to play and call the system. But she didn't have the human touch." If true, she fooled me: I found her warm and witty, gracious and generous, and still able to call a spade a shovel when circumstances warrant.

After several years in state government in New York, she landed a position with the Civil Service Commission. For a woman who suffered for many years with a serious case of "Potomac fever," Ginny's civil service made her realize when she spoke with me in 1995 at her home in upstate New York that

> in the ten years I've been in state government, I've been able to do more than if I'd won in 1978, and been in the Assembly all this time! What have I done? I've been a confidante of a governor who sat there for the last ten years. I am now the highest-ranking Democrat in a Republican administration, dealing with personnel. I am the *highest*-ranking Democrat in the executive branch of New York state government today. The one they didn't want to give the job to. [Laughs] . . . I deal with labor issues; I deal with merit and fitness; I deal with things like domestic partners. The last thing I did, in my job, was to get the sign-off from the governor and the director of the budget in the Cuomo administration, and the comptroller, to get domestic partners solidified, so that [Gov. George] Pataki couldn't come in and undermine that. So, if I'd been sittin' in the Assembly, could I have done that? . . . I didn't run in 1986 because if I had won, I would have been one voice of many.

However, Apuzzo also offered, "Now, will I ever run for political office again? One thing that **Barney Frank** will tell you, and anybody else you talk to who's a politician, never say never."

By the end of 1996, Apuzzo became an associate deputy secretary at the U.S. Department of Labor; on October 1, 1997, the White House appointed Apuzzo to serve as President Bill Clinton's assistant for management and administration, becoming the highest ranking openly gay or lesbian government official in American history. Ginny finally "cured" her lifelong "Potomac fever," albeit by a circuitous route. However, late in the spring of 1999, Apuzzo resigned her White House position (where one of her duties was oversight of its intern program), and she planned to return to NGLTF in September to assume the Virginia Apuzzo Chair for Leadership in Public Policy at the Policy Institute.

Ginny also takes current lesbian and gay leaders to task for failing to articulate a vision around which the community can unite. In Dennis Altman's 1982 *The Homosexualization of America, the Americanization of the Homosexual*, Apuzzo said,

> After ten years there is an unbecoming amount of evidence that we have not found an agenda, that we have not forged tools to get us an

> agenda, and that we are in danger of failing in our commitment to our own community as well as to all others with an investment in our participation in social change. . . . What we lack is the willingness within our movement to assess, to evaluate, and to demand accountability.

More than a decade later, the issue still lay on her heart, as she told me,

> The politics part of our community is a very complex series of competing and conflicting voices that tend to almost be like a web. . . . And there is a real need to go beyond that, and to look to questions of vision. Questions of strategy. And I think we need to ask those questions of people who put themselves in the positions like that. . . . I think those are important questions. It's absent. And I think it needs to be articulated.

Yet she undoubtedly loves the lesbian and gay community, proudly remarking in a 1985 *Advocate* interview, "I never stop marveling at the beauty and courage and generosity that is this community." In a 1994 speech in Dallas, she reiterated,

> Let [history] say of us that we loved one another fully, fiercely, and deeply and that we fought to save each of our lives, and we treasured those lives. Let it say of us that we built a community that would live on after us to care for and teach and learn from our young people. Let it say of us that we cherished our time together and that our work was a hymn to life.

When I asked Ginny what people didn't know about her that she wished they did, her answer charmed me: "They probably don't know that I really just want to be in musical comedy. [Laughs] I really would. I feel like I've missed my vocation as a musician, and musical comedy person, somewhere along the line." While I'm certain she would have done it very well (it's hard to imagine Apuzzo *not* doing something well!), her continued contribution to this movement is greater than any role she could play under a proscenium arch. Better yet, it's the real thing.

Note

1. In *Virtual Equality*, Urvashi Vaid quoted Ginny as speaking of the experience: "Access! It's wonderful. I remember the first time I went to the White House. Loved it! I was so excited. You know what? It's another house. It's a

nice place to send postcards from. But if you don't go in and come out with more than coffee under your belt you've got a problem."

28

ALLAN SPEAR

I didn't want to live a lie, I wanted people to know who I was. I didn't want to worry about who knew and how I should relate to this one or that one. This one may know, and that one may not. I didn't want all that. What I worried about most was that I would be typecast; I would be viewed simply as a gay man and nothing else. That was not all I saw myself as being. I never wanted to be, and never have been, a full-time professional gay person. I never had much interest in national gay politics or wanted to work for a gay organization. I had a whole lot of other things that I wanted to do with my life. I wanted to be open as gay, but I didn't want that to be all anybody ever thought of me as being. I wanted to be able to have positions and be taken seriously on a whole range of issues, and do a lot of things that didn't have anything to do with gay rights. So, I was afraid that coming out as gay would be so spectacular that it would overshadow everything else.

—Allan Spear, interview with Scott Paulsen, 1993

Unless you live in Minnesota or really know your national politics, you probably wouldn't recognize Allan Spear if he passed you on the street. You probably wouldn't know that this unassuming man held one of the highest elected political offices by an openly gay person in the United States, and that his sexual orientation proved no barrier to his political career. Spear arguably embodies the American Dream: Work hard, do your job well, add a bit of luck, and enjoy your success.

Allan Henry Spear was born on June 24, 1937, in Michigan City, Indiana, the older of two boys. Spear recognized his homosexual orientation around 1950, when Mattachine began taking its first tentative steps toward sunlight, although sexual activity for Allan did not follow until several years later. Spear told me,

> I hardly knew the name for what I was. And when I did first realize what it was, and I started going to the library to look it up, I was horrified by what I found. Because it was always in books about sexual pathology, and homosexuality was viewed as one of those deep, dark sexual perversities. And so—God, I didn't want to be that! . . . It would have been nice not to have had a young adulthood that was almost barren of sexual and romantic experiences.

Following his graduation from high school, Spear attended Northwestern University for a year before enrolling at Ohio's Oberlin College in 1955 (where he gave the commencement speech in 1997). As Spear told me,

> Oberlin is a place that long had a very strong civil rights tradition. I went to Oberlin, and I probably was already kind of ready for it, but Oberlin really kind of influenced me on that. . . . Oberlin had a program, a one semester exchange, where three, four Oberlin students would go spend a semester at a black college in the south, and then a couple of students from those colleges would come up to Oberlin. . . . Why did I choose to do it? I was already obviously interested enough to want to do that. . . . This was right after the 1954 Supreme Court decision, which I thought was wonderful. And there were no sit-ins yet, but the Montgomery [Alabama] bus boycott had happened, and I followed all that with great interest. So I decided to go. . . . I spent the second semester of my junior [year] at Fisk in Nashville. And so lived in an all-black environment in the Jim Crow South. I had all kinds of experiences, as you can imagine, in terms of trying to test the color line. I traveled with black friends into Georgia, and we tried to test the color line and all kinds of stuff. And it was great excitement and adventure for a nineteen-year-old kid, believe me.

Allan would not make the connection linking his interest in Negro civil rights with his own oppression as a Jew and as a homosexual until later in his life. After graduating from Oberlin with a B.A., Spear studied at Yale University, earning a masters and completing a Ph.D. in 1965. His doctoral thesis became his only book, *Black Chicago: The Making of a Negro Ghetto, 1890-1920*, published in 1967. Also while at Yale, Spear saw a psychiatrist who he hoped would "cure" his homosexuality. The good doctor told Allan that his real problem was his inability to relate to women; if only he would let down his guard with women, his homosexual fantasies would disappear. In Spear's words, "They didn't, of course."

In 1964, Spear moved to Minneapolis to teach history at the University of Minnesota, assuming his career lay in teaching. As fate dictated, he was no more prescient about the tumultuous '60s than anyone else. His liberalism and sympathy for the underdog caused Spear to champion a variety of causes on the U. Minn. campus in the mid- to late-'60s, including prison reform, anti-Vietnam War efforts, and his organizing of Black Panther Party support groups in Minneapolis.

In 1968, after a few years away from the Democratic Party to explore some far-left political options, fellow supporters of liberal Democrat Eugene McCarthy encouraged Spear to run for the Minnesota legislature. He recalls, "I got the [Democratic] Party endorsement, because the McCarthy people had taken over the local party, but I then lost in the general election, and probably deserved to lose—I wasn't really ready. It was too quick, too sudden. But then I stayed in Democratic Party politics between '68 and '72." By June 1972, Minnesota's redistricting plan "put the University community together in a single district, and it was a *very* liberal district. . . . A lot of students, a lot of faculty people, you know. And so it looked like a winnable district for me." While no incumbent held that seat, the November election beckoned little more than four months away. His quick declaration for that seat was the first (but not the last) example about which Spear told me, "I think that in each of the major turning points in my political career, what saved me was my ability to make a decision quickly, and not hem and haw too much about it." Within two weeks, Spear secured the Democratic endorsement for the state senate seat. Allan believes his opponent in the general election, liberal Republican John Cairns, knew Allan was gay, but the fair-minded Cairns chose not to use that information against Spear. (Allen joked, "I'm one of the few Democrats in the United States who got elected on George McGovern's coattails.")

Once elected to the Minnesota State Senate, there remained the matter of how and when to disclose his sexual orientation. He began inching his way out of the closet in 1972 with help from local gay activists such as Jack Baker and Steve Endean. Spear told Paulsen:

> The most difficulty I had was coming out at the age of thirty-five and learning how to establish relationships. One of my friends later told me [that it appeared to him as though I] was almost going through adolescence again. . . . I had [more] trouble coming to terms with the issue of establishing, learning how to have and develop interpersonal relationships, than I did with the public aspect of it.

Spear even served as the principal speaker at Minneapolis Gay Pride in June 1974, but his turning point came when voters elected Elaine Noble to the Massachusetts House of Representatives that November, the first open lesbian to win statewide office. Spear publicly came out on December 9, 1974, in a front-page article in the *Minneapolis Star*, Minnesota's largest newspaper. Admitting that Noble's victory made him feel a little less lonely, the timing made Spear the first openly gay person to serve a state constituency.

Fortunately for Spear, his disclosure did not negatively impact his district's voters, although his visibility made him a luminary in gay circles. As Spear recalled to me,

> I became an instant celebrity in the gay community when I came out. . . . I was a front page story in *The Advocate*, and I was instantly deluged with invitations. I went to Ann Arbor [Michigan] in January [1975, to speak with Noble]; I went to [New York gay activist Howard Brown's] memorial service, I think in February; in June of that year I was the keynote speaker at the Los Angeles Gay Pride; and all these things blew my mind a little bit. . . . I looked down Hollywood Boulevard—it's just packed, jammed on both sides with people, and there I am, waving to the crowd—"Oh, my God, what am I doing here?"

However, Spear accurately identified the constituency who elected him to do a job for them, and it wasn't the gay community:

> After a few months of this, it died down a little bit. But I also realized that I had to balance it off. So I kind of toned it down a little bit after those first few months, and did a little bit less, especially as my reelection was coming closer in '76. It was the first time I was going to run as an openly gay person, and I knew I could not be seen simply as a gay celebrity. So I tempered it, I stopped doing quite so much of it. But the first year was kind of heady.

As it turned out, once voters easily reelected the now openly gay Spear in 1976, no opponent in his district could effectively use his homosexuality against him.

Another firestorm in which Spear involved himself was the referendum to repeal St. Paul's gay rights protections following Anita Bryant's victory in Dade County (Miami), Florida, in 1977. Anita and her allies won consecutive victories in the spring of 1978 in St. Paul, Wichita (Kansas), and Eugene (Oregon) until fair-minded voters halted the momentum in Seattle (Washington) and statewide in California that November. Bryant hardly impressed Spear, who told Paulsen, "She just became a symbol of our opposition. She was also not very smart. She said things that were really ignorant and stupid, so she really became a symbol of the know-nothingness we were up against." It didn't help that the gay community in the Twin Cities experienced considerable internecine warfare when Jack Baker's outrageous political antics divided the moderates from the radicals, providing a dis-united gay front. Spear had recently suffered a painful loss on a Twin Cities gay rights bill in 1977, about which *Out for Good* painted a vivid picture:

> Standing on the Senate floor afterward, a bitter Allan Spear denounced the vote as a victory for "bigots." The bill had been killed, he said, by "a campaign of vilification led by people who call themselves Christians." A mild, owlish man, an academic by profession, Spear was barely in control of his emotions, and when he had finished speaking, Steve Endean led him from the chamber into a private room, where he broke down and wept.

In its wake, Spear described the St. Paul loss as "just really heartbreaking."

Spear's next political milestone came in 1982. Ten years earlier, redistricting had created a seat tailor-made for him; this time, it blew that district to bits:

> [In] '82, we had to run again, even though it's just a two-year term, because of redistricting. And this time my district got splintered badly. The city was losing population—we were down from eight to six districts in the city. My district was divided up. I had no place to run except against another Democratic incumbent if I had stayed over there, so what was I going to do? And I thought for a while, "OK, I've been in ten years, and my district's gone. It's time to quit and go back to being a history professor." I thought that for about a week. And then, of course, people [were] saying, "Oh no, no, no." I remembered [gay legislative colleague] Karen Clark was one who just came to me and said, "It's not an option. . . . There are lots of people around here that we can do without, but you're not one of them." . . . So there's this district over here on the other side of town from where I lived then. The incumbent Democrat announced that he was not running for reelection, so here was an empty seat over here. Now, do I move across town, become a carpetbagger, and try to run in this district? . . . This is a more affluent district than the one over by the university. There's a lot of so-called limousine liberals over here. . . . So anyway, this was the second time when I think being able to make a decision quick helped me.

Spear moved across town, dissuaded all Democratic opposition, and handily defeated his Republican challenger by more than twenty points. But the situation created some anxiety for Spear; he described as one of the most traumatic days of his life "the day that the new district maps came out in 1982, and I went and looked at that map, and I don't have a district any more."

Later that same year, Allan met the person he calls "the great love of my life." He had dated other men before, but Junjiro ("Jun") Tsuji became Spear's first long-term live-in relationship. The two men met through a friend of Allan's (then Jun's recent ex-lover). A dinner party for three soon turned into a tête-à-tête for two. Jun owns and manages a very successful hair salon at the other end of town from their home. When I visited their lovely home in Minneapolis, Allan and Jun put me up for two nights, and I saw their relationship as very caring and sweet, as one would hope a longstanding relationship would be.

After twenty years in the state senate, Spear set his sights on obtaining the presidency of the Minnesota Senate. The incumbent president was leaving the senate; while Spear's closest competitor for the seat had two years' seniority on him, Allan's colleagues considered his opponent's extreme conservatism and homophobia outré for a Minnesota Democrat. (Some also perceived Spear's opponent could not handle the job.) In the Minnesota Senate, members of the majority caucus (in this case, forty-five Democrats) vote among themselves, and the entire senate in effect rubber-stamps the caucus's choice. Spear, as usual, did his homework, counted the votes ("One thing you learn in politics; 'Maybe' means 'No,' and 'I haven't decided yet' means 'I'm not going to support you'"), and garnered a 25-20 victory on January 5, 1993. Spear explained that his role as senate president made him the chief presiding officer, "and I make the parliamentary decisions, and I do have some power in that, but I'm not the most powerful person in the senate by any means. . . . Being president is not so much power, [but] it's very high visibility. It's a very visible position, because you're up there presiding all the time." While the general senate still had to confirm Spear's presidency every two years, Spear correctly anticipated that he would retain that post for the balance of his political life. When I met with Spear in the summer of 1995, he was debating whether to run for one more four-year senate term in 1996. He told me,

> There's no doubt that if I run next year, that will be my last term. Because by the time I finish that, I'll be sixty-three years old. And very frankly, I'm going to be ready to retire. I'm not a person who wants to work until I'm seventy-five. . . . I'm ready to kind of gracefully phase out into the golden years, or the sunset years, or whatever you want to call them.

(Indeed, Spear ran and won in 1996, and he did not seek reelection in 2000.)

Despite his success, even Spear found himself sometimes deflecting unwarranted criticism. In *Trailblazers* he noted,

> There are people in the gay community who disapprove of the kind of [role] model that I have been, saying that I am an assimilationist—that although I'm out as a gay man, I have not sufficiently emphasized my gayness, and that I'm too mainstream. If other people want to develop different models, I don't have any problems with that. This is who I am. I am not comfortable in the role of the flaming queen or the flamboyant homosexual that some, including a few elected officials with different personalities, have chosen to play.

Yet he also points out, "The major part I've played in changing public opinion is being accepted to the point where my gayness now is almost a secondary part of my life and career."

In addition to Spear's longevity in office as an openly gay man, he avoided any taint of scandal in over two decades of political service, unlike so many of his peers. While Allan acknowledged smoking an occasional joint ("everybody did that a little bit in the '60s") and a few random encounters with other men ("Sure, after I came out in '72, I started going to the bars, and a little bit to the baths. I occasionally would run into somebody, you know, and went home with somebody"), he never exercised egregious judgment: "I certainly didn't pick up underage hustlers. . . . It wasn't a matter of not being caught. I just didn't do it."

In a July 2000 *Advocate* article, while admitting surprise at the lack of speed of forwarding gay issues ("I certainly anticipated that progress would have come more quickly. I certainly did not expect that it would take twenty years to pass basic human rights protections in Minnesota"), he added that passage of an amendment that included gay people in the state's human rights law in 1993 remained his "proudest legislative achievement."

Not just a successful politician, Spear truly seemed happy and contented when I met with him. In politics, few people rise to the top who remain "good guys," but Spear did so. I hope the citizens of Minnesota realize how valuable a treasure he is, and they continue treating him with the respect he has earned. Unlike so many tales in this book (and in life), it is nice to have one that ends with the phrase, "and they all lived happily ever after."

29

CLEVE JONES

Randy [Shilts] and I, I hate to say it, are a lot alike. We are both egotistical. We both need to prove. We are both members of this little club of gay white men of middle-class backgrounds who believed that we could stop the epidemic. Randy believed that his journalism, his investigations, his reporting, would expose misdeeds and the stupidity of the government. And Larry Kramer believed that his play would outrage people. Martin Delaney believed that he would find a cure. Cleve Jones believed that the Quilt would bring the walls of Jericho down. And we all failed.

—Cleve Jones, 1995

Most of the people about whom I've written are considerably older than I. Not that there's anything wrong with that; I like older people. (Besides, I'm getting older every day!) Fortunately, I grew up in a family that viewed age as accumulated wisdom. But in the early stages of putting this book together, I often wished to speak with one of my contemporaries about his or her experiences that might more closely reflect my own. In January 1995, that wish came true when I spoke with Cleve Jones. In his relatively short lifetime, he has seen and experienced more about gay liberation than most people his age, myself included. I wondered what had become of Cleve Jones, at that time out of the limelight for several years. He did not disappoint me. Cleve and I sat for a long interview at his home on the Russian River only two weeks after torrential rains flooded the entire area; while the flooding damaged the house across the street, it did not reach his home. I found it a fitting metaphor; while the storm surrounds him, somehow Cleve generally manages to keep one step ahead of impending disaster.

Cleve Edward Jones was born on October 11, 1954, in West Lafayette, Indiana. His only sibling, Elizabeth, followed eight years later. Cleve identified his sexuality rather early in his life; he spoke to me of a group of friends in Pittsburgh, Pennsylvania with whom he used to masturbate during puberty. But there came a time when joy turned to fear. As Cleve wrote in his 2000 memoir, *Stitching a Revolution*,

> One night we were camping out and somebody said, "Let's jack off," and I was thinking, *Yeah, let's.* Then somebody said, "No, we can't do that anymore, we're too old. If you keep doing it that means you're queer." I remember, as if it were yesterday, feeling a terrible chill, a clenching in my gut, my throat tightening. *That's it,* I realized with dread. *I am one of those. That's the problem. I'm a queer.*

While he enjoyed the same-sex encounters, being the class sissy proved painful; Cleve also shared with me about the young man, Carl Ketchum, who beat him up on his first day of junior high school (Buddy Whiting and Sean Bogan performed the same function for me):

> This guy tormented me. He was the first person to call me a fag. He beat me up over and over and over. And when we moved away from Pittsburgh in 1968, as we pulled out, I remember thinking, "I will never come back here; I will never see these people again." Years went by, and so much of what I am is because of Carl Ketchum.

Scottsdale (Arizona) High School was worse; Cleve recounted to Randy Shilts how other students used him for a punching bag and dunked his head into toilets before he transferred to Phoenix Country Day School, a private institution.

Cleve's parents, Austin and Marion, seemed helpless in the face of such brutality: "My mother told me that once they even bought me a toy gun for Christmas. And she used to buy me bulkier clothes to make me look bigger, because she just didn't know what to do." The only benefit to this brutality became Cleve's early self-identification of his sexual orientation: "I think when I was about fourteen, I put it all together and I knew I was a homosexual."

Only a few years later, given an opportunity to speak about being gay before a class, the painfully shy Jones discovered to his surprise how much he loved public speaking. Shortly thereafter, he signed up to speak before a psychology class at Arizona State University, where Cleve's father chaired the psychology department. (Marion worked as a choreographer.) That was how Cleve's parents discovered his homosexuality at age seventeen. "And he freaked, and my mom freaked. . . . I could not ever imagine that they did not already know. Because I'd been called a faggot by everybody for so many years, I just assumed that everybody knew." While Cleve's parents asked him to leave home, he defends their position at that time: "You have to remember the context here. I'm talking '72, and I had grown my hair very long, and I was taking LSD. It wasn't just that I was a homosexual. I subscribed to all sorts of revolutionary ideals. And so they just freaked." Cleve stressed that all of those fences have been long mended; his parents are now his best friends, as well as fellow AIDS activists.

After a year's study at ASU, Jones moved to San Francisco in 1972. In the KQED documentary *The Castro*, Jones recalled how the City's magic transformed his world:

> This was a different planet. Everything about San Francisco was different. From the glitter in the sidewalks to the way the fog rolled in, to the fact that you could see other people on the street that you knew were gay. I immediately fell in love with a man, and I knew something was different. And that really was the beginning of a real, major change in my life.

His internal liberation expanded as he marched in the Gay Freedom Day Parade that year, realizing a personal goal of his for several years. He began spending time in the Castro Street area, then a rising gay/countercultural community, partaking of all the delights available, including drugs, alcohol, and sex: "I still think of myself as a sexual liberationist. It's that being part of the core of our movement was sort of this hippie, antiwar movement leftover thing. We were very counterculture. We were very much into shock value and pushing the limits." Cleve also waxed nostalgic in *The Castro*:

> There was an innocence about it—a naïveté, really—about the whole thing, that I think gets lost now. People talk about the bathhouses and the sex clubs, and things like that, and it all sounds very tawdry and jaded. But I don't remember it that way. I remember it as being terribly exciting, terribly romantic, and very much about the individual exploration and liberation that was occurring in our lives.

In 1973, Jones wandered into Castro Camera, owned by Harvey Milk. Meeting Milk transformed Jones's activism, and gave him an effective platform for the rest of his life.

> He gave me access to power. You know, if I wanted to make something happen now, I had this ally who could really pull strings and push buttons for me. It was exhilarating to be around him, because he was so unapologetic, and so caught up in the wonder and the romance of what we were doing. And this is gone; it does not exist any more, at all. But we were new. . . . I was so proud that he liked me. And I just—I'm still—I miss him. You know, I still think about him, even though I didn't know him for that long a period of time. But he really touched people.

Along with his parents and longtime activists **Del Martin** and **Phyllis Lyon**, Jones cited Harvey as the most influential person in his life.[1] Harvey quickly recognized Cleve's talents, and he groomed him into an effective mover and shaker in San Francisco's gay community.

After San Francisco voters elected Milk to the Board of Supervisors in 1977, Jones became one of Harvey's supervisorial aides. Equally at home in front of the camera or behind the scenes, Cleve became one of the most effective activists in contemporary U.S. gay history. Historian **John D'Emilio** wrote of Jones in *Making Trouble*,

> I was impressed by a very special quality that Cleve had. He knew how to reach people *exactly* where they were, and move them forward. He did this in conversation on a one-to-one level, but he could also do this with large groups, even a whole community. Cleve could take the frustration, or the despair, or the cynicism of a group, reach inside, and turn it into positive, constructive, committed energy directed toward liberation work.

Harry Britt lovingly referred to Jones as "the Media Queen." Be that as it may, Cleve actively participated during San Francisco's heyday of gay visibility in 1977 and 1978.

Cleve credits Anita Bryant as

> definitely responsible for me being an activist. I'd always been interested in politics, but you know, I was a horny little kid at that point, and all I was really doing was going to the bars and dancing every night. I was leading a very hedonistic, sort of gay hippie experience. It was pretty exciting and very different from today. It was still very romantic then. . . . I got involved in what I think was my first real serious project, which was I organized the very first conference in California to deal with this new threat [against California's gay public school teachers], and it was before [then-State Senator John] Briggs had qualified for the ballot or even started circulating petitions. And so I organized a student conference from San Francisco State University, and we had representatives from twenty-two California campuses, which was a big deal in those days, and we began laying the

> groundwork for the campaign. . . . And so I never met [Bryant], but she propelled me into activism.

After Briggs's petition qualified for statewide consideration, the "No On 6" campaign began in earnest. Cleve helped start the first San Francisco group, Bay Area Committee against the Briggs Initiative (BACABI), to respond to Briggs's threat; ultimately members of the Socialist Party dominated BACABI, and another group, San Franciscans against Proposition 6, took the middle ground. Cleve recognized the gravity of the Briggs initiative:

> Prop 6 was terribly important because, for the first time, we had something that all of us could agree on. You didn't have to be a leftist, you didn't have to be a right-winger, you didn't have to be a woman, you didn't have to be a man, you didn't have to be a Democrat or Republican—this was a terrible attack against all of us that we thought we would lose, that would have devastating impact, that our people would be fired, would be dismissed, would be jailed. And so I think that that was an incredible turning point. And in San Francisco, you can sort of see it as an example of what happened statewide. We'd had these little Democratic clubs, but suddenly we had a focus—we had this huge surge of people coming out of the closet, and deciding to be visible and take political action.

That action resulted in Proposition 6's statewide defeat in November 1978. The crucial victory stopped the juggernaut, coming on the heels of antigay initiative successes in the previous two years in Dade County, Florida; St. Paul, Minnesota; Wichita, Kansas; and Eugene, Oregon. San Francisco's triumph, combined with the simultaneous successful effort in Seattle, Washington, slew the antigay dragon for the time being. The outcome both pleased and surprised Jones:

> We never thought we'd win. Ever. . . . We were sure we would lose, because it seemed to go right to the heart of the straight world's fear of us, as sexually aggressive child molesters. . . . The campaign was very exciting because we, of course, knew we would lose, and so we thought, well, we will use this as an education, and we will go door-to-door, and we will mobilize a classic, grass-roots campaign. And we'll lose, of course, and then we'll have a big riot, but we'll educate people in the meantime, and for the first time, we'll have a real discussion of this issue. . . . Instead, what we'd found was that we'd created this rather potent political machine.

The time for rioting came soon thereafter, when anger exploded into rage.

The luster of the Prop 6 win soon faded in the wake of the Jonestown (Guyana) massacre in mid-November, followed just two weeks later by former San Francisco supervisor Dan White's assassination of Harvey Milk and George Moscone. Cleve had been working at City Hall earlier that morning before returning home to retrieve some information. On his way back to City Hall, Jones heard only that Mayor Moscone had been shot. Harvey had given Cleve a key to the back door to the supervisors' offices; Cleve used it that morning because "there were cops everywhere." Jones opened the back door,

> and went in and looked down the hallway, and I saw [Milk's] feet sticking out of the door of Dan White's office. I knew it was him because he had these big old clunky wingtips with a hole in the bottom. . . . And the blood everywhere. I had never seen a dead body before; it was pretty horrifying. There was a cop there, and he moved the body and the head—I just felt so ripped off. Because Harvey was "Daddy" for me, you know. He was one of the few people in my life who was older and more experienced.

Even though numbed by shock, Jones organized the "semi-spontaneous, secretly-organized-by-me-behind-the-scenes" march and candlelight vigil that evening; although only seventeen, and not "out," I will never forget the outpouring of love and grief as thousands upon thousands crowded the City's streets, walking silently in remembrance of two men dead at the hands of a self-righteous, tortured colleague.

The Dan White jury compounded Cleve's loss six months later when it returned a verdict of voluntary manslaughter. What does Cleve remember of the White Night Riots that followed that evening?

> I was down there at the very beginning. I led the march down to City Hall. And ran ahead and got there, and was on the steps. But as the crowd came in, the police freaked. They charged up to put a line up in front of the doors. And in doing so, they knocked over the generator [for the sound system] and ripped up the wires that led to the podium. And that terrified me—I mean, they didn't do it deliberately, just in their haste—because I realized we didn't have a sound system. And I took a bullhorn and spoke to the crowd through the bullhorn. Then I jumped down trying to get the generator going again, and could not get back on the steps. Then the struggling began. Harry [Britt] spoke; [Supervisor] Carol [Ruth Silver] spoke. [Activist] Amber Hollibaugh spoke; she said, "I think we ought to do this more often!" Harry was insipid; Carol was insipid; I was insipid, but nobody even heard what I said.

I asked Jones about that night's violent reaction, one of the few times the gay/lesbian community collectively has responded with violence (Stonewall in 1969 and California governor Pete Wilson's veto of AB-1 in 1991 are the other noteworthy instances to date). He said, "I think the potential for violence is still there, but I think most of us feel more powerful. I rarely feel the sort of personal rage that would lead me to break a window or burn a police car."

In 1980, Jones became the first openly gay legislative aide in the country, working for Leo McCarthy, speaker of the California State Assembly. By 1981, Jones joined San Francisco assemblyman Art Agnos's team as an administrative assistant, and he worked on gay civil rights legislation. A bright political future lay ahead of him. But Jones's next great battle came against AIDS/HIV. Despite the tantalizing possibilities, Cleve wrote in *Stitching a Revolution*, "I didn't want to leave Castro Street. Castro was my home, its natives my people. And now there was something wrong. We didn't know exactly what it was, when we could stop it, or even how we'd survive. But I had no other choice."

Cleve was among the first gay leaders in San Francisco to acknowledge the gravity of the situation, in response to a meeting with dermatologist Marcus Conant in January 1982:

> He believed that [AIDS] would prove to be a virus similar to hepatitis in form, and sexually transmitted, and fatal. And perhaps a new virus. And that we had to educate the community. And I was—I knew immediately—that dinner—I knew I was infected, I knew it! It was like, bam, right in the fucking forehead; you're going to die, everybody you care about is going to die. I just saw it exactly, what was going to happen. I remember leaving there, walking down Market Street and thinking, "Millions of people are going to die, and this will become the calamity of my generation."

An August 1983 *Newsweek* article quoted Jones as saying, "The AIDS epidemic is clearly an appalling disaster to our people. As a sexually transmitted disease . . . this epidemic is forcing us to reevaluate how we live and how we love. There are a whole lot of us who are frightened by that."

Despite his fear, Cleve chose to enter the fray. Agnos's office financially backed Cleve as he founded and directed the Kaposi's Sarcoma Research and Education Foundation (later becoming the San Francisco AIDS Foundation) before AIDS even had a name. What did one say then to people who called requesting information?

> We told them that we thought it was sexually transmitted, that hepatitis was probably a good model, and that we didn't know how to treat it. And the main efforts during those first years [were] simply to find physicians who were willing to care for these people, who

> weren't homophobic or afraid to touch somebody like that. And then as more and more people got seriously ill and died, creating the systems to care for them. . . . I would have volunteers for during the day, and then in the evening, physicians and nurses would come in and call these people back, and at least track them and hold their hand. There wasn't much more that we could do then. . . . That time was before we had the antibody test, and before the virus was identified. People just can't imagine the level of terror and confusion that existed then. And that was the period where I was spit at, and called a fascist. And people looked at ionizers in the bars, and wondered if that was the cause, you know? It was just terrifying.

Cleve voluntarily left the KS Foundation about a year after he established it. "I'm a dingbat, OK? Then I was a *total* dingbat. I had no interest in running an agency. . . . They needed an administrator, and it needed to be yuppified, it needed to be professionalized. And that's not me." Perhaps that ambivalence explained **José Sarria**'s comment to me regarding Cleve: "I think that he was not honest. I just don't believe him. . . . I think he benefited Cleve Jones rather than the idea. I may be way off base on that, but maybe I'm not." Jones also describes himself as "often crippled with self-doubt. I'm a lazy, disorganized person, and I'm often unclear of my own motives. *But*, every now and then, I just see something really clearly, and I know what to do." Within a few years, Cleve's vision transformed AIDS awareness among straights and gays alike.

In 1985, after Cleve received his HIV-positive diagnosis, he took an eight-month hiatus to Hawaii, where he acknowledged his alcohol dependency. On November 27 of that year, seven years to the day after the Milk-Moscone assassinations, Cleve planned to memorialize the event for the eighth consecutive year when suddenly,

> I picked up a copy of the [San Francisco] *Chronicle*, and it had a headline that a thousand San Franciscans had died of AIDS. I was just struck by the fact that, of those thousand, the vast majority had lived and died within a ten-block radius of where I was standing [at Castro and Market Streets], and there was no evidence. And I said to my friend Joseph [Durant], "You know, if this was a field with a thousand corpses lying in the sun, then people would look at it and they would understand. And if they were human beings, they would be compelled to respond." But there was no such evidence, and there was no such response. And I got really obsessive about this idea of evidence, because I knew I was standing there in the middle of this tragedy that was hidden behind these Victorian façades and cafés and bars and boutiques.

> So on the twenty-seventh, Joseph and I had a big stack of cardboard and these black magic markers. People showed up, and we asked them to write down the name of one person they knew who had died of AIDS. . . . We climbed up on these ladders with big rolls of tape, and covered the whole façade [of the U.N. Building] with these placards. I was looking at this patchwork, and I watched the crowd, and it was very weird, 'cause it was cold, and it was raining. Many people realized that they had an ex-roommate's name up there somewhere. I was just really struck by this almost palpable yearning that I could sense in the crowd, of people wanting to find a way not only to grieve and to remember, but also to try to communicate to the rest of the world what was happening! . . . And I thought of making something like a quilt. And I was immediately flooded with memories of my grandmother and my great-grandmother, and the quilt that my great-grandmother made in 1952, two years before I was born—a warm, comforting, nonthreatening, middle-class, middle-American sort of symbol. That was the idea.

Cleve made the first 3' x 6' panel in his backyard in February 1987 to honor his friend Marvin Feldman, who died of AIDS on October 10, 1986. From that humble beginning, the Quilt has grown and grown, and has been visited by more than twelve million people. In *Stitching a Revolution*, Cleve wrote,

> We had no idea the Quilt would last beyond that day. I was looking for a symbol to focus the nation on the epidemic at a time when many of us had lost hope. I hoped it could be a tool for healing families divided by homophobia and believed it might unite the nation against the plague. But I saw it mainly as evidence, as mediagenic proof of the enormity of the crisis killing thousands.

However, not everyone immediately embraced the concept: In *After Stonewall*, **Robin Tyler** mused, "At the 1987 March, people would bring their ideas, and they'd want to get it sponsored by the March. It was about a quilt, some kind of quilt they wanted to bring. Quilting. They thought it was a sewing bee. And a quilt, you know. And none of us really understood it." Finally it clicked for **Barbara Gittings**:

> I didn't know what to make [of it] at first. It had this funny name. The Names Project. I didn't understand what it was until I actually walked onto the field, and saw. And started to walk around, and see also the reaction of other people who were looking at the panels. This was the first time that anyone had ever done this kind of memorial. I think the Quilt, our AIDS Quilt, is one of the most inspired ideas of the Twentieth Century.

First displayed in full on Jones's thirty-third birthday with 1,920 panels, by 1999 the Quilt comprised over 44,000 panels.

The Quilt has provided extraordinarily powerful testimony for the first generation to experience AIDS worldwide. Nominated for a Nobel Peace Prize in 1989, it has been memorialized in books, a play, and an Academy Award-winning documentary (*Common Threads*), and by 2000 the idea had expanded to include thirty-eight international affiliates, from Thailand to Brazil, Guam to Israel. While he defends the Quilt from critics who have opined that its time has passed, or believe it an ineffective, passive symbol, even Jones expressed his ambivalence regarding the Quilt:

> I think the Quilt is the best idea I ever had, and I'm very proud of it. And I have all the cynical feelings that the critics have about it. I think the Quilt is an incredible symbol of our failure. And by "our," I mean *all* of us. I mean America, I mean the gay community—we've failed at a lot of levels here, or our kids wouldn't be getting sick with this disease. Was it our fault? No. But have we succeeded? Have we created a new generation of homosexuals that love themselves for what they are? There's still a real battle out there.

The Quilt even brought Jones back in touch with his nemesis. Remember Carl Ketchum?

> Whenever there's a Quilt display, I always get letters and photographs that people want me to have. And there was this letter that had been left on the Quilt [in Pittsburgh]. It said, "Please deliver to Cleve Jones." And it said, "Dear Cleve: Just didn't want you to think that no one in Pittsburgh remembered you. Thank you for everything you've done. Signed, Carlton Ketchum." And I'm looking at this letter, and I got sick to my stomach, and [had] this weird feeling. And I called up my mother, and I said, "Does the name Carlton Ketchum mean anything to you?" She paused for a minute, and then she said, "That son of a bitch." She remembered him. And so I called, and his wife answered the phone—"Hello?" "Is Carlton Ketchum in?" And she said, "No, who's calling?" I said, "This is Cleve Jones." And she, like, started crying. And [she said], "I'm so glad you called. You know, he's going to be so sorry he missed your call." His brother had just died of AIDS, and his sister's a lesbian. And it's just so odd, and karmic, and circular, and weird. But this guy tormented me as a child, and later found out he had gay people in his family, and lost a brother to the epidemic, and now his whole family is part of the struggle, and his parents know my parents, and we're together. Bizarre!

While the gay community's initial denial became painfully evident, Cleve acknowledged that, through AIDS, good has come from evil.

> It's ironic to me, but I think in many ways the epidemic has accomplished for us things that we might not have achieved. Because of the epidemic, America was forced to acknowledge its gay children, usually on our death beds. So, in families all across the country, people discovered that their children were homosexuals, and they learned that at the time of greatest suffering. And they saw how we responded. It was also the first real test of everything we'd said. We'd said we were a community. We called ourselves a community before there *was* a community. We called ourselves a community when we were going to unnamed bars that you had to enter from an alley in the back. . . . But I think that the epidemic, more than anything else, transformed the movement.

After the Quilt, Jones still had other great ideas up his sleeve. He cocreated the New Pacific Academy in 1990 to introduce young people across America to effective gay activism, and (with designer Gilbert Baker) conceptualized the mile-long Rainbow Flag at Stonewall 25 in New York City in 1994. (Unfortunately, ill health caused Cleve to miss seeing it displayed in person.)

How has Jones survived so long with HIV?

> I have no idea. I think part of it's genetic. My family's healthy, there's little cancer, they live a long time, given half a chance. I gave up drugs and alcohol. I smoke pot now and I drink a little bit, but I gave up serious abuse of my body. But I do think it's attitude. The closest I've come to death was this past year [1994]. And what happened to me was that last spring I became depressed. And I've never understood depression before; never realized what an incredibly debilitating disease it is. I always thought of it as some emotional thing that—"Now get over yourself, girl! Just snap out of it—get a job, girl!" That would be my attitude in the past. But when I got pneumonia, I became terribly, terribly depressed, and stayed in bed for six months.

On the day I met with him, Cleve received news from his doctor that his new medication boosted his T-cells from seventy to 350 in a matter of weeks; the news left Jones feeling he had received a new lease on life. As of the end of 2000, Cleve is still around, still fighting. Indeed, in the September 2000 issue of *POZ*, Cleve exulted, "Right now, I'm on my three-drug combo, I'm doing great, I'm undetectable for the first time, I have more T cells than ever. . . . So I'm healthy. I have a beautiful home. I have the possibility of a future, and I find it all quite incomprehensible."

What's the biggest misconception about Cleve? "I don't think most people know what a romantic I am. I think a lot of people think of me as a fairly hard-boiled, cynical person, because of my political work. But I think that was a small part of me." How would Jones like to be remembered?

> I wanted my life to be different—I wanted it to have adventure and romance, and I wanted it to be exciting, and I wanted to touch other people's lives. And I never would have predicted how that would unfold. But I did it. And I may not be around much longer. I'm not really frightened about it—you catch me on a day when I've just had wonderful medical news!—but this summer, you know, in the midst of all this depression and fear and everything, I still felt that I used my life well. There [are] a few people I wish I had been kinder to, but there's not much I would change. So I guess I would like to be remembered as somebody who did something with his life, and had a good time, and saw the world. I touched people.

In *Stitching a Revolution*, he summarized the unparalleled changes that occurred in twenty-five years:

> I joined the gay liberation movement in 1972, when I was seventeen years old. There were no openly gay or lesbian elected officials then, no openly gay or lesbian characters on television, and participants in the Stonewall Day marches rarely numbered more than a few hundred. Homosexuality was illegal in almost every state, and the bars that provided the only opportunity for gay people to meet were harassed continually by the police. . . . [Our myriad accomplishments] in such a short period of time, during years in which tens of thousands of us were killed, is certainly the greatest possible testament to the power and solidarity of our united community.

He added in a March 2000 *Echo* interview with Ken Furtado,

> I would say I've had a love affair with the gay and lesbian movement all my life and I've managed to have a long relationship with the quilt (laughs). I've had an extraordinary life and I feel very blessed—I know that sounds trite. When I was a little kid I loved reading autobiography and history and I remember thinking I wanted to have a life worth writing a book about. [*Stitching a Revolution*] is what turned out.

Cleve certainly has touched my life, and his actions probably have touched yours, too. Especially in creating a memorial we all wish didn't need to exist, Jones surely will live in the collective consciousness of the gay men of my generation long after he departs this earth.

Note

1. In a December 1999 *Associated Press* piece, Cleve pointed out how the movement has evolved in the last decades of the twentieth century: "I think that were Harvey Milk able to come back today, he would be amused that our movement's two top goals are the right to marry and the right to be in the military. In the '70s we were about dismantling the patriarchy and exploring personal liberation and we were not trying to be like straight people. We were radicals!"

30

HARRY BRITT

I've never seen myself as a politician, Paul. I was an activist, and when you get an activist elected to something, to me, what you do as an activist who occupies an office, is you use it as an organizing place. An activist doesn't do things *for* people; an activist provides a space within which people can organize for themselves . . . . [As supervisor], I was thrown into an endless series of totally impossible situations, where people, in trying to do the right thing, were just fucking up so badly. And I was supposed to fix it. . . . And in terms of my own self-esteem, I learned early that you can't be loved by everybody.

—Harry Britt, 1994

In 1978, gay San Franciscans reveled in a series of hard-won political victories, including the election of openly gay Harvey Milk to the Board of Supervisors and the defeat of the antigay initiative, Proposition 6. Suddenly, on November 27, former supervisor Dan White shot and killed both Milk and Mayor George Moscone. The assassinations created an emotional upheaval in the City surpassed only by the advent of AIDS/HIV. White's action irrevocably changed the lives of many people, gay and straight. A pleasant but shy activist turned reluctant politician emerged from the tragedy, and he shrewdly built on Harvey Milk's political power to the gay community's advantage. I interviewed Harry Britt at his apartment, across from San Francisco's notorious Buena Vista Park, in May 1994.

Harry Greer Britt was born on June 8, 1938. He spent his early years in Port Arthur, Texas, where he served as both a local and regional president in the Methodist Youth Foundation. In a May 1980 interview with Winston Leyland for *Gay Sunshine*, Britt shared,

> I can recall having homosexual fantasies as early as the age of five, but there was nothing in my history that offered me any sort of guidance as to how to deal with those. . . . I assumed I was the only person who had these fantasies and it was best not to allow the world to see them.

As he told Carl Maves in a January 1987 *Advocate* interview, "the first guy I ever had any sort of physical affection with died of cancer a few months later. I was 12 years old, and that was a terrible lesson to me, that you'd better be good if you want to survive." Britt spent thirty years "being good," but it failed to provide him emotional fulfillment. Harry found solace only in religion; as he told Lenny Giteck in a February 1979 *Advocate* article, "The Methodist Church was where I could express the kind of feelings for people that men weren't supposed to have. The church is basically a women's institution, and it's where I felt most comfortable."

Britt spent three years at Duke University, graduating with a B.A. in 1960. Upon his return to Port Arthur, Harry married Fran, his minister's daughter, and he became a minister himself, serving congregations in Port Arthur and later in Chicago. But his inner conflict manifested itself in his body; during the marriage, Britt smoked four packs of cigarettes a day and ballooned to 270 pounds as he attempted to sublimate his homosexual desires. Finally, Harry could stand the internal tension no longer. His marriage having ended in 1967, Britt left the church, moved to Dallas for three years, and then in October 1971 relocated to San Francisco. As if to begin his life anew in the City, Harry started "to explore transactional analysis, bio-energetics, Esalen, Gestalt, all that confluence of alternative psychological thought that was going on out here. I wanted to move beyond the religious context my life had had for so many years."

Britt didn't come out until 1974, around the time he moved to San Francisco's then up-and-coming gay mecca on Castro Street. There, as Randy Shilts described it in *The Mayor of Castro Street*, "For Harry Britt, being gay in the Castro in 1975 meant buying a sun lamp, losing one hundred pounds, joining a gym to pump up his sagging pectorals, and changing from glasses to contact lenses." Britt made up for lost time between 1975 and 1978, discovering himself and making peace with his sexuality. Leaving his ministerial background far behind, Harry delivered mail in the Castro (**José Sarria** told me that "Harry

Britt was my mailman, when I lived on York Street. Very nice young man, and I must admit, I tried to seduce him, by offering him coffee and cake on his mail delivery. But he never accepted"), moved to 2 Castro Street, and worked as a night auditor for a local hotel. While he dipped a toe in the turbulent waters of local gay politics, including becoming president of the San Francisco Gay Democratic Club in January 1978, Britt did not abstain from more pressing pursuits; as Shilts recounted, "Harry did not come to Castro Street for politics, he just wanted to cruise." Britt told me,

> I got into this business [politics] very reluctantly. . . . I came to California to do the things you do in California, and was doing them. I was working, all that stuff. Just working four hours and four days a week, and just enjoying nature and learning about being gay at the age of thirty-four. So I didn't need any of this shit. Really did not need it.

Shortly before Milk's assassination, Britt considered attending law school, having successfully completed the necessary testing. Instead, history called him for another purpose. (I attended law school for a semester; we both agreed he didn't miss anything.)

After Harvey Milk's election as District Five supervisor in November 1977, Britt was shocked to learn that Milk had included him on a list of potential successors to Harvey's supervisorial seat should something happen to Milk while in office. While Harry and Harvey instinctively seemed to agree on political matters, Britt had no political aspirations at the time. Shilts wrote that "[f]ew of Harvey's intimates took Harry Britt seriously as a potential successor. His political experience was largely limited to Milk's campaigns and their own fledgling Democratic club. His long sideburns and Texas drawl convinced most that he was an unrefined yahoo, ill-suited for the role as the city's chief gay spokesperson."

Milk transferred his list onto an audiotape, which would substantially alter San Francisco gay politics. In the aftermath of Milk's assassination, many lesbian and gay leaders endorsed Harvey's aide, Anne Kronenberg (also mentioned on the tape), to accede to Milk's supervisorial seat. But Anne's age (just twenty-three) and newly appointed Mayor Dianne Feinstein's political antipathy toward her conspired against Anne to deny her the seat, to the gay leadership's chagrin. As Harry remarked,

> Anne was not [Dianne's] kind of gay person. It was a style thing. She wanted someone who had held responsible positions, preferably in government, and there just weren't any gay people who had had that

> opportunity. And the ones who had had that opportunity were the ones that were [Milk's political enemies in the gay community].[1]

As Britt tells the story, Feinstein "was prepared to appoint a person, whose name I've never divulged to anyone, and will not now, that was totally unacceptable to me, and our people. The person that she was thinking about appointing was a—just a totally unacceptable person. Nice guy. Friend of mine. Gay, but—very conservative and not out of the gay movement. . . . She called me in, saying that that's what she had decided to do. And I said, 'No, we can't have that. And before you do that, I'll take it.'" **Del Martin**, however, presented a different version to me:

> Dianne called us, and wanted to know, "What's your second choice [for Harvey's seat]?" And we said, "We don't have any." And we really wanted Anne. . . . This was going on and on and on, and she hadn't made a decision. And so finally, Harry Britt went to see her, and he said, "I'm my second choice." And that's how he got the appointment. And he didn't talk to Anne; he didn't talk to anybody else. He just did it.

Cleve Jones believes that

> Harry betrayed Anne Kronenberg. You know, he betrayed all of us. He cut a deal behind our backs. . . . The issue is that you have a community—there has been a very clear consensus that we're going to support Anne Kronenberg, and we're gonna push for her. Harry unilaterally, on his own, without discussing it with very many people beyond the folks at SEIU [Service Employees International Union], broke ranks. . . . And the community, many of us were, you know, outraged and shocked.

Feinstein appointed Britt to Milk's former seat on January 8, 1979.

Regardless of how he attained the position, Harry encountered several problems during those first months in office. Not only did he introduce issues such as rent-control legislation, which gentrified San Franciscans (including gays) disdained, but Harry simply wasn't Harvey. "People wanted Harvey back," Harry sighed. Additionally, Britt battled "a whole set of gay leadership that was jealous of me, including everybody who wrote for the newspapers. That was always a huge problem for me. I just could not get the word out." Publisher David Goodstein's comments in an August 1984 *Advocate* editorial didn't help matters any:

> I like Britt; everyone likes Britt. He is a very nice man. A former Methodist minister, he is sincere, dedicated and sweet. But he does not cut the mustard. When leadership is required, Britt's opinion does not carry the weight it should, and there are no adverse consequences when his wishes are thwarted. Apparently, he doesn't want to risk offending anyone.

In *Cities on a Hill*, Frances FitzGerald commented, "The former minister and civil rights activist had the political and intellectual credentials to succeed Milk. He was a thoughtful man with a good deal of charm. . . . Britt, however, lacked Milk's extraordinary political energy and his sheer chutzpah." (As Jones echoed in *Stitching a Revolution*, Britt was "a tad deficient in the charisma department.") Or, as José Sarria explained,

> Even if [Harry] had stood on his own merit, I mean, that's something. But you have to follow in the footsteps of the biggest martyr the gay community has seen, you know, really to date. How much more difficult does that make it to do your job? And I think that one of the things that made it very difficult for Harry, in a lot of ways, was trying to follow after Harvey. I mean, how do you follow an act like that?

On May 21, 1979, the Dan White jury returned its verdict; instead of first- or second-degree murder, it convicted White of the lesser charge of voluntary manslaughter, for which he received a sentence of seven years and eight months. Harry pointed out to me that the jury delivered its verdict

> on a Monday, so the Board of Supervisors was in session at the time the verdict came out. There wasn't a lack of availability of people to deal with the riots. Everyone was there. We were all talking to one another, what to do. So it's not like there was one person who did something or didn't do something. Everybody was in contact with everybody. Basically, we all were of one mind as to what needed to happen. We wanted a protest, but not destruction of City Hall.

In the wake of the verdict's announcement, Britt angrily acknowledged that

> Harvey Milk knew he would be assassinated. He knew that the lowest nature in human beings would rise up and get him. But he never imagined that this city would approve of that act. It's beyond immoral. It's obscene. This is an insane jury. [Dan White's] homophobia had something to do with this verdict—and it *was* murder.

The City's gay community in particular vented its outrage on City property; during the White Night Riots, as they were later known, rioters smashed windows at City Hall, systematically torched several police cars, and destroyed over $300,000 in property. Despite the best efforts of gay leaders, including Britt, no one could deter the violence. Later that evening/morning, police took their revenge when they assaulted Castro Street gay bar patrons, many who had left City Hall when the confrontation turned violent. Harry Britt admitted disappointment with his own performance: "The things I had said to the press up to that point were pretty stupid. I said things like, 'They won't think we're a bunch of hairdressers anymore,' and stuff like that. Just anger, but it wasn't my job to be angry, or my job to be cruel, and I was." Miraculously, despite several injuries among both police officers and civilians, no fatalities occurred.

Harry's greatest political tests came during his first supervisorial campaign in 1979. Having obtained his position by appointment, Harry had never run for citywide political office. Many pundits considered Britt the weakest of several supervisorial incumbents, but Harry knew that following Harvey's assassination the race would prove crucial for San Francisco's gay community. Britt won a runoff against Terence Hallinan, a straight scion of one of San Francisco's first families. (Despite pundits' dire predictions, among incumbent supervisors, voters returned only Britt and John Molinari [who ran unopposed].)

Shortly thereafter, San Francisco's voters reverted to citywide elections from the short-lived district elections; Harry now had to woo and carry not only District Five's voters, but all of the City's voters at large,

> which meant that all of a sudden I needed 80-90,000 votes, which is quite a big leap up from ten [thousand], when you've spent all your time concentrating to build a base and offending the conservatives all over the city. . . . So it was a rather remarkable effort by a whole group of wonderful people that enabled me to survive in 1980.

San Franciscans comfortably reelected Britt supervisor on November 4, 1980. From that point forward, Harry never faced a serious threat in his supervisorial races. In the 1989 elections, Britt received more votes than any other candidate, and accordingly he served a two-year term as president of the Board of Supervisors.

Britt, however, may never have fully reconciled his inner conflicts regarding his political career, telling me, "I made a commitment to five years, when I took the job. I told the people around me, look, this is not me. I'm a quiet, sort of shy fellow. I do not like all this stuff. This is not my world. But I'll stay there for five years. . . . I ultimately stayed fourteen." In 1982 Britt proposed the nation's first domestic partnership ordinance; Mayor Feinstein vetoed it (a lesser-reaching version finally passed in 1991). Yet Britt fought even more fiercely in the '80s against AIDS/HIV during its earliest days. Not only did Britt grapple for funding beyond the local level and for recognition of the gravity of the situation during the first half of the decade, he also contended with his personal grief over the losses the virus inflicted, including his friend and aide Bill Kraus.

> I just couldn't—there was just an empty place in my—you know, 'cause the dying kept going on and on and on. I mean, you know, we could do stuff, we could lobby, but basically getting money, locally at least, was not that hard. The damn disease just kind of kept coming, and, you know, everybody wanted to do everything right.

Harry received mixed reviews regarding his job performance. **Hal Call** told me,

> I think Harry did a good job, as good a job as anybody else could do on the Board of Supervisors in his time here. I have nothing but praise for him, and admiration. He had a hard job to fill, and he's been subject to criticism by some people that—you know, there's an awful lot of people in the community who want more than maybe they're entitled to.

Allan Spear noted, "I didn't agree with a lot of the things he said, but I liked him." José Sarria recalled,

> Harry was not really political material in the beginning. But Harry was smart. And Harry was likable. And [John] Molinari took him under his wing. And Harry learned. And I think Harry ended up being a good politician. Sometimes he was a little wishy-washy. It takes balls to say no, when everybody is saying yes. But he ended up being well-respected.

Cleve Jones also remarked that, "I think for someone who was so unqualified to be thrust into the position, that he did a good job with it. But he was not qualified, because he was not comfortable with himself." (Several people along the way also commented to me on Harry's penchant for "the horses.")

In 1987, Britt ran for state assembly. Despite eight years in office, Britt had earned a reputation as a political "outsider"; opponent Nancy Pelosi, despite having never held office before, belonged to the "Burton machine," and was perceived a powerful, effective "insider." (**Phyllis Lyon** surprised me when she opined, "Harry would have been an embarrassment to the gay community nationwide if he'd gotten into Congress!") Pelosi defeated Britt in that race. Harry finally stepped down from politics in 1992, after San Francisco voters elected lesbians Roberta Achtenberg and Carole Migden to the Board of Supervisors in 1990.

When I spoke with Harry, he occupied the position of Harvey Milk Chair of Activism and Social Justice at New College of California in San Francisco.

> I basically came to New College because I love to teach, and because it's a place that I really could sort out the meaning of all this stuff. And so I've got sort of a basic course that I'm teaching this fall called The Politics of Alienation. And it's an effort to sort of tie the Harvey Milk perspective on politics and social change with people like W.E.B. DuBois and [leaders like] Malcolm X. Mainly, I teach political history.

Harry told me that of all his many jobs over the years, he enjoys teaching at New College most.

I unintentionally startled Harry when I asked him about his love life:

> Well, if you mean my sex life, it's not very good. But if you mean my love life, I feel—that's been the other good thing about being supervisor. There's been so much at stake so many times, with so many people, that you really develop some really strong relationships. . . . So I feel more surrounded by people that I think really care about me than I ever have in my life. Certainly more than when I was in the church. A lot more. And that's wonderful. . . . Being loved, or being in loving relationships, you really have to sort of get to know yourself. I never was good at doing that. . . . And you have to learn that it's OK to react the way that you react, and to actually do it. And I acted out my growing up in a very public stage, and sometimes it got ugly. But, basically, I feel very good about who I am now.

Now that the inordinately modest Britt has left the limelight, he agreed to let me interview him for only two reasons I could fathom: He wanted an opportunity to talk about Harvey Milk, and he genuinely wanted to help me. Having served his community decently and honorably, he now seems to have found his niche in teaching. But while many people can teach history, Harry Britt made history.

Note

1. Many San Francisco gay leaders considered the other two people Milk mentioned, Bob Ross and Frank Robinson, unsatisfactory for the position.

31

DAVID CLARENBACH

We made an important strategic decision. We formed the issue in the way we felt we could get the best results. We did not ask the Catholic Church to resolve the theological issues involved, or to even answer the question, "Is homosexuality good or bad, to be encouraged, discouraged, sinful or not sinful?" We asked if bigotry or discrimination against *any* group could be tolerated, and when that is the question that is posed, the answer is a universal, "No, it cannot be tolerated." . . . The lesson that I learned, growing up in Wisconsin, which is the home of the Green Bay Packers and Vince Lombardi, is that the best defense is a good offense. And you never, in politics or in football, want to be put on the defensive.

—David Clarenbach, 1995

Given that most lesbian/gay movement activity nationwide during the last half-century has emanated from New York City, San Francisco, and Los Angeles, it may surprise the uninitiated to learn that the first successful statewide antidiscrimination legislation based on sexual orientation originated on neither coast.[1] Thanks largely to the determination of an extraordinary young legislator, Wisconsin's assembly and senate (home of '50s' rabid anticommunist witch-hunter Joseph McCarthy) passed such a bill into law on February 25, 1982, still the most exhilarating day of that legislator's life.

Now openly gay, David Clarenbach served in the Wisconsin State Assembly for nearly two decades before becoming executive director of the Gay and Lesbian Victory Fund in the summer of 1995. When I met with David in Washington, D.C., that August, the gay press continued to criticize his earlier decision not to declare his sexuality, and they questioned his nearly decade-long relationship (and four-year marriage) with a woman during that time. We talked about those things and many more; his charm, forthrightness, and intensity captivated me.

David Eric Clarenbach was born on September 26, 1953, in St. Louis, Missouri. By the '60s, David and his family (including an older and a younger sister) had moved to Madison, Wisconsin. His mother, Dr. Kathryn Clarenbach, served as the National Organization for Women's (NOW) first board chair; his father, a World War II veteran, participated in Madison's antiwar community and supported Eugene McCarthy at Chicago's 1968 Democratic National Convention. In his formative years, David's parents demonstrated an unconventional relationship:

> From a personal standpoint, to know that my mother was the one that went out and made speeches, and went on trips, and my father was the one who made sure to be at home when we came home from school, and he made sure that there was dinner on the table and that there was groceries in the refrigerator and that we got to bed on time, seemed totally natural to me. . . . They had a very respectful relationship. There was never a time that I saw any expression of unhappiness or disrespect as a result of my mother's prominence, and it wasn't because they hid it well. It really was because there was a basic tenet of respect.

At age ten David visited Washington, D.C., and he began to believe himself called to become a member of Congress, preferably succeeding his Second District congressman, Bob Kastenmeier. A hardworking lad, Clarenbach did everything in his power to turn that belief into reality, actively working in Madison's civil rights and anti-Vietnam War movements while in his mid-teens. Shortly after turning eighteen, Clarenbach ran for the Dane County Board of Supervisors; after the incumbent died of a heart attack mid-race, David defeated three other candidates to obtain the seat. (Thanks to the Constitution's Twenty-Sixth Amendment, effective January 1, 1972, he could cast a vote for himself in the election!) Two years later, David won a state assembly seat, leading pundits to dub him the wunderkind of Wisconsin electoral politics. Did Clarenbach's unprecedented early victories surprise him? Given his background as a political animal, David told me that "it did not seem unnatural."

Upon entering the Wisconsin legislature in 1975, Clarenbach championed many liberal causes, following in the footsteps of heterosexual African-American Milwaukee legislator Lloyd Barbee, who introduced a bill to provide for gay marriages as early as the '60s. According to David, "Part of the reason that [Barbee] felt comfortable leaving the legislature, I believe—and he's told me this—is that there was someone to whom he could pass the baton." Clarenbach did not disappoint him; David continued laying the groundwork for successful sex reform bills. Instructively, it took David eight years to achieve his first legislative success in the treacherous arena of sexual politics.

Simultaneously, Clarenbach wrestled with publicly acknowledging his homosexuality, a dilemma that took him more than two decades to resolve. Clarenbach's friend and fellow midwestern politician, **Allan Spear**, met Clarenbach at the National Alternative Policy Conference shortly after Spear came out in 1975. There, Spear told me, David

> came up and said, "I'm David Clarenbach, and I was just elected to the legislature in Wisconsin last year . . . and I wanted to meet you because I'm gay, too." . . . But then he went on to tell me that he was not yet out. . . . So I saw him from time to time during the '70s. He was up here once with his boyfriend, and he called me, and we had dinner together and all kinds of stuff, and I said, "David, when are you coming out?" And he would always sort of hem and haw . . . Well, there were two reasons he always gave. One was his mother. . . . He thought it would [bother her]. (**Jean O'Leary** confirmed Spear's account, calling Kathryn Clarenbach "one of the biggest homophobes" at Houston's International Women's Year Conference in 1977.) And secondly . . . he said, "When Bob Kastenmeier retires—he's going to retire one of these days—I want to be his successor." And he said, "That district includes not just Dane County, but a bunch of rural counties surrounding Dane, and I can't get elected if I'm out."

Not surprisingly, Clarenbach's take differed somewhat from Spear's:

> I got elected to public office in 1972. That was the year that **Barney Frank** got elected to public office. No one ran for public office as an "out" official at that time. . . . I would say a vast, vast majority of the state legislature knew that I was gay. I had a partner. You know, the Capitol was in my district. I mean, it wasn't like I was exactly walled up in my house . . . or out in some big city, where I could blend in.

While actively fighting for his causes, David chose a pragmatic route, possibly believing constituents and legislators would find him less effective if he declared his sexual orientation. Perhaps, as **Holly**

Near suggests, no word or phrase yet exists that accurately describes Clarenbach's sexual orientation. Also like Near, Clarenbach does not self-identify as bisexual, believing "the public would not accept that kind of label." As executive director for the Victory Fund, certainly David found it politically expedient to self-identify as gay, but circumstances largely forced that label upon him, insensitive to the complex person behind it.

Following 1982's antidiscrimination bill, signed by Republican governor Lee Dreyfus, Clarenbach shepherded a "consenting adults" bill through the Wisconsin legislature in 1983, signed by Democratic governor Anthony Earl. David remarked afterward, "The last chapter of major sex-law reform in Wisconsin has been closed." Also in 1983, his colleagues elected Clarenbach, still in his twenties, speaker pro tem of the Wisconsin State Assembly.

During the '80s, Clarenbach began a relationship with, and later married, attorney Heidi Nass. Some observers felt Heidi served as a "cover" for David's sexual orientation; speaking with friends in Madison around the time of David's congressional race, Spear asked them, "'Is he gay?' Well, they said, 'We're not sure what David is anymore.' And they told me he had married this woman. And so then I was real surprised." David knew that following his heart to marry a woman could have political repercussions:

> It was a marriage of *inconvenience*, is what it was. I mean that quite sincerely. We decided not to disclose that we were married. . . . [The response was] "Well, you know, that's as obvious as the nose on my face why he's doing that! Why he suddenly wants to become straight." Well, that is—hurtful, and disrespectful, and implies that I would use another human being for a ten-year period for political purpose— And that violates the underlying tenets of the gay rights movement. That who you are and who you love should not make any difference, and you should not be judged on the basis of who you love and how you love. . . . There were segments, not just of the gay and lesbian community, but of the constituency at large, who felt—who reached a conclusion, jumped to a conclusion, that— "Well, he's not being honest." And that, I think, was terribly unfortunate, and terribly wrong. But had an effect.

The couple separated in 1994.

When Clarenbach ultimately ran for Congress in 1992, not even the most clairvoyant politician could reasonably have anticipated the results. Allan Spear begins the story:

> Finally, you know, David miscalculated on the congressional seat. Because what he didn't see is that Kastenmeier was not going to re-

tire, but Kastenmeier was going to be beat. And so what happened in, I think, 1990, was that Kastenmeier was upset by a Republican [Scott Klug], which no one expected—it was just a real upset. And so there was David, having waited all these years for Kastenmeier to retire, and instead Kastenmeier was defeated, and so now he's got a Republican incumbent.

Clarenbach continues the saga: After Kastenmeier's defeat,

I prepared almost immediately following the 1990 election to give up my seat in the legislature, and to run for Congress. . . . I laid what I had thought was the groundwork to be taken seriously, and as a viable candidate against what was now an incumbent Republican. . . . Well, I chose to run in the Year of the Woman, and the Year of the Outsider. And I was neither! . . . I served in the leadership of the assembly for ten years; longer than anyone served in any leadership in the assembly ever. Speaker pro tem was the second spot in the pecking order. . . . I raised more money than any [primary] challenger in the country, in 1992. I, in fact, scared the most likely primary contender out of the race. . . . So I sort of thought, well, yes, I have this kind of token [primary] candidate. And our polling said that no one knew her.

Spear picks up again: David

was challenged for the Democratic primary by [a Native American] woman, named Ada Deer. . . . As I understand it, the liberals in Madison were really divided because, on the one hand, David had been this champion, but on the other hand, in this age of identity politics, it was Ada Deer, an Indian woman—the chance to elect the first Indian woman to the United States Congress. And this was one [instance] where David probably would have been better off had he been "out." Because if he had been out, then it would have been an Indian woman versus an openly gay man, so the identity politics would have kind of neutralized.

David finishes the story: "I had a general election strategy. And Ada Deer had a primary election strategy. . . . Her primary strategy was perfect. And it worked. And she beat me handily." However, Deer lost to incumbent Klug in the general election. How did Clarenbach handle the defeat, his first in two decades of electoral politics?

Well, as Morris Udall said when he lost the Wisconsin [presidential] primary, and had therefore to withdraw, "I slept last night— for the first time, I slept like a baby. Every two or three hours I woke up crying." . . . I was prepared to lose the election. I did not expect to lose the primary. And to be honest, the scars have yet to heal. . . . I

> could have, and was well prepared to be defeated by the right wing, by the enemy. But not by my own party, or my own constituency.

The most traumatic day of David's life came when he recognized his lifelong dream of becoming a member of the U.S. Congress would not materialize.

Clarenbach told me he does not see himself running for electoral office again. Yet David pointed out to me that, in contrast to most politicians, he "had, in some ways, the good fortune to have my first career, and an extraordinarily successful one, and one in which I can be very proud of, beyond a doubt, come and go before I reached the age of forty." His only regret?

> Why didn't I [leave Madison and the assembly seat] earlier? And why didn't I come out? Why didn't I set aside the trials and tribulations of the electoral, political world as a candidate? . . . When you're a candidate for public office, you *do* have to spend half of your time raising money, and the other half glad-handing people that you either don't know or would rather not know!

Following his defeat, Clarenbach moved forward, working as a political consultant and as the interim executive director of the Madison AIDS Support Network before the Gay & Lesbian Victory Fund selected him as its executive director. When I interviewed David, he had held the position for less than two months, yet at that time he told me, "I have to say that I have never been involved in a more exciting or a more important project."

While he started with great promise, something apparently went awry; within two years, David stepped down from the position. Unfortunately, at that time I also lost track of Clarenbach, and I could not discover the circumstances surrounding his departure from the Victory Fund. Not until the end of 2000 did I discover that Clarenbach remained in D.C., as he was apparently volunteering with the Mary-Helen Mautner Project for Lesbians with Cancer there.

After more than two decades in the public eye, I wondered what people didn't know about Clarenbach that he wished they did: "I love baseball, and the Green Bay Packers. . . . I find humor and comedy to be my best release. And that I don't think it would be lying to say that, with enthusiasm, I've looked forward to practically every day of my life." How would David like people to remember him? "I would like people to know that I was honest, and hard-working, and tried to make a difference."

Often a prophet is without honor in his hometown. Not Clarenbach. Upon receiving news of his Victory Fund appointment, the *Wis-*

consin Light, the state's major gay newspaper, proudly ran an editorial that stated,

> Here is a man of great dynamism, of wide talents, who has used all that and more for the good of our community. He has worked tirelessly here in Wisconsin and he will take all that to Washington to use nationwide now. . . . We have reason to know what a great, good heart David has, a man full of love, who has shown it in so many ways the world will never know. It is that kind of man with that kind of inner reserves of strength who we, as a nationwide community, need now. Thankfully he has accepted the challenge before him now.

When I began this journey, I shared the gay media's general cynicism of "gay leaders" in mainstream politics. Meeting people like David Clarenbach, **Urvashi Vaid**, and Barney Frank restored my faith in the integrity and decency of the women and men who represent my community on the political front lines. A very good feeling indeed.

Note

1. Prior to 1982, California and Pennsylvania issued executive orders banning antigay discrimination, but these largely symbolic orders carried little force.

32

BARNEY FRANK

> **Given the mistakes I've made and the silly things I did, including the business with the hustler, people have been nicer to me than I had a right to expect at all. Society's changed. I made a mistake to stay in the closet as long as I did and today, I don't see how people can do it. When I was 30 or even 40, I never really thought that it would have been possible for me to be living my life completely as a gay, living with another man, doing everything other couples do and have a fairly unconstrained political career. I have no complaints. I think I'm very lucky.**
>
> —Barney Frank, interview with Tracy Sypert, *Frontiers*, September 6, 1996

Any lesbian or gay man who voluntarily reveals his/her sexuality takes a calculated risk, since s/he cannot know how those about whom one cares will greet such a revelation. Depending on one's profession, issues concerning job security may arise. But what if your job requires the goodwill and approval of more than half a million constituents? Can you afford to take that risk?

In 1987, Massachusetts representative Barney Frank took the plunge. His timing may have proven propitious: Not only were several reporters aware of Frank's homosexuality (yet waiting for him to publicly acknowledge it instead of "outing" him, as likely would have occurred less than half a decade later), but some of Barney's actions had created an unpleasant skeleton sharing his closet, which threatened to jeopardize his career. (He told Jeff Ofstedahl in a 1996 *Echo Magazine* article, "I was going crazy trying to live a duel [*sic*] life. I was doing stupid things. Coming out was the best thing I ever did.") Frank's revelation regarding his sexual orientation on the front page of the May 30, 1987, *Boston Globe* wasn't the first by an American politician, but as one of the highest ranking officials to do so, he has since developed one of the nation's strongest voices on gay rights matters. On a lovely morning in August 1995, I spent an entertaining and enlightening hour with Barney Frank at his regional office in Newton, Massachusetts.

Barnett Frank ("my parents always called me Barney, and I finally changed it legally") was born on March 31, 1940, in Bayonne, New Jersey, to Samuel and Elsie Frank. Of his three siblings, his elder sister, Ann Lewis, has held several important Democratic Party offices, including campaign communications director of President Bill Clinton's reelection campaign. Because Barney told Rick Harding in an April 12, 1988, *Advocate* interview, "I don't do feelings for publication. Feelings are private. I have this constant tension between what gets left private and what gets made public. I've got to keep my feelings private," I asked Frank far fewer personal questions than I asked any other interviewee. However, regarding his childhood, he volunteered, "I can remember the attraction [to males] as early as the first grade, but that's thinking back. I remember the day I realized I was gay I was thirteen. Very depressing." (Frank's first sexual encounter with another man would not occur until 1968.) He also told Claudia Dreifus in a February 1996 *New York Times Magazine* article, "I think I always wanted a political career, but I didn't think it would be possible as a young person. Actually, as much because I was Jewish as because I was gay."

After graduating from Bayonne High in 1957, Frank attended Harvard University, earning a B.A. in 1962, and serving as a teaching fellow there until 1972.[1] After assisting Boston mayor Kevin White from 1968 to 1971 and Representative Michael Harrington in 1972, later that year Frank won a seat in the Massachusetts House of Representatives. Yet his victory extracted an emotional toll: As he told Dreifus, "When I first ran for office, I made a decision that I would sacrifice a private life for politics." He added in *After Stonewall*, "in 1972, it was inconceivable to me that you could win office, and be out." In 1973, his freshman year, Frank laid his reputation on the line when he sponsored an ultimately unsuccessful gay rights bill in the Massachusetts legislature, becoming a "straight liberal friend" of his state's gay community. Frank served four terms in the State House (and simultaneously earned a law degree from Harvard in 1977) before graduating to the U.S. House of Representatives in 1980. Despite his success, it seems he rubbed some of his colleagues the wrong way, admitting to Neil Miller in *In Search of Gay America*, "I discovered when I left the Massachusetts legislature, I wasn't as well-liked as I thought. People thought I was too acerbic. I've tried to be more liked [in Congress]."

A sterner political test arose in 1982 when, as a result of redistricting, circumstances forced him to run against a fellow incumbent, Republican Margaret (Peggy) Heckler. In the waning days of that race, Heckler's camp attempted a whispering campaign regarding the Democratic congressman's sexuality, but Frank defeated Heckler with a convincing 59 percent of the vote. Having comfortably secured his congressional seat, Frank told Miller that he began "living my private life as a gay man without too much concern." Still, Barney chose not to identify his sexual orientation publicly, and he remained a subject of much speculation.

By 1986 the rumors progressed from vague murmurings to printed allegations. Former congressman Bob Bauman wrote in 1986's *The Gentleman from Maryland*, "the witty liberal, Barney Frank, appears at Washington's annual Gay Pride Day in a tank top with his usual young companion and their picture appears in the [Washington] *Blade* without comment." Not surprisingly, as Barney told Rick Harding,

> I was asked "Are you gay?" in connection with Bauman's book, and I didn't want to say yes in that context. I didn't want the stories to be: "Here is this book about a man who has sex with people who are under the legal age, who—by his own admission—gets beaten up a lot, who is an alcoholic; and, oh, by the way, one of the people who is like him is Barney Frank." No . . . that ain't me.

But by now Frank knew he soon would have to reveal his homosexuality publicly, although not as a preemptive strike against intruding journalists. (Barney shared with me, "every journalist with whom I had discussed this made it clear to me that they had no intention of outing me until and unless I decided I wanted to be outed. . . . I am very proud of having come out voluntarily with no sense that I would be forced to that.") But in a September 1989 *Newsweek* interview with Eleanor Clift, Frank revealed,

> I told my mother [I was gay] in 1984 because I was afraid she'd hear it from somebody else. I was 40 years old before I told my siblings. . . . The most satisfying public life is no substitute for private life. I reached the point where, as my public life got better, it became more agonizing because of the disparity. . . . I had really great confidence in my job skills, and abysmal social self-confidence.

He ultimately spoke out to honor a colleague, bisexual Connecticut Republican representative Stewart McKinney, who died from AIDS-related causes in the spring of 1987. Again Frank told Harding, "I liked and respected Stew a lot, and I was depressed about having this kind of scuffle about whether he was or wasn't gay or bisexual. I didn't want that kind of debate to happen over me. I think I probably said at that point, 'OK, that's it.'" (More recently, he told Tracy Sypert, "I said to myself, 'Shit, suppose I get hit by a truck tomorrow. I can't have this [speculation]. I'm coming out.'") After the *Boston Globe* article Frank could not turn back—and never has.

As Frank correctly deduced, his admission did not fatally damage his career: In 1988, he won comfortably in the general election in his decidedly liberal district. Instead, his next serious political threat came from his unsavory past, and it nearly derailed his career.

Some closeted homosexuals take risks that seem mind-numbing to those open about their sexuality, and Frank proved no exception. As *Out for Good* explained, in the early '80s both Frank and fellow closeted Massachusetts Democratic representative Gerry Studds permitted themselves "almost no gay life. Both men were intellectual, driven, socially awkward and defined by their work. Neither one knew how to relax. Neither of them really dated nor allowed himself the prospect of romance, and both of them had sex lives which were either austere or furtive, and bound to get them in trouble." In 1985, desiring affection and sex but unable to obtain them in a socially sanctioned manner, Barney responded to a *Washington Blade* escort ad, and he paid $80 to engage in sex with Stephen Gobie, seventeen years Frank's junior. As a result of the encounter, Frank decided to pursue a relationship with Gobie, a choice he would later regret.

Unbeknownst to Frank, Gobie was a hustler. Over the next two years or so, Barney and Steve's relationship quickly soured. As Frank told me, "Actually, the relationship, very soon after I met him, stopped being sexual after the first couple of months. Because he was basically straight. He had a straight girlfriend for much of the time." Gobie also had a drug problem, which only exacerbated Frank's discomfort. Barney later described his charitable actions as "thinking I was going to be Henry Higgins," and he confessed that trying to help Gobie "was the biggest mistake I ever made." As Barney explained to me,

> When I decided to come out in the spring of 1987 my relationship with Gobie was still a perfectly good one. At no point did it remotely occur to me that he would turn on me as he did. In fact, what happened was that after his probation ended, he apparently went back to his drug habit and it was this that led to his effort to destroy me more than two years after I'd come out.

Indeed, Frank testified before the House Ethics Committee[2] that his relationship with Gobie "is something I should not have done. . . . I did not handle the pressures of having a public life [and] of being a closeted gay man nearly as well as I should have." Ultimately, Barney noted,

> The Ethics Committee found that I had violated the rules in two respects: by lying about how I had met [Gobie] in a memorandum I had sent to a private attorney, who, unbeknownst to me, passed it on to a prosecutor; and by letting [Gobie] use my car and get parking tickets which I had voided as was my right as a member of Congress if they had been incurred in official business.

The House of Representatives, having weathered its share of sex scandals in the '80s, took umbrage when the allegations surfaced. Its members decided on July 26, 1990, to reprimand a chastened Frank, who apologized on the House floor for his poor judgment: "There was in my life a central element of dishonesty. Three years ago I decided concealment wouldn't work—I wish I had decided that long ago." Despite "reprimand's" harsh tone, Barney received a comparatively light punishment; his colleagues on the House Ethics Committee earlier weighed more severe options, specifically censure and expulsion.

At the time, few predicted Frank could rise above the scandal: **Urvashi Vaid**, then NGLTF executive director, commented, "This has been painful for gays, and it will have an impact on some people's attitudes toward us," but she also admitted that throughout the investigation Frank handled himself "with an impressive amount of honesty and dignity." (She later added in a November 1997 *OUT* interview with Michelangelo Signorile, "I admire Barney a lot. He's been incredibly effective on key issues, like immigration. He's a very smart strategist.") While the issue never disappeared entirely (and while the entire Gobie episode produced the most traumatic days of Barney's life, telling me, "I don't remember that much from that period. When he was making these terrible accusations, and I realized that these terrible accusations were being treated as if they were true . . . ."), Frank put the matter behind him quickly and in impressive fashion, especially having just entered a visible, committed relationship, falling in requited love for the first time.

Frank met Herb Moses in a very different way than he met Gobie. Herb sent Barney a note in August 1987, which read in part, "'Gee, I was really impressed. I think we have a lot in common. And I'd like to talk to you.' . . . And the pottery studio where he worked was a block from my house in Washington. So he came over one night. And we hit it off well, and I started dating him." After ten and one-half years, the couple separated in the summer of 1998. Between the influence of Moses (a federal employee who worked at the Department of Agriculture) and the fresh air Barney breathed after leaving his stuffy closet, stability surfaced in Frank's heretofore disheveled personal life. (Reporters often use "disheveled" to describe Frank's appearance as well. Unlikely ever to pass as an *International Male* model, he spoke to me of the popular misperception that he is a walking fashion "don't": "I think there's a cultural lag about my dress. . . . The coats are kind of good [but] they don't look so good. I wrinkle things; I ruffle things. I think if people would see me at 9:30 or so . . . .")

Now that Frank had come out and dodged the potentially fatal bullet that might have destroyed a lesser man's career, he set out to accomplish some of the best work of his political life. While Larry Kramer, in one of his nastier tirades, had the effrontery in 1992 to tell Victor Zonana, "Barney Frank is probably the most useless congressperson on gay issues that we have. Just because he's openly gay, we're supposed to kiss his ass. Well, he does fuck-all for us. He does fuck-all for AIDS," Frank

> secured a $200 million dollar plus increase in the presidential request for AIDS research. I was also the major advocate for increased AIDS research money on the House Budget Committee while I was on that committee. In addition, I was the leader in fighting in the House against right-wing efforts to interfere with AIDS research and prevention by imposing antigay riders, and I was the leader in the fight to preserve the parts of the Americans with Disabilities Act protection for people with AIDS.

His efforts also resulted in lifting the ban on immigration into the United States against gays and lesbians in 1990, granting U.S. asylum to those persecuted on account of their homosexuality in 1994, supporting transgender rights, defending assisted suicide, and attempting to overturn other discriminatory policies that affect the lives of many individual lesbians and gays, as well as his "official" constituents. (I can vouch for his generosity in support of lesbian and gay causes—he spoke with me, a journalist of no reputation whatsoever.)

Along the way toward trying to create a better country, Frank earned a reputation as one of the best debaters in Congress. Where did he learn his debating skills?

> Look, you have certain talents; you have certain weaknesses. . . . I have very few nonverbal skills. I have no musical talent; I have no manual dexterity. But I do have good verbal skills. . . . Debating is not debating, I believe. It's thinking that's important. I mean, it's not clever ways to say it. I find that most people tend to think much more

emotionally and inconsistently. And that's the problem. People over-argue their case."

Frank has taken his share of hits from his political enemies over the years (including Texan Dick Armey, whose ill-chosen "Barney Fag" comment in 1995 and "if there is a dick army, Barney Frank would want to join up" in 2000 won him no Brownie points with Frank). More recently, responding to particular acts of Republican mean-spiritedness, Barney threatened to expose certain closeted gay Republican elected officials. (To date, he has not needed to carry out his threat—Barney's mere acknowledgment usually sends his political foes, like cockroaches, scurrying away from the threat of such harsh glare.) Ironically, Frank even tried to help heterosexuals set their affairs in order by sponsoring the Anti-Hypocrisy Act, designed to end criminal prosecution for sex acts between consenting adults in the U.S. Armed Forces.

An ambitious realist who would like to become president of the United States "because I care a lot about public policy. And that is the position in this world where you can have more of an impact on public policy than any other," Barney also flatly stated, "There's obviously no remote possibility. I mean, it's like making me permanent pope." Despite his impressive successes, many in the gay community clobbered Frank in 1993 when they disagreed with his political tactics.

When in May 1992 Arkansas governor Bill Clinton declared his intent to strike the ban on open gays serving in the military if voters elected him president, the gay community watched his candidacy with increased interest; when he proved victorious, many were elated. Despite his good intentions, Clinton failed to comprehend the severity of homophobia in upper military echelons, as well as in Congress. Consequently, he found himself committed to a battle he could not win. Shortly before Clinton took office in January 1993, Frank told Chris Bull,

> I begged [HRCF and NGLTF] to get a letter-writing campaign going.[3] . . . They thought that having a president on your side means you've won. Having the president on your side is a necessary condition, but it's not a sufficient condition. I told the groups, "You're deciding what to have for dessert when we haven't even killed the chickens for dinner yet."

Instead of accepting political defeat, Clinton attempted a "half-a-loaf-is-better-than-none" approach.

In May 1993, Frank proposed a compromise, dubbed "Don't Ask, Don't Tell, Don't Pursue," to replace Georgia senator (and fellow

Democrat) Sam Nunn's "Don't Ask, Don't Tell" policy propounded earlier that year. For that action, the gay press and others widely accused Frank of capitulating to the enemy, and excoriated him for offering an alternative to Clinton's original promise. **Jim Kepner** told me, "I think Barney Frank made an awful mistake in—during the negotiation period, you don't give your minimum bid. And that came close to seeming like treachery, and many in the gay community felt it was that way." Sergeant **Miriam Ben-Shalom** was characteristically blunt:

> Everybody made such a big deal out of Congressman Frank. Well, where the heck was he? He was the one who came up with "Don't Ask, Don't Tell." And I've oftentimes wondered how these people who developed this "principled compromise" [would] feel, if they had to live under that kind of stricture themselves. . . . As a matter of fact, it is a worse policy than the old one that was in effect, because "Don't Ask, Don't Tell" doesn't have any guidelines.

In a June 1993 *Advocate* op-ed piece, even Urvashi Vaid criticized "the debacle of Democratic weasels in the Senate pandering to homophobia as well as the painful sight of Barney Frank defending a sellout on the military ban." (In contrast, **Rita Mae Brown** wrote in *Rita Will* that Frank's "political acumen is never to be underestimated," and shrewd politico **Allan Spear** told me, "I think he did the right thing.")

When I relayed the gist of these comments to Frank, he expressed his frustration:

> People said that, right? I must be really stupid to those people. I could be uncertain about stuff. But I did know more about negotiating that thing than most of them. . . . I think I probably held off the last deal for a few weeks, because we thought maybe we'd get a better one. . . . After the March [on Washington in April 1993] came and went, and there was no significant useful political activity, then it was clear that a deal was being formulated without us.

Frank expounded on this subject in a June 1993 interview with David Rayside:

> Being able to effect a compromise—that's a basic rule with [Congress]. I can say, "By the way, my position is, only a total lifting of the ban is acceptable; now let me negotiate a compromise." Nobody around here is stupid enough to let you do that. . . . I saw a compromise coming, and I saw that compromise being negotiated without any of us. You can't be part of the compromise if you are not willing to compromise.

His action fit his general philosophy, delineated in a spring 1996 *Harvard Gay & Lesbian Review* article:

> It's bad enough having to plead, trade, and argue for rights that we should be able to take for granted. And as with any cause that is important, it's especially aggravating to have to argue with someone who you think should know better. . . . I understand how frustrating it is to have to persuade someone who should know it already that ending officially sanctioned homophobia is very important. I wish that it weren't necessary. But I also wish that I could eat more without gaining weight, and that I could work as long and hard today as I could 25 years ago without getting tired. But I restrict my food intake and say no to invitations and proposals that I would like to accept. And I spend time pushing my friends to do better when I wish I could simply insist that they behave appropriately and have them instantly respond.

More specifically, in *Uncommon Heroes* Frank said,

> I knew I was right. The difficult thing about the military situation was realizing that we were going to lose if we didn't find a middle ground. That was hard. But I knew reaching a compromise was the best thing. A lot of people disagreed with me, but I'm used to disagreeing with people on my own side.

Frank also assumed a high-visibility position on the House Judiciary Committee when in 1998 it reviewed President Clinton's dalliance with intern Monica Lewinsky and his subsequent denial of the relationship's sexual nature before a grand jury. Having experienced congressional discipline himself, Barney emerged as the Democratic voice of reason, and he was quoted in an October 1998 *Frontiers* article contrasting his experience with the president's: "I [acknowledged my actions] right up front. I said, 'This is true, and this is true.' I think the president would be in a better situation if he'd done that. . . . He made the mistake of denying it all." In an October 1998 *Advocate* article, Barney also stated, "While the president's behavior may indicate a character flaw, I don't think it raises to the level of an impeachable offense—not even close."

In 1998 Barney briefly reentered the dating pool before he began a new relationship that October, and he underwent coronary bypass surgery on June 30, 1999, after suffering chest pains. Asked about Bill Clinton's legacy in an April 2000 *Advocate* interview, Frank replied, "Clinton will play in history a role comparable to—but better than—John F. Kennedy on race. While he did not do everything I would have liked . . . he is the first president to act on the principle that sexual orientation discrimination is wrong." Despite having publicly criticized the Millennium March on Washington, *Frontiers* reported that "Although [Frank] showed up to speak, he left after long delays in the six-hour rally." (Frank explained in *The Advocate*, "It's not so much that I was annoyed at having to wander around for a couple of hours. . . . The speakers were so unfocused. No one really laid out a political strategy or how we are going to achieve our political goals in the election. A lot of people will be returning home without the information they needed.")

An hour one-on-one with a serving elected official for whom you are not a constituent is a rare honor. As one of my shortest interviews, it forced me to ask fewer questions than I would have liked. But unlike the stereotypical politician, prone to giving broad, evasive non-answers in response to questions, Barney stayed on point throughout. When he didn't want to answer a question, he told me so, and I respected his right not to answer. (He's not named Barney *Frank* for nothing!) When we spoke, Barney was one of three openly gay congressmen, but before the 1996 elections Gerry Studds retired and Wisconsin representative Steve Gunderson decided not to run against another Republican in a primary race. While Republican representative Jim Kolbe from my then-adopted state of Arizona came out in 1996, he and Barney, practically polar opposites on the political spectrum, served as the only openly gay members of the 105th Congress (despite rumors that they have plenty of closeted company).[4] While meeting with Barney, I developed quite an admiration for his savvy and ability on behalf of both his official and "unofficial" constituencies. And given his sharp wit and words, I am profoundly grateful Frank is on *my* side.

Notes

1. In his autobiographic novel *The Best Little Boy in the World*, Andrew Tobias pseudonymously wrote of a fictional character he later acknowledged as being based on Frank: "I would see the older bachelor faculty residents of the college trying to pick the same kind of friendly fights. They never fooled me. I knew exactly what they had in mind, or I thought I did. And when I saw myself acting like that, a perverted dirty old man of thirty-one—the future looked bleak." More than a quarter-century later, in *The Best Little Boy in the World Grows Up*, Tobias described Frank as "one tough, brave cookie."

2. Interestingly, Frank himself called for his investigation before the Ethics Committee, telling me, "I knew [Gobie] was lying, and I wanted a forum in which I could prove it. I knew that the most damaging things he was saying weren't true. . . . I had decided, in my own mind, I wouldn't run again. But I

had to also never contemplate quitting. Because if I'd quit, I wouldn't have had the forum. And the Ethics Committee [investigation] would have ended. And then people would have thought that the charges were true. So that's why I wanted the Ethics Committee investigation."

3. As Frank explained to Dreifus in 1996, "People on the left are more likely to say, 'Well, wait a minute, writing letters is nothing. We need a demonstration.' That is absolutely backward . . . . The first choice is to exercise political power, to scare them into voting the right way. Direct action is what you do when you have no power." Barney the politician does not fear criticizing those seeking easy solutions to difficult problems, telling a *Mother Jones* interviewer for a May/June 1995 article, "The gay community has tended to fuse cultural self-expression with political tactics. . . . Too much of our energy has gone into cultural self-expression, and not enough into conventional politics." Consistent with that philosophy, in 1998 Barney also questioned the effectiveness of a planned national March on Washington in 2000, stating, "It's going to be a terrible waste of energy and resources. I don't even begin to understand how it helps." Responding to such comments, in June 1999 then-MMOW producer **Robin Tyler** wrote, "So, Barney Frank, when you say public marches are not necessary, are a waste of time, I happen to strongly disagree with you. . . . [African-American Democratic Presidential contender Jesse Jackson] was right when he said that pressure must come from within and without. We're marching to keep the pressure on our elected officials. . . . We do not yet have one of the civil rights that we demanded in 1979."

4. Happily, they were joined in the 106th Congress by Wisconsin Democrat Tammy Baldwin, elected in 1998.

PART V

CREATING A NEW WORLD

33

JACK CAMPBELL

One of my heroes in the gay movement is Jack Campbell of Miami, the man who founded the Club Baths chain. He has given selflessly to the movement without ever asking for anything in return. Everything he earned in the bathhouses he has repaid a hundred fold back to the community.

—Leonard Matlovich, *Matlovich: The Good Soldier*, Mike Hippler, 1989

Contemporary gay American history has consistently overlooked Jack Campbell's good works. While even the conservative Leonard Matlovich appreciated Campbell's service, many people can't see beyond "Jack the bathhouse owner" to "Jack the aspiring politician" or "Jack the philanthropist." Others develop myopia focusing on his business and political skills, ignoring other aspects of Campbell's life. It seemed to me no historian ever looked objectively at Campbell, or accurately assessed his movement contributions. Jack and I spent a couple of hours together at his home in a Miami suburb shortly after Thanksgiving 1994.

The son of a doctor and a nurse, John Willard Campbell was born in East Grand Rapids, Michigan, on December 5, 1932. He received an undergraduate degree in accounting from the University of Michigan, and he earned a masters degree in business from Ohio's Kent State University. Campbell first engaged in sex at age fourteen, a not particularly sexually precocious age considering his later vocation. But politics ran in his blood: Jack told me, "I had a great-grandfather who was a state senator, and my father's father was a sheriff. . . . And an uncle who was a city commissioner."

Religion also played an important role in Jack's youth through what Jack believes was the greatest influence of his life. When Campbell and his family attended Fountain Street Baptist Church, its youth minister, Bob Houser, broadened young Jack's horizons.

> My senior year in high school, we took what was called the workshop tour, and one of the things we did was stopped at Hyde Park, New York, and Mrs. [Eleanor] Roosevelt had lunch for us at her little cottage. . . . And she arranged for us to go to the top of the U.N. Secretariat building, under construction at the time. We went to Washington, and of course our congressman—you may have heard of him—Gerald R. Ford? He arranged for an audience with a Supreme Court justice. I was very interested in politics at a very young age, from grade school. So I think it was because of Bob Houser.

Campbell described Fountain Street Baptist as "very liberal"; Houser knew of Campbell's homosexuality, but he didn't hold it against him. Consequently, Jack harbors no bitterness against organized religion, unlike many gays and lesbians whose experiences proved injurious.

In 1965, after graduating from Kent State, Campbell was "managing an art theater—porn films—in Cleveland Heights." The theater chain decided to open another theater on Cleveland's west side, so Campbell moved with it. "And I moved my YMCA membership from downtown to the west side Y, and there was—this was in the Little Finland area—there was an old Finnish sauna which was for sale. The man had had a heart attack, and I bought it—the whole building and the bathhouse—for less than it cost to put a whirlpool bath in a bathhouse." (Cleveland's previous gay bathhouse had closed in 1960.) Jack drew on his own knowledge, according to *The Other Side of Silence*: "I had been to San Francisco and so I knew that bathhouses didn't have to be so dumpy, like the ones in New York and Chicago. I specifically wanted a better, cleaner atmosphere." Campbell's $15,000 investment and his logic were sound: "I figured I just knew enough people that just if I ran it as a hobby, you know, it would do well. Well, it did so well that within a year I had to open a second place in Cleveland."

As the sexual revolution began to flourish in the mid-'60s and '70s, Campbell's Club Bath Chain (CBC) also expanded. Campbell opened his third bathhouse in Toledo:

Jack: [A]nd from that nucleus in northern Ohio, we just expanded in all directions. For a long time, we would just go into a city on the outskirts of a major metropolitan area, like Toledo was close to, but not in, Detroit. We went to a place near Chicago; to Newark, New Jersey, rather than to New York City.

Paul: And the reason behind that?

Jack: Well, we found that there were places where there were bathhouses that were just dumps, you know, owned by straights who certainly liked the gay business but wouldn't spend a penny to improve 'em. And we didn't want to go in and challenge the Everard Baths in New York City, or the Lincoln Hotel Baths in Chicago. For a long time, we thought we had to go into an area where there had been a bathhouse, where there would be clientele already broken into the idea—

Paul: [Laughs]

Jack: —of the charms and the necessities of bathhouses.

Once Campbell solidified his financial base, he began working within the established gay movement, helping Don Dickman found the Ohio Mattachine Society in 1967. Ohio Mattachine attempted to meet the social and emotional needs of its members, and he worked with the Ohio state legislature to abolish its sodomy laws; Jack told me Ohio Mattachine was "partially responsible for getting Ohio to become a reformed jurisdiction."

As CBC continued to flourish in the north, Campbell shrewdly gambled: "And then we decided, well, let's go south—there are no bathhouses in the South. So we went into Atlanta." The Atlanta venture succeeded, as did establishments in many other cities across the United States and Canada. While an element in the gay community has always looked upon bathhouses with distaste if not downright hostility, they provided a place where gay men could explore their sexual desires and fantasies in a safe environment. In the '80s several Chain links separated, but not before Campbell and others fought the most galvanizing gay civil rights battle in the United States.

On January 18, 1977, the Dade County (Florida) Metro Commission approved legislation sponsored by newly elected commissioner Ruth Shack that provided countywide gay civil rights protections. This disturbed singer/second-runner-up to Miss America/orange juice pitch-woman Anita Bryant; Shack's husband Dick had served for many years as Bryant's agent, and Anita had supported Ruth's campaign. Anita purportedly feared avowed homosexuals teaching her children because she perceived that gays "recruit" children to become homosexual. Thus, gay civil rights protections became a political hot potato.

Bryant and others, chiefly from the religious community, initiated a widely publicized referendum to overturn the progay legislation. As a result, the issue of homosexuality received unprecedented nationwide media exposure. Jack Campbell had moved to Miami in 1972; holding significant financial resources as well as more political clout than any other openly gay person in Florida, he fought Anita and her allies. He even found some sympathy in his heart for Bryant, revealing in a June 1977 *Newsweek* article, "A lot of people think she's doing this for publicity, but I don't doubt her sincerity or her motives for a moment. I know how Baptists think. There's just this feeling that homosexuals are not God's chosen people."

However, Campbell realized the Florida gay community's political abilities fell short of New York's and California's: "We didn't have any gays here who knew anything about politics. Other than the fact that I had run a campaign for state commissioner [in 1975], and Bob Kunst had run for county commissioner, we really didn't have people that were that involved in running campaigns." Accordingly, with *Advocate* publisher David Goodstein's help and funding, strategists such as Jim Foster and speakers/public figures such as Leonard Matlovich went to Florida to confront Anita's coalition. Unfortunately, many viewed the outsiders as "carpetbaggers." (Indeed, *The Other Side of Silence* recorded Campbell's recollection that "more money ultimately came in from the San Francisco Bay Area than from all of Florida.") Seven out of ten Dade County voters revoked the antidiscrimination referendum on June 7, 1977.

What does Campbell recall of that time? Perhaps most fascinating is the information Jack discovered after the battle ended. "I went to dinner with the Shacks, and I met the guy who had been some cigarette man, and he told me that he and Anita had had an affair while they were in a production in New York City years ago," Campbell recalled. And Bryant's husband, Bob Green, "was known to have homosexual activities. He didn't do it here [in Miami], but he was well known up in central Florida." While the Shacks knew this information, "they didn't think that we were going to lose," so they didn't share it with those fighting the referendum.

In 1978, acting on a tip from soon-to-be mayor Dianne Feinstein, a San Francisco undercover cop arrested Campbell on pimping charges in response to a *Bay Area Reporter* classified ad he placed seeking escorts for hire. Fearing the impact on California's Proposition 6 (similar to the Florida referendum) of the spectacle of a Campbell felony trial, Jack pled guilty to a misdemeanor. He said his attorneys "pled it out so it was similar to being found in a bawdy house." Since Campbell still resided in Florida, he believed the plea bargain a wise strategy: "It wouldn't affect me one way or the other."

At the peak of the Club Baths' success in 1983, with forty-three facilities in North America, Jack considered expanding into Europe. However, the advent of AIDS required changes in traditional aspects of the bathhouse milieu; for public health reasons, bathhouse institutions such as orgy rooms and "glory holes" were no longer sustainable. While Jack claims to have supported AIDS education by 1985, Randy Shilts reported in *And the Band Played On* that in May 1983, Jack "brushed off questions about the baths' role in the epidemic by insisting that most of Florida's AIDS cases were Haitians, and it wasn't a problem for gays." In retrospect, it seems easy to blame bathhouse owners for failing to take steps to retard the virus's transmission earlier in the epidemic. In fairness, absent sufficient knowledge about HIV or how it spread, few businessowners were willing to abandon or radically alter their facilities or the services they offered based on rumors and half-truths.

Campbell reflected on the uncertainty of how AIDS would impact his livelihood and that of other Club Baths owners:

> We experienced a precipitous decline after Rock Hudson announced that he had AIDS [in 1985]. By that time, we had had some internal problems. We sort of split up into two camps. One camp thought that we needed to not only educate our patrons, to provide free condoms, but also to do away with orgy rooms and areas where they had anonymous sexual activity, to brighten them up, and to add facilities more like a regular health club or gym.

On July 1, 1985, these ten facilities became the Club Body Centers. (Later, four others followed.) And the other camp? "They didn't want to do the education work," Campbell told me. "They felt that doing educational work was an admission that we were the breeding grounds for [AIDS]." Campbell sold them to individual owners, who were then free to decide as they wished within local restrictions, if any.

Over the years, Campbell's philanthropic nature and savvy business acumen benefited many gay organizations, including the Human Rights Campaign Fund (now HRC), National Gay Task Force (now NGLTF), Gay Rights National Lobby and National Gay Rights Advocates (both defunct), and the Gay Games Federation. Yet Campbell has received virtually no community recognition for his generosity. When I asked him why he doesn't receive more credit for his good works, Jack said, "Well, I really don't seek credit. I mean, I don't ask people for it. . . . I'm not looking for credit. I want results." Campbell seems to have made peace with his public persona, and he recognizes he is unlikely to receive the acclaim due him because of the way he earns his living. Yet **Ginny Apuzzo** strewed verbal valentines when I spoke with her about Campbell:

> Jack's a wonderful guy. He has been a consistent supporter of virtually every idea that has been generated on behalf of the community's interest. I genuinely believe that Jack loves this community. I think it's his first and most certainly lasting love. And he does it always with good humor. I have never seen Jack get bad-tempered, or carry a grudge, or put toxins into the mix about people. . . . I think Jack, like all of us, gets enamored with the accoutrements of power. But I think that Jack is a gay liberation person.

Southern Florida voters thwarted Jack's political aspirations, as several times he ran unsuccessfully for local political office (Miami city commissioner in 1975, an aborted Florida State Senate run in 1986, Florida House of Representatives in 1986, and Miami mayoral race in 1989). Instead, Campbell influenced national Democratic politics, serving several times as a Democratic National Convention delegate. Much as he enjoys politics, Campbell explained that in the future, "I definitely will not run for public office. Too much of a fishbowl."

Of Jack's fifteen lovers when I met him in 1994, Glenn Swann, Campbell's lover for six years beginning in 1985, received the most exposure. The bisexual HIV-positive Swann, twenty-six years Campbell's junior, modeled and performed in gay erotica. Swann met Campbell through fellow performer Rick "Humongous" Donovan and his then-companion, San Diego Imperial Court Empress Nicole Ramirez-Murray. Campbell told me his relationship with Glenn disintegrated primarily due to Swann's drug problems: "He used to tell me about the Martians up there on the roof." According to Campbell, Swann returned to San Diego and got his life together: "He went into a religious thing, a mission or something, where he went through rehabilitation." When I met Jack, his lover was young, attractive Alex Sanchez.

Campbell made gay news headlines in the summer of 1997, resulting from his encounters with serial killer Andrew Cunanan. In a *Fort Lauderdale Sun-Sentinel* newspaper article, Jack acknowledged meeting Cunanan three times, and having sex with him on one occasion in August 1996—the year before Cunanan killed designer Gianni Versace in Miami. The article also revealed that three days after Versace's slaying, Campbell received a telephoned death threat, which he believed came from Cunanan.

Jack would like to be remembered "for helping as much as I can to see our community make progress." While Campbell unquestionably influenced the movement, controversy has dogged his steps along the way. But, as I've learned through composing this book, every story has two sides. Jack's deeds deserve to speak for themselves.

34

DAVID KOPAY

> **I know that I had no choice but to come out. I was emotionally a mess at the time, and it was one way of getting rid of all my anxieties. Gay athletes have to have the opportunity to be open about themselves, and professional sports has the responsibility to make it possible.**
>
> —David Kopay, *The David Kopay Story*, 1977

Many little boys dream about becoming professional football players, although I never did; thanks to his bad knees, my father, the high school quarterback, steered me in a different athletic direction (for which I remain eternally grateful). But for all the boys who dream that dream, only a select few ever achieve it, even fleetingly. Some of those boys-becoming-men, not only in football but in other sports, also carry a secret: They dare not tell anyone about their homosexuality, lest someone forbid them from playing the game they love and earning an enviable salary while doing so. They may not know that a male athlete stepped forward in 1975 to acknowledge his homosexual orientation when the topic lay shrouded in innuendo and discussed in whispers. Almost a decade before the most famous contemporary openly lesbian athlete, Martina Navratilova, made her public disclosure, and well before athletes such as Glenn Burke and Billy Bean (baseball), Bruce Hayes (swimming), Rudy Galindo (ice skating), Amelie Mauresmo (tennis), Greg Louganis and David Pichler (diving), and Muffin Spencer-Devlin and Patty Sheehan (golf) shared their experiences, David Kopay shattered stereotypes about both athletes and gays. I spoke with Kopay shortly after Gay Games IV in New York in June 1994, in which we both participated.

David Kopay was born on June 28, 1942, in Chicago, Illinois, to Anton and Marguerite Kopay, sandwiched between his older brother Tony and his younger brother and sister, Gary and Marguerite. When David reached fourth grade, his family moved from Chicago to North Hollywood, California.

By his own admission, David did not grow up in a happy home environment: "I do not remember a time in our house when there was not some kind of fight going on between my parents. Not once do I remember them exchanging any kind of love words. What I most often heard them call each other was, 'You son of a bitch.'" A child of devout Catholics, young David had a difficult time with the church, especially as it pertained to sex: "I learned a lot about fear and guilt through the church, and very little about compassion and love." Nonetheless, David chose to attend a Claretian seminary for one and a half years.

In 1961, Kopay entered the University of Washington on a football scholarship. In 1964, Kopay's senior year, he cocaptained his squad, which played in the Rose Bowl that year. Academically, during the off-season Kopay earned a degree in history, and he considered applying to law school. But the hazings Kopay endured from his Theta Chi fraternity brothers terrified me:

> Hell Week—or hazing—came during the spring. The pledges had to scrub all the floors, paint almost every wall in the house, wear 'dingle bells' around their cocks and Kotex belts soaked in molasses without taking them off the whole week. . . . The pledges went through an exhausting routine of calisthenics—running in place, upsy-downsies, then they'd be broken down into relay teams for races, running with their mouths full of bitter alum water until a bucket had been filled, or picking up an olive off a block of ice with the crack of their ass and running with it. The loser had to eat the olive.

The other fraternity brothers also brutally paddled Kopay, like the other pledges; later he took his turn paddling others. Why withstand (and inflict) such torture?

> Maybe it's the same kind of peer pressure that kept professional athletes in the closet. It's really an intense kind of peer pressure, to be this stud, fucking the ladies, and not the guys. Not to be called a sissy, not to be called a wimp. . . . Looking back on it, I couldn't believe it when it was happening—the intensity of all the working-out activities, in this downstairs basement, and the heat that used to be generated, and really, the sexual energy, too. . . . But somehow it just

> kind of—it was brotherhood, you know. Something that kind of kept us together.

During college, Kopay also discovered sex, first with a woman, and later with a fellow male athlete.

Despite Kopay's fine college career, football's professional leagues did not draft him upon graduation. But the desire to play burned within him, and Kopay muscled his way onto the San Francisco Forty-Niners in 1964 as a free agent. He played ball for ten years in the National Football League (often as a member of the "suicide squad" or special teams) as a Detroit Lion, Washington Redskin, New Orleans Saint, and Green Bay Packer. Kopay also joined the short-lived World Football League in 1975, where he played on the Southern California Sun team. Professional football players in those days made only a fraction of today's lucrative salaries; as a football player, Kopay never made more than $32,000 a year. He agreed with me that finances might explain why so few athletes come out during their careers, and virtually no athletes in team sports; even Kopay admits, "If I'd had a lot more money, possibly I would have never spoken out." Kopay also knew his limitations as an athlete; speaking of Navratilova, he told me, "She was a real star. I was, like, a good ballplayer, but I wasn't any star."

At the suggestion of his analyst, Kopay married a woman in the early '70s. Despite their affection for one another, the marriage ended in divorce. I asked him whether he had contacted his ex-wife in recent years: "I talked to her about three years ago and had a wonderful talk—it was like, we were going to get back together and be friends, and I never heard from her after that. It's kind of sad. I didn't take any steps. I don't know what to tell you. I'd like to be friends." Kopay also involved himself for a short time in a degrading relationship with a married man, but he found that kind of pairing unfulfilling.

After so many years of punishing his body, by 1975 his career wound down. Now he could admit in public what he had explored in private: his homosexuality.

Also in 1975, a *Washington Star* editor assigned young sports writer Lynn Rosellini to write a series of articles about homosexuality in sports. While several athletes willingly acknowledged their homosexuality "off the record," not one would reveal his/her name. Despite its guardedness, Dave rejoiced at Rosellini's first article: "I could not believe I was reading those words. I sat there choking back laughter and tears. Homosexuality was finally being discussed openly and—something I never expected to see—on the sports page." Kopay had wrestled with his sexuality for many years before deciding to discuss the matter in print:

> I'd been thinking about it for a long time. Many people in the sports world already knew I was gay. My family knew. And I knew how difficult and frustrating it is to try to lead a double life. I was tired of compromising myself. When Lynn told me she needed my story to lend credibility to her series, I decided to do it. It was the right time.

Kopay's reading of Patricia Nell Warren's ground-breaking first book, *The Front Runner*, about a gay Olympic athlete and his coach/lover, "really pushed me over the edge on that." Kopay contacted Rosellini, whom he knew through her father, Albert Rosellini, governor of Washington while Kopay played at the university. The story broke on December 11, 1975.

No impulsive decision, Kopay anticipated what his honesty might sacrifice: his dreams of coaching; financial security; his relationship with his family. However, his need to tell the truth outweighed the possible personal repercussions. Later he told Robert McQueen in a 1976 *Advocate* interview,

> The impact amazes me. Look at all the incredible people who have made the same statement—doctors, lawyers, politicians, artists, performers, writers, military people, educators, businesspeople, to say nothing of just ordinary people who are openly gay and successful and happy. All I did was run around with a football under my arm for ten years.

In the same interview, Kopay continued, "Perhaps I was a catalyst in destroying a myth people felt secure believing in. [Rosellini's] series forced them to think about their own sexuality, how they should or shouldn't respond to it and to other people's. Hopefully they'll begin responding in more compassionate and understanding ways." Openly gay writer Merle Miller commented of Kopay's revelation, "This is history; he has killed a stereotype overnight."

But Kopay paid the price for his admission. Despite his skills, coaching jobs never materialized. As that door closed, he hoped to obtain the cushy sales rep jobs several players developed through their football contacts, but that didn't fly either: "When I first spoke out, then a lot of companies were too worried about them being identified as a gay company if they hired me." Kopay also related to McQueen in 1976, "I didn't realize how negative the reaction from my family would be." While his disclosure initially strained several family relationships, his sister and younger brother always supported him; Kopay's parents' and older brother's attitudes softened over the years.

An articulate Kopay avoided the stereotypical "dumb jock" label. But when he first came out, many in the gay community expected him to know more about current gay issues than might be considered reasonable, given his apolitical background. Certainly at the beginning, Kopay exhibited political naiveté. **Del Martin**, along with **Troy Perry** and Leonard Matlovich, spoke with Kopay in Texas in 1978 while all four raised funds for California's "No On 6" campaign. Del remembered both Kopay and the trip with chagrin: "I went with these three jocks. And Dave Kopay, in his speaking and so on—He even embarrassed the men! It was just unbelievable. . . . His talk was—all sex. And the jargon, and so on. And it was really embarrassing to people!" In contrast, writer Michael E. O'Connor wrote of Kopay in *Torso* magazine in October 1989, "Dave Kopay is sincere. And very likeable. A big teddy bear of a guy."

I personally experienced both sides of Kopay, the soft-spoken gentle man and the self-absorbed narcissist. So did **Rita Mae Brown**, who met him shortly after he emerged from the closet. But Rita Mae placed the blame for Kopay's failure to live up to great expectations as a gay hero/role model squarely on the shoulders of the men leading the movement at that time: Dave

> just made a real effort to do good for other people. He's extremely good looking; he's easy to be around; you can't help but like the guy. He could have been so important to us, in so many ways. And instead, all the guys did was hit on him. Instead of taking this man aside, and realizing, "Look here. This is a valuable person to us." Educate him. Don't try to get in his pants, you know. Realize that he has an enormous amount to learn. . . . But nobody helped him. . . . [T]he movement made a tremendous mistake with Dave.

And according to Dick Schaap, the biographer of athlete Tom Waddell, who "came out" shortly after Kopay, "Tom admired his courage but not his style. Tom feared that Kopay confirmed more stereotypes than he destroyed."

In 1977, Kopay and writer Perry Deane Young completed David's autobiography, *The David Kopay Story*. While it didn't affect my life as much as it affected the lives of others, it certainly showed me an additional lifestyle option besides drag queen, motorcycle man, and Castro clone. Kopay told O'Connor,

> I know what the book's done for a lot of people. I mean, it's done a lot of good for *me*, but it's also *legitimized* so many people in a way. I don't know, it's hard to say what it *does* do for different people. Sometimes I feel embarrassed by it all. I mean, it's kind of funny being famous for what comes naturally. Yet I'm not ashamed of it at all; I know it's the best thing I've ever done and maybe ever *will* do!

The David Kopay Story became a *New York Times* best-seller for ten weeks; Edward Alwood's *Straight News* reported it "the first book about a sports figure ever to appear on the list."

Perhaps because of years of hiding his sexuality, or perhaps because of his family background (or perhaps for neither reason), Kopay sometimes failed to harness an explosive temper. Even Young, who worked closely with Kopay, wrote of Dave's anger: "What would cause that look of absolute rage? A wrong turn or a question worded in a way that offended Kopay."

After completing his book, Kopay relocated himself in San Francisco in 1979, living with openly gay writer Armistead Maupin for three months and briefly selling cars. He moved to Fort Lauderdale for a time, remodeling homes, and then he accepted a job from one of his uncles at Hollywood's Linoleum City, where Kopay has earned his living for several years as sales manager. A more interesting job than one might think, much of Kopay's work goes into large-scale projects such as Hollywood sound sets and the like. Kopay remains hopeful someone will turn his life story into a television biography; he told me in 1994 that he had recently heard some rumblings to that effect again for the first time in several years, but I saw no such program by the end of 2000.

In stark contrast to places like **Frank Kameny**'s or **Jim Kepner**'s, not a paper or object sat out of place in Kopay's immaculate but small West Hollywood apartment. Likewise, Kopay has kept his body in enviable good shape; despite his fragile knees and incipient arthritis, he still can swim ("but it's so boring") and ride a Lifecycle, and he watches his caloric intake. However, even given the toll football took on his body, Kopay said that given the option, he probably would do it again: "I wish sometimes that I would have known that there were some other outlets, so I didn't have to *do* that, so that I wouldn't have known what it was."

In his book Kopay wrote, "I still hope to find a 'main man,' a meaningful sexual relationship with a best friend. . . . But at this time in my life what I want most is a real commitment of love with another man." I found no indication that such a relationship ever developed; Kopay told me, "I don't have a lover, but I have some loves in my life."

Does Kopay regret his outspokenness? In 1988 he closed the update to his book, "I feel so lucky in choosing the path I did. Would I speak out again if I had a choice? Absolutely. It's the best thing I've ever done, may ever do in my life. I feel so fortunate to be alive and well. I'm going to continue to speak out as long as I can talk." But in 1994 Kopay asked me, rhetorically,

> Why haven't any other athletes come out? I don't know why they haven't come out. I know I felt so desperate that I needed to come out. I also felt angry that I really wasn't getting any interviews for coaching jobs, and lots of rumors going on about me. I competed and really succeeded at every level—don't tell me I couldn't compete as a coach.

He added in an August 2000 *Advocate* interview, "I now think it may take another 25 years before an all-pro American ballplayer announces he's gay while in the sport." However, in the intervening years, I hope Kopay has been pleased with recent revelations by athletes in several sports.

While assembling this profile, a memory returned to me. I saw David Kopay for the first time at the Long Beach Pride Festival, probably in 1985; a friend of mine, probably a fellow Gay Men's Chorus of Los Angeles member, kindly pointed him out to me. I remember watching him, still an attractive man, walk alone into the sunset, and my sudden feelings of pathos. Having met him, in some ways I still feel sorry for him; Kopay is not the sort to surround himself with hordes of good friends (and hangers-on) and, like many others I interviewed, to some degree lives on past glories. But I believe David carries no self-pity. Maybe life hasn't treated Kopay fairly, but I sensed no bitterness. Kopay knows his coming out broke ground for every gay athlete who followed, which now includes many. I am grateful to him for that; I hope they are, too.

35

HOLLY NEAR

When I started being in relationships with men again, I could have done what some famous people had done, which was to immediately try to get on major networks, and say, "Well, my lesbianism was a phase. And this is my new boyfriend." Well, I didn't want to do that. And as far as I was concerned, if I was more useful being a lesbian, that was fine with me, because I don't care! You know, it's not an insult to me to be a lesbian, so I had no need to say I wasn't. . . . But the fact was, I felt that it was absolutely unnecessary to announce my heterosexuality until a new wave of visible, outspoken, lesbian, cultural people came along, that it wasn't time to leave a gap. Well, now those people have come along. But I still sing lesbian songs from the stage. It seems like a natural part of my life.

—Holly Near, 1995

I'll begin with the criticism to get it out of the way: "What's Holly Near doing in this book? She's not a lesbian any longer!" Well, that depends on one's worldview. Near lives her life in ways that eschew labels of any kind; for example, she believes no language yet exists to accurately describe her erotic nature. Certainly she willingly self-identified as a lesbian when music industry bigwigs considered such designation anathema to the kind of mainstream musical/theatrical career her talent otherwise might have dictated. But as one of the pioneers of the "women's music" genre in the '70s, Near and others revolutionized the way lesbians related to the world and one another, and Near's openness regarding her sexuality catalyzed many lesbians to claim their sexuality through the messages her music revealed. No less an impeccable lesbian feminist than **Charlotte Bunch** told me, "I think it's a really narrow view, to see Holly as selling out. I think what Holly has done to mainstream gay and lesbian consciousness to people who are politically progressive has been extraordinary." Holly remains a challenging presence in the music world, and so I include her here.

Holly Holmes Near was born on June 6, 1949, in Ukiah, California, two hours' drive north of San Francisco, and she grew up in nearby Potter Valley. Anne and Russell Near parented four children; Holly was born behind her sister Timothy, and ahead of her brother Fred and sister Laurel, respectively. She considers herself privileged to have grown up in a very liberal family ("We did weep for the Rosenbergs in my household, and we did listen to Paul Robeson") surrounded by a conservative community, and in an environment where her parents and siblings encouraged her performing gifts (writing, singing, dance, and stage direction among them) while developing their own. Yet a tug-of-war on Holly's emotions grated even then.

Music played a central role very early in Holly's life: Her Worldwide Web biography (www.hollynear.com) notes that "Near's love of performing began at age seven when she auditioned for a talent contest put on by the Veterans of Foreign Wars singing 'Oh, What a Beautiful Morning' from *Oklahoma*." In an interview with Harriet L. Schwartz published in the May 1998 issue of *Lesbian News*, Near acknowledged, "I have sung for as long as I have eaten and put my socks on in the morning. I was given a voice. It wasn't that I wanted to be a singer and I had to develop a voice. I was handed a voice on a silver platter—came into the world with it." Her childhood musical influences included "The Weavers, Odetta, Edith Piaf, Judy Garland, Elvis Presley, Rosemary Clooney, Miriam Makeba . . . and our own." In her touching autobiography, *Fire in the Rain . . . Singer in the Storm*, Near recounted auditioning before a Columbia Records representative at age ten, and flying across the stage at twelve at the Redwood Empire Fair as a juvenile Peter Pan (placing second behind a seven-year-old space-suited tap dancer).

In high school, Holly experienced small-town fame not only by playing Eliza in *My Fair Lady*, but also simultaneously by becoming football royalty. Holly acknowledged her awareness that

> it was a compromise. I had this huge need to feel accepted, and to be popular. Being a football princess was symbolic of popularity. And then I had this whole other life where I was involved in music and theater, which was not considered terribly cool. . . . So it was a way

> for me to get some kind of mainstream popular acceptance. And that's about what it meant to me. . . . Somehow it would tell me that, even though I was smart and assertive and talented, I was also helpless and pretty and desirable.

Unable to afford tuition at an eastern college, at age eighteen Holly attended UCLA for a year; she remembers the school as "a factory" and the experience "lonely." However, it provided a springboard for her acting career: "Music was the first love, but I thought in order to do musical theater, which was really my love, I would need to know acting and dance, so I took both of those." A zaftig young woman, she later described herself as "very much in demand. There weren't many chubby, twenty-year-old character actresses in Hollywood." She acted in a few television episodes (including *The Mod Squad* and *The Partridge Family*), and some mostly forgettable films, including *The Magic Garden of Stanley Sweetheart* in New York (where one reviewer described her as "the most charming" of the title character's numerous sexual encounters), and later in the movie version of Kurt Vonnegut's *Slaughterhouse Five*. But suddenly, perhaps on the brink of a more traditional Hollywood path to success, she remained in New York, joined the cast of the play *Hair*, and shortly thereafter traveled with Jane Fonda and Donald Sutherland, among others, in an antiwar show entitled "Free the Army" (FTA). FTA first played near U.S. service bases during the Vietnam War era, and then the show toured throughout the Pacific. Holly's FTA experiences helped her think even faster on her feet, and they afforded her an opportunity to bring her multiple talents before diverse audiences. In addition to her theatrical abilities, Near began to showcase her tremendous diversity of musical styles, including folk, peace, pop, country, musical theater, jazz, and feminist songs.

Returning to Los Angeles, Holly failed to secure a standard recording contract, despite her promising experience and obvious talent; "one label representative told [my agent] that I wouldn't become a successful pop vocalist because there was no element of submission in my voice." Not one meekly to suffer such rejection, she "decided to make an album of political songs and get it out of my system," founding Redwood Records in 1972 and releasing her first album, *Hang In There*, in 1973. For a small, independent label, and despite many growing pains and setbacks along the way (telling Elizabeth Shaw Green in a February 1983 *Frontiers* article, "I didn't know how to make a record when I first started. I didn't know what the hell I was doing! But I didn't know I didn't know"), Redwood experienced phenomenal success. Redwood Records made sixteen Holly Near albums, selling over 1.5 million copies (not counting Redwood's works with other artists). Near raised over $10 million for various causes, and, in 1989, along with her business partners Joanie Shoemaker and Jo-Lynne Worley, she transformed Redwood Records into Redwood Cultural Work, a non-profit arts organization.

Holly's journey into "women's music" intensified in 1975, when she, Margie Adam, Cris Williamson, and Meg Christian joined to perform a concert in Los Angeles, which later blossomed into the "Women on Wheels" tour. Today, thoughts of that tour conjure bittersweet memories for Holly; despite the music's brilliance, the four artists could not agree on the details of recording the concert for posterity:

> We were all fighting with each other by the time the show got up on the stage; started out friends, and we couldn't agree on anything by the time the show actually began. The music had already been rehearsed and prepared, and the show was together, so we were in the wings, we were not adoring one another, we walked out, and we did a great show, night after night, but we couldn't agree on who would own the recording, or who should record it, or who should produce it, or any of those things. So it didn't happen. And I wish we had taken a fifth party and said, "Record this, put it in a vault, and in twenty years, we'll bring it out."[1]

Initially, only Holly avowed heterosexuality among the Women on Wheels artists, but during the course of the tour she and Meg Christian "accidentally" fell in love. She admitted, "It was one of those loves of one's life that you hear about in movies. It wasn't healthy; it wasn't kind; it wasn't sensitive to the people around us. [Laughs] But I'll treasure it always." To pursue the relationship, both Christian and Near had to extricate themselves from another committed relationship; Holly now reflects on her behavior at that time as "inappropriate" because of the pain it caused those in its immediate vicinity. **Ginny Berson**, Christian's lover of four years at the time, felt some of that anguish. When I reminisced with Ginny about Meg and Holly's affair, she took the high road, saying, "It was not easy for me. And I'm sure it wasn't easy for [Holly]. Part of the difficulty for me was believing that it wasn't OK to feel how I felt. That there was no place for this sort of thing in the revolution. And so that made it much harder for me to deal with it all. . . . I mean, Holly does good work. She always has."

But for the nascent women's music movement, and for Holly and Meg, the relationship created an ethereal magic. "When Meg and I looked at each other on stage, you could hear the first hundred rows sigh, you know, because— Where could women go to see two women look at each other like that, you know? . . . But there was a lot of pressure to live up to everybody's fantasies." After three-and-one-half turbulent years, during which both lovers made several self-discoveries, including confronting issues of alcoholism and codependency, the relationship ended at Meg's behest. With difficulty, Holly continued forward.

Near gravitated toward coalition work with several different people and groups, including Inti-Illimani, a Chilean men's ensemble; folk singers Pete Seeger and Arlo Guthrie; Argentinian Mercedes Sosa; a black women's group, Sweet Honey in the Rock; Ronnie Gilbert of The Weavers; Afrikan Dreamland, a male black reggae group; The Flirtations, a gay group; and guest appearances with many of the gay and lesbian choruses (GALA) flourishing around the country.[2] Holly discussed the difficulties of processing issues in coalition work in her autobiography, and she described the process to me this way:

> Let's say you're putting together an event, and you have a panel of people you're inviting, and you have an hour's time in order to put the panel together. Well, if all you know is white men, it's going to be easier in that hour to gather white men to be on the panel. And, to me, even though that person putting on the panel is good-hearted, and maybe understands the limitation of the panel, he will go ahead and do it that way anyway. And somebody who is on a somewhat more complicated path may do it that way the first time. But they won't ever do it again. . . . And sometimes they'll do it wrong again and again, and kill themselves over it—they'll be in a state of despair over their inability to have their work reflect their vision. Whereas liberals, I don't think, agonize quite as much over it. They feel guilty, but they don't agonize in the same way that I think people who really want their work to reflect their vision agonize. And my life, as joyful and as exciting and as productive and all of the things it has been—still, there's moments—hours, days, years of agony, that I oftentimes could not have my work be as good as my vision.

When Near wrote "Singing for Our Lives" in 1978 to honor slain San Francisco supervisor Harvey Milk, a song many consider the gay movement's definitive anthem, did she know at the time that she was writing a work that would become renowned?

> No, I was writing a little folk song to get us through the night. I saw my work, aside from the fact that it was how I made my living, as a tool. I needed to keep my repertoire and my performing skills tuned so that I could play Carnegie Hall, and be an artist. And then I could let go of those standards, and climb up on a truck bed, and sing to striking nurses outside a hospital. If I didn't have a song to sing, I would write one, on the spot, or change a verse to meet the needs of that moment in time. So that was the spectrum of my challenge to myself as an artist, and I don't do it as much any more, but when I

> was at the height of all that, I was very good at, just on the spot, writing songs and verses to meet the needs of the moment. It was an exciting job to have! And you have to be able to just throw it away afterwards. You can't have the music be precious when you're working that way. You don't copyright it. You just toss it. It's there, people grab hold of it, what with their picket sign in one hand, and their song in the other. And then it's over, and you move on to the next one.

Holly's music—and her vision—have taken her from England, Scotland, Germany, Japan, Portugal, and the Philippines to Okinawa, Cuba, Vietnam, El Salvador, and Nicaragua. Near's vision also afforded her the opportunity to present a one-woman show in 1992, directed by her sister Timothy, that theatricalized the experiences Holly detailed in her autobiography.

Holly also talked with me about the self-induced pressure to excel:

> I was the brilliant kid from very early on, and I didn't really learn how to fail. I've always wished that I'd known how to go and play a game and be the worst in the game. Somebody has to be the worst. I'd always go to the game I was the best at, and I was very controlling about getting involved only with that at which I was the best. What a sad thing! It should be fun to be the worst at something. We should all get to do that. It's such relief. Now I'm trying really hard to do some things I'm not any good at, because one has to get rid of that pressure in order to learn. However, being so ambitious made me a prime candidate for service—and burnout.

In 1984, Near experienced the "burnout" she had anticipated. The breakdown coming in bits and pieces for some time, Holly admits to preoccupation with her work and resistance to make the lifestyle changes necessary to prevent it. First her voice began to falter, followed by her entire body. Finally, by 1985, Holly knew she had to take better care of herself. She told me, "I was as out-of-control as I've ever been. It was like on those trains, if you pull that brake switch. I feel that my brake switch got pulled, and everything screeched, and all the luggage fell on my head, and all the drinks spilled. And it was a mess, but it was good; I needed to have a mess in order to instigate change in my life." She began working arduously

> with a kinesiologist-chiropractor and with healers. I tried acupuncture and massage and Alexander technique and yoga. I consulted a surgeon, a neurologist, and worked with a physical therapist. I let a lover into my life. I went on a stimulant-free diet, no sugar, alcohol, or caffeine. I spent a lot of time alone trying to get to know myself apart

> from my work. . . . There was no walking on water. I rowed every inch to get across the river.

Holly also had to learn how to rest; given her active spirit, that task may have proven the most difficult. She also said that "getting well was the hardest work I had ever done." As a result, in 1995 Near described her journey to me as putting her "in the place now where I'm really enjoying replacing some of those familiar ways with new systems. It's taken me ten years to do it, but it's really delightful. By doing less, I'm doing more. Instead of running around in circles to get from A to B, I just go from A to B."

Holly and I also spoke about her sexuality. She shared a "very loving" **Robin Tyler** joke with me regarding her sexuality: "Holly has really been a challenge for me. Because now, when I say I'm a lesbian, I have to say I'm a lesbian who sleeps with women!" Examining her feelings and identifying her heart's leading has always challenged Holly, particularly as her sexuality remained fluid:

> When I started having a relationship with a man again, the hardest part for me was fearing that I would somehow betray [the lesbian community's] trust. And there was a part of me that just said, "This is ridiculous! Every intelligent woman should be a lesbian!" It was more a problem with my own intelligence than anything else, you know. I just couldn't believe that I had heterosexual tendencies again!

In her autobiography, Near

> figured I was a grown-up now. I could decide when and with whom to make love without asking the permission of ten thousand dykes. Oh, but it isn't true. I was letting other people's judgment throw me into an identity crisis that I wasn't having. I doubt that any single time in my life has been more emotionally stressful.

At one point, after she again sexually involved herself with men, Near described a conversation with a man in Mexico: "I told him I was lesbian . . . well, I am except when I'm not. He asked if I was bisexual. I said I didn't feel like a bisexual. I felt like a lesbian when I was with a woman, and a lesbian making love to a man when I was with a man." In some ways, the issue remains unresolved for Near:

> I think that I'm far enough away now from my last lesbian relationship that I probably don't feel quite that way any more. Or at least I wouldn't use that language. . . . Sometimes I fall prey to language

> just because I get tired, you know? . . . Language oftentimes leads us to war. And I see it happening around sexuality.

In her book, Near concluded, "I needed to end my part in the co-dependency that might have developed between me and the lesbian community. We didn't owe each other political correctness. We owed ourselves meaningful lives."

In between her travels to the corners of the earth, Holly lives in a small home in Ukiah "in a really sane and healthy domestic situation" with Pat, a charming man. "Tired of jumping from relationship to relationship," Near hopes she and Pat will stay together, but she doesn't rule out the possibility of involving herself in a relationship with a woman in the future.

While Near has explored many options in the performing arts, she still would like to perform an entire concert with an orchestra and sing in a jazz quartet. "I used to think I wanted to play the lead in a grand Broadway musical, but I don't really want to do that any more. This is going to make me sound lazy, but it's too much work. . . . The thought of doing a show eight times a week! I don't know that I'd want to do that to myself."

We also discussed leadership in minority communities, especially in the lesbian and gay communities:

> The women's movement has a terrible time finding leaders! And I think that we came out of an era where people actually didn't respect leaders, and nobody wanted—you know, there was certainly a time in the women's movement where nobody wanted anybody to do anything better than anybody else; to function on the lowest common denominator in order not to hurt anybody's feelings. We were struggling with concepts of equality. . . . The leaders that I'm looking for now don't come out of a singular community. I don't think that a leader from a singular community can take me where I need to go as we approach the millennium. . . . Someone rising out of a singular community cannot be a world leader. I'm looking for fifteen or twenty people who find each other, and come to a position of leadership together. That would be really unique and powerful.

Yet Near herself has led ably, influencing the lives of many other lesbian and gay community workers, including "men's music" pioneers Ron Romanovsky and Paul Phillips. Charlotte Bunch pointed out, "I think Holly tried to bring what it means to be successful in the world and bring it together with being political, and committed to her causes. And I think she has a great deal of integrity about that."

Since I interviewed Near, she has hardly rested on her musical laurels. Holly recorded a duet with Mary Travers for Peter, Paul, and

Mary's *LifeLines* album, helped Ronnie Gilbert celebrate her seventieth birthday in 1996 with their joint album, *This Train Still Runs*, and recorded an album of old standards in 1997's *With a Song in My Heart*. (Fine music lovers should not overlook this simply beautiful and timeless album; likewise for Near's 1987 collection of love songs, *Don't Hold Back*.)

In 1998, Near permitted herself a "semi-sabbatical," noting on her website, "I am enjoying a break from 25 years of a non-stop schedule. It is giving me time to think, time to let in new ideas, time to prepare for whatever is coming next." (What came next included two new releases, *Edge* and *Simply Love*, the latter a comprehensive retrospective of '70s and '80s feminist songs, including her own.) And without experiencing biological motherhood, children play an important role in Holly's life. Speaking of her partner Pat's two daughters and two grandchildren and Holly's own five nieces and nephews, she states, "I inherited children. It has been good for me, for them, and for their parents."

As a writer, I can tell you only so much about Holly Near; the written word seems inadequate to do her justice. Listen to her music; read her book; spend an evening with her if she comes to your town. Experience Holly Near's bountiful gifts. It may not change your world, but then again, it just might.

Notes

1. In another version of the story, Margie Adam recalled in *The Girls Next Door* that Holly quashed the recording, arguing "that four white women with privilege should not get still more validation for our work, when there were so many equally talented women disadvantaged by race and class who still had not had the opportunity to record at all."

2. She received the first GALA Legacy Award in 1996 "in recognition of unique contributions to the Lesbian and Gay Choral movement."

36

MIRIAM BEN-SHALOM

The Army taught me how to be strong. If you wonder why I was able to fight all those years, it's because of the qualities of leadership and courage that the Army instilled in me. It was part of their training. . . . I think the Army allowed me to find myself. I finally had a sense of who I was. . . . The Army raised a fighter. Big mistake. And they spent seven million dollars keeping me out of the military. I could have been on their side.

—Miriam Ben-Shalom, 1995

Strong, stubborn, proud, driven. How else could one describe a woman who battled her government for nearly a decade and a half, refusing it to deny her right to serve her country before exhausting every possibility? How about intelligent, funny, light-hearted, and sweet? As I spoke with her in Milwaukee, Wisconsin, in the summer of 1995, it seemed that Miriam Ben-Shalom possessed two almost totally disparate personalities. She treated me with incredible kindness during my brief stay with her, and she wields a finely honed wit. We had a marvelous time together before and after recording our interview. But the combination of the memories of her shabby treatment and my gentle probing tapped a wellspring of anger over her treatment by the army during her prolonged ordeal when Miriam's government decided her lesbianism rendered her unfit to serve her country.

Miriam Ben-Shalom was born on May 3, 1948, "in the back seat of a car, in Waukesha, Wisconsin." She was "raised wonderfully well," the oldest of a family of six (three brothers, two sisters). Miriam told me, "There is something about Wisconsin and the darkness during the winter that either makes a person turn, or they go deep. And I can't say that I've turned—perhaps it might be said that I run deep."

She first recalled identifying her attractions to females as early as fifth grade. "But I wouldn't have been able, in all fairness, to say that I was a lesbian or it was sexual, because it wasn't. I can say that in high school I had an enormous crush on—are you ready?—of course—the female gym teacher. Her name was Miss Gazelle. I mean, I would have died for her!"

Ben-Shalom is also a mother; her daughter, Hannah, is, in Ben-Shalom's words, "A well-grounded and open woman. She's a wonderful 'kid.' She is strong in her own right. And what I appreciate about her a whole lot is that she's turned out to be a very honorable human being, and that, perhaps, is the biggest compliment of all. . . . I am proud of her, more than anybody can ever possibly know."

What about the U.S. Army Reserves appealed to Ben-Shalom when she joined in 1974? "I was looking for a career, you know. I was a single parent, and just—it was an option. . . . I was looking for something to do with myself—what I could do, and so I thought I'd try the army. So I went into the reserves—you stick your toe in the bathtub water. And I found I liked it very much." In her initial service interview, she answered "No" to a question about homosexual tendencies, adding, "I don't have tendencies—I am one." Then why did the army accept her anyway? "I think they saw me as sort of like a female equivalent of a heterosexual male, who would harass and otherwise try to—without ever realizing that my system of ethics and my morals are much different."

Ben-Shalom served with distinction and without difficulty until she came out to a newspaper reporter in Fort Leonard Wood, Missouri, in 1975. As Miriam explained, she and another woman "were the first two female drill sergeants ever. We got our hats the old-fashioned way; we earned them." As a result, a news article profiling both women appeared: "I guess I was developing a sense of my own pride in who and what I am. . . . I felt it was the thing to do, because I was asked, 'Who are you? Who are you?' Well, I was a chaplain's assistant, who was getting my bachelor's degree in Hebrew Studies." And she defined herself as a "radical lesbian feminist." Even though her provocative remark did not receive public dissemination at that time, a television interview with three of Ben-Shalom's male classmates revealed that Miriam's lesbianism didn't matter because of her soldierly competence. Miriam's choice not to serve in silence obviously discomforted the army, which honorably discharged her in November 1976. At that point, most people would cut their losses and move on. Not for the first time, the army underestimated Miriam Ben-Shalom.

Why did Ben-Shalom keep fighting after receiving an honorable discharge (when the army easily might have awarded her a general or dishonorable discharge due to her sexual orientation)?

> Because I wanted my job back. . . . I felt that since I had [done] no harm to anyone, and I was conducting myself appropriately, that it was morally repugnant and morally bankrupt to take my job away from me. I really liked serving my country. I liked being a soldier. I would have gone active duty. I would have been happy to do twenty, thirty—as many years as I could have in the service of my country.

Thus began a fourteen-year struggle with enough twists and turns to fill any daytime drama.

Miriam and Hannah toured the country to publicize Miriam's dismissal among gay and women's groups, and they solicited donations to fund her court challenge. Despite the support and the funds raised on her behalf, Miriam confessed, "it was extremely disheartening to me, because of [similarly discharged gay soldier] Leonard Matlovich and his unwillingness to account for all the money that was raised [during his earlier tour], and stuff. It made it very hard, and I almost gave up." During this time, Miriam also earned her B.A. (1977) and M.A. (1981) in English from the University of Wisconsin.

When Ben-Shalom filed suit against the army at trial court level in 1978, that court found in Miriam's favor. On May 20, 1980, U.S. District Court judge Terence Evans ruled that the army violated Ben-Shalom's First Amendment right to free speech—in effect, her assertion of her lesbianism did not predispose her to criminal acts (i.e., expressing her sexuality overtly with another woman)—as well as her Ninth Amendment right to privacy of personality. Miriam thus won the first successful challenge against the U.S. Armed Forces, but the gay media largely failed to credit her accordingly. (Having deemed Matlovich the "poster boy" for the gays-vs.-the-military fight, perhaps they preferred to keep matters simple. Or, worse, perhaps they didn't want to acknowledge the stereotypicality of a lesbian drill sergeant.) Miriam remains disturbed about the publicity Matlovich's victory received in relation to her case:

> Leonard Matlovich won in September of 1980. My decision . . . came down in May of 1980. . . . And what irritates me is that historian after historian—and it's usually white males who don't want to give credit where credit is due—will try to credit Leonard Matlovich, when, in fact, it was a midwestern woman who first won, and who subsequently became the first openly gay person in history to go back in

> the military. . . . I don't frankly give a damn. But I hate inaccuracy in history, and I don't much like where credit is given where no credit is due. . . . It was not a white, gay male who first won, and it has not been white gay males who established the precedents for the victories that you're seeing now. [In fellow African-American soldier Perry Watkins's words,] it was literally "a nigger and a kike."

Judge Evans ordered the army to "reinstate" Ben-Shalom, but the army chose to disregard the court's order. By 1983, as the army continued its intransigence, Ben-Shalom again brought suit, this time accusing the army of contempt of court. Not until August 18, 1987, did the Seventh Circuit Court of Appeals affirm the lower court's ruling forbidding the army to ban Miriam from serving her country. As Randy Shilts reported in *Conduct Unbecoming*,

> For seven years, the government had refused to reinstate her, contending that it was not sure how to interpret the earlier order to reinstate Ben-Shalom, which led the court to observe tersely, "We are baffled by the [secretary of the army's] asserted confusion over the word 'reinstatement' in the 1980 order. The District Court specifically ordered that the Army 'reinstate [Ben-Shalom] as a member of the Army Reserves with all duties, responsibilities and privileges earned prior to her discharge.' The order could hardly be clearer."

Finally, under threat of a $500 per diem fine, the army reenlisted Ben-Shalom to serve the remainder of her original stint, which she did from September 12, 1987, until August 11, 1988. While permitting Miriam to serve should have lain all the army's unfounded fears to rest (as well as demonstrated its policy's inherent irrational prejudice), the army instead appealed the Seventh Circuit's decision.

Following the army's belated reinstatement, Miriam explained,

> From 1987, August, until the end of February, the very last day of February in 1990, I was the only acknowledged homosexual in any branch of service in this country. Were there others? Of course there were. But I was the only acknowledged one. And the army didn't die. I got a commendation as an openly gay person; I got a promotion as an openly gay person. I was constantly given superior enlisted efficiency ratings, and stuff like this. I was rated, when I was finally put out, in the upper 5 percent of all soldiers in the Eighty-Fourth Division.

Never, through all the arguments and court battles and rhetoric, did the army allege that Ben-Shalom performed unsatisfactorily.

In the spring of 1988, while still on active duty, Ben-Shalom formally requested reenlistment. On April 7, the army refused, arguing that while the courts had ruled Ben-Shalom could *say* she was a lesbian, army regulations forbade her from *being* one.

Shortly thereafter, the court battles began resolving themselves in Miriam's opponents' favor. In his August 7, 1989, decision for a unanimous three-member panel of the Seventh Circuit Court of Appeals, Judge Harlington Wood, Jr. ruled that Miriam's statement acknowledging her lesbianism offered "compelling evidence" that she had engaged in homosexual acts and would do so again. His inaccurate ruling particularly galled Miriam: "I have to live with that for the rest of my life, that I've been convicted of and punished for telling the truth. . . . That's like saying you're a white heterosexual male, you might do a rape. That's what really hurt."

Miriam appealed the Circuit Court's ruling to the U.S. Supreme Court. On February 26, 1990, it refused to hear her case; the Seventh Circuit ruling would stand unchanged. Her response? "I feel devastated. I feel outrage. I feel angry. What in the name of God do I need to do to be a citizen of this country and be fit to serve her?" But her fight to return to U.S. military service had exhausted all legal avenues for redress. To demonstrate the capriciousness of such laws, her good friend Perry Watkins secured his court victory the same year Ben-Shalom lost, but it had no far-reaching application in other cases pertaining to gay servicepeople, including Miriam.

The battle took a personal toll. Ben-Shalom told Mary Ann Humphrey in *My Country, My Right to Serve*,

> I've had "Nazis" threaten my life. . . . I've lost so much . . . lost my house, custody of my daughter for a while, employment. It's real hard to get a job when you're on the front page of the newspaper and people think that you're highly radical and highly adversarial. I was shot at in Indianapolis . . . somebody loosened the lug nuts on the drive wheel of my truck . . . I had my brake linings cut.

When I spoke with her in July 1995, she remained seriously in debt as a result of her protracted legal wrangling:

> There has been very little [organizational] support; nobody cares. You know, I have some good friends who have cared . . . . But, in fact, nobody has ever said, "Geez, she's been paying off all these legal fees herself, working three jobs." I mean, all last year, I worked seven days a week—four and then two nights a week. I didn't have a day off.

However, in 1994, she received a $25,000 Anderson Foundation Award, which allowed her metaphorically to "plug the holes in the boat and keep it afloat, you know. And not have to pump water with such fierceness."

For many years, Ben-Shalom taught as a substitute in Milwaukee's public high school system, working with emotionally disturbed and developmentally disabled kids, among others. She now teaches in the West Bend School District. She has also taught at Milwaukee Area Technical College for sixteen years as a communication and English instructor, and she has taught in a male prison for young offenders. Did her training as a drill sergeant adequately prepare her for teaching? "Yeah, in some ways . . . . I end up going to a lot of alternative programs because they think that I would be able to handle some situations." However, even Miriam has not mastered all situations: Frequently hassled for being a Jew (more than for being a lesbian), Ben-Shalom suffered a permanent partial disability when a student assaulted her. With her lover Karen and a gay male couple, she also ran an antiques and collectibles shop, where I saw her "in action" on the Sunday afternoon I interviewed her.

In addition to fighting the army, Ben-Shalom has also expended considerable energy at various times clashing ideologically with the women's and gay movements' established positions:

> One of the reasons why the women's movement hasn't done as much as their potential would indicate [is] because there are people who want to process, and there are doers. I'm a doer. . . . Give me a job; I don't have time. . . . And I can accept people who are different than me, but I have no patience with people who cannot accept me as I am.

Of the gay movement, she says, "Now I do think we've reached a point where the only fights that people want to fight are the ones that they know they will win." Nevertheless, she remains active in her community, working with Milwaukee's PrideFest Committee. And to my delight, in 1999 Arizona Central Pride, Phoenix's gay pride parade committee, chose Miriam as its grand marshal, a role she filled with quiet power and grace despite the heat—even in April, Arizona is a world apart climactically from Wisconsin!

Politically, in 1992 Ben-Shalom ran for U.S. vice president on the Queer Nation ticket (with drag queen Joan Jett Blakk running for president). Both the Clinton administration's "Don't Ask, Don't Tell" military policy and the gay leadership's response to it disappointed Miriam:

> If President Clinton had shown the strong kind of principled leadership, and raw leadership, and said to our community, "OK, I'm writing the executive order. Quietly. You shut up. I'm gonna do it. Let it

> go." And then said to the military, "Here's the executive order. I'm your commander in chief. If you don't like it, I want your resignation letter inside of twenty-four hours." There are some who would have harrumphed and rattled their sabers and postured a little, but soldiers are soldiers, and they will take orders.

Speaking of the gay leadership at the time, she commented,

> The Campaign for Military Service [where Miriam worked in Washington, D.C., in 1993] was doomed because it did not have enough military people working for it, and for those of us who were working, we were not listened to. . . . Basically, you know, it was a lot of people who didn't know very much about the issue. And it was very frustrating. That, and they started talking about "principled compromise." And I watched people just, you know, sell veterans and active duty people from our community right down the creek. At one point, I literally stood up and said, "How many more pieces of our lives will you sell out? Will you toss out? Where is the principle here?" . . . HRCF and NGLTF themselves were not totally committed to the issue. They really did not take it seriously. And there wasn't a real good spirit of cooperation going on.

In fairness, Ben-Shalom acknowledged her temper: "It takes a lot to provoke it, but once it gets provoked, it's like I flare, and then I let it go. . . . I think that's probably my greatest weakness."

What does Miriam want? Besides desiring to own a Harley-Davidson motorcycle, Miriam confessed,

> This is silly, but just once in my life, I would like to be pretty. I'd like to see a cure for AIDS soon! I wish I could do more to help people, and I live for the day—no, my fantasy is that I *will live* to see the day when what a person is privately won't matter at all. . . . That the competency of a person for a job will be all that matters. And I wish Jesse Helms, Jerry Falwell, and the Reverend [Fred] Phelps would all disappear immediately.

If Ben-Shalom had the power, what would she change about the gay and lesbian community?

> First of all, I'd give us a swift kick in the ass, and tell us to stop being so damn sexist and so damn racist, *and* homophobic. The second thing I would do is say, "Respect those who have come before you, and listen to their history, because if we don't learn now, history is doomed to repeat itself again." And the third thing I would say is, you can't sit around on your laurels thinking nothing is going to happen.

Her bluntness reflects one part of her personality; in her earlier days, "It was like, 'Up against the wall, redneck asshole.' I have mellowed with age—I'm just like, 'Up against the wall, you redneck' now, and leave off the 'asshole.'"

When I asked Miriam how she would like to be remembered, she told me, "If they would say of me, she was a good soldier and she served her country well, it would be enough for me. Or, conversely, if they would say that I was a person of honor and integrity, it would be enough." The army acknowledged the former; I'll vouch for the latter. The last word goes to her fellow Wisconsonian, **David Clarenbach**, who said of her: "Miriam Ben-Shalom should be on the front cover of every gay newspaper. . . . She is the hero of our movement."

37

VIRGINIA URIBE

I thought that I could change things overnight, when I first started. I thought all kids would be healed, and everybody would come out of the closet. Now, you know, that lasted about thirty seconds. [Laughs] So I've had to reconcile myself that [my work is] a step.

—Virginia Uribe, 1994

Virtually everyone agrees that perpetrators commit child abuse against some of the most vulnerable members of our society. Except, perhaps, the Rev. Lou Sheldon or a member of his Traditional Values Coalition, who blithely accept systemic abuse of gay/lesbian children in the public schools, and who believe that teaching that lesbians and gays are neither mentally ill nor inherently more sinful than nongay people equates to proselytizing for homosexuality. As the founder of the Los Angeles Unified School District's Project 10, a dropout prevention program for gay and lesbian youth, Dr. Virginia Uribe learned a lot about Rev. Sheldon and the TVC ("I believe that he's a child abuser if there ever was one, in the things that he says, and the messages that he puts out"). However, this grandmother (whose partner calls her "the biggest scaredy-cat in the world. The only thing she's not afraid of is the right wing!") might never have mustered the courage to confront them but for the plight of one student at Fairfax High School, two blocks south of West Hollywood, where Dr. Uribe began teaching science in 1959.

Chris H., a seventeen-year-old black student, arrived at Fairfax High in 1984 after bouncing among several schools in the Los Angeles public school system. Although a good student, liked by his teachers and generally successful in his interactions with other students, from his first day on campus Chris received physical abuse from some students, and verbal harassment from some Fairfax staff. As a result, administrators transferred Chris out of Fairfax. While in the process of claiming her lesbianism, Dr. Uribe became aware of the abuse Chris suffered at the hands of unenlightened students, staff, teachers, and administrators. Ultimately unable to help Chris, Uribe resolved to develop and administer a program to better serve lesbian and gay students in her district. Thus Dr. Uribe began to advocate for gay and lesbian youth ("I don't even know what 'open' [about one's homosexuality] means. . . . For me, it means, are you an advocate? Are you willing to put up a poster? You know, are you willing to do something?"), and devised Project 10.

Dr. Virginia Uribe ("Gina") began life as Marilyn Virginia Rubino, born in Los Angeles on December 20, 1933. As a child she dreamed of an adventurous life: "I wanted to be a detective, or I wanted to be a spy, I wanted to be a soldier. [Laughs] All kinds of things that were not very ladylike." At that time, society severely restricted women's career opportunities; most of the graduates of her alma mater, Immaculate Heart College in Los Angeles (where Uribe received her B.A. in 1955 and her M.A. in 1962), chose careers in teaching, nursing, or social work. Had she been born male, Uribe believes she would have ventured into politics; her grandfather, the most influential person in her life, played an active role in Democratic circles. Fortuitously, Gina chose teaching: "Teaching has been very good to me. It turned out to be just a wonderful choice for me. But it was not something I had a burning desire to do from when I was a little kid." In 1988, Uribe received her Ph.D. in Psychology from Sierra University.

While she recognized early in her life that she loved women, she had no frame of reference regarding lesbianism: "I tried very hard not to identify with that term." Before confronting her internal homophobia in the mid-'60s, Gina tackled misogyny as demonstrated by her local Catholic church hierarchy. When Uribe's beloved Immaculate Heart nuns attempted to follow Pope John XXIII's teachings to modernize the church, their local conservative superior, one Cardinal McIntyre, defied the pope and declared Immaculate Heart to no longer constitute a religious order. McIntyre's demonstrated misogyny caused Gina to question her faith, and she ultimately left the church.

Uribe married and bore two children before she began to acknowledge her true sexual orientation at age thirty-five, an agonizing process for her. Under the best of circumstances divorce generates pain; in Gina's case, her ex-husband twice unsuccessfully attempted to have the courts declare Gina an unfit mother because of her lesbianism. Lost among the personal wrangling and political posturing of others was Gina's abiding love for her children and grandchildren: "I'm a real Italian, family person." Both Uribe and Gail Rolf, a health teacher at Emerson High, and Gina's life-partner since 1989, have supportive families who nurture them and honor their relationship.

Dr. Uribe began Project 10 by cautiously approaching her principal, Warren Steinberg, with her idea. Steinberg pleasantly surprised Gina when he told her, "We're public school educators. And we serve the needs of all of our children. And this is a need." His support "gave me a lot of courage"; combined with the support of members of the Los Angeles School Board, Uribe continued pressing forward.

Why did Dr. Uribe stick her neck out for gay and lesbian kids when other lesbian and gay teachers chose to look the other way? "I'm not going to take upon myself unnecessary heroism. I was older. From a pragmatic standpoint. I guess in the back of my mind, I'd always thought, you know, if things got too horrible, I could just retire." A television piece on an openly gay physics teacher in her district also encouraged and inspired her. But while the tremendous support from administration she received from the very beginning encouraged (and amazed) Uribe, reaction from her fellow lesbian/gay teachers disappointed her. In her naiveté, Gina's discovery that Fairfax's closeted homosexual teachers feared her efforts dismayed her: "I thought here I am, breaking down the barrier, that everyone can just follow through. And it just didn't work that way at all." While the situation at Fairfax improved, Gina believes most of its gay teachers remain closeted.

Next, Gina had to sell Project 10 to the students. In a news article with Kieran Prather, Gina described the beginning weekly rap groups:

> I saw here the students I had been reading about. Though very intelligent and dedicated, they were still performing badly. They had poor self-images and had become isolated; many went to private counseling, and some had attempted suicide. I had never really seen kids as damaged as those gay and lesbian kids.

As Gina recalled, "At first [the gay Fairfax students] thought it was kind of crazy. . . . [But t]hey took to it. I mean, we started having our little lunch, and we had formal meetings, and we got to where there were about twenty-five or thirty kids that would come. They thought it was wonderful." While some of the heterosexual students initially worried the publicity might cause people to think Fairfax served *only* gay students, Gina described it to me by 1994 as "a nonissue." Most of the districts in the Los Angeles public school system have adopted a Project 10-type program of their own, focusing on education, reduction of verbal and physical abuse, suicide prevention, and dissemination of accurate AIDS information. Uribe's partner Gail Rolf became Project 10's full-time coordinator following Gina's retirement.

But retirement hasn't restricted Uribe to a rocking chair; on the contrary, a May 2000 *Frontiers* article reported that

> [a]fter running the program from her Pasadena home for nine years, Uribe retired (some say she works all the harder now) to head Friends of Project 10. Her goal is to secure a $2.5 million endowment to ensure the funding of the various scholarships, leadership programs, and other events the Project operates.

By a quirk of fate, this very nonthreatening woman became a person the TVC loves to hate:

> The nastiness all comes from organized groups. And when that first descended on me, I didn't know that there were such groups. I thought I was the first person they had ever attacked! That was hard! And they're so nasty! Awful, lying, terrible people! And I had no idea what kind of tactics, the smear tactics and things that they would employ.

But they failed to recognize Uribe's greatest personal strength: "My ability to carry forth my idea in the face of opposition. My clarity of what I want to do."

Dr. Uribe also participated in programs with the EAGLES (Emphasizing Adolescent Gay and Lesbian Education Services) Center, a separate high school begun in the early '90s for lesbian and gay kids who cannot successfully integrate into a traditional school setting. From a practical standpoint, Gina knows that many EAGLES Center students "aren't gonna graduate if they don't go there! They're gonna be dead, or on the street. But philosophically, I would like to see the schools open up, and be more sensitive to their gay and lesbian students. And see that they're not harassed, and that they find a welcoming environment in their own high school." Dr. Uribe served as a chaperone at the EAGLES Center's first gay/lesbian prom at the L.A. Hilton on May 20, 1994; approximately 150 kids had a great time after Project 10 supporters raised the money for the event from nondistrict sources. Gina pointed out that New York City's Harvey Milk School equates to the EAGLES Center, but unfortunately New York has no program comparable to Project 10 for mainstream students.

How does Uribe think she will be remembered?

> I don't know. Maybe they'll think of me as that little old lesbian grandma in Pasadena. I think my greatest contribution in Project 10 is

> to have opened the door of discussion. I mean, that doesn't seem so great now. But ten years ago, nobody, ever, ever, ever, talked about this. And I think [I'll be remembered for] that opening up, just saying these words.

The Project 10 handbook quotes Erik Erikson: "Some day, maybe, there will exist a well informed, well considered and yet fervent public conviction that the most deadly of all possible sins is the mutilation of a child's spirit." In Ginny Vida's *New Our Right to Love*, Uribe wrote, "In my mind, Project 10 should not be controversial. We are talking about life and death issues. If we lose these children, we lose them to death or to the streets. We can no longer allow unchallenged discrimination and crippling self-hate to be the legacy of our gay and lesbian youth."

I know that the wisdom and caring of someone like Dr. Uribe, who would have shown me by example that my being gay was OK, would have soothed at least some of the pain I felt during my teen years. I don't envy our children growing up today; between drugs and gangs, poverty and broken homes, they face more uncertainty on any given day than I ever did in my comfortable white, middle-class suburb. But in the inner city of Los Angeles, Dr. Uribe fights the good fight for our children, who deserve every bit of effort we can expend on their behalf.

38

BRENT NICHOLSON EARLE

The younger generation doesn't have the—should I say "benefit"—of having lost most of their friends, to be able to know why they need to practice safe sex. I mean, if I was to have unsafe sex now, I would feel I was spitting on the graves of my friends. . . . It's a great pain in my heart, because, you know, I love the gay community. I love being part of it. But it hurts a lot. It hurts when I realize that I ran around America, and it still wasn't enough to get the message out.

—Brent Nicholson Earle, 1994

One of the many horrors of Acquired Immune Deficiency Syndrome has been the sense of personal loss for those of us who remain. When I spoke with Brent Nicholson Earle as he passed through Phoenix in May 1994 during The Rainbow Roll for the End of AIDS, I intuited a very powerful sense of loss in Brent's life. Simultaneously, I felt his incredible internal joy. We spoke at length of many people no longer with us who had touched his life. But even their absence could not quench the energy, the passion, and the joy Brent radiates.

John Robert Brent Nicholson was born on January 21, 1951, in Niagara Falls, New York. Brent, his elder sister, and their parents lived in Lockport, New York, during Brent's childhood. In a moving 1989 *People* article profiling him, Earle spoke of his relationship with his father ("Memories flooding back. How I never could tell him I was gay. How he never could tell me he loved me. How badly he wanted me to play sports with him, and all I burned for was the stage") and his mother's background ("Where does her compassion come from? Perhaps her twenty-seven years as a teacher, or growing up the daughter of a Methodist missionary, living for eight years in China as a child and then on a Cree Indian reservation in Canada"). After Brent's father's death from cancer in 1980, Brent's acknowledgment of his sexual orientation estranged him from his father's family, while his mother's extended family continued to love and support him. As a result, he dropped his two first names and added his mother's maiden name to become Brent Nicholson Earle. Speaking of his family's internal relationships, Brent says, "I think sometimes parents and children kind of get divided up a little bit. And my sister was definitely a Nicholson, and I was definitely an Earle."

Brent's most satisfying moment as an actor came in Tucson, Arizona, in 1971, performing the role of Larry in *The Boys in the Band*: "It's a part that's not a flashy role, but I apparently turned it into one. I kind of got some of the best reviews in Tucson." However, he soon discovered Tucson circa 1971 hardly constituted a hotbed of gay activity: "I thought the gay life in Tucson was so great, and the community was energized—basically, it was the play that had created this whole festive environment out at the bar and everything. And there was only one bar at the time." Earle's most thrilling moment as a playwright occurred when a Milwaukee theater company produced two of his works: "It was very exciting to see my work actually produced with a professional company." But Earle's real claim to fame came through his efforts to raise awareness and money to halt the spread of AIDS.

Why running as a medium to convey the message? It certainly wasn't a natural fit:

> I was, at best, a recreational runner. I'd heard about the Gay Pride Run in New York City, in the summer of early 1984. And it was a whole process. '82 to '84, along with the onset of AIDS, was also much more of a blossoming and a feeling like I needed to start becoming more a part of the gay community. And being a part leads you to doing something about it, not just being a part of it. I had been so caught up with my career in New York as an actor, and as a writer. And although I was part of the community, I didn't participate in anything.

During this period, Earle transitioned out of a fourteen-year relationship.

> At the same time I heard about this Gay Pride Run, and I thought, "Well, I've never run a race in my whole life." And I went down and I entered the race. And I don't even remember what prompted me to

do this, but the night before the race, I got my racing number, and it was number 605. And I placed the names of five friends who had died of AIDS on that race number. And—little did I know what kind of impact that was going to have on me. Because the next day, as I was running that race, they came to mind. And not only did they come to mind, but I suddenly felt an overwhelming sense of gratitude. To be alive. To be able to still see the world around me, feel the wind on my face. To be able to run. It was the summer of the [1984] Olympics, and I got into watching the Olympics. And I kept saying, "I'm gonna join that running club [Front Runners]." And so I finally did do it. I no sooner had joined than I got an application for their second benefit run. And I thought, "I should do this. And I should get my friends to pledge for however many miles I run." And so I did that. And on the 13th of October, 1984, I ran around Central Park. The longest distance I'd ever run, twelve miles. It felt so good when I realized I had raised $400, just by running twice around Central Park. And through a series of events that happened that day, the idea of the Run was born.

He continued in the *People* article with his April 15, 1986, journal entry:

So how did you get the idea for the run? they ask everywhere I go. What should I give them? The simple version? That my grief and anger were so great I *had* to pound them out through my soles? Or the more truthful, confusing one? That by Oct. 14, 1984, the night the idea flashed in my head, my acting career was all but dead; that a short, balding man with dark zealot's eyes has almost no chance on TV or on Broadway? . . . And that I came home from a club at 3 A.M. that night, full of this ravaging emptiness, and sat on a chair and suddenly heard myself sobbing and pleading for help from my father, four years dead of cancer? And that I heard his voice reply, "Follow in Terry Fox's footsteps," and knew immediately what that meant, knew that Terry Fox was the Canadian who lost a leg to cancer but still raised $40 million to fight the disease by running across his country on an artificial limb in 1980, the run eventually cut short by his death? And that maybe it wasn't really my father's voice bidding me to run, but mine?

Brent continued in our conversation,

Within weeks after having decided to do this, I got up at a Front Runners business meeting, after being a member of the club not even quite two months, and made this announcement that I was planning to run around America, and could use any help and advice that anybody would offer. The looks, like, "Mary, what is— You're gonna run around America? Do you know what you're trying to do?" But fortunately, there were some incredible people in that club who really took me at my word, and helped me, and supported me.

With his friends' assistance, Brent created the American Run for the End of AIDS (AREA) in 1984, and he began trekking around the United States on March 1, 1986. But he didn't go alone:

I called [my mother] up, barely a few weeks after I'd made the decision to do it. And said, "Oh, Mom, you're not gonna believe what I'm doing now." She said, "What's going on now?" And I said, "Well, I'm planning to run around America to fight AIDS." "Well, I guess I'm gonna have to come with you." And I went, "*What?*" "Well, who's gonna take care of you when you're doing this? Who's gonna do your laundry? Who's gonna cook for you?" And I said, "Well, maybe you've got a point there." [Laughs] And so I didn't fight her on it. And she became a spokesperson in her own right.

Brent and Marion set out in a Winnebago and, with AREA executive director Bill Konkoy, hit the road for twenty months, ending October 31, 1987. During that time, Brent ran over nine thousand miles, spreading a message of hope and awareness.

To his chagrin, in the mid-'80s Brent quickly found AIDS fundraising a particularly difficult proposition. Despite his best efforts, no major company would financially sponsor the initial run, and he encountered difficulties working with several AIDS organizations he endeavored to assist.

I have a lot of problems with a lot of the AIDS groups. You know, I find that they're self-perpetuating. It's like, I take great pride in the fact that the name of my organization is the American Run for the *End* of AIDS. I mean, I would love to be out of business. [Laughs] . . . [AREA] isn't much of a fund-raising event. It's basically had to become more of a visibility—you know, inspirational event. . . . But fortunately, the money that we did raise had a lot of efficacy, in that we raised it in those little communities that we went through. We raised about $300,000 in the run around America, which stayed in those communities. That money went a long way."

Following the run, Brent turned his energies to the AIDS Coalition to Unleash Power (ACT-UP) in New York City:

ACT-UP was only six months old at that time, and I started to tap in regularly. And got involved. It was the spring after I returned from the run, and first got arrested. At the first anniversary demonstration for ACT-UP on Wall Street—Wall Street II. And it was a very scary

> experience, but a very empowering one. And I've been arrested several times since. And it's very important work."

Earle hoped he might evade an HIV diagnosis; his first test while on the run came back negative. "But I didn't wipe my brow with relief, or heave a great sigh. My lover of fourteen years was already sick. I mean, he'd had an ARC [AIDS-Related Complex] diagnosis. I said, 'I can't be negative! The virus is hiding away somewhere, the antibodies haven't developed,' whatever." Doctors proved Earle's suspicions correct, declaring him HIV-positive on June 12, 1989. How did the diagnosis change his life? "Once I received my HIV-positive test, I felt more a part of the community that I'd been fighting for for so long. And that whole Damoclean sword, like the other shoe, had finally dropped. And I didn't have to dread that coming. Whatever was going to come."

Despite the limited financial success of his first run, in 1990 Earle ran from San Francisco to Vancouver, British Columbia, Canada, on the Rainbow Run for the End of AIDS to meet the participants at Gay Games III. In 1991, not long after that trip, Earle's mother died. The tremendous loss for Brent, always very close to her, made the Rainbow Roll in 1994 without her that much more emotionally difficult for him.

> Even that first little fundraiser in New York. Suddenly, everywhere, you know, selling T-shirts and this sort of thing, I was looking over my shoulder for her. You know, 'cause she was always there with me. And—this was the first time I'd done anything like this without her. I miss her terribly every day, but especially on this.

From April to June 1994, Brent strapped on rollerblades and assembled a team to skate over 4,500 miles from San Francisco to New York to greet the athletes at Gay Games IV and the marchers of Stonewall 25. (In retrospect, the group concept proved a wise decision; a week before our interview, Earle took a very nasty spill near Santa Barbara, and he was still healing from a resultant severe hip injury, from which he later recovered.) Brent discussed with me the differences between the Rainbow Roll and his earlier efforts:

> The coordination is a nightmare! . . . Before it's always been a solo effort. I mean, *I* was always the one out on the highway. I was the athlete. I was the one that was pounding the pavement, and the spokesperson. And it's been very tough since I had the accident, 'cause I haven't been able to skate at all. . . . But that's all overridden by the incredible camaraderie of this group. And I'm so grateful to have each and every one of them along."

Since Gay Games V organizers planned to hold the 1998 Games in Amsterdam, the Netherlands, I wondered if Brent had worked on his long-distance swimming. He laughed: "Oh, I don't think I'm gonna swim across the ocean!" (Funny—I wouldn't have put it past him.) AREA continues its work, still producing the Annual Rally and Candlelight March in observance of World AIDS Day on December 1, 2000, and planning the International Rainbow Memorial Run from San Francisco to Sydney, Australia, for Gay Games VI in November 2002.

Like so many gay men living in the age of AIDS, Earle has endured numerous losses. In a 1990 *Advocate* article, Brent spoke of losing nearly one hundred loved ones to AIDS. In addition to Allan, Brent's former lover, and Bill Konkoy, the director of his original run around America, Brent also especially misses Tom Waddell, founder of the Gay Games ("Tom Waddell probably has been the greatest inspiration in my life") and artist Keith Haring, the two men to whom Earle dedicated the Rainbow Roll. Brent shared with me,

> I carry a great deal of despair in my heart. . . . My friend Terrah, who was the road manager on my first two runs, and who's working on [the Rainbow Roll] as well, doing advance work, said that possibly I'm doing this to process some of the grief that I haven't processed. And she's probably very right.

During all his years of traversing the United States, Earle encountered America's constant and willful denial of the impact of AIDS. "There's denial in the straight community, there's been denial in the gay community. You have to approach it from different angles, but it's still the same enemy we're fighting. And I think, still, even in this day and age, twelve years into the epidemic, denial is still one of our worst enemies."

Brent's greatest personal strength? "Probably my tenacity. Or my optimism." His greatest weakness? "I'm an actor. So I need to go to the dramatic. And the dramatic can lead you into the negative sometimes. It can lead you down that tunnel of despair." What do people not know about Earle? "Well, I guess maybe that I'm the same as everybody else. That I'm nobody special. That what my message is, is that we each have within us to do whatever it takes to get the job done. That if we just reach out, and have courage to put ourselves out there, the rewards are just tremendous."

I did not set out to write a book about heroes. However, I consider myself privileged to have met many heroic figures throughout my travels for this book. On the initial run, Brent took inspiration from Bonnie Tyler's song, "Holding Out for a Hero." I expect Brent would tell me the real heroes are his friends and loved ones who have fought the virus, and that he considers them his heroes. I don't care. Despite—or because of—his modesty, I will always love and admire Brent Nicholson Earle, my very special hero.

39

URVASHI VAID

I love the exchange of ideas; I love ideas; I love arguing with people, and changing my ideas. I think I am radical, in the sense that I'm progressive. I mean, I don't feel like I've done that much radical stuff, personally. But I can see that, you know, standing up and disrupting [President George] Bush's speech as Executive Director was, in context, a radical thing to do for the head of a national gay and lesbian organization.

—Urvashi Vaid, 1995

No one can fairly deny that white men of a certain sociopolitical class have dominated the lesbian and gay movement in the United States for the past half-century. While in some cases GWMs actively discouraged participation by lesbians, lower-middle-class persons, and people of color, far more often it has been benign neglect and/or gay organizations' failure to articulate a vision that addressed their daily concerns that has kept them away. Psychologist Abraham Maslow pioneered the construct known as the hierarchy of needs, exemplified within the GLBT community in which gay white men of means often deal with "higher" level needs, such as love and belongingness, esteem, and self-actualization, while other community members struggle to meet basic physiological and safety needs. Despite the constant presence of non-white, nonwealthy participants in the movement since its inception, the '80s brought a greater range of voices into the choir. By 1989, one could fairly argue that the chorale's director was a young American lesbian of Indian heritage. Despite *Time* magazine's singling her out as one of fifty leaders under age forty to watch in the future and Women.com's selecting her in 2000 as one of only twelve women whose actions it thinks will have an impact in the third millennium, she represented both the symbolic representation of how far the movement had come and how far it had (and has) to go.

Urvashi Vaid (rhymes with "plaid") was born in New Delhi, India, on October 8, 1958. At age eight, she and her family (novelist/professor father, teacher/poet mother, and two older sisters) moved to upstate New York. The university town of Potsdam provided a fishbowl experience for young Urvashi and her family, who could hardly blend into their surroundings (children asked Vaid if she lived in a teepee).

Following her high school graduation, Vaid attended Vassar College in Poughkeepsie, where she discovered her lesbianism. While she identifies her sexual attraction to females from age ten, her passion for feminism led to her self-discovery. At Vassar,

> I was getting more and more involved in feminism. And I think the experience of meeting and coming into contact with self-identified lesbians was very exciting and eye-opening for me. And I found myself like drawn, very drawn, to these women on campus who were dykes. And [they] came to the Women's Center, where we worked. And [I] eventually ended up in bed with one of them.

A year later, at age nineteen, Vaid fell in love with a woman, "and that cinched it for me. I thought, 'I have never felt this kind of emotional, sexual completion. Ever. And I'm a lesbian.' And I knew it, from that moment on. There was no doubt." Vaid graduated from college in 1979, and she soon moved to Boston. There she continued to hone her political skills for the benefit of the lesbian and gay community.

Upon her arrival, Vaid wasted no time becoming involved in Boston's feminist, lesbian, and gay communities. Perhaps most influential (and certainly longest lasting) was her participation with *Gay Community News*, a progressive, nonprofit weekly newspaper first published in 1973. Vaid's participation began casually in 1980, but she continued to assume more responsibilities: "I started out as a Friday night stuffer, stuffing papers on a weekly basis. Then I was a Thursday night proofreader. . . . Then I became a board member, which meant that I was there every day! [Laughs] Doing volunteer work." Simultaneously, Urvashi earned a law degree from Northeastern University in 1983 ("I went into law school in part because I knew I had to make a living. And I didn't think I could make a living doing activist stuff"). Upon completing her studies, Vaid relocated to Washington, D.C., serving as a

GCN "stringer" for two years. As Vaid described *GCN*, "In its heyday, I think it was . . . the one rag that every activist in the grassroots read. . . . It was a really amazing collection of people at *Gay Community News*. And they shaped my politics tremendously." After several years away from *GCN*, in 1992, Vaid returned to its board, and she helped to restructure the weekly paper into a quarterly magazine.

Her years in Boston excited yet exhausted her:

> I was involved with *GCN*; I was going to law school full-time; I was really involved with this Vassar feminist group called Boston Brighton Green Light . . . . I was very involved with GLAD, Gay and Lesbian Advocates and Defenders, as a volunteer; I was involved with the Boston Lesbian and Gay Political Alliance . . . . I think I went to bed about 1:00 and woke up about 7:00 every morning! 'Cause we had 8:30 classes. Ridiculous! But it was so much fun!

After earning a law degree, Vaid spent the next few years in D.C. working with the ACLU's National Prison Project, but she never lost her love for gay/lesbian organizing. In 1986, she joined NGLTF as its public information director. In 1988, Vaid cofounded the first Creating Change Conference, "a skills-building and political discussion-type space" designed to share practical application of strategies successful in other locales. Several years later, its mission and energy still excite Vaid: "I always get pumped up when I go. . . . You just have to walk into a room where people are really doing the front-line work in Montana, or Idaho, and you're talking about their excitement, and you get caught up in it. . . . It's really encouraging; it's hopeful."

As identity politics played an even greater role in gay/lesbian organizations by the mid-'80s, not belonging to the dominant culture provided Vaid a different and valuable perspective. When I asked what she, a lesbian of Indian-American heritage, brought with her that a WASP gay male didn't, she recognized that her bicultural background, her one-generation-removed immigrant status, and the culture clash that resulted within her family over her "Americanization"

> has allowed me a great deal of sensitivity to seeing both sides of situations. I'm also a Libra, and I happen to be very on-the-one-hand/on-the-other-hand. [Partner/comic Kate Clinton] says I'm an Indian Libra. I'm like a statue of Shiva. You know, with all these hands. [Laughs] It's infuriating until you get to know me!

In a more serious vein, she added,

> there were many situations in Washington where I'd be the only woman in the room. Sometimes the only person of color in the room.

> And it's annoying, because you don't want to always have to carry that stuff. . . . But I also feel like it's a responsibility to bring it up, therefore representing this whole group of people who aren't there.

In her 1995 book, *Virtual Equality*, she also related a painful episode shortly after NGLTF named Vaid executive director: A wealthy gay man and potential donor told the group's associate director of development that he was frankly appalled that the board chose "that radical woman, who's practically a nigger." Urv wrote,

> I do not remember what I did when I heard about this comment; I probably fumed and laughed at once. But I can still feel the sting of this man's distrust. He had never spoken to me, had no idea of my values, my background, ideas, or abilities, but because I was "practically a nigger" in his eyes, he would not bother to learn those things.

Vaid took the reins from NGLTF's Jeff Levi in 1989, becoming the group's first female executive director. Observers quickly perceived her to be more politically radical than her predecessor. Interestingly, at the time of NGLTF's announcement, Vaid allegedly said, "You might see my role [within the group] change. I probably won't be the one yelling from behind a bullhorn anymore." However, less than a year later, on March 29, 1990, the Secret Service removed Vaid from an audience of gay and AIDS activists at the National Leadership Coalition on AIDS when she openly challenged President George H.W. Bush regarding his failure to implement a proactive national AIDS policy.

While NGLTF's membership and its funding during her tenure increased, both Vaid and her critics found the organization's growth rate insufficient. In retrospect, Vaid believes

> the doors to gay and lesbian funding have really cracked and opened since I left Washington . . . . In 1988 [to] 1992, it was like pulling teeth to get people to give to gay organizations. I still think it's a challenge; I still think people are much more comfortable spending $100 on a pair of Doc Martens than they are spending $100 on a gay organization.

Urv and I spoke about why, as late as 1995, no really successful national gay organizations had emerged:

> The average gay person doesn't necessarily interact with the National Gay and Lesbian Task Force, or the Human Rights Campaign Fund [now HRC], except when we come to solicit money from them. So most people get the attitude, "Well, what do you do?" When anybody

> who's trying to pass a local gay rights bill, or experiencing discrimination and fighting it in the courts, can tell you what the national organizations do, because they personally know what it's about! . . . Part of our problem is we haven't created the sense of identification, or constituency, among people who aren't in crisis. . . . It's partly a responsibility of people on the national end of things to communicate more effectively what they're doing.

Despite the example of AIDS funding demonstrating the lesbian and gay community's philanthropic generosity, Vaid points out that

> there are many, many people who could be giving much more than they do. . . . We haven't created that kind of tithing obligation. If ten percent of queer, middle-class money were going to gay/lesbian institutions—then we wouldn't have a funding crisis! We just wouldn't. But the fact is, some people are giving 10 percent, and most people are giving one or two, if that.

In a June 1997 *Advocate* piece, Urv also justifiably criticized gays and lesbians for their failure to participate more actively in the political process:

> This gap between gay individuals and the gay political movement is the responsibility of both sides to address. Discomfort with those who are most visible in gay politics keeps some people from identifying as activists. Newly out gay people often want to distance themselves from those who have come before. "We are ordinary, normal gays," they say, "not activist gays." . . . The antidote to people's discomfort with who speaks for gay and lesbian people is not avoidance but involvement. If you don't like what you see, change it. But don't carp about it from the sidelines.

After three-and-one-half years in one of the most visible gay organizational positions, Vaid voluntarily resigned her post in December 1992, telling Todd Simmons in a 1995 *Advocate* article, "Basically, I wanted a life." (However, Vaid returned to NGLTF in the spring of 1997, assuming directorship of the Policy Institute from **John D'Emilio**. Toward the end of 2000, she announced her departure to take a job at the Ford Foundation.) Her decision also meant she could more fully develop her relationship with Kate Clinton, at the time a long-distance romance begun in February 1988 at the lesbian and gay "War Conference." In my experience, rarely do both members of a successful couple carry such high profiles in nonrelated work fields. How do they make their relationship work? Urv explained, "We definitely bring to the relationship a really strong sense of self. . . . I also think we both are nurturing people. You know, we have that side. So we can give as much as we can receive." In 1998, Kate praised Urv: "It helps my comic inspiration to live with a conspiracy theorist. . . . She is an incredible spotter of trends. She wakes up smart every day." Asked in 2000 whether they had ever had a commitment ceremony, Clinton cracked, "No, honey. We signed mortgage papers in New York City and it was like, 'This is our ceremony.'" She further added, "I would register as domestic partners for health insurance benefits, but I have no interest in marriage." And while Kate may not include jokes about Urv that mention her by name, Vaid sees her fingerprints in Clinton's routines, telling *Lesbian News* in November 1999, "She doesn't mention my name, but she sure uses the material!"

Despite Vaid's absence from national gay politics, organizers asked her to speak at 1993's March on Washington. There she orated, "The gay rights movement is not a party. It is not a lifestyle. It is not a hairstyle or a fad or a fringe or a sickness. It is not about sin or salvation. The gay rights movement is an integral part of the American promise of freedom. We are the descendants of a proud tradition of people asserting their dignity." She also flung down the gauntlet at the Christian Conservative movement, contrasting its aims with those of the GLBT movement:

> We believe in democracy, in many voices coexisting in peace, in people of all faiths living together in harmony, under a common civil framework known as the U.S. Constitution. Our opponents believe in monotheism—one way, theirs; one God, theirs; one law, the Old Testament; one nation, supreme, the Christian, White one. Christian supremacist leaders like Bill Bennett and Pat Robertson, Lou Sheldon and Pat Buchanan, these supremacist leaders don't care about morality—they care about power! They care about social control! And their goal, my friends, is the reconstruction of American democracy into American theocracy.

In her personal life, she has discovered a South Asian gay and lesbian community in the United States that previously had remained largely invisible, acknowledging in a 1995 interview with Surina Khan in *The Harvard Gay & Lesbian Review*,

> I feel like I had no space in which to be an Indian lesbian, to be who I was, until very recently. Simply because there was no South Asian gay/lesbian community. . . . Since you and I last talked I feel much more connected to being Indian. And really I credit a lot of that to this emerging South Asian queer movement and the things that people have been writing.

After receiving a reported $250,000 advance, in October 1995 Doubleday released Vaid's *Virtual Equality: The Mainstreaming of Gay and Lesbian Liberation*. I found the book an excellent primer (even though I quibbled with Urv about certain historical errors), but I was disappointed not to find any "new" strategies or magic formulas to guarantee liberation (admittedly an unfair expectation). When I interviewed Urv in August 1995, she had completed the book and eagerly anticipated its release. Unfortunately, I found the book's critics unduly harsh and dismissive of Vaid's efforts—perhaps they, like I, expected more than *Virtual Equality* could fairly deliver, itself a form of flattery. On the other hand, *Virtual Equality* received the American Library Association's 1996 gay/lesbian/bisexual book award for nonfiction.

In a summer 1999 *Harvard Gay & Lesbian Review* interview, Vaid expressed her concern about the Millennium March on Washington; while prefacing her remarks by saying, "I am not against national marches; I love national marches," like **Barney Frank**, Urv believed "at this moment we don't need a symbolic gesture like converging on Washington. We need pragmatic political action, and I don't think the march is pragmatic." Remarks in other publications that year indicated Vaid's desire to make more time for personal matters in her life, even if they cut into her political involvement.

Given her reputation as an intense political animal, casual observers don't see Urv's warmth and charm; she put me at ease instantly. (Having flown from Boston to Provincetown in a nine-seater airplane, I needed all the putting-at-ease I could get!) Urv's musical tastes (which run to punk and hard rock, with a special place in her heart for Patti Smith) may also surprise some. Urv mentioned an *Outweek* magazine article which described her participation "in this *ghastly* punk band! Horrible, horrible, bad music! [I] could barely play. I played an implement. Not an instrument. [Laughs] A musical implement." Vaid's physical presence also surprises the unexpectant. As she told me,

> Actually, interestingly, one of the things people say to me the most when they see me: "I thought you'd be taller." [Laughs] You know, I'm like 5'2"! I think they have this impression of this kind of big, brassy dyke kind of thing. [Laughs] And, you know, I'm light enough, and I can be as pushy as the next dyke. But I'm also, like, a shrimpy short girl.

Asking a series of questions to so many people, I was bound to trip up at least once by asking the wrong person the right question. When I asked Urv what she thought she would be remembered for, she correctly pointed out, "I'm too young for that! I'm thirty-six right now, and so, maybe in twenty more years . . . . I have a lot more work to do,

I hope to do." A sizeable segment of the les/bi/gay/trans community hopes so, too: Even as she minimized her national presence since 1992, a 1995 *Advocate* poll revealed that 26 percent of respondents felt Urv should lead the gay and lesbian movement, not only putting her first among the eight choices (including "None of the Above"), but well ahead of such luminaries as Larry Kramer, Camille Paglia, and David Geffen. Amazingly, even Kramer, often more caustic than Drano, said in a 1992 *Advocate* interview that Vaid, "who probably has the best heart of all of us, is just a loving, lovable, delectable person who suffers physically when gays or lesbians are in any way harmed." (But he then spoiled the accolade by claiming, "She was unable, somehow, to get this part of her character across to millions.")

Urvashi Vaid retains a voice with something to say, and a political presence with which the Right must reckon. Given her age, a later edition of this book focusing on the next twenty-five years of lesbian and gay liberation very well may include her updated profile; certainly her energy and passion show no sign of flagging.

SELECTED BIBLIOGRAPHY

Abbott, Sidney, and Barbara Love. *Sappho Was a Right-On Woman.* New York: Stein and Day, 1972.

Adair, Nancy, and Casey Adair. *Word Is Out*. San Francisco: New Glide Publications, 1978.

Adam, Barry D. *The Rise of a Gay and Lesbian Movement*. New York: Twayne Publishers, 1995.

Altman, Dennis. *Homosexual Oppression and Liberation*. New York: Discus, 1971.

———. *The Homosexualization of America, the Americanization of the Homosexual*. New York: St. Martin's, 1982.

Alwood, Edward. *Straight News: Gays, Lesbians, and the News Media*. New York: Columbia University Press, 1996.

Alyson Almanac 1994-95 Edition. Boston: Alyson Publications, 1993 (1989).

Alyson Almanac. Boston: Alyson Publications, 1990 (1989).

Alyson, Sasha, ed. *Young, Gay and Proud.* Boston: Alyson Publications, 1980.

——. *You Can Do Something about AIDS*. Boston: Stop AIDS Project, 1988.

Andrews, Nancy. *Family*. San Francisco: Harper, 1994.

Bannon, Ann. *Beebo Brinker*. Tallahassee, Fla.: Naiad, 1986 (1962).

———. *Journey to a Woman*. Tallahassee, Fla.: Naiad, 1986 (1960).

———. *Odd Girl Out*. Tallahassee, Fla.: Naiad, 1986 (1957).

———. *Woman in the Shadows*. Tallahassee, Fla.: Naiad, 1986 (1959).

Basile, Vic, and John Scagliotti, executive producers. *After Stonewall: From the Riots to the Millennium* (documentary). New York: First Run Features, 1999.

Bauman, Robert. *The Gentleman from Maryland: The Conscience of a Gay Conservative*. New York: Arbor House, 1986.

Bawer, Bruce. *A Place at the Table: The Gay Individual in American Society*. New York: Poseidon, 1993.

Beard, Rick, and Leslie Cohen Berlowitz, eds. *Greenwich Village: Culture and Counterculture*. New Brunswick, N. J.: Rutgers University Press, 1993.

Bender, David, and Bruno Leone, series editors, William Dudley, book editor. *Homosexuality: Opposing Viewpoints*. St. Paul, Minn.: Greenhaven, 1993.

Berkley Publishing Group. *The Gay and Lesbian Address Book*. New York: Berkley Publishing Group, 1995.

Bernstein, Samuel, ed. *Uncommon Heroes: A Celebration of Heroes and Role Models for Gay and Lesbian Americans*. New York: Fletcher, 1994.

Bérubé, Allan. *Coming Out under Fire*. New York: Plume, 1990.

Biren, Joan E., and Moonforce Media Producers. *A Simple Matter of Justice* (documentary). 1993.

Blasius, Mark, and Shane Phelan, eds. *We Are Everywhere: A Historical Sourcebook of Gay and Lesbian Politics*. New York: Routledge, 1997.

Blue, Adrianne. *Martina: The Lives and Times of Martina Navratilova*. New York: Birch Lane, 1995.

Boyd, Malcolm. *Are You Running with Me, Jesus? A Spiritual Companion for the 1990s*. Boston: Beacon, 1990.

———. *Are You Running with Me, Jesus?* New York: Holt, Rinehart and Winston, 1965.

———. *As I Live and Breathe*. New York: Random House, 1969.

———. *Edges, Boundaries, and Connections*. Seattle, Wash.: Broken Moon, 1992.

———. *Gay Priest*. New York: St. Martin's, 1986.

———. *Go Gentle into That Good Night*. Columbus, Miss.: Genesis, 1998.

———. *Half Laughing/Half Crying*. New York: St. Martin's, 1986.

———. *Look Back in Joy*. Boston: Alyson Publications, 1990.

———. *Malcolm Boyd's Book of Days*. New York: Random House, 1968.

———. *Take Off the Masks*. Philadelphia: New Society Publishers, 1984.

Brandt, Kate. *Happy Endings: Lesbian Writers Talk about Their Lives and Work*. Tallahassee, Fla.: Naiad, 1993.

Brelin, Christa, ed. *Strength in Numbers: A Lesbian, Gay and Bisexual Resource*. Detroit: Visible Ink, 1996.

Bronski, Michael, ed. *Outstanding Lives: Profiles of Lesbians and Gay Men*. Detroit: Visible Ink, 1997.

Brown, Howard. *Familiar Faces, Hidden Lives*. New York: Harcourt Brace Jovanovich, 1976.

Brown, Rita Mae. *A Plain Brown Rapper*. Oakland, Calif.: Diana, 1976.

———. *Rita Will*. New York: Bantam Books, 1997.

———. *Rubyfruit Jungle*. Toronto, Canada: Bantam Books, 1983.

———. *Starting from Scratch*. New York: Bantam Books, 1988.

———. *Sudden Death*. Toronto, Canada: Bantam Books, 1983.

Brownmiller, Susan. *In Our Time: Memoir of a Revolution*. New York: Dial, 1999.

Bullough, Vern. *Homosexuality: A History*. New York: New American Library, 1979.

Bunch, Charlotte. *Passionate Politics: Feminist Theory in Action*. New York: St. Martin's, 1987.

Bunch, Charlotte, and Sandra Pollack, eds. *Learning Our Way: Essays in Feminist Education*. Trumansburg, N.Y.: The Crossing Press, 1983.

Burkett, Elinor. *The Gravest Show on Earth: America in the Age of AIDS*. New York: Picador USA, 1995.

Clarke, Lige, and Jack Nichols. *I Have More Fun with You than Anybody*. New York: St. Martin's, 1972.

———. *Roommates Can't Always Be Lovers*. New York: St. Martin's, 1974.

Clendinen, Dudley, and Adam Nagourney. *Out for Good: The Struggle to Build a Gay Rights Movement in America*. New York: Simon and Schuster, 1999.

Cohen, Marcia. *The Sisterhood*. New York: Simon and Schuster, 1988.

Contemporary Authors Autobiography Series. vol. 2. Detroit: Gale, 1990.

Cory, Donald Webster. *The Homosexual in America: A Subjective Approach*. New York: Paperback Library, 1963 (Greenberg, 1951).

———. *The Lesbian in America*. New York: Tower Publications, 1964.

Cory, Donald Webster, and John P. LeRoy. *The Homosexual and His Society*. New York: Citadel, 1963.

Crew, Louie, ed. *The Gay Academic*. Palm Springs, Calif.: ETC Publications, 1978.

D'Emilio, John. *Making Trouble: Essays on Gay History, Politics, and the University*. New York: Routledge, 1992.

———. *Sexual Politics, Sexual Communities*. Chicago: University of Chicago Press, 1983.

———. *The Civil Rights Struggle: Leaders in Profile*. New York: Facts on File, 1979.

DeBold, Kathleen, ed. *Out for Office: Campaigning in the Gay Nineties*. Washington, D.C.: Gay and Lesbian Victory Fund, 1994.

Deitcher, David, ed. *The Question of Equality: Lesbian and Gay Politics in America since Stonewall*. New York: Scribner's, 1995.

Denneny, Michael, Charles Ortleb, and Thomas Steele, eds. *The Christopher Street Reader*. New York: Coward-McCann, 1983.

Duberman, Martin B. *In White America*. Boston: Houghton Mifflin, 1964.

Duberman, Martin. *About Time: Exploring the Gay Past*. New York: Meridian, 1991.

———. *Black Mountain: An Exploration in Community*. New York: E.P. Dutton, 1972.

———. *Cures: A Gay Man's Odyssey*. New York: E.P. Dutton, 1991.

———. *Male Armor*. New York: E.P. Dutton, 1975.

———. *Midlife Queer: Autobiography of a Decade, 1971-1981*. New York: Scribner's, 1996.

———. *Stonewall*. New York: E.P. Dutton, 1993.

Duberman, Martin, ed. *A Queer World*. New York: New York University Press, 1997.

DuPlessis, Rachel Blau, and Ann Snitow, eds. *The Feminist Memoir Project*. New York: Three Rivers, 1998.

Dupre, Jeff, director. *Out of the Past* (documentary). Inverted Pictures, 1997.

Dynes, Wayne R. *Homosexuality: A Research Guide*. New York: Garland Publishing, 1987.

Echols, Alice. *Daring to Be Bad*. Minneapolis: University of Minnesota Press, 1989.

Ehrenstein, David. *Open Secret*. New York: William Morrow, 1998.

Epstein, Rob, and Richard Schmiechen, producers. *The Times of Harvey Milk* (documentary). Black Sand Productions, 1984.

Faderman, Lillian. *Odd Girls & Twilight Lovers: A History of Lesbian Life in Twentieth-Century America*. New York: Penguin Books, 1991.

Farrell, Lorena Fletcher, ed. *Lambda Gray: A Practical, Emotional, and Spiritual Guide for Gays and Lesbians Who Are Growing Older*. North Hollywood, Calif.: Newcastle Publishing, 1993.

Faulkner, Sandra, with Judy Nelson. *Love Match: Nelson vs. Navratilova*. New York: Birch Lane, 1993.

FitzGerald, Frances. *Cities on a Hill*. New York: Simon and Schuster, 1986.

Fletcher, Lynne Yamaguchi, and Adrien Saks. *Lavender Lists: New Lists about Lesbian and Gay Culture, History, and Personalities*. Boston: Alyson Publications, 1990.

Forward Focus Productions, Ltd. *God, Gays, & The Gospel* (documentary). 1984.

Gardner-Loulan, JoAnn, Bonnie Lopez, and Marcia Quackenbush. *Period*. Volcano, Calif.: Volcano, 1979, 1981.

Gershick, Zsa Zsa. *Gay Old Girls*. New York: Alyson Books, 1998.

Giard, Robert. *Particular Voices: Portraits of Gay and Lesbian Writers*. Cambridge, Mass.: MIT Press, 1997.

Gorman, Michael R. *The Empress Is a Man: Stories from the Life of José Sarria*. New York: Harrington Park, 1998.

Greif, Martin. *Gay Book of Days*. New York: Carol Publishing Group, 1989 (1982).

Grier, Barbara, and Coletta Reid, eds. *The Lavender Herring: Lesbian Essays from* The Ladder. Baltimore, Md.: Diana, 1976.

Hansen, Joseph. *A Few Doors West of Hope: The Life and Times of Dauntless Don Slater*. Universal City, Calif.: Homosexual Information Center, 1998.

Hippler, Mike. *Matlovich: The Good Soldier*. Boston: Alyson Publications, 1989.

Hogan, Steve, and Lee Hudson. *Completely Queer: The Gay and Lesbian Encyclopedia*. New York: Henry Holt, 1998.

Humphrey, Mary Ann. *My Country, My Right to Serve: Experiences of Gay Men and Women in the Military, World War II to the Present*. New York: HarperCollins, 1990.

Humphreys, Laud. *Out of the Closets: The Sociology of Homosexual Liberation*. Englewood Cliffs, N.J.: Prentice Hall, 1972.

Hunter, John Francis. *The Gay Insider USA*. New York: Stonehill Publishing, 1972.

Hurewitz, Daniel. *Stepping Out: Nine Walks through New York City's Gay and Lesbian Past*. New York: Henry Holt, 1997.

Jay, Karla. *Tales of the Lavender Menace: A Memoir of Liberation*. New York: Basic Books, 1999.

———, ed. *Dyke Life*. New York: Basic Books, 1995.

Jay, Karla, and Allen Young, eds. *Out of the Closets: Voices of Gay Liberation*. New York: A Douglas Book, 1972.

Jennings, Kevin, ed. *Becoming Visible*. Boston: Alyson Publications, 1994.

Johnson, Pamela S. *Profiles Encourage: Conversations with Twenty Women*. Austin, Tex.: Banned Books, 1988.

Jones, Cleve, with Jeff Dawson. *Stitching a Revolution: The Making of an Activist*. New York: HarperSanFrancisco, 2000.

Kaiser, Charles. *The Gay Metropolis: 1940-1996*. New York: Houghton Mifflin, 1997.

Karvoski Jr., Ed. *A Funny Time to Be Gay*. New York: Fireside, 1997.

Katz, Jonathan Ned. *Gay American History: Lesbians and Gay Men in the U.S.A*. New York: Harper and Row, 1976.

———. *Gay/Lesbian Almanac*. New York: Harper and Row, 1983.

Kepner, Jim. *Rough News—Daring Views: 1950s' Pioneer Gay Press Journalism*. Binghamton, N.Y.: Harrington Park, 1998.

Kopay, David, and Perry Deane Young. *The David Kopay Story*. New York: Primus, 1988.

KQED. *The Castro* (documentary). San Francisco, 1997.

Lamson, Peggy. *In the Vanguard*. Boston: Houghton Mifflin, 1979.

Lee, John Alan Ph.D., ed. *Gay Midlife and Maturity*. New York: Haworth, 1991.

Legg, W. Dorr, ed. *Homophile Studies in Theory and Practice*. San Francisco: ONE Institute Press and GLB Publishers, 1994.

Legg, W. Dorr, ed. [Marvin Cutler pseud.] *Homosexuals Today 1956: A Handbook of Organizations & Publications*. Los Angeles: ONE, Inc., 1956.

LeVay, Simon, and Elisabeth Nonas. *City of Friends*. Cambridge, Mass.: MIT Press, 1995.

Leyland, Winston, ed. *Gay Sunshine Interviews*. vol. 1. San Francisco: Gay Sunshine, 1978.

———. *Gay Sunshine Interviews*. vol. 2. San Francisco: Gay Sunshine, 1982.

Licata, Salvatore J., Ph.D., and Robert P. Petersen, eds. *Historical Perspectives on Homosexuality*. New York: Haworth, 1981.

Loughery, John. *The Other Side of Silence: Men's Lives and Gay Identities: A Twentieth-Century History*. New York: Henry Holt, 1998.

Loulan, JoAnn. *Lesbian Passion: Loving Ourselves and Each Other*. Duluth, Minn.: Spinsters Ink, 1987.

———. *Lesbian Sex*. Minneapolis: Spinsters Ink, 1984.

———. *The Lesbian Erotic Dance: Butch Femme Androgyny and Other Rhythms*. San Francisco: Spinsters Book Co., 1990.

McGarry, Molly, and Fred Wasserman. *Becoming Visible*. New York: Penguin Studio, 1998.

Malibu Sales. *The Historic March on Washington* (documentary). 1987.

Malinowski, Sharon, and Christa Brelin. *The Gay and Lesbian Literary Companion*. Boston: Visible Ink, 1995.

Marcus, Eric. *Making History: The Struggle for Gay and Lesbian Equal Rights, 1945-1990, an Oral History*. New York: HarperCollins, 1992.

Mariposa Film Group. *Word Is Out: Stories of Some of Our Lives* (documentary). Adair Films, 1977.

Marotta, Toby. *The Politics of Homosexuality*. Boston: Houghton Mifflin, 1981.

Martin, Del. *Battered Wives*. New York: Pocket Books, 1979.

Martin, Del, and Phyllis Lyon. *Lesbian/Woman*. Volcano, Calif.: Volcano, 1991.

Mass, Lawrence D. *We Must Love One Another or Die*. New York: St. Martin's, 1997.

Maupin, Armistead. *28 Barbary Lane: A Tales of the City Omnibus.* New York: Harper & Row, 1990.

———. *Back to Barbary Lane: The Final Tales of the City Omnibus.* New York: HarperCollins, 1991.

Miller, Neil. *In Search of Gay America: Women and Men in a Time of Change*. New York: Harper and Row, 1989.

———. *Out of the Past: Gay and Lesbian History from 1869 to the Present*. New York: Vintage Books, 1995.

Millett, Kate. *A.D.* New York: W.W. Norton, 1995.

———. *Flying*. New York: Simon and Schuster, 1974.

———. *Sexual Politics*. Garden City, N.Y.: Doubleday, 1969.

———. *Sita*. New York: Farrar, Straus and Giroux, 1976-77.

———. *The Loony-Bin Trip*. New York: Simon and Schuster, 1990.

Mixner, David, and Dennis Bailey. *Brave Journeys: Profiles in Gay and Lesbian Courage*. New York: Bantam Books, 2000.

Morris, Bonnie J. *Eden Built by Eves: The Culture of Women's Music Festivals*. Los Angeles: Alyson Books, 1999.

Myron, Nancy, and Charlotte Bunch, eds. *Lesbianism and the Women's Movement*. Baltimore, Md.: Diana, 1975.

National Museum and Archive of Lesbian and Gay History. *Gay Almanac*. New York: Berkley Books, 1996.

———. *Lesbian Almanac*. New York: Berkley Books, 1996.

Navratilova, Martina, with George Vecsey. *Martina*. New York: Alfred A. Knopf, 1985.

Near, Holly. *Don't Hold Back*. Oakland, Calif.: Redwood Records, RR413.

———. *Fire in the Rain*. Redwood Records, RRC-402.

———. *Hang in There*. Redwood Records, RR3800.

———. *Simply Love.* Ukiah, Calif.: Calico Tracks Music, CTM0003.

———. *Singer in the Storm*. Chameleon Records, D2-74832.

———. *With a Song in My Heart*. Lansing, Mich.: Calico Tracks Music, CTM-CD-9701.

Near, Holly, and Ronnie Gilbert. *This Train Still Runs*. Berkeley, Calif.: Abbe Alice Music, AAH0696.

Near, Holly, with Derk Richardson. *Fire in the Rain . . . Singer in the Storm*. New York: William Morrow, 1990.

Nelson, Judy Hill. *Choices: My Journey after Leaving My Husband for Martina and a Lesbian Life*. New York: Carol Publishing Group, 1996.

Nestle, Joan. *A Fragile Union: New and Selected Writings*. San Francisco: Cleis, 1998.

———. *A Restricted Country*. Ithaca, N.Y.: Firebrand Books, 1987.

Nestle, Joan, ed. *The Persistent Desire: A Femme-Butch Reader*. Boston: Alyson Publications, 1992.

Nestle, Joan, with John Preston, eds. *Sister and Brother: Lesbians and Gay Men Write about Their Lives Together*. San Francisco: HarperSanFrancisco, 1994.

Nichols, Jack. *Men's Liberation: A New Definition of Masculinity*. New York: Penguin Books, 1975.

———. *Welcome to Fire Island: Visions of Cherry Grove and the Pines*. New York: St. Martin's, 1976.

———. *The Gay Agenda: Talking Back to the Fundamentalists*. Amherst, N.Y.: Prometheus Books, 1996.

Oberholtzer, W. Dwight, ed. *Is Gay Good?* Philadelphia: Westminster, 1971.

Perry, Rev. Troy D., and Thomas L.P. Swicegood. *Profiles in Gay & Lesbian Courage*. New York: St. Martin's, 1991.

Perry, Rev. Troy D., with Thomas L.P. Swicegood. *Don't Be Afraid Anymore: The Story of Reverend Troy Perry and the Metropolitan Community Churches*. New York: St. Martin's, 1990.

Perry, Rev. Troy, with Charles L. Lucas. *The Lord Is My Shepherd and He Knows I'm Gay*. Austin, Tex.: Liberty, 1987 (1972).

Poirier, Paris, director. *Last Call at Maud's* (documentary). Water Bearer Films, 1993.

Post, Laura. *Backstage Pass: Interviews with Women in Music*. Norwich, Vt.: New Victoria Publishers, 1997.

Preston, John. *A Member of the Family: Gay Men Write about Their Families*. New York: Dutton, 1992.

———, ed. *Hometowns: Gay Men Write about Where They Belong*. New York: Dutton, 1991.

Rayside, David. *On the Fringe: Gays and Lesbians in Politics*. Ithaca, N.Y.: Cornell University Press, 1998.

Richards, Dell. *Lesbian Lists: A Look at Lesbian Culture, History, and Personalities*. Boston: Alyson Publications, 1990.

Richmond, Len, with Gary Noguera. *The New Gay Liberation Book*. Palo Alto, Calif.: Ramparts, 1979.

Ringer, R. Jeffrey, ed. *Queer Words, Queer Images: Communication and the Construction of Homosexuality*. New York: New York University Press, 1994.

Rutledge, Leigh W. *The Gay Decades: From Stonewall to the Present: The People and Events That Shaped Gay Lives*. New York: Plume, 1992.

———. *The Gay Fireside Companion*. Boston: Alyson Publications, 1989.

———. *The New Gay Book of Lists*. Los Angeles: Alyson Publications, 1996.

Sang, Barbara, Joyce Warshow, and Adrienne J. Smith, eds. *Lesbians at Midlife: The Creative Transition*. San Francisco: Spinsters Book Co., 1991.

Scagliotti, John, executive producer; Greta Schiller, director; Robert Rosenberg, codirector. *Before Stonewall* (documentary). Before Stonewall Inc., in association with the Center for the Study of Filmed History, released by David Whittier Promotions, 1985.

Sears, James T. *Lonely Hunters: An Oral History of Lesbian and Gay Southern Life 1948-1968*. Boulder, Colo.: Westview, 1997.

Shilts, Randy. *And the Band Played On: Politics, People and the AIDS Epidemic*. New York: Penguin Books, 1987-88.

———. *Conduct Unbecoming: Gays and Lesbians in the U.S. Military*. New York: St. Martin's, 1993.

———. *The Mayor of Castro Street: The Life and Times of Harvey Milk*. New York: St. Martin's, 1982.

Signorile, Michelangelo. *Queer in America*. New York: Random House, 1993.

Silva, Rosemary. *Lesbian Quotations*. Boston: Alyson Publications, 1993.

Simpson, Ruth. *From the Closet to the Courts: The Lesbian Transition*. New York: Penguin Books, 1976.

Singer, Bennett L., ed. *Growing Up Gay: A Literary Anthology*. New York: The New Press, 1993.

Spear, Allan H. *Black Chicago: The Making of a Negro Ghetto 1890-1920*. Chicago: University of Chicago Press, 1970.

Stein, Marc. *City of Sisterly and Brotherly Loves*. Chicago: University of Chicago Press, 2000.

Stewart, Stephen. *Positive Image: A Portrait of Gay America*. New York: William Morrow, 1985.

Stone, Pamela M., ed./Roxanne May, photographs. *Friends, Lovers, Husbands*. Phoenix: Triangle Productions, 1994.

Streitmatter, Rodger. *Unspeakable: The Rise of the Gay and Lesbian Press in America*. Boston: Faber and Faber, 1995.

Stryker, Susan, and Jim Van Buskirk. *Gay by the Bay: A History of Queer Culture in the San Francisco Bay Area*. San Francisco: Chronicle Books, 1996.

Summers, Claude J., ed. *The Gay and Lesbian Literary Heritage: A Reader's Companion to the Writers and Their Works, from Antiquity to the Present*. New York: Henry Holt, 1995.

Teal, Donn. *The Gay Militants*. New York: St. Martin's, 1971.

Testing the Limits. *Voices from the Front* (documentary). 1991.

Thompson, Mark, ed. *Gay Soul: Finding the Heart of Gay Spirit and Nature with Sixteen Writers, Healers, Teachers and Visionaries*. San Francisco: HarperSanFrancisco, 1995.

———. *Leatherfolk: Radical Sex, People, Politics, and Practice*. Boston: Alyson Publications, 1991.

———. *Long Road to Freedom: The Advocate History of the Gay and Lesbian Movement*. New York: St. Martin's, 1994.

Thompson, Mark. *Gay Body*. New York: St. Martin's, 1997.

———. *Gay Spirit: Myth and Meaning*. New York: St. Martin's, 1987.

Timmons, Stuart. *The Trouble with Harry Hay: Founder of the Modern Gay Movement*. Boston: Alyson Publications, 1990.

Tobias, Andrew. *The Best Little Boy in the World Grows Up*. New York: Ballantine Books, 1998.

Tobias, Andrew [John Reid pseud.]. *The Best Little Boy in the World*. New York: Ballantine Books, 1973.

Tobin, Kay, and Randy Wicker. *The Gay Crusaders*. New York: Paperback Library, 1972.

Tyler, Robin. *Always a Bridesmaid, Never a Groom*. University of New Mexico, Albuquerque: Harrison and Tyler Publications, Olivia Records, 1979.

———. *Just Kidding*. Cleveland, Ga.: Harrison and Tyler Productions, 1985.

Vaid, Urvashi. *Virtual Equality: The Mainstreaming of Gay and Lesbian Liberation*. New York: Anchor Books Doubleday, 1995.

Van Gelder, Lindsy, and Pamela Robin Brandt. *The Girls Next Door: Into the Heart of Lesbian America*. New York: Touchstone, 1996.

Vida, Ginny, ed. *Our Right to Love: A Lesbian Resource Book*. Englewood Cliffs, N.J.: Prentice Hall, 1978.

———. *The New Our Right to Love: A Lesbian Resource Book*. New York: Touchstone, 1996.

Waddell, Tom, and Dick Schaap. *Gay Olympian: The Life and Death of Dr. Tom Waddell*. New York: Knopf, 1996.

Wallace, Irving, Amy Wallace, David Wallechinsky, and Sylvia Wallace. *The Intimate Sex Lives of Famous People*. New York: Delacorte, 1981.

Wallace, Mike, correspondent, and Harry Morgan, producer. *The Homosexuals* (documentary). New York: CBS Reports, 1967.

Weinberg, Dr. George. *Society and the Healthy Homosexual*. New York: St. Martin's, 1972.

Weiss, Andrea, and Greta Schiller. *Before Stonewall*. Tallahassee, Fla.: Naiad, 1988.

Weissman, Aerlyn, and Lynne Fernie, directors. *Forbidden Love* (documentary). New York: Women Make Movies Home Video, 1992.

White, Edmund. *States of Desire: Travels in Gay America*. New York: E.P. Dutton, 1983.

Witt, Lynn, Sherry Thomas, and Eric Marcus. *Out in All Directions: The Almanac of Gay and Lesbian America*. New York: Warner Books, 1995.

Wolf, Deborah Goleman. *The Lesbian Community*. Berkeley, Calif.: University of California Press, 1979.

Woog, Dan. *School's Out: The Impact of Gay and Lesbian Issues on America's Schools*. Boston: Alyson Publications, 1995.

Yeager, Ken. *Trailblazers: Profiles of America's Gay and Lesbian Elected Officials*. New York: Haworth Press, 1999.

Young, Perry Deane. *Lesbians and Gays and Sports*. New York: Chelsea House Publishers, 1995.

Zahava, Irene, ed. *Lavender Mansions: 40 Contemporary Lesbian and Gay Short Stories*. Boulder, Colo.: Westview, 1994.

Zwerman, Gilda. *Martina Navratilova*. New York: Chelsea House Publishers, 1995.

INDEX

Note: All bolded names in this index have photos/illustrations in the center spread.

ABOUT THE AUTHOR

Paul D. Cain acknowledged his homosexuality in 1984 and has served his community as an activist ever since. After singing with the Gay Men's Chorus of Los Angeles from 1984-1986 (while graduating as valedictorian with a music degree from California Lutheran University in Thousand Oaks), he moved to Phoenix, Arizona. While generally employed as a legal secretary, Cain served the lesbian/gay community in a multiplicity of capacities, most notably as executive director of Phoenix's Lesbian and Gay Community Switchboard from March 1992 to April 1993.

In March 2001, Cain joined his partner of twelve years, Kurt L. Jacobowitz-Cain, in Reno, Nevada. He currently works as a blackjack dealer at a Reno casino.

Cain dabbled in writing for many years before attempting to write *Leading the Parade*, his first book. He also currently writes a monthly column for *Reno Tahoe Outlands*, a gay magazine, and he periodically contributes articles for GayToday on the Web.